Maurice Walsh is
from Ireland: Fore
tion. As an award-wi....
Africa, Asia, Latin America, ...
His essays, reviews and reportage have appeared in *Granta*,
the *London Review of Books*, the *Dublin Review*, the *New
Statesman*, and other newspapers in the UK, Ireland and the
US. He was Knight Wallace Fellow at the University of Michigan in 2001, and Alistair Horne Fellow at St Anthony's College, Oxford 2010/11. He teaches journalism at Brunel
University in London.

Futher praise for *Bitter Freedom*:

'Our commemoration of 1916 has drawn forth so much good
new work, but for breadth of scholarship, empathy with oft-
neglected, intimate and human stories, and above all for the
grace and elegance of the writing, *Bitter Freedom* stands out
– a beautiful book, beautifully and informatively written.'
Michael D. Higgins, President of Ireland

'This is probably the best overview of the revolutionary era in
the current crop of books prompted by the "decade of centenaries". It is superbly crafted and a joy to read. It is particularly suited to an international audience wishing to know
more about the Irish revolution but provides many insights
for those of us who think we are fairly familiar with the subject.' Padraig Yeates, *History Ireland*

'Invigorating . . . Vivid and incisive, his approach highlights
discontinuities and contradictions among the revolutionaries.'
Roy Foster, *Spectator*

'Mau   ye for the

illuminating detail of everyday lives in extremis . . . The great strength of Walsh's book is its breadth of vision. His book challenges parochial tendencies in the revolutionary story.' Feargal Keane, *Prospect*

'This compelling book . . . manages to make large and abstract arguments while conveying a sense of the lived experience of the Irish revolution. With one hand, Maurice Walsh widens his lens, while simultaneously he applies a magnifying glass with the other. The result of this dexterity is an arresting set of Big Pictures interspersed with a sequence of vivid miniatures.' Alvin Jackson, *Tablet*

'[Walsh] stretches the canvas of history into a beautifully realised story, one that is as human and cultural as it is political and military.' Neil Hegarty, *BBC History Magazine*

'A vivid and highly engaging account of events in Ireland during the most turbulent and transformative period of history of the United Kingdom.' *History Today*

'What sets apart Maurice Walsh's hugely readable new book is that he places the political upheaval . . . within a broader European context, so we view the Irish revolution not as a stand-alone event, but as part of a wave of change that was sweeping across Europe. Walsh's book provides a fascinating and detailed examination of Ireland at that period . . . crammed with insights into the characters who shaped a revolution.' Dermot Bolger, *Sunday Business Post*

'Walsh is a fine writer and has a novelist's feel for pace and colour.' Diarmaid Ferriter, *Irish Times*

---

by the same author

THE NEWS FROM IRELAND:
FOREIGN CORRESPONDENTS AND THE IRISH REVOLUTION

Bitter Freedom

Ireland in a
Revolutionary World
1918–1923

MAURICE WALSH

FABER & FABER

First published in 2015
by Faber & Faber Ltd
Bloomsbury House
74–77 Great Russell Street
London WC1B 3DA
This paperback edition published in 2016

Typeset by Faber & Faber Ltd
Printed in England by CPI Group (UK) Ltd, Croydon CR0 4YY

A CIP record for this book
is available from the British Library

ISBN 978-0-571-24301-3

2 4 6 8 10 9 7 5 3 1

In memory of
Michael Walsh (1899–1974)

Contents

Illustrations

Chronology

1918

11 November Armistice between Germany and the Allied powers
ends First World War

14 November Tomáš Masaryk elected president of Czechoslovakia

16 November Hungary proclaims itself a republic

14 December UK general election voting: Lloyd George's Liberal
and Conservative coalition wins a huge majority;
Sinn Féin wins 73 of Ireland's 105 seats

1919

15 January Spartacist uprising crushed in Berlin,
Rosa Luxemburg shot

18 January Peace conference opens in Paris

21 January Irish parliament, Dáil Éireann, inaugurated in Dublin.
Two policemen killed in an ambush by Irish Volunteers
at Soloheadbeg in County Tipperary

5 February Charlie Chaplin, Mary Pickford, Douglas Fairbanks,
and D. W. Griffith launch United Artists film studio

8 March Anti-British riots erupt in Cairo

23 March Mussolini launches Italian fascist movement

1 April Following his escape from Lincoln Prison in February,
Eamon de Valera elected president of Dáil Éireann

13 April In India, 379 protesting civilians massacred by British
troops at Amritsar

14–25 April General strike in Limerick sees the formation of the
Limerick soviet

11 June De Valera arrives in New York at the start of an
eighteen-month tour of the United States

23 June	Detective Inspector Hunt shot dead in Market Square, Thurles
28 June	Treaty of Versailles signed
30 July	Detective Patrick Smyth of G Division of the DMP shot by IRA Squad in Dublin [dies 8 September]
12 September	Dáil Éireann declared illegal
19 December	Viceroy Lord French survives assassination attempt in Dublin

1920

2 January	Ex-servicemen recruited to reinforce the Royal Irish Constabulary; they become known as the Black and Tans
15 January	Sinn Féin scores big successes in local government elections
13–17 March	Attempted right-wing coup fails in Germany
20 March	Lord Mayor of Cork, Tomás Mac Curtain, shot dead at his home
26 March	Retired magistrate investigating Dáil finances, Alan Bell, shot dead in Dublin
3 April	Hundreds of tax offices and abandoned police barracks burned by the IRA
12 April	General strike in support of hunger strikers at Mountjoy Prison in Dublin
19 July	Sectarian rioting begins in Derry; 19 killed over several days
21 July	Expulsion of Catholics from Belfast shipyards sets off three days of violence
25 July	French troops occupy Damascus to begin French mandate in Syria
27 July	Auxiliary Divison of the RIC is launched, made up of ex-British Army officers
6 August	Dáil Éireann declares boycott of goods from protestant firms in Belfast
9 August	Restoration of Order in Ireland Act gives military sweeping powers including trial of civilians by court martial

22 *August* Assassination of Detective Inspector Swanzy in Lisburn sparks renewed violence in Belfast

20 *September* Black and Tans ransack Balbriggan in County Dublin

14 *October* One of the Soloheadbeg ambushers, Sean Treacy, shot dead in a street battle with Auxiliaries and British intelligence agents in Dublin

25 *October* Terence MacSwiney, Lord Mayor of Cork, dies in Brixton Prison in London after 74 days on hunger strike

1 *November* IRA volunteer, Kevin Barry (aged eighteen), hanged for the murder of a British soldier in the first execution since the 1916 Rising

2 *November* The Republican Warren G. Harding, an isolationist, wins the US presidential election

21 *November* IRA Squad organised by Michael Collins kills 14 suspected British secret service agents; Black and Tans kill 12 during a football match at Croke Park

28 *November* 18 Auxiliaries killed in an ambush at Kilmichael, County Cork

10 *December* The American Mamie Smith becomes the first black singer to make a gramophone record

11 *December* Following an IRA ambush in Cork, Auxiliaries and Black and Tans set fire to large parts of the centre of Cork city

23 *December* British parliament passes the Better Government of Ireland Act, creating two parliaments, one for Southern Ireland (covering 26 counties) and another for Northern Ireland (6 counties)

1921

1 *January* The destruction of seven houses in County Cork by military order signals the start of official reprisals.

7 *March* The Mayor of Limerick, George Clancy, and the former mayor, Michael O'Callaghan, shot dead at their homes

24 *May* General election for parliaments in Northern and Southern Ireland: Sinn Féin candidates returned

unopposed to 124 of the 128 seats in the south; in Northern Ireland, Unionists win 40 seats, Sinn Féin 6 and Nationalists 6

25 May   Custom House in Dublin set on fire in IRA attack on headquarters of Local Government Board and burns for five days, destroying thousands of administrative records.

22 June   George V opens Northern Ireland parliament and calls for reconciliation in Ireland.

11 July   Truce between British forces and IRA comes into effect

14–21 July   Lloyd George meets de Valera in London three times to explore grounds for peace talks

9 October–   Anglo-Irish conference opens at Downing Street
6 December   to negotiate final settlement of the Irish question

6 December   Anglo-Irish Treaty signed in London at 2.10 a.m.

14 December   Dáil Éireann meets to debate the treaty

16 December   British parliament ratifies Anglo-Irish Treaty

1922

7 January   Dáil Éireann approves the treaty by 64 votes to 57

16 January   Michael Collins, as chairman of the Provisional Government of the Irish Free State, takes formal control of Dublin Castle

2 February   James Joyce's novel *Ulysses* published in Paris

11 February   Four Special Constables from Northern Ireland and one IRA man killed in clash at Clones railway station in County Monaghan

27 March   Anti-treaty convention representing almost fifty brigades of the IRA meets in Dublin

29 March   Police suspected of involvement in the killing of Catholic publican Owen McMahon and four members of his family at their home in Belfast

13 April   Anti-treaty IRA units occupy Four Courts in Dublin

25–29 April   13 Protestant men shot dead in County Cork

1 May   Over £750,000 taken by anti-treaty forces in bank raids

16 June   General election results in victory for pro-treaty candidates; constitution of Irish Free State published

22 June	Field Marshal Sir Henry Wilson shot dead outside his London home
28 June	Assault on the Four Courts by Provisional Government forces begins civil war
30 June	Republicans in Four Courts surrender; fighting continues in Dublin
5 July	Cathal Brugha fatally wounded as anti-treaty forces are defeated in Dublin
20 July	Limerick and Waterford occupied by Provisional Government forces
10 August	Provisional Government troops enter Cork
12 August	Arthur Griffith dies of a cerebral haemorrhage
22 August	Michael Collins killed, aged thirty-one, in an ambush in County Cork
25 August	W. T. Cosgrave becomes chairman of the Provisonal Government
28 August	Large crowds attend the funeral of Michael Collins in Dublin
24 September	'Battling Siki' defeats Georges Carpentier in Paris to become world light heavyweight boxing champion
28 September	The Dáil approves military courts empowered to impose the death penalty
10 October	Catholic bishops denounce anti-treaty campaign, declaring that killing government soldiers is murder
17 November	Four men shot by firing squad in Dublin in first executions of republicans
24 November	Erskine Childers executed for possession of a revolver
6 December	Irish Free State established
7 December	Northern Ireland parliament votes to remain in United Kingdom
7–8 December	One member of the Dáil is shot dead and another wounded in Dublin; in retaliation, the government executes four republican prisoners
10 December	Arson attack on the home of Sean McGarry, a member of the Dáil, leads to the death of his son.

1923

20 January 11 republicans executed

29 January House of Sir Horace Plunkett, one of the founders of the Irish co-operative movement, burned by republicans in one of several attacks on the homes of newly appointed senators

10 April Chief-of-staff of the anti-treaty IRA, Liam Lynch, dies aged thirty-three, after being shot by Free State troops in the Knockmealdown mountains in County Tipperary

24 May De Valera issues ceasefire order to anti-treaty forces

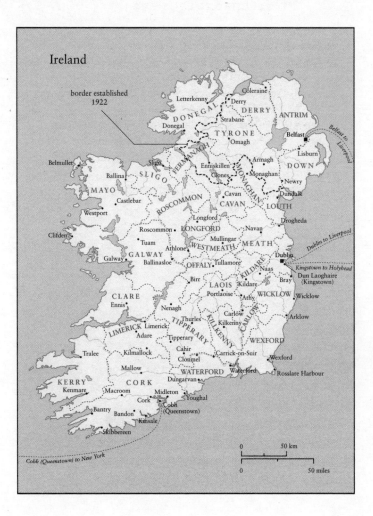

Ireland

border established
1922

Letterkenny
Coleraine
Derry
DONEGAL
DERRY
ANTRIM
Donegal
Strabane
TYRONE
Belfast
Omagh
Belfast to Liverpool
Lisburn
Belmullet
Sligo
FERMANAGH
Armagh
DOWN
Ballina
Enniskillen
Newry
MAYO
SLIGO
Clones
Monaghan
MONAGHAN
Dundalk
Castlebar
ROSCOMMON
Cavan
LOUTH
CAVAN
Westport
Longford
Drogheda
Clifden
Roscommon
LONGFORD
Navan
Dublin to Liverpool
Tuam
Mullingar
MEATH
Athlone
WESTMEATH
Dublin
Galway
GALWAY
OFFALY
Tullamore
Kingstown to Holyhead
Ballinasloe
Naas
KILDARE
Bray
Dun Laoghaire
(Kingstown)
Birr
Kildare
CLARE
LAOIS
WICKLOW
Wicklow
Ennis
Portlaoise
Athy
Nenagh
CARLOW
Arklow
Thurles
Carlow
LIMERICK
TIPPERARY
Kilkenny
Limerick
KILKENNY
Adare
Tipperary
WEXFORD
Cahir
Kilmallock
Clonmel
Carrick-on-Suir
Wexford
Tralee
Mallow
WATERFORD
Waterford
Dungarvan
Rosslare Harbour
KERRY
CORK
Midleton
Youghal
Kenmare
Macroom
Cork
Bantry
Bandon
Cobh
(Queenstown)
Kinsale
Skibbereen

Cobh (Queenstown) to New York

0	50 km
0	50 miles

Prologue: Two Funerals

Just before 1.30 p.m. on Sunday, 30 September 1917, six members of the Irish Volunteers in military uniform prepared to carry the coffin of their comrade, Thomas Ashe, down the steps of City Hall in Dublin to a waiting hearse piled with wreaths. Ashe – the commander of the most successful Irish military operation of the failed Easter Rising of 1916 – had died the previous Tuesday in hospital after being force fed on hunger strike in Mountjoy Prison while serving a sentence for seditious speech. In the days after his death the city was tense; rumours circulated that other prisoners on hunger strike might die. Men and women wore black and small boys wandered the streets selling photographs of the dead martyr and copies of the poem he had written in Lewes Gaol in Sussex after the Rising: 'Let me carry your Cross for Ireland, Lord!' In a series of elaborate processions, Ashe's body was taken from the hospital to the Pro-Cathedral and then to City Hall, where he lay in state, guarded by Volunteers in their illegal uniforms, as thousands of mourners filed past his coffin. All these events had been meticulously planned by the new leaders who had emerged after 1916 – Eamon de Valera, Michael Collins, Richard Mulcahy – and thousands of people had gathered in Dublin for the crowning spectacle, the funeral procession to Glasnevin Cemetery.

The start time itself would be an act of defiance. Less than a year previously the House of Commons had voted to end the custom whereby Dublin Mean Time was twenty-five minutes behind Greenwich Mean Time, in accordance with the later sunrise in the west. The entire civilised world, the British government declared, was divided into hourly time zones, so why should Ireland be an exception? But the timetable for Thomas Ashe's funeral had been advertised according to the old, dissonant time. As the crowds lining the streets waited for the cortège to set off at 1.30, the minute hands on the public clocks around them crept towards 1.55. Since midday, City Hall had been closed to the public so that Ashe's family could remain with the body. Before the coffin was carried outside, a priest from Kerry recited the Rosary in Irish. Only a few days earlier this same litany, recited during evening devotions in a Dublin church, was credited with inspiring the remarkable recovery of speech and hearing by Private Francis Donaghy of the Royal Irish Regiment, who had lain deaf and dumb in St George's Hospital with shell shock after fighting for Britain and her allies on the battle-fields of France.

The prisoners who carried Thomas Ashe's body to the hearse had been in gaol with him in Lewes. The coffin was draped with the green, white and orange tricolour, the flag first raised above the General Post Office in Dublin seventeen months earlier when an Irish Republic was proclaimed. Up ahead fifty Irish Volunteers had arranged themselves in formation to lead the procession to Glasnevin Cemetery, three miles to the north across the River Liffey. Following them were more than a hundred Catholic priests, led by two Capuchin fathers who had given the last rites to the leaders of the Easter Rising executed just over a year before in

Kilmainham Gaol. Alongside the hearse two rows of Irish Volunteers in uniform – looking not unlike soldiers of the Great War – stood ready with their rifles reversed. Behind it a horse pulled a cart carrying more wreaths. And then came the carriages carrying the chief mourners, Thomas Ashe's father, brother and sister; the official car of the Catholic Archbishop of Dublin, its blinds drawn; the Lord Mayor's carriage and, snaking far back along the street, dozens of other carriages carrying elected officials from all parts of Ireland, waiting their turn to jolt forward.

All morning people in uniforms, sashes and emblems had been gathering in the surrounding streets to join the procession. Now they stretched out in a long line to march solemnly behind the carriages: brass bands from the Dublin Fire Brigade, boys from Na Fianna (an Irish nationalist version of Robert Baden-Powell's Boy Scouts), women from Cumann na mBan, the support organisation for the Volunteers, hundreds of primary-school teachers, all varieties of trade unionists from butchers to brushmakers, widows and relatives of those who took part in the recent insurrection, men and women from the Gaelic Athletic Association, carrying hurley sticks over their shoulders. As this long column moved off down Dame Street, the thousands of men and women lining the pavement removed their hats. The hearse passed Dublin Castle, the administrative centre of British power in Ireland, where just the previous Friday night an audience of wounded soldiers had been treated to a concert in St Patrick's Hall. Tricolours hung from the windows of houses and offices, many of them inscribed with a cross. On the pavement men made their way through the crowd handing out reprints of a letter from the Catholic Bishop of Killaloe in the previous day's *Freeman's Journal* condemning 'the slow killing of poor

Thomas Ashe'. He had been subjected, the bishop wrote, to 'the sort of cruelty we are accustomed to hear of as possible only in the ancient Bastille, or the dungeons of Naples or the black prison of Russia' and the world would soon see 'in these hideous atrocities what the triumph of English culture means for small nationalities'.

Half a mile away, on the other side of the river, the English writer Douglas Goldring had taken a taxi to Dublin's principal thoroughfare, Sackville Street, to await the arrival of the cortège. There were so many people that his driver had to lean out of the window to plead with the spectators to move aside and let them through. As the car crawled through the crowd Goldring spotted people he knew: a friend who appeared to be accompanied by an English staff officer in mufti; a well-to-do Dublin doctor; intellectuals from the city's literary soirées; and the wife of a tobacconist dragging along 'her three rather grubby little boys'. Finally, the taxi came to a halt near Lord Nelson's Pillar and Goldring joined the spectators. He watched a gang of schoolboys across the street climb the remaining wall of a building destroyed by shellfire during the suppression of the Rising the previous year and sit dangling their legs as they waited for the funeral procession to pass. Such was the demand for vantage points that people with houses along the route were able to charge spectators for window seats. Although City Hall was less than fifteen minutes' walk away, it was an hour before Goldring saw the procession turn into Sackville Street, advancing silently, save when one band or another struck up a rebel melody. The presence of the archbishop's car and the Lord Mayor's carriage lent, he thought, a touch of official dignity to the spectacle; a foreigner, Goldring suspected, might conclude that this was the funeral of a famous soldier rather than a convicted criminal.

In the middle of the marchers a home-made banner appeared above the heads of a group of schoolchildren, so small that their heads were barely visible; the words 'In Memory of Thomas Ashe who died for Ireland' had been embroidered on the cloth in black thread. When the last of the marchers had passed and his taxi was reversing into the street, Goldring drew alongside the British officer he had noticed earlier. 'Oh yes, we do just the same in India,' Goldring heard him say to his companion. 'We always give the natives a free hand with their religious rites.'

The procession finally reached Glasnevin Cemetery just before four o'clock, the crescendo of Handel's Dead March from *Saul* and chanting priests reaching the crowd already inside. Volunteers controlled the entrance and only those holding permits were allowed to gather around the newly dug grave. After the tricolour was removed and folded, the coffin was lowered into the ground and the assembled priests intoned the *Miserere-Benedictus* beneath a waft of incense. Many mourners wept as they recited the Rosary. When the last murmurs of prayer faded, Michael Collins, in his vice-commandant's uniform, issued a command in Irish to the captain of the firing party lined up by the graveside. Raising their rifles, they fired three volleys towards the sky. A bugler sounded the Last Post and Collins, standing at the head of the grave, his back to a Celtic stone cross, pushed out his jaw to give the oration. Its brevity was a jolt to an audience accustomed to set-piece funereal eloquence. Even when repeated in English his speech had taken less than a minute. 'Nothing additional remains to be said. That volley is the only speech it is proper to make above the grave of a dead Fenian.'

Ernie O'Malley, a twenty-year-old medical student at University College Dublin, had marched to the cemetery with

'F' Company of the Dublin Brigade of the Volunteers. He carried a revolver inside his coat and his pockets were full of ammunition and field dressings because he and his friends were sure that the police and the army would never allow the Volunteers to defy the law and march in formation in their uniforms, carrying weapons. O'Malley spent the day manning a cordon across a quiet road near Glasnevin wondering what was happening in other parts of the city. In the evening, when the crowds had long gone, his company's turn came to march past Ashe's grave and then back into the city once more before being dismissed. They felt elated and that this was the beginning of something that could not be reversed. 'The Volunteers had held the streets of the capital, had kept order, had marched in the forbidden formations, and had worn uniforms. A firing squad had carried rifles and fired volleys.' That evening many people who took part in the procession crowded into the Bohemian picture-house in Phibsboro on the north side of the city to watch highlights of the funeral, which for ten minutes showed Dublin as the capital of a nation apart.

9 March 1918

On the morning of Wednesday, 6 March 1918, the Irish MP for Waterford, John Redmond, died of heart failure in a nursing home in London while recovering from an operation for gallstones. At sixty-two Redmond personified Irish constitutional nationalism. A country gentleman with the appearance of 'a tamed and weary hawk', he was the leader of the Irish Party at Westminster, where his great-uncle and his father had served as MPs. Redmond's body was taken to Westminster Cathedral, where it lay covered in the flag of the home-rule movement – a golden harp in yellow on a green field – which had also been draped on the coffin of his brother, Willie, who had been killed in France less than nine months previously. The Irish in London – many of them soldiers home from the front – came to pay their respects. The following morning, the Archbishop of Westminster, Cardinal Francis Bourne, led a solemn High Mass before a congregation thronged with Irish clergy but also the great and the good of London. King George V sent a personal representative and the British prime minister David Lloyd George, the Conservative leader Bonar Law and other members of the government were present. The previous day Lloyd George had recalled in the House of Commons how one of his earliest memories of being an MP was an old member pointing to Redmond and saying, 'There goes one of the most respected members of this House.' Redmond's support for the war had given him a great place in the affection of Britain, the prime minister said. But the last time Lloyd George had seen the Irish leader, Redmond looked a broken man with death written on his face. In September 1914 Redmond appeared to have achieved his life's ambition when home rule for Ireland was passed into law, its implementation suspended until the conclusion of the world war just declared. But the draining conflict that followed had made Redmond and his parliamentarians appear marginal and irrelevant. The Easter Rising in 1916 was a direct challenge to his right to speak for Ireland.

News of Redmond's funeral arrangements was published on Friday, 8 March. His coffin was to be taken by boat to Ireland and then by train along the east coast to his home town of Wexford. It was no longer certain that the remains of the leader of constitutional Irish nationalism would be received with the respect that might have been expected for a dead chief. Some of Redmond's supporters worried that feelings were running so high against him that the funeral might provoke humiliating demonstrations. A new hunger strike by Sinn Féin prisoners demanding political status was under way in Dublin; there were warnings of 'another Thomas Ashe tragedy'.

A small crowd gathered on the platform at Euston station when Redmond's body was put on board the 8.45 p.m. mail train to Holyhead. Special carriages were reserved for Mrs Redmond and prominent leaders of the Irish Party and for the wreaths that had amassed in Westminster. Two priests recited the Rosary on the platform, and while the mourners were responding, the train pulled out of the station. It was raining heavily when the mailboat arrived at Kingstown early the following morning. Flags on the other ships in the harbour flew at half mast. Members of the National Volunteers, the quasi-military units still loyal to the Irish Party, were in charge of managing the crowd gathered on the pier. Many people wore black rosettes and a badge with a photo of Redmond. Officials from Dublin Castle had come to pay their respects: Sir Bryan Mahon, the commander of British forces in Ireland, and Sir William Byrne, the undersecretary in the Irish administration. There was a brief wait while leading figures in the Irish Party boarded the steamboat to offer their condolences to the Redmond family and then Mrs Redmond appeared with her son, Captain William Redmond, in his army uniform. A bell tolled in a nearby church as the coffin was carried past a few dozen men from Captain Redmond's regiment, the Royal Irish, and put on the train that would take him home to Wexford.

The engine draped in crape pulled its carriages south along the coast through the wealthy southern suburbs of Dublin and then down to the resort of Bray (where Charlie Chaplin was playing at the picture-house in *The Vagabond*), along the cliff edge with the 'sea thundering below' and down into County Wicklow through the village of Woodenbridge, where Redmond had made his famous promise to support the Allied war effort. It passed silent crowds standing in the rain on bridges, at level crossings and at little stations along the line. Benedictine nuns from the Belgian town of Ypres, whom Redmond had helped to find refuge during the war, knelt in the fields around their convent as the train passed. As it stopped in one small town after another a handful of people would come forward and kneel in prayer by the carriage carrying the coffin. But that same week in the towns and villages along the Dublin–Wexford line, through which the Redmond funeral party made its melancholy journey, people were reading in their local papers about big meetings of Sinn Féin clubs and the opening of new branches. In Arklow the winner of the Sinn Féin club raffle received a full-sized portrait of Thomas Ashe.

The train reached Wexford North station at half past ten and was met by the mayor and leading public figures from the town. All shops and businesses were closed and life-size pictures of Redmond were displayed along the streets. Thousands of people had gathered around a monument to Redmond's great-uncle, who was credited with giving the town its railways, steamships and harbour, even its public institutions. The bells of both Protestant and Catholic churches tolled as the procession made its way through the town. At the Church of the Immaculate Conception the organist played Chopin's Funeral March as the coffin was carried up the centre aisle. After solemn High Mass it was carried out of the church by some of Redmond's constituents from Waterford.

A band from the Royal Irish Regiment led the procession to the family vault followed by soldiers and sailors who had served in the war, among them a contingent from the American navy. Sixty priests marched in front of the hearse and alongside it in full uniform were two columns of members of the Irish National Foresters, a Catholic welfare society aligned with Redmond's party.

At the graveside John Dillon, Redmond's loyal lieutenant, said time would do justice to Redmond's life's work; even people in Ireland who misunderstood him would come to appreciate his greatness. Redmond, Dillon said, had 'left the whole of England friendly to his country's freedom'. Later a member of Wexford Corporation followed Dillon when paying tribute to Redmond. The late leader had been hounded out of public life, Mr D. R. Keating said, by lay people and clerics who had stooped to a cesspool of slander. However, at a meeting of the Sinn Féin club in nearby Kilmacanogue Mr C. M. Byrne asked if Ireland was the only country in the world that feared to change leaders who had proved false to the trust of the people. During the war all the great powers had changed and rechanged their statesmen and generals; all the more reason, Mr Byrne said to applause, why Ireland should scrap the leaders who had failed them.

Benito Mussolini would not have been surprised that developments across Europe during the First World War were invoked at a meeting in a tiny village in the south-east of Ireland. 'The whole earth trembles,' the future dictator of Italy wrote at the time. 'All continents are riven by the same crisis. There is not a single part of the planet . . . which is not shaken by the cyclone. In old Europe, men disappear, systems break, institutions collapse.' In a country where the public funeral had become a political art form, the farewells to Ashe and Redmond – one triumphal, the other tinged with defeat – dramatised the local symptoms of the global upheaval Mussolini described. It would have been odd if Ireland had remained untouched by such an all-consuming storm. And yet, the story of the culmination of Ireland's independence struggle has too often been told in a claustrophobic Anglo-Irish setting, with the global war a mere backdrop to events that were uniquely heroic or uniquely disastrous depending on a point of view often inflected by contemporary politics.

Nationalist movements across the world were taking advantage of the immense pressure on the empires that contained them. Why would Ireland have been different? According to the Czech leader Tomáš Masaryk, the war had turned Europe into 'a laboratory atop a vast graveyard'. The experiment launched by the independence movement in Czechoslovakia and led by Masaryk and his followers matched Ireland's in almost every detail. Radical Czech nationalists protested that Austria-Hungary had repressed the democratic demands of the people, almost wiping out their language and their sense of nationality until a spirited band of intellectuals, styled as the 'Awakeners', reinvigorated interest in their own history and national culture, defining themselves as the antithesis of the Habsburgs. When the war began many Czechs supported the Austrians, but the radicals saw the conflagration as an opportunity to win independence. 'Our future is in us, ourselves!' proclaimed a nationalist newspaper in 1914, echoing the meaning of 'Sinn Féin', 'we ourselves'. Czechoslovakia was placed under military rule during the war. Moderates who wanted to accommodate the empire lost ground. Like the leaders of the Easter Rising, Masaryk was convinced that without an army they would 'obtain nothing from anybody', so he recruited a Czechoslovak legion from among the thousands of Czech soldiers in the Russian army. His movement established a shadow state and lobbied assiduously for international recognition.

Masaryk's lieutenant, Edvard Beneš, put Czechoslovakia's successful struggle for independence down to its ability to respond to the transformative moment created by the war: 'We adjusted our movement to the scope of world events.' The scale of Ireland's adjustment to the revolutionary world of 1918 is often muted in histories that focus on the template established in the late nineteenth century: Protestant resistance to Catholic demands for self-government and the rivalry between constitutional nationalists striving for Irish home rule at Westminster and the violent conspiratorial separatists of the Irish Republican Brotherhood. John Redmond's success on the eve of the First World War in making home rule for Ireland inevitable was the springboard for more radical nationalists to launch an insurrection proclaiming a republic. And the Easter Rising they organised in 1916 created a national vocabulary to match that of the combatants on the western front – blood sacrifice, an assertion of a nation's manhood and a commitment to honour the dead by fighting on to realise their dreams. A political movement dismissed not long before as a relic of the past now looked very modern.

The Irish revolution was part of the unravelling of empires provoked by the First World War but the state born at its conclusion was unique in western Europe. Czechoslovakia and the other new states in the east emerged from collapsed or defeated empires. Irish independence was wrested from a victorious world power expanding the territory it controlled across the globe. The arrangements finally agreed for the establishment of the Irish Free State were deeply influenced by the changing nature of Britain's imperial mission. The first dent in the integrity of the British Empire – so flawed and traumatic for Irish revolutionaries – inspired movements from India to Palestine: in his clandestine fight against the British protectorate in 1940s Jerusalem the young Yitzhak Shamir used the *nom de guerre* 'Michael' in homage to his hero, Michael Collins. And even in countries where little is known of what happened between 1919 and 1921, the Irish War of Independence has forever fixed Ireland in the popular imagination as an anti-imperial nation. But the price of freedom was partition and enormous challenges for a small country in a modern world where many believed isolated states were an anachronism. The astonishing rise of the United States as a global economic power seemed to confirm this view.

Fixated on de-anglicising Ireland, the revolutionaries who fought for Irish independence did not appear to notice the beginnings of the Americanisation of the entire world. Writing on the fiftieth anniversary of the Easter Rising in 1966, the Irish taoiseach, Seán Lemass – who had fought in the General Post Office as a sixteen-year-old – suggested that historians in 2016 would be able to 'detect some at least of the influences already operating, which will eventually decide the kind of country we will become, even if we today are not aware of them, or can only faintly detect their effects'. The traces of Ireland's future in the twentieth century are all to be found in the dramatic years of the independence struggle because the new state emerged into a world that was revolutionary in every sense. The ideal of creating a distinctive Irish civilisation came up against Ireland's openness to the currents of modern life flowing across all the new borders: jazz, cinema and the lure of America, as well as the influence of London. The hopes, dreams and bitter disappointments of the revolutionary years affected everyone in Ireland whether they fought or not. On election day 1918 they prepared to stake their place in the post-war world.

I

Victory of the Rainbow Chasers

Some people noticed the women, the novelty of it all. In the election that changed Ireland for ever on that Saturday morning, 14 December 1918, they turned up at polling stations in a steady stream from 8 o'clock, the first time women had ever entered polling booths in Britain and Ireland and put a mark on a ballot paper. By mid-afternoon in Dublin, as twilight crept up on a mild showery day, more women than men had voted (although this might have been influenced by the decision to give most workers the day off and the fact that the pubs were still open). In a village in South Tyrone, in the north of Ireland, a woman aged a hundred arrived to claim her vote and was almost carried to her ballot paper. Some reports chose to emphasise how even determined women betrayed uncertainty about their new status as voters, citizens with a say in determining the fate of Ireland in the post-war world. In some polling stations women asked the clerk to mark their papers; in others they brought their friends to help them put the X in the right place or held up their ballot papers for inspection to make sure they had marked them correctly. That morning's *Irish Times* recognised that the women would be vital to the outcome. An editorial urged spouses to relax temporarily the normal domestic regime: 'If any woman pleads domestic engagements, her husband should tell her that on this one occasion his dinner is less vital than her vote,' the editorial advised. 'If any man is disposed to thinking voting "a bother", his wife should insist on leading him to the poll.'

The women voters the *Irish Times* had in mind, those who might pay heed to what the paper had to say, were the wives of men who would vote for unionist candidates dedicated to keeping Ireland within the United Kingdom. But these were not the people who would decide what this election would mean for Ireland. Everybody knew where the real challenge was coming from: the new movement that had swept the country since the 1916 Rising, Sinn Féin. In addition to extending the franchise to women over thirty, the Representation of the People Act passed in February 1918 had also given the vote to all adult males over twenty-one. The Irish electorate had nearly tripled from 700,000 to 1.9 million. The implications of this experiment in mass democracy were set to be even more dramatic in Ireland than in Britain. Sinn Féin was taking on the constitutional nationalist party that had argued Ireland's case for home rule in Westminster for nearly forty years. If they won, the Sinn Féin leaders were promising not to take their seats in the House of Commons but instead to establish an Irish parliament in Dublin.

Sinn Féin supporters were running a far more visible campaign than their opponents, carloads of canvassers crisscrossing the country in pursuit of votes. In an age newly enthralled by speed, when racing drivers were popular heroes and automobiles had suddenly become objects of desire, the Sinn Féin convoys marked the party out as modern and exotic, with a flair for organisation, youth and vigour. It was not an accidental image. Back in 1908 – the year Henry Ford launched the Model T – a Sinn Féin election poster portrayed

John Redmond, the leader of the Irish Party at Westminster, as a forlorn cabbie in a horse and carriage watching a car emblazoned with 'Sinn Féin' on its side – 'that infernal machine with the foreign name' – stealing his customers. Now young men and women were driving all over the country condemning the world-weariness and cynicism of their elders. A well-read landowner who watched them thought they were 'exactly similar in appearance and manner with those who must have carried through the French Revolution'.

In rural towns speakers told their audiences of farmers, shop assistants and labourers that the world was changing: the war had set the stage for the rise of small nationalities all over Europe. Was Ireland going to be the only one left out? A candidate in Cork spoke of 'a wave of democracy in the world'. Sometimes Sinn Féin speakers talked about establishing an 'Irish republic' and sometimes about more nebulous ideas of 'freedom' and 'sovereign independence'. In the words of the Sinn Féin propagandist Aodh de Blácam, whatever form it took, the ancient Irish nation about to be reborn would be both thoroughly up to date – 'the world's working model of a modern Catholic state' – and a champion of lost ideals in an age of greed, 'a medieval fragment in the modern world'. Ireland would stand for spirituality against the materialism of the imperialists. It would reject the debased conditions of the crowded industrial cities of Britain or America – where millions of Irish emigrants lived and worked – in pursuit of rural simplicity. High ideals could also be compatible with personal advancement. In an independent republic, a Sinn Féin speaker told a rally in Tipperary, open competition for jobs would leave the highest position open to the humblest individual with merit. 'They used to deride us[,] call us foolish boys and rainbow chasers,' another speaker crowed, 'but the platform is full of the best elements of the town, the workers and the hard-headed businessmen have combined to win Ireland's freedom through Sinn Féin.'

Where had this insurgent party come from? Four years of global war had reshaped Ireland's ancient quarrel about the terms on which it could be independent from Britain and whether everyone on the island could be reconciled to independence. Even before 1914, when the military became the mapmakers of the world, Ireland was already a country of competing armies. There were nearly 30,000 British soldiers stationed in Ireland in addition to 12,000 armed policemen. When it looked as if the British government was certain to concede the long-running Irish nationalist demand for home rule, Protestants in the north-east established their own militia, thousands of men marching and drilling with rifles illegally imported from Germany. They threatened to declare a provisional government in defiance of both London and the new administration that would sit in Dublin. In response, the nationalists in the rest of Ireland, mostly Catholics, formed their own volunteer force.

When the war started in Europe, John Redmond delivered speeches in which he urged these volunteers to join up to fight for Britain and her allies, envisaging the Irish contingent as the equals of the Australians, South Africans and Canadians: nations within the empire, fighting for the king against the barbarous Prussians. Redmond believed the experience could convince the Ulster Protestants that there was nothing to fear from home rule after all, that Ireland could be a self-governing nation *and* a loyal member of the empire. 'No people can be said to have rightly proved their nationhood and their power to maintain it until they have demonstrated their military prowess,' Redmond declared. The Irish had shown they could fight – 'Irish blood had reddened the earth of every continent' – but 'never until now have we as a people set a national army in the field'. The Irish nation could come into its own, Redmond thought, through a blood sacrifice on the side of the Allied cause against Germany: 'It is heroic deeds entering into their traditions that give life to nations – that is the recompense of those who die to perform them.'

A minority of the nationalist volunteers refused to follow Redmond, insisting that the empire's cause was not Ireland's. Far from joining the Allies, they argued, Irish nationalists should take advantage of British involvement in a major war to strike their own blow for complete freedom. In Redmond's view, these dissenters – spouting old saws that 'England's difficulty is Ireland's opportunity', rhetorical leftovers of previous failed attempts to achieve Irish independence by force, such as the abortive Fenian uprising of 1867 – were out of touch with the times and would soon be irrelevant. If, as many believed, the war in Europe would be over by Christmas, Ireland would shortly have its own parliament, its nationhood restored. Redmond looked forward to thousands of his volunteers returning from a victorious war to line up proudly in Dublin for the opening of a new home-rule parliament.

But the war did not turn out as Redmond hoped. It was not just that it lasted four years instead of four months, so that the prospect of Irish home rule seemed as far away as ever. Although over 200,000 Irishmen signed up and some 35,000 died, the Irish soldiers were never recognised as a distinct unit in the way Redmond wished. Farmers made money from increased food prices but workers languished in unemployment. Enthusiasm for enlisting fell away; the Pope declared that the war was futile. As early as 1915, ordinary people began to fear that they would be conscripted to become anonymous cannon fodder in a slaughter that had no end in sight.

On Easter Monday 1916 a small group among the minority of volunteers who had always opposed Redmond's call to arms launched an insurrection in Dublin against British rule. Led by members of the secret revolutionary organisation the Irish Republican Brotherhood (IRB), and supported by the socialist James Connolly and his small Irish Citizen Army, they took over the General Post Office in the centre of Dublin and several other strategic buildings. Standing outside the post office, their spokesman, the poet and teacher Patrick Pearse, addressed the people of Ireland: 'In the name of God and of the dead generations from which she receives her old tradition of nationhood, Ireland, through us, summons her children to her flag and strikes for her freedom.' He also claimed the attention of the rest of the world: 'In every generation the Irish people have asserted their right to national freedom and sovereignty . . . again asserting it in arms in the face of the world, we hereby proclaim the Irish Republic as a Sovereign Independent State . . .'

Denis Johnston, the fourteen-year-old son of a judge who was a moderate supporter of home rule, lived the privileged life of a member of the southern Protestant establishment in a comfortable house on Lansdowne Road, not far from the rugby ground. At Easter 1916 he had returned for the holiday from his Scottish boarding school. As he went to bed on Easter Monday rumours reached the suburbs about the dramatic events unfolding in the centre of Dublin. He was awoken at half past midnight by his father switching on the light. 'You'd better get dressed,' he said. 'The house is being occupied.' When Denis came out to the landing and peered down into the hallway he saw a tall figure in a slouch hat and a green uniform, with a bandolier across his shoulder. It was clearly a class of person he had never encountered before, but instead of a terrifying revolutionary Denis saw 'an honest round face and an embarrassed smile'. Afterwards, the thing he remembered most about the intruders was how politely they behaved. They apologised for disturbing the Johnstons; any damage they might unavoidably be forced to do would be compensated by the Irish Republic. Denis's father was particularly alarmed by their proposal to knock a hole in the wall of a bedroom so that they could escape quickly into the neighbouring house if attacked. He reasoned with them until they were finally dissuaded from remodelling the house. Then the Johnstons and their captors sat amid the displaced furniture to have tea and bread and butter. The next day the rebels had moved on, leaving uniforms, rifles and ammunition behind. When soldiers arrived to save the loyal population from the rebels, the commander of the detachment of Sherwood Foresters made to reassure the Johnstons that the rebellion would be crushed. 'Never fear, madam,' a soldier told Denis's mother, 'we'll take no prisoners.' Denis remembered that her face puckered up and she answered caustically, 'I don't know what you mean, they were very nice, civil boys.'

The Crown forces bombarded the rebels and forced their surrender within six days. The centre of Dublin was in ruins; nearly 500 people had been killed, half of them civilians, and 2,500 wounded. Pearse justified the Rising in terms similar to those in which Redmond had championed Irish participation in the world war: it was a blood sacrifice to rouse the Irish people to seize their freedom. At first the nation seemed apathetic, even hostile. But that a woman of Mrs Johnston's class and outlook was impressed by the demeanour and gallantry of the rebels suggests that even those who regarded the insurrection as reckless folly saw some symmetry between the republican volunteers and the soldiers fighting in France. The execution of fifteen of the leaders of the Rising, including Pearse, over ten days in May 1916 turned ambiguous admiration for their misguided valour into a sense of outrage. A few weeks after his house had been occupied, young Denis Johnston noted that the public mood was sour: 'They were still shooting rebels and people were getting fed up with it.' There was mounting disgust that the socialist leader James Connolly, who had been badly wounded in the GPO, was 'being apparently nursed around in hospital in order to get him fit to be shot'. The regime of military government that followed the Rising was deeply resented. By the autumn of 1916 Irish soldiers fighting on the western front were enraged by what they were hearing about conditions at home. The nationalist MP from Belfast, Joe Devlin, who had followed his leader John Redmond in encouraging thousands of northern Catholics to fight for the Allies, told the House of Commons he was receiving streams of angry letters from the Irish troops. The general thrust, Devlin said, was that they had not enlisted to fight a war on behalf of small nations so that Ireland would be run by a military dictatorship.

By then the executed leaders had been converted into martyrs, their pictures displayed in shop windows, on the walls of humble cottages and on Mass cards and calendars circulating all over the country. The Rising was styled the 'Sinn Féin rebellion' merely because this small political party was one of the most well known of the fringe radical nationalist groups. Its founder, an obsessive polemical journalist called Arthur Griffith, had fought for the Boers in South Africa and returned to Ireland advocating passive resistance to British rule and economic self-sufficiency. But within a year the survivors of the insurrection had used the name to harness the new angry public mood over the executions, military rule and the fear of conscription. The Sinn Féin movement now embraced the people who had taken up arms in 1916 and were ready to do so again, advocates of passive resistance such as Griffith, and disillusioned members and supporters of Redmond's party. It asserted itself as the new, energetic voice of Irish nationalism, blessed with the authority of 1916, no longer deferential or accommodating to British statesmen and parliamentary procedure. In a series of by-elections in 1917 Sinn Féin began to challenge Redmond's Irish Party, a once powerful political machine that had grown rusty and out-dated. At the end of 1917 there were nearly as many Sinn Féin clubs in Ireland as Catholic parishes.

The new movement had created an unlikely political celebrity. Eamon de Valera was a tall, gaunt mathematics teacher, born to an Irish mother and a Spanish father in New York but raised from infancy by his grandmother, aunt and uncle in a cottage in rural County Limerick. The only commandant to survive the Rising, because the executions were halted before his turn came to face the firing squad, he possessed a unique authority among his comrades. To the public he was a living relic of the dead martyrs. De Valera won a by-election in Clare for Sinn Féin in 1917 campaigning in his Volunteer uniform, but his popularity did not spring solely from his power as an emblem of a now sanctified insurrection. He also possessed a calculating political brain. A young priest who campaigned for him was impressed by his first glimpse of de Valera on a platform, his 'lean, hard face' scanning the crowd to estimate its strength. He took this to mean that de Valera was a realist, not a dreamer. More significantly, for all his talk about the ancient wrongs done to Ireland, de Valera was uniquely skilled in the now essentially modern techniques of advertising. Despite rumours about his parentage, he turned his exotic origins to his advantage. 'His romantic foreign name was a great asset,' the priest later recalled. 'If he had been plain "Michael Murphy" he would not have had half the appeal to the Irish people.' Observing de Valera, the veteran Irish nationalist William O'Brien noticed how he was able to project a personality, 'the subtle blend of virility and emotion which the Americans mean when they speak of a "magnetic man"'. Soon, de Valera was getting fan mail. 'We had candles lighting in every window the night you were elected,' a seven-year-old boy wrote to him from Kerry.

De Valera's achievement was sustained by the organisational work of others who would shortly become powerful figures in the revolutionary movement. Michael Collins had been a post-office clerk in London before he returned to Ireland to fight in the Rising. Only twenty-six when released from an internment camp in Wales, he was already determined that the military folly of the insurrection should not be repeated. Future violence should be based on a political organisation with much broader support, he believed, and carefully escalated to provoke a draconian response that would turn the public against British rule. Collins deployed his prodigious business and managerial skills to looking after the families of the remaining prisoners. He built up a sophisticated welfare network that not only provided prisoners and their dependants with money, food and support but also raised more than £100,000 in donations, a large portion of it from the United States. The National Aid Fund served as a training ground for the activists who would soon attempt to build an underground government with its own bureaucracy.

And its humanitarian appeal gave the cause a far greater reach while at the same time popularising Sinn Féin. Through his indefatigable work for the fund, Collins groomed a cadre of loyal followers awed by his dynamism and made himself an indispensable figure in the coming revolution.

As Sinn Féin swept the country in its motor cars, winning a string of by-elections, the authorities in Dublin Castle fretted that the country was becoming ungovernable. They banned meetings, confiscated weapons and censored the mail. The surge of support for Sinn Féin could not have come at a worse moment for the British war effort. An offensive by the German army in the spring of 1918 won so much French territory that Paris came within firing range of German artillery. Desperate for manpower, the cabinet decided to extend conscription to Ireland. Politicians in London had become exasperated by the scale of dissension in Ireland and many had convinced themselves of the need to suppress the disorder. Ray Stannard Baker, the American journalist who had been sent by President Woodrow Wilson on a secret mission to report on the state of European opinion, went to a dinner party in London attended by 'English people of the better sort' and was shocked to find how many of his fellow guests agreed that in Ireland 'a little blood-letting will do no harm'.

Choosing to join in a coalition of the willing to fight for the rights of small nations might have had plausible idealistic appeal in 1914 (especially if Ireland might thereby win recognition for its own nationhood); being dragooned by diktat to save the collapse of the increasingly unpopular British war effort in 1918 was something else entirely. All nationalists united against compulsory enlistment. Sinn Féin and the trade unions would have been expected to resist but even the Irish

Parliamentary Party could no longer support the war effort on those terms. Fearing an outbreak of 'brutal military savagery' the new leader of the Irish Parliamentary Party, John Dillon, led his MPs out of Westminster and back to Ireland to join their bitter rivals Sinn Féin in the anti-conscription campaign. *Punch* magazine now depicted the Irish MPs as terrorists carrying sickles, guns and bombs in parliament. It was an absurd caricature based on shopworn prejudice, but any of the Irish MPs who saw it would have realised the uncomfortable truth that they were now aligning themselves with a campaign led by Sinn Féin and the militants of 1916. Abandoning Westminster had been Sinn Féin policy all along. Now it appeared to be not just an audacious gesture but a respectable one as well.

The leaders of the anti-conscription campaign drafted a pledge to be signed by churchgoers in every parish in Ireland: 'Denying the right of the British government to enforce compulsory service in this country, we pledge ourselves solemnly to one another to resist conscription by the most effective means at our disposal.' A general strike – one of the first in western Europe – was called for 23 April and observed everywhere except in the north.

The Irish Volunteers prepared for battle. Private houses were raided for arms; gelignite was stolen from quarries. A plan was drawn up to resist conscription in every town and village, with barricades to prevent troops from taking away men eligible for military service. Part of the plan required the blockading of police stations but the British government worried that even the Royal Irish Constabulary might mutiny. In Galway W. B. Yeats heard that young men were buying crowbars and hatchets to break up railway lines and cut down telegraph polls. Elsewhere members of the Volunteers were sleeping out at night to avoid being arrested. Yeats warned a senior Liberal politician that there would be a bloodbath if the British military tried to force men into the army. His friend (and co-founder of the Abbey Theatre) Lady Augusta Gregory, Yeats wrote, was 'convinced that the women and children will stand in front of their men and receive the bullets'.

Conscription was never introduced in Ireland, although the threat remained for the last six months of the war. To stymie any resistance, more than seventy prominent members of Sinn Féin, including virtually the entire leadership, were arrested in May 1918 on trumped-up charges that they were plotting with German agents. Public meetings were banned, the Irish Volunteers was declared an illegal organisation, newspapers were censored and printing plants destroyed. Until he was arrested in the round-up de Valera deftly combined his life as a dangerous revolutionary with the routine of a respectable bourgeois, plotting subversion in committee rooms in Dublin and commuting by train to his home in the middle-class seaside town of Bray, with a season ticket for his bicycle. When he was imprisoned in England, he filed his tax returns from his cell, taught his fellow prisoners Irish, studied maths, served Mass in the prison chapel and said the Rosary every night.

Not long before, a young member of Sinn Féin, Rosamond Jacob, had gone to watch de Valera speak in her home town of Waterford. Rosamond combined her commitment to Sinn Féin with a passionate interest in the cinema. Her diary was as likely to contain a detailed account of the programme at the local picture-house as a report on a political meeting. She found Charlie Chaplin 'delicious' in *A Dog's Life*, which played to a full house in September 1918. She was looking forward to a significant birthday: on 13 October she would be thirty and old enough to vote. For years Rosamond had

championed women's suffrage and was not afraid to be direct
with men in Sinn Féin who opposed it or ignored it, no matter
how powerful they were. What caught her attention watching
de Valera speak in Waterford was not his determination to
defy a police ban, or his growing fame – in her diary she was
far less complimentary about him than she would be about
Charlie Chaplin. Instead, she noted his unthinking conven-
tionality: 'He had the usual way of saying "men" & "every
man" etc., as if there were no women in the country.' Rather
than being flattered into silence when invited to join de Valera
for tea at his hotel after the speech, she was emboldened to
confront him about his omission. De Valera was regretful that
he had not acknowledged women; but, he protested, it was so
easy to forget! He wished, he told Rosamond, that he could
always have someone there to prompt him when he was making a speech. 'I said', Rosamond recalled in her diary, 'I didn't
think he should require prompting at this time of the day.'

Nobody who knew Rosamond would have been surprised
that she had been so blunt with such a forbidding figure. She
was well aware herself that people considered her tactless.
Pride in her strong opinions competed with self-doubt about
her ability to read a situation correctly. Above all, she worried
that she lacked charm and scared off men. Still living at home
with her widowed mother, cultural and political activism was
her only opportunity for an independent social life. In this,
she was like many young people in Ireland in the early twentieth century for whom the surge of interest in the many
strands of the movement to celebrate Irish culture was as
much a pastime as an assertion of identity. She learned Irish
and went to the summer schools run by the Gaelic League.
She joined Irish dancing classes, mastered some tunes on the
uilleann pipes and attended hurling matches. What marked

her out was that she was a Quaker in a movement that was overwhelmingly Catholic. Her father had been an anti-imperialist, an agnostic and an Irish nationalist. Even among Quakers, familiar with a culture of dissent, the Jacobs were considered eccentric. It was easy to see why she felt so intensely that she was always an outsider ('I wish I could go somewhere where I wasn't known and believed beforehand to be mad,' she had confided to her diary after attending a Quaker meeting) but she probably underestimated how others of her own age were torn in different directions by the times, under pressure to choose between their taste for Irish dancing or American movies, religious scruples or the new freedoms opening up for young women, cricket – the sedate game of the English colonisers – or hurling, the vigorous sport of Irish patriots. On visits to Dublin Rosamond cast off the restrictions of a sheltered upbringing by mixing with a set of vaguely bohemian nationalist feminists, eating in a vegetarian restaurant and, thrillingly, smoking her first cigarette. On her thirtieth birthday she received a bicycle pump, a green scarf and a large photo of Eamon de Valera.

That autumn, the worldwide influenza epidemic that had first been reported in the newspapers in June as 'a mysterious war disease' was claiming victims all over Ireland. On one day at the end of October, there had been dozens of funerals in Dublin, 'cortège after cortège' moving slowly towards Glasnevin Cemetery. People with jobs that brought them into contact with the public – shop assistants, auctioneers, commercial travellers, prison warders – ran a greater risk of being infected. In the crowded hospitals and workhouses, nurses and doctors themselves were bedridden. Several teachers had also died. In some areas farmers were afraid to go to markets in town in case they exposed themselves to infection. One doctor estimated that three-quarters of the deaths of people under thirty were directly or indirectly caused by the flu. The authorities appeared helpless. At the height of the epidemic, the Local Government Board, which controlled the health services in Ireland, could only encourage flu victims to have fewer hot meals and stoke smaller fires.

The poor official response was a gift for Sinn Féin. As the epidemic cut down the party's own activists, they were memorialised as fallen patriots. When James Corrigan, a twenty-seven-year-old teacher in the midlands, succumbed to the flu at the end of October 1918 his life was presented as a paragon of energy and service: he had been a member of Sinn Féin, an officer in the Irish Volunteers, a champion hurler, the secretary and driving force of the local branches of the Gaelic Athletic Association and the Gaelic League, and a devoted Catholic. 'His mind was filled with the purest and loftiest ideals,' his obituary eulogised, 'emanating from a soul burning with patriotism, and faithfully irradiating the piercing light which constitutes Irish nationality. He fully realized that national liberty was not a toy to be bartered away, but an ideal to be purchased only by wading through the deepest suffering and pain.'

By midday on 11 November, as the news spread that the war was over, the streets of Dublin filled with crowds celebrating under a cloudless blue sky. Bands of soldiers passed through the city singing 'It's a Long Way to Tipperary'. The shops began to close to allow employees to join in and soon all the streets from the General Post Office in Sackville Street to St Stephen's Green on the south side were packed with a dense crowd. Students from Trinity College commandeered a hearse and placed in it an effigy of the Kaiser wrapped in the Sinn Féin tricolour. Kevin O'Shiel, a young barrister who had studied law at Trinity and switched during the war from supporting home rule to joining Sinn Féin, watched the commotion with distaste but also disdain. It would not be long, he believed, before these jingoes and imperialists waving their Union Jacks would get the shock of their lives. Everyone was now predicting a Sinn Féin victory.

On election day, people marvelled in towns, villages and cities as fleets of cars bedecked in green-white-and-orange flags sped by, carrying Sinn Féin supporters to vote. Douglas Goldring arrived in Limerick in the south-west to find the city in a state of excitement, with motors trying to edge through the crowds in the main street: 'Ford cars, covered with dust and filled to overflowing with gesticulating young men, dashed here and there.' There were reports that the young supporters of Sinn Féin had locked their fathers and mothers in their homes to prevent them getting to the booth and voting against change. There were many stories of personation, people voting in the names of the dead. One member of the Irish Volunteers in County Meath estimated that he had voted thirty times; each time he was met with a friendly smile by the presiding officer, and the poll clerk would laugh and ask, 'Whose name is it this time?', before giving him his ballot paper. At polling stations around the country, members of the Irish Volunteers – in the eyes of the public, Sinn Féin's army – lined up in formation as if they and not the Royal Irish Constabulary were the guardians of law and order. In several areas the Volunteers were allowed to accompany the police to guard the ballot boxes when voting ended.

It would be two weeks before the votes were counted to allow time for the return of the ballot papers sent to the soldiers still in France and the Middle East. But within days the word was that Sinn Féin had swept the board and the Irish

Party had been routed. When the results came in Sinn Féin had won 73 seats, the Unionists 26 (almost all in the north-east) and the Irish Parliamentary Party was reduced to 6. 'I have looked in vain for any policy from the Sinn Féin Party,' Father Michael Maher, a Catholic curate in Thurles and a diligent observer of politics, recorded in his journal. 'They have not said what they are going to do after their return for the constituency except to appeal to the Peace Conference and to abstain from Parliament, apart from these two intentions they have sketched no modus operandi.'

President Wilson had arrived in Paris for the peace talks to settle a new world order. The day Ireland voted he had made a triumphal procession down the Champs-Élysées. Soldiers had trouble holding back the dense crowds; people clung to roofs and tree branches to get a glimpse of the president. His wife was almost invisible under bouquets of flowers in the open-topped carriage. Students and soldiers waved the star-spangled banner and cheered, '*Vive Wilson! Vive l'Amérique.*'

2

The American Spirit

A couple of months after the armistice had ended the First World War, the American writer John Dos Passos found himself in a small Spanish village. Early one murky morning he went to buy bread at a little bakery illuminated by gaslight. As he waited to pay for his loaf, his eyes were drawn to a photograph of a man with a long, lean face pasted on the wall behind the counter. He recognised the American president, Woodrow Wilson. The old woman behind the counter noticed him gazing at the image on the wall; her eyes shone as she confided to Dos Passos, 'He will save us all, with his Americans.' The writer did not need much more evidence that Wilson had gripped the imagination of ordinary people across Europe. He had seen the president's portrait many times during his travels in the previous months. In Italy they burned candles before it; in Germany it had replaced pictures of the Kaiser. In Spain, the previous year, even before the war had finished, they were naming squares and children after Wilson.

The cult of Wilson had not happened overnight; nor was it spontaneous. Once the United States decided to enter the war 'to make the world safe for democracy' in 1917 Wilson's government had embarked on an enormous propaganda campaign to acquaint Europeans with the president's idea that the disaster of the war also meant that the era of autocratic governments immune to popular will was finished. The world must now be reshaped according to democratic American values. Two million American troops arrived in Europe to fight but they also served as a demonstration of how a mass democracy inspired progress, vigour and efficiency. When their arrival in French ports provoked enormous traffic jams, the American troops simply redesigned the ports to relieve the congestion, winning both admiration and envy for their blithe indifference to local propriety. The same reputation for resourceful daring had been won by the American relief operation in Belgium, run by the millionaire mining engineer Herbert Hoover, who became known to his staff as 'the chief' and who after the armistice directed the distribution of over a billion dollars' worth of food supplies to starving civilians in Europe, bypassing the 'pinheads of bureaucratic Europe' and using the same principles for humanitarian relief as he employed in his multinational mining empire. It was not for nothing that the Americans called the conflict in Europe 'the big show'.

As the war ended the demobilising American soldiers lingered to acquaint themselves with the old world. Thousands passed through Dublin, so many that they occupied their own hostel and their special concerts and dances became a feature of life in the city in the months after the war. As they walked around Dublin chewing gum – a practice that had taken off in Europe only since their arrival – they could, if they looked hard enough, detect numerous touches of American influence on Ireland. The first Rotary Club in Britain or Ireland was established in Dublin in 1911, five years after the business fraternity with the motto 'He Profits Most Who Serves Best' was founded in Chicago. You could, for four shillings, book a table at a 'jazz tea' at a respectable Dublin residence or watch the Tallaght Jazz Band at the fashionable Café Cairo on Grafton Street. And if you were uncertain of your dance steps the newspapers advertised private tuition from visiting London instructors. Henry Ford was a name everybody recognised (in Elizabeth Bowen's novel of the revolutionary years, *The Last September*, an English visitor, Mrs Vermont, observes that in Ireland 'they seem to take Fords so seriously'). The great man was investing millions of pounds in a factory in Cork that he promised would employ two thousand people – work was well under way building it and in a few months the first Fordson tractor would roll off the assembly line. Some were arguing that Ford's investment was only a taste of the bright prospects that would emerge when transatlantic trade resumed after the war – Ireland's future was American. The nationalist politician J. J. Horgan believed that Ireland was a natural base for American companies chasing European markets: 'If we can enlist the support of American capital now seeking a foreign outlet, and adopt American business methods and machinery, the speedy development of Ireland is certain. Mr Ford is perhaps after all only an indication and a forerunner of what is to be.' For the *Irish Times* the American spirit was an epoch-changing moment that would dwarf the worldwide influence of the French Revolution: 'We are on the eve of such a time of spiritual and political and social adventure as the world has not yet known . . . America not England will be the interpreter of the thoughts and visions of the world re-born.'

Now the messiah of progress had come to Europe. Wilson had arrived in the French port of Brest the day before the election in Ireland, the first sitting American president to visit Europe, and enjoying, as John Maynard Keynes was later to recall, 'a prestige and a moral influence throughout the world unequalled in history'. When not in conference with his officials during the nine-day crossing on board the USS *George Washington* (a German ocean liner converted by the US navy into a transport ship during the war) Wilson had spent his time watching films. It might seem a curious pastime for a man regarded as a puritanical egghead but he was fascinated by cinema and how he could harness its power to his own purpose. He had noted shrewdly that 'since it speaks a universal language, it lends itself importantly to the presentation of America's plans and purposes'. By three o'clock in the afternoon, when the guns started to boom to announce the Wilsons' arrival and the *George Washington* slowly emerged from an escort of British, American and French battleships, thousands of people had gathered in Brest to watch him disembark. The town was decorated with American and British flags and people stood on roofs and hung out of trees to get a glimpse of Wilson. The French foreign minister, Stephen Pichon, told him, 'We are so thankful you have come to give us the right kind of peace.'

Irish nationalists were sure that 'the right kind of peace' meant recognition for an independent Irish state. In New York on the eve of Wilson's arrival in Europe, Cardinal John Joseph O'Connor addressed thousands of Irish Americans in Madison Square Garden. Surely, he protested, the Irish people, faithful Catholics for generations, could not be denied their freedom when the whole world was now acknowledging even the Bolsheviks? In December, forty Irish town councils pledged support for Wilson and invited him to Ireland (though it would be some time before American presidents appreciated the advantages of discovering or concocting an Irish genealogy). Many of these declarations were joint requests by the Irish Parliamentary Party and Sinn Féin; as was frequently the case by that time the constitutional party now spoke the same language as the movement about to supplant it. The Irish Party leaders sent an appeal to Wilson insisting that Ireland deserved to be free like other small nations. 'Every national question today is international,' it proclaimed.

The context in which Irish leaders pressed their claims for recognition of their nationality had been transformed by the war. In 1914 Ireland's cause seemed a parochial dispute within the United Kingdom; now, in 1918, empires had collapsed and the world was being reordered according to the 'national principle'. New nations were springing up all over Europe: Poland, Ukraine, Finland. Sinn Féin argued that limited self-government for Ireland within the United Kingdom was now an anachronism. It did not matter any more that home rule had been approved by the British parliament, the Sinn Féin leader Arthur Griffith wrote in 1917; Ireland's gaze and ambitions had moved beyond London and what could be achieved there: 'Ireland is out of the corner where for generations she had been hidden away from the world. She is no longer an island lying behind England – she is again politically, as well as geographically, part of Europe.'

Griffith's words were a reflection of how Wilson's rhetoric had encouraged an upsurge in national claims all over Europe from the ruins of the Habsburg, Ottoman and Russian empires. In many places nationalists had been through the same arguments that had raged in Ireland over how to approach the war. Each country had its own Redmonds and de Valeras debating the merits of co-operation or resistance. In Bohemia or Croatia or Slovenia some argued that a supportive attitude to the Habsburgs in the war would yield generous concessions to self-government afterwards and that to take advantage of the war by launching an uprising would be folly and bound to fail. Many also regarded the empire as a guarantee of law and order. But more radical nationalists believed the war presented a unique opportunity to strike a blow for freedom and formed secret committees to plot revolt, joined by socialists prepared to set aside class warfare temporarily in favour of the national question. As the war worsened, the moderates were condemned as collaborators. By 1918 the most radical nationalist elements were in the ascendant.

This new gospel of self-determination was also travelling far beyond Europe. In imperial Japan films showing Wilson's face were banned for fear of provoking unrest, particularly in Korea, which had been occupied by Japan in 1905 and was where anti-colonialist agitators were already making comparisons with Ireland. In May 1919 over a million Koreans took part in demonstrations calling for independence. When they were violently suppressed, word went around that Wilson himself would lead a fleet of American battleships to intervene on the side of the protestors. In China a collection of Wilson's speeches became a bestseller. And in Egypt anxious British diplomats relayed to London the news that Wilson's ideas were being talked about 'in the remotest villages'. Wilson made it respectable to be anti-imperialist – he blamed the old imperial powers and their secret treaties for starting the war and offered a new vision of an international community of nation states. The world had changed so much that a few days before the armistice both Britain and France had publicly declared that they now wanted the world to be composed of 'national governments and administrations deriving their authority from the initiative and free choice of the indigenous population'. This was mainly directed at an

Arab audience but nobody in Ireland would have missed its propaganda possibilities. At Buckingham Palace during his visit to London at the end of December, Wilson declared that 'the two "great nations" [the United States and Britain] were called upon to "organise the moral forces of the world" in accordance with "the right and justice" they represented'. Reading the reports of the excitement generated by Wilson's arrival in London, an Indian intellectual imagined the 'wild delirium of joy' that would follow if he chose to visit Delhi or Shanghai: 'It would have been as though one of the great teachers of humanity, Christ or Buddha, had come back to his home.'

Wilson's assertion that Britain and the United States were of the same mind in how to reorder the world should have been a warning to Sinn Féin that self-determination was a panacea to be introduced only in the defeated empires. National movements and their putative armies were already physically altering the map of the continent, delineating – often in blood – the new frontiers that the cartographers and diplomats at the peace conference would be asked to endorse. But Irish nationalists were in a far weaker position than their counterparts in Eastern Europe because Britain's victory meant the empire was beyond challenge. By now sitting in a cell in Gloucester Prison, Arthur Griffith persisted in arguing that Woodrow Wilson's good will was essential to any hope that Ireland might have of a hearing at the peace conference about to begin in Paris. In a memo written in January 1919, he dismissed those who were presciently casting doubt on Wilson's sincerity when it came to self-determination for Ireland. British propagandists, Griffith thought, would use any slights directed against the American president by Irish nationalists to claim that Ireland was hostile to his plans for a new world order. It would be more politic, Griffith wrote, to row in behind Wilson: 'Our attitude should be that Wilson is a sincere man striving to give effect to his programme of freedom for all nations and struggling against all the forces of tyranny, imperialism and lusty world power which are seeking to dominate the Peace Conference. That Ireland therefore supports him heartily and seeks to strengthen his hands.' Better still, Griffith advised, Wilson should be flattered by Ireland's renowned literary resources: 'Mobilise the poets. Let them address Wilson, and let them remind him in their best verse that he has the opportunity and the duty of giving the world true peace and freedom.' Even more pointedly they should remind him that 'all his ideals fail if Ireland is permitted to remain enclosed'. Griffith drew up a detailed strategy for enlisting support at the peace conference. Sinn Féin delegates should remind South American states of the Irish military geniuses who had helped liberate them from Spain. Similarly the Serbs should be reminded that their leader in the war against Turkey was called Colonel O'Rourke. Liberia and Haiti should have it explained to them that Ireland was the only European country that never engaged in the slave trade. Above all, it should be demonstrated beyond doubt that 'the case of Ireland against England surpasses by far the case of any other country in Europe, against foreign domination'.

Despite Wilson's optimism that self-determination would deliver peace, the breakdown of the old order and the chaotic competition for sovereignty was merely one reminder of how fragile liberal civilisation had become after four years of unprecedented slaughter. In Russia the war had produced a new leadership determined to start a world revolution. In defeated Germany and Austria, where revolutionaries were marching in the streets, shortages of meat, milk and flour raised the prospect of famine; nearly a third of all children born in Berlin were dead within a few days. The spread of Bolshevism was a major preoccupation among the victorious powers. In an election speech in Dundee in November 1918 Winston Churchill warned his audience that civilisation was being extinguished in Russia by the Bolsheviks, who 'hop and caper like troops of ferocious baboons amid the ruins of cities and the corpses of their victims'. That same month the *New York Times* declared that the most pressing post-war question was 'how far Europe is infested with Bolshevism'. Labour disputes were breaking out everywhere. In August 1918 even police officers in London had gone on strike in an attempt to form a trade union. And in January 1919 thousands of British soldiers protesting the speed and terms of their demobilisation mutinied in Calais and formed strike committees. Although the crisis was eventually defused, British intelligence officers worried about a Bolshevist plot to infiltrate the army. In Ireland the Congress of Trade Unions was recruiting thousands more members; barmen, hotel workers and agricultural labourers had all participated in strikes by the time of the armistice in an attempt to get a share of the fruits of the war and the boom that followed. Then on Saturday, 25 January, shipyard workers in Belfast walked out, supported by the men who ran the power stations. Within days factories closed down, trams stopped running and theatres and cinemas were shut. Belfast became, the *New York Times* reported, 'a dead city, a city of candles'. In the following months coalminers, cotton workers and railwaymen went on strike in Britain. From Spain it was reported that anarcho-syndicalists had joined forces with Catalan nationalists demanding home rule.

It was tempting for observers everywhere to link all these events together: who was to say that the conditions were not ripe for the realisation of Lenin's dreams of world revolution? In April 1919 Rosamond Jacob took the train to Dublin from Waterford to attend the Sinn Féin convention. Among the delegates she heard lots of gossip about intrigue and competing factions at headquarters. To lift her spirits she went to a talk on 'Bolshevism and Feminism' delivered by a speaker called Mr Cogley. He told his audience that every country in Europe would soon have to choose between Bolshevism and 'the present state' of disorder. Although revolutionary Russia was not nearly as powerful as it appeared, many across Europe agreed that the choice was either Wilson or Lenin. The American president seemed to offer a path between the old imperialism and the dangers of revolution. Woodrow Wilson's plan was to revive the post-war Europe so that it would become a peaceful market for American commerce. His promise was that liberal democratic states were the best guarantee of this Ford-friendly world.

Ostensibly the outcome of the First World War had left Britain best placed to be Wilson's ally in imposing his vision on the world. In December 1918 Sir Charles Munro, commander-in-chief of British forces in India, wrote to Sir Henry Rawlinson, the commander of the Fourth Army, 'Now that it is all over, and the Empire stands on a pinnacle built by her tenacity & courage – never did our reputation stand so high.' But victory came at a price. The outcome of the peace settlement vastly extended Britain's traditional empire: a quarter of the world's population now lived under the British Empire. This imposed many new military commitments on the British government. Some of these obligations, such as participation in the occupation of Germany, were a direct consequence of the war. Others were the result of a deliberate policy to get hold of the possessions of rival empires that had collapsed. Extra forces would have to be found to control the new protectorates of Palestine, Mesopotamia and German East Africa granted to Britain at the peace conference. Controlling the Persian Gulf had long been considered to be essential for securing India – now it was important as a source of oil too. It was not long before a series of uprisings and rebellions put pressure on the ability of the British military to respond. In March 1919 there was an uprising in Egypt; English residents were dragged off trains and beaten to death. In April Afghan fighters invaded India and 3,000 troops were sent to the frontier provinces to repel them. By the middle of 1920 the British were dealing with a rebellion in Mesopotamia. Maintaining the armed forces to control the empire was a huge drain on Treasury resources: by 1918 the military accounted for more than 80 per cent of government expenditure and during the course of the war income tax had increased sixfold to pay for it. This was hardly tenable in a country committed to building homes fit for heroes.

A major cause of all this trouble was the extent to which the idea of national rights was now universally acclaimed. This was not just the result of Wilson's fame. Even before Wilson arrived in Europe to promulgate self-determination, many British thinkers had been celebrating the 'nationality principle', not just in defence of Belgium from German invasion but as a solution for the problems that had caused the war. 'There can be no good international system,' Bertrand Russell wrote in 1917, 'until the boundaries of states coincide as nearly as possible with the boundaries of nations.' Championing nationalism had also been useful for less idealistic purposes during the war, to stir up discontent among the peoples of the enemy empires (the attempt to conflate both impulses was the cause of T. E. Lawrence's public angst). It was naive to think the clock could be turned back at the end of the war. The Egyptian uprising was ignited by the exclusion of Egyptian nationalists from the peace conference at Versailles. No longer could nationalist politicians be easily isolated, especially in an empire based on globalisation. The very nature of the modern empire, connected more than ever before by the technologies that it boasted were its gift to world progress – telegraph, telephone and wireless signals, shipping lines, the spread of the English language itself – now made it much easier for nationalists to spread their message. Manifestos, declarations and petitions were now intended for world consumption. It was not just the Irish who discovered the value of their diaspora: Koreans, Chinese and Indians in the United States and Britain were mobilised in support of independence campaigns back home.

This was a disturbing scenario for British policymakers; 'the whole world is rocking', as the secretary of state for the colonies, Lord Milner, put it. It was particularly tricky because a misstep or false move in dealing with one set of nationalist demands could reverberate across the empire, skewing the management of other hotspots in ways that might be impossible to predict. Reaction in Britain to concessions in Ireland might affect how the British government could negotiate with the Egyptians, and slippage there might encourage what the British saw as Indian extremists. The government feared a domino effect that might unravel the empire just when it should have been most secure. It was easy to see how, struggling to contain all these outbreaks of anti-colonial disaffection in a still chaotic world, it might feel besieged and detect a pattern, 'a world movement which takes different forms in different places, but is plainly discernible on every continent and in every country', as the British foreign secretary, Arthur Balfour, described the threat in 1919. The government was beginning to realise that the carve-up of the territory of the defeated empires might be the last time they could indulge territorial ambitions, once the currency of empire building. The weariness and anxiety induced by the complications that undermined apparent triumph can be detected in a Foreign Office memo written in 1926: 'We have got all that we want – perhaps more. Our sole object is to keep what we want and live in peace . . . The fact is that war and rumours of war, quarrels and friction, in any corner of the world spell loss and harm to British commercial and financial interests . . . whatever else may be the outcome of a disturbance of the peace, we shall be the losers.' Sinn Féin was preparing to defy a victorious empire suddenly afflicted by the tribulations of a condition that would become known later in the twentieth century as imperial overstretch.

Challenges to Britain's rule across its global territories might have been difficult enough to deal with but they co-incided with an even more fundamental shift in world politics. The empire was also forced to adapt to a world in which the very idea of imperialism had been discredited. This refashioning had begun well before the war. Some of the impetus for this came from the British Empire's white-settler colonies – Canada, Australia, New Zealand and South Africa – now known as the dominions. Throughout the late nineteenth and early twentieth centuries they had become more nationalistic, rejecting control or interference from London and asserting their constitutional independence. At the same time they had also grown more attached to the empire as a great union of white nations sharing a common British culture. The novelist and politician John Buchan reflected in 1907 that Britain was now the 'Mother Country', first among equals in a family partnership bound together by blood ties and common ideals. The First World War was a watershed in the relationship between London and its dominions. They sent more than a million soldiers into combat and the experience had sharpened their sense of national identity. In 1917 the dominion leaders demanded full recognition from London as autonomous nations – a short step from equal status with the 'Mother Country' within the empire. When the armistice came each dominion was entitled to send its own delegation to the peace conference.

The British Empire was also developing a new image more suited to the era of mass electorates to counter the appeal of Bolshevism across the world and the American critique of imperialism as a danger to world peace. It had to deal with a new language of international relations emphasising co-operation and understanding between nations. Moral arguments – diehard conservatives would have said pretensions – now seemed to carry enormous weight. It was exasperating for those who celebrated the British Empire's great victory in the war to realise that to prosper in the new world it could no longer afford to look like an empire. How could it justify itself? Instead of boasts about the extent of its territory and its military achievements, the British Empire was now represented by its supporters as a harbinger of civilisation and good government to the lawless corners of the globe. The days of brutality and exploitation were in the past; now Britain would nurture and develop its subject peoples. Reflecting on her job as an official in the new colonial mission in Mesopotamia, Gertrude Bell reached the same conclusion: 'Truly we are a remarkable people. We save from destruction remnants of oppressed nations, laboriously and expensively giving them sanitary accommodation, teaching their children, respecting their faiths.'

The very language of the peace conference – where the former colonies of the vanquished powers were allocated to the victors as protectorates and trusteeships – was designed to smooth the rebranding of the British Empire as a commonwealth. The figure who personified the new idea of empire was the South African general Jan Smuts. Only twenty years earlier he had been beloved by Irish nationalists for leading the Boers in a war against the British that he tried to extend to India in order to weaken imperial will. Defeat and accommodation with the British set him thinking about a different kind of empire, a confederation of autonomous nations rather than a land-grabbing cartel, held together by a shared civilisation. As a member of the imperial war cabinet he had become a celebrated figure in the imperial metropolis. C. P. Scott, the editor of the *Manchester Guardian*, described him as the most popular man in Britain. In 1917 he received the freedom of the City of London and seven other cities, as well as honorary degrees from six universities, including Trinity College Dublin. 'The British Empire', Smuts declared during the war, 'is not founded on might or force, but on moral principles – on principles of freedom, equality and equity. It is these principles which we stand for to-day in this mighty struggle.' At the peace conference in Versailles it was Smuts who solved the problem of how to deal with Germany's former colonies by fleshing out a system for running them under the League of Nations. The mandate system fitted nicely with the new image of benign imperialism. The big powers would become trustees or guardians of countries incapable of self-government, untrained and destitute peoples who, in the view of Smuts, would need 'much nursing' before they could be considered candidates for independence. The system made little difference to how these mandates were run – their populations might hardly have noticed the switch from one colonial ruler to another. But the adoption of a new word to make an old regime legitimate did mean that Britain had to spend more time justifying how it ran its empire both at home and to the rest of the world, especially to sceptical Americans. In an article published in the American magazine *Foreign Affairs* in 1922, Phillip Kerr explained that the purpose of the British Empire was to defend backward peoples unable to cope with modern civilisation. He chose as an example of this helplessness the chief of Swaziland, who, Kerr wrote, had signed away his country's resources to foreign traders for a consignment of gin. The empire would defend these vulnerable peoples against unscrupulous exploiters, bringing law, justice and sound finance to governments, and irrigation and sanitary works to impoverished peasants. Americans should realise, Kerr advised his elite readers in Washington, that unless the civilised peoples took control, the backward races would end up in ruins. The British genius for governing backward peoples was also the answer to the many demands that the establishment of a world government would be the only way to avoid another global slaughter. Smuts and others argued that the British Commonwealth already was the nearest thing to a global administration promoting international values. As the Romans had once laid the foundations for European civilisation, British ideas would now underpin a world civilisation.

These ideas seem airily remote from the concerns of the Volunteers drilling in fields in rural Ireland, invoking the heroes of previous rebellions against British rule rather than contemplating the changing nature of empire. But the shape of the new world emerging from the war would have a decisive influence on their aspirations. The loud proclamations that imperialism had changed made British conduct in Ireland more susceptible to public opinion both at home and abroad; bad publicity could make life awkward for the political elite in London. And the question of whether the new British Commonwealth was radically different from the rapacious empire that Irish nationalists detested, a new partnership of equals accommodating national aspirations, would become a divisive issue when the revolutionaries came to negotiate the terms of independence. Another idea associated with Smuts was also vital for Ireland's case in the post-war world. Self-determination was for civilised peoples, not barbarians – both he and Wilson disapproved of any European country becoming a mandate ruled by a superior power. So a nation's standing in the world depended on whether they were classed as 'civilised' or 'savage'. In an age of pan-Africanism and pan-Arabism, fear of Asiatic hordes or a 'tide of colour' meant that lines would be drawn on racial grounds. Smuts saw himself as the leader of a white civilisation on a savage continent and his struggle since the Boer War was to make South Africa – and himself – a leading player in a worldwide alliance of white peoples, the British Commonwealth. All that remained was for the United States to take its place in the grand coalition of white men. Where would Ireland fit into this scheme? In a letter to *The Times* on 5 May 1919, Erskine Childers, the former English officer and bestselling spy novelist who had become Sinn Féin's chief propagandist, accused the British government of 'making war, literally, on the principle of freedom' in Ireland. The Irish, Childers wrote, were the only white nationality in the world being denied self-determination. In Paris, Britain had set about fixing boundaries and frontiers of huge complexity all over Europe, dealing with nationalities that Lloyd George admitted he had scarcely heard of before.

'Is she in the same breath', Childers asked, 'to decline to deal with Ireland, whose uninterrupted historical identity and boundaries nobody can mistake? Ireland, the last unliberated white community on the face of the globe?'

3

Message to the World

In January 1919 Denis Johnston, now seventeen, would often cycle into the centre of Dublin and make his way to the North Wall, the port where steamships arrived from Liverpool and Glasgow, to watch demobilised soldiers returning to Ireland after their discharge from the army in Britain. He liked to watch the men coming up the steps from the quay and to scan the expressions of the 'white-faced women' craning over the wall in search of someone they recognised. There were often people who stood at the wall and waited until the boat was empty, then turned away in despair because nobody came running to greet them. One day he stood eavesdropping on two elderly women and a younger companion staring down onto the quay and talking about the possibility that 'George' might appear from the boat unloading below. Finally one of them shouted, 'There's George!' and they fixed their eyes on a man carrying his knapsack up the steps, a wide smile on his face now that he had noticed that someone had come to greet him. 'Well, my word, such excitement!' Denis noted in his diary. 'They kissed him and hugged him and pawed him all over. They felt his kitbag and his arms and nearly went mad with hysterics and weeping.'

Did George or any of the other soldiers stepping off the boats at the North Wall have much of an idea of what had become of their home since they left to fight for the freedom of small nations? They had sailed away to the front from a country preparing for home rule, an idea most would have understood to mean freedom, even though Ireland would still be part of the British Empire. Then they had heard of the rebellion, the proclamation of an Irish republic, the destruction of the centre of Dublin by the forces in whose uniform they served and Irish leaders facing firing squads in the green uniforms of a new Volunteer army. The Easter Rising could seem a confusing and distant event to many Irish soldiers serving with the Allies. One soldier wrote home, 'We heard that there was a rebellion in Ireland, and we were having to send soldiers there instead of the war; we thought this was odd, as we were a lot of Irishmen in the firing line.' Now they were slowly returning to discover that the new men and women from Sinn Féin had displaced the political leaders whose names and faces were familiar to them and that they were about to establish their own parliament in Dublin without any sanction from the British government. The city seemed a tranquil enough place. Apart from the ruined buildings in and around Sackville Street a casual visitor might think that Dublin had returned to normal and the Rising had been forgotten. It was even difficult to spot the signs of the revolutionary movement preparing to defy the British Empire. A grubby, limp tricolour hung from a window on Harcourt Street, off fashionable St Stephen's Green, where Sinn Féin had its headquarters. Less than a mile away, nearer the quays of the River Liffey, Dublin Castle, the seat of British rule, appeared not to be disturbed by this upstart rival. And if the returning soldiers had chosen to reacquaint themselves with Dublin by taking a stroll in the magnificent Phoenix Park, where the Lord Lieutenant of Ireland had his residence on the other side of the Liffey to the north-west, they might have caught sight of one of the most colourful figures of the war on the western front.

Field Marshal Viscount French of Ypres had been famous for touring the front line on his white horse, rallying the troops and listening attentively to the laments of injured and dying men. But the field marshal had not had a good war. Placed in charge of the first British Expeditionary Force to counter the German invasion of Belgium, his troops had been forced into a desperate retreat, to the dismay of his superiors in London. Later on he had failed to break the German lines, feuding with General Haig and Lord Kitchener over tactics. French resigned his command when it became clear to him that the politicians thought he was incompetent (the prime minister, Herbert Asquith, had been heard criticising him in front of *waiters* in a railway dining carriage). He was made commander-in-chief of British Home Forces in 1915 and worked hard to become a trusted adviser to the cabinet, all the time intriguing against Haig's conduct of the war. French had sent General Maxwell to put down the Easter Rising, so when the conscription crisis erupted he appeared to be the man with the resolve to quell the protests. Lord French was appointed Lord Lieutenant of Ireland in May 1918, with a brief to act like a military governor.

With the war concluded he had scores to settle. When his official duties permitted – and his married mistress was not visiting from England, giving mild scandal to the gossipy elite of Dublin society who patronised the Viceregal Lodge – Lord French worked on his memoirs, attacking Haig, Asquith and all the others who he believed had let him down. Taking charge in Ireland had restored French's self-respect; when they needed a tough military man to put an end to sedition they had turned to him. His experience in colonial wars all over Africa would be invaluable in crushing opposition when the government gave the order to conscript Irishmen for the army. French was also convinced he possessed special insight into Ireland's troubles. Although he had been born on a country estate in Kent, his father's ancestors were Irish and he owned a house near the original family seat in County Roscommon. He regarded himself as more Irish than the Sinn Féin leaders. Conscription, he believed, would not just provide the army with extra bodies but would also rid Ireland of the 'useless and idle youths' who would have emigrated but for the war and instead of labouring on the waterfront in New York were having their heads filled with dangerous nonsense by political agitators. Indeed, he believed the Irish were at heart a biddable people who were being led astray; just as he had won the affection of the soldiers under his command, French was certain he could also win the hearts of the Irish people, who admired strong leadership. A family story recounted how French's official car once stalled in the vicinity of a horse fair in rural Ireland. As the driver tried to restart the engine, a menacing crowd who had recognised the viceroy surrounded the car. Undismayed, Sir John got out and began to wander through the fair with his bow-legged gait, stopping to appraise the horses for sale and offering a cavalry officer's commentary on their quality. This display turned the crowd in his favour, and when the engine was revived they cheered him as he drove off.

To Sir John, this kind of experience was more instructive than Sinn Féin's showing at the general election. Like his friend, Walter Long, the colonial secretary, he believed republicanism was just a euphemism for Bolshevism. In the intelligence reports that formed his world view as Home

Forces commander, Irish unrest had been conflated with anti-war agitation, pacifism and trade-union militancy, just one strand in a network of menace. He was not opposed to limited self-government for Ireland, but this could be conceded only when order was restored. Freeing the mass of the people from the grip of the extremists – 'swine' in French's eyes – would require strong measures: martial law, the suppression of Sinn Féin and other nationalist organisations and the internment of troublemakers. He was particularly taken with the idea of using aircraft to police the countryside. Lord French's Ireland was noticeably militarised; public meetings were allowed only with special permission, cultural organisations such as the Gaelic League were banned and there were hundreds of arrests for minor displays of dissent or defiance. On a trip to Dublin in the autumn of 1918, to make speeches encouraging men to join the army voluntarily, the writer G. K. Chesterton was taken aback at the number of soldiers in the streets: 'I knew, of course, that we had a garrison in Dublin, but I had no notion that it was so obvious all over Dublin. I had no notion that it had been considered necessary to occupy the country in such force, or with so much parade of force.' While he was attending an outdoor nationalist music festival in County Cork, Chesterton watched a military plane appear overhead and drop flares near women and children listening to the performers. The scene reminded him of the technological militarism of the Germans that had aroused such indignation in Britain: 'the flying men, the flame, the selection of a mixed crowd, the selection of a popular festival . . . It was as if the whole British army in Ireland had dressed up in spiked helmets and spectacles, merely that they might look like Prussians . . . These Christian peasants have seen coming westward out of England what we saw coming westward out of Germany. They saw science in arms; which turns the very heavens into hells.'

French would have been horrified by the idea of himself as the Kaiser's doppelgänger. His ideas about pacifying Ireland came not from some Prussian strategy book but from the imperial experience of fighting small wars against recalcitrant subjects. He relied on a small coterie of advisers, many of them members of the Kildare Street Club on St Stephen's Green, a recreational redoubt of the landlord class and officers recently returned from colonial campaigns. A favourite comparison in the after-dinner talk here was between Ireland and India, another country where fanatics were trying to undermine the empire. Differences were acknowledged, of course; Ireland must be ruled with more kindness than was suitable when dealing with Asian peoples. But the army must always be on top. From an armchair in the Kildare Street Club, all the political fervour in the countryside was evidence of criminal conspiracy.

To contradict this view, even if you were a high official, could be a fatal career move. The inspector general of the Royal Irish Constabulary, General Sir Joseph Byrne, sought to complicate the hysteria of those who read the police reports and concluded that Ireland was a frightening hotbed of disorder. He distinguished between what he called real crime and the criminalisation of political activity. Ireland, according to Byrne, would be revealed as a much more peaceable place if the arrests and prosecutions of people taking part in sincere political action were halted, and thus subtracted from the crime statistics. Moreover, he argued, the influence of extreme republicans would then falter. Byrne told his superiors that the government would have to negotiate with Sinn Féin eventually because it represented a wide and deep swathe of Irish public opinion. This analysis confirmed the suspicion of those around Lord French that Byrne was endowed with an overly active intelligence for the role assigned to him. He was at first sidelined and then sent on indefinite paid leave (it was more than two years before a sinecure was found to justify his salary, when a vacancy arose for the governorship of the Seychelles). With Byrne gone there was no more talk of conciliation. Lord French even shocked his unionist cronies by drawing parallels with the Boer War, enthusing how 'we wired them all up inside concentration camps'. This, he asserted, would be the only way to settle the Irish business.

Not that Lord French thought only about military solutions – after pacification would come reconstruction. His officials toured the country asking businessmen how to revive the economy. They elaborated schemes to develop mines, bogs, fisheries and forestry, to improve drainage and rebuild harbours. Lord French was particularly keen on giving cash and land to demobilised soldiers so that they would not be seduced by Sinn Féin. But who would implement these utopian plans? Lord French would have to turn to the Irish administration in Dublin Castle, where he must have suspected he was not held in high esteem. The chief legal official, W. E. Wylie, privately sympathised with the politicians who forced the field marshal from his command in France. 'A dear old man Lord French,' he wrote. 'A kindly, honest Gentleman, brave and courteous but I often wondered how the first British Expeditionary Force . . . ever got back from Mons in 1914.' However, there was a bigger problem than the management of a collection of fusty civil servants. The truth was that French presided over a creaking administration of such notoriety that for all nationalists, radical or moderate, the iniquity of British rule in Ireland was summed up in the words 'Dublin Castle'. The name was a misnomer, since the Castle was a complex of grand but secluded buildings on a ridge overlooking the south bank of the River Liffey; all that remained of the original thirteenth-century Norman fortification were two old towers. Over the centuries it had been the seat of British rule in Ireland: it had housed a prison and the royal mint, as well as the viceroy's residence, apartments to accommodate the monarch during royal visits and galleries and ballrooms where the city's elite socialised in occasional splendour. By the early twentieth century its workaday aspect was the warren of offices occupied by civilian and military officials. A senior civil servant recalled that as he worked in his room one day he was startled by the sound of breaking glass from the Upper Castle Yard: 'A lady who wished to call attention to her grievances was walking round armed with a heavy stick smashing the ground-floor windows in her progress.' Tom Kettle, a moderate home ruler who would die fighting for the Allies at the Battle of the Somme, described the Castle administration as a parasitic bureaucracy: 'Under its regime, the nation has had as much to say to its own public policy as a Durbar-elephant has to say to the future of India.' Irish MPs who were happy to patronise Westminster boycotted the Castle and the Viceregal Lodge, their own non-violent contribution to delegitimising British rule in Ireland.

Even Lord French's diehard confidant, Walter Long, agreed that the Irish administration 'was wholly divorced from the people', and Lloyd George acknowledged after the 1916 rebellion that the system of government in Ireland had broken down. Endless inquiries had recommended reforms to the system but nothing was done. The byzantine complexity of its departments, boards and subdivisions meant that officials were perpetually unsure where authority lay. Treasury officials in London regarded the civil servants across the Irish Sea as archaic, extravagant, lazy and incompetent. Certainly their own representative in Dublin, Maurice Headlam, was no administrative dynamo: he had failed the exams for the Indian civil service and took the job in Dublin only because the posting would give him opportunities for excellent fishing. At the Kildare Street Club he ingratiated himself with the owners of country estates so that he could win invitations to spend weekends by their riverbanks. The cumulative combination of dilettante administrators and their distant detractors in London made for a chronic bureaucratic insensitivity to Irish realities large and small, illustrated by a Treasury proposal to save money by exterminating the herd of deer in the Phoenix Park.

But even the most disinterested and enlightened measures to improve life in Ireland were undermined by the perception that the Castle was regarded as the last bastion of diehard unionist rule. The prejudice against Catholics displayed within its walls could be shocking even to loyalists who went to work there. When Anthony MacDonnell, a Catholic from a County Mayo landowning family, was appointed as undersecretary for Ireland in 1902, he quickly discovered that the popular notoriety of the Castle was not a mischievous invention. After his first day in the office he complained to his wife that he could not stand the atmosphere of 'suspicion and espionage'. Revealingly, he compared the feuding between Catholic and Protestant civil servants to the hostile relations between Hindus and Muslims in India. Two decades later a thoroughly establishment official could be suspected of subversion because he was friendly with Catholic bishops. Most local councillors would never set foot in Dublin Castle.

They preferred to do business with officials from the agencies that administered health and agriculture, in convivial surroundings such as the paddock at Punchestown races or the showgrounds of the Royal Dublin Society during Horse Show week.

Beneath the small, all-powerful, top layer of civil servants, thousands of other employees of the British state in Ireland were entirely alienated from British rule. Teachers, customs officials, post-office workers and even policemen were sympathetic to Sinn Féin to varying degrees. Local magistrates could not be relied on to return the right verdicts in political cases. Many of those who emerged as leading revolutionaries had earned their living as civil servants. In this sense, the British Treasury could rightfully be said to be subsidising subversion, although it was Inspector General Byrne and not Lord French who drew the correct conclusion from this paradox. Rather than dealing with the reality of political feeling in Ireland, Lord French suggested that all government employees should be forced to take a loyalty oath. He was convinced that his tough regime would prevail, welcoming assassination threats as proof of his effectiveness. As for the plan by the newly elected Sinn Féin MPs to establish a national assembly in Dublin, he regarded it as a joke, the puffed-up self-importance of déclassé politicians playing at being statesmen on the world stage, not realising that the rest of the world would laugh. What would be best for them, Lord French reasoned, was to experience the disappointment of having their upstart parliament ignored. Then the temporary fascination of the mass of the people would dissolve and Ireland would return to a state of loyal normality.

But the Sinn Féin landslide had created a novel situation and as the new year began nobody could be certain what would happen. It was not just unionists who scoffed at Sinn Féin's claim that their newly elected MPs would stay in Dublin and establish their own parliament instead of taking their seats at Westminster. For one thing, many of the new MPs had already crossed the Irish Sea involuntarily and were imprisoned in gaols around Britain (34 of the 69 elected representatives were incarcerated). At a secret meeting just after the election Michael Collins used this as a reason to argue for the postponement of any attempt to convene an assembly in Dublin. There were other options open to them. One was to go to Westminster but to refuse to take their seats, gaining public attention by their distracting presence, 'haunting' the House of Commons, as the veteran Irish parliamentarian Tim Healy put it. This was taken as such a serious possibility that the London police were instructed to be on the lookout for Sinn Féin MPs who might turn up at the opening of parliament, and prevent them from creating a disturbance. Any of them wanted for crimes were to be arrested. There was some talk in government circles that if the Sinn Féin members did not take their seats, their constituencies could be handed over to the defeated candidates from the Irish Party (as if they were ever likely to risk taking up that offer). The only thing on which most people agreed, from commentators to the curious public, was that it could take months to work out what Ireland's future under Sinn Féin might look like.

To curious observers arriving from abroad to assess the intentions of the new Irish politicians, Sinn Féiners certainly did not look like statesmen in the making. Just about the first thing most reporters must have entered in their notebooks was how shabby the party's offices appeared. Neither did the young people making up parcels to send to the prisoners in

England look like architects of an Irish national assembly – though the young woman with short hair and a cigarette certainly offered a symbol of a generational change. Many of the leaders came across as intense characters and professed to be teetotallers. A young Dublin activist called Harry Boland, who managed to be pleasant and enthusiastic as well as earnest, turned up in many of the reports as the face and voice of Sinn Féin. His message was that the ramifications of what was happening in Ireland would spread worldwide. There would be no peace in western Europe, he warned, 'so long as Ireland remained under the heel of the English oppressor', although he added the clarification that although he hated England, he liked many Englishmen. Boland and his friends conveyed an impression that Sinn Féin was calm and not at all in a panic about the daring ambition of the plan that they were committed to delivering.

But the pressure of events dictated that they must make decisions soon. The new session of parliament in London would open on 4 February 1919, so it would obviously look good if they were able to set up a rival assembly in Dublin before then. Even more importantly the peace conference was scheduled to open at Versailles on 18 January. A functioning, credible assembly, where Ireland's elected representatives could be seen to be acting like legislators in any other self-respecting state, would enhance their claim that the nation was a perfect fit for self-determination. On 11 January Lloyd George had crossed the Channel in a British destroyer and taken a train from Calais to Paris. For the next six months his home would be a luxurious flat on the rue Nitot and his attention would be entirely consumed by making a new alliance with the United States – now Britain's creditor – while protecting and expanding the British Empire by acquiring the most coveted territories of the rival empires that had collapsed during the war (already Britain had made a secret agreement with France to divide the Ottoman empire, opening up the oil riches of the Middle East to British control). One of the first things Lloyd George did in Paris was to give Canada, Australia, South Africa and New Zealand separate representation at the peace conference. Even India was to have its own delegation, led by the British secretary of state for India, Edwin Montagu, because Indians were clearly not mature enough to conduct their own affairs. Nonetheless, President Wilson's adviser, Colonel House, believed all this autonomy might mean the 'eventual disintegration of the British Empire'.

In Redmond's dream this might have been how Ireland would have emerged from the war with its own government and equal standing with the other dominions in the Hall of Mirrors, helping to carve up the world. Instead Sinn Féin needed to play make-believe and convince the peacemakers from outside the hall that Ireland had managed to turn itself into a new state ready to separate from the British Empire. So the meetings to draw up plans for the new assembly in the weeks after the election were all about how to put on a show that would demonstrate to the world (and perhaps only as an afterthought to the people of Ireland) that Lord French was like the caricature of a Habsburg princeling, a relic of a bygone age now usurped by a properly modern democratic legislature. Long afterwards, one of the men involved in planning the new assembly confessed that his long experience of producing plays served him well in stage-managing the opening of the Dáil Éireann, as the parliament was to be called, using the ancient Irish words for a council of elders. When they discussed the functions and procedures for the assembly they employed the familiar usages of British parliamentary tradition: whips, committees, standing orders. To be seen as credible was to adopt the norms of Westminster decorum; but to be seen as modern would require the proclamation of solemn, even soaring, foundation statements extolling independence, freedom and democracy, and social reform, the kind of documents that could be framed and hung in the lobbies of public buildings. Hence the 'Declaration of Independence', the 'Message to the Free Nations of the World' and, drafted at the last minute in the face of much opposition, the vaguely socialistic 'Democratic Programme'.

Given the uncertainty that surrounded Sinn Féin's actual intentions, it is remarkable how much public excitement was generated in Dublin on 21 January, the day set for the Dáil to meet in the largest room in the elegant eighteenth-century townhouse that served as the official residence of the Lord Mayor of Dublin. A long queue formed in Dawson Street outside the Mansion House. Inside, soldiers from the Dublin Fusiliers, who had just returned from France, were finishing their lunch in a great room whose walls were festooned with Union Jacks with a rendition of 'God Save the King'. Some of those standing out on the street in the gathering gloom were invited guests; others had received tickets for entry from the new Dáil deputies (as they would now be known instead of being referred to as members of parliament). There were fifty priests and two US naval officers and several soldiers from the dominions. Maire Comerford, a young Sinn Féin activist from County Wexford, later wrote that she heard people in the queue talking of dead patriots and 'the first coming of the English to Ireland'. An English reporter was impressed at how many people were obsessed with the significance of the occasion. From a window in a building across the street the chief commissioner of the Dublin Metropolitan Police, Colonel Wedgeworth Johnstone, and the inspector general of the RIC, Sir James Byrne, looked down on the crowds gathering outside. A police raid earlier in January had yielded copies of the proposed constitution for the Dáil and the Declaration of Independence. Lord French deemed them to be so self-evidently ludicrous that the day before the Dáil was due to meet, the government removed the requirement for a police permit. Still fearful that there might be an attempt to arrest the deputies en masse, the organisers had prepared an emergency drill to rescue the main leaders. As it turned out, the police, helped by good-natured volunteers, kept the traffic running smoothly.

Photographs of the scene in the Round Room, built in 1821 to receive King George IV, vindicate the choice of venue. Although spectators significantly outnumbered members of the assembly (since so many of those elected in December were in gaol) the crowded circular auditorium at once gave the impression of an august forum that had been meeting for decades. Deputies sat together on sofas in the centre of the room under the spotlights; ladies seated around them and in the balcony wore hats. There was an impressive collection of journalists from Britain and the rest of the world – at least fifty – with their pens and notebooks ready to record the historic moment, a sight that reassured the stage managers that the event would not be the laughing stock their detractors predicted. Besides, the press interest proved that it was just as possible to win international attention from Dublin as from London. At 3.30 p.m. the new members of the assembly filed in through the central doors. To one reporter present they looked not like dangerous revolutionaries, more like the audience at a concert.

Only deputies elected on the Sinn Féin ticket had chosen to come to the Mansion House, so there were no unionists, no members of the old Irish Party and no representatives of the Labour Party, which had stood aside at the election. In theory the Dáil was the nucleus of a potential one-party state; in fact, beneath the camaraderie and emotion there was no uniformity of opinion among the delegates. Political operators mingled with secretive guerrilla strategists, rhetoricians sat beside civil servants, some were anti-clerical and many were happy to be the political proxies of the Catholic Church. There were men present who would be forgotten, some who would die in front of firing squads and others who would become rich and successful in the new state. Already there were signs of cabals and coteries; strong personalities were emerging who were attracting their own bands of followers. All sat solemnly to hear the speaker, Cathal Brugha, announce that they were engaged in the most important work in Ireland's history. As he spoke, the dozens of visiting journalists, the dominion soldiers looking on and even several of the new members of the Dáil would have been lost in incomprehension, for Brugha delivered his opening address in Irish. There might be people, he said after a few minutes, who because of the foreign education system did not understand their own language, so for their benefit he would speak a few words in English: 'We desire that there shall be no cheering whatever.'

The Declaration of Independence was read in Irish, then in French and, finally, in English. For seven hundred years, until the Irish Republic had been proclaimed on Easter Monday 1916, English rule had been based on force, fraud and military occupation. The Irish people had seized their first opportunity to declare their allegiance to the Irish Republic by voting overwhelmingly for Sinn Féin in the 1918 election. Now, their elected representatives were ratifying the establishment of the republic. The declaration was a mixture of the hackneyed and the modern. God had given our ancestors the determination to persevere in the face of ruthless tyranny. International peace now depended on Irish independence. For Maire Comerford, watching it was a pivotal emotional moment. She repeated the words of the Declaration to herself as it was read out, and felt she had committed herself to an irrevocable step: 'We had burnt our boats now. There was no going back.'

The drafters of the 'Message to the Free Nations of the World' felt the need to point out that Dublin was the capital of Ireland, 'the point upon which great trade routes between East and West converge', before continuing in the new language of the Wilsonian world. At 'the dawn of the promised era of self-determination' Ireland believed in 'the fundamental principles of international law' and 'frank co-operation between the peoples for equal rights against the vested privileges of ancient tyrannies' because peace could not be guaranteed by empires but by the free will of free peoples. (A new post-imperial world would need freedom of the seas and ergo Irish independence so that the country's 'great harbours' – still to be developed – would not be a British monopoly.) Ireland, it pointed out, was not some newly minted Ruritania just brought to life by some hasty redrawing of lines on a map but one of the most ancient nations in Europe 'who had asserted nationhood by force of arms in every generation'. The deputies called on every free nation to support the vindication of the Irish Republic at the peace congress. It would be for the civilised world to judge between English wrong and Irish right.

The final document to advertise Ireland's claim to be a modern, progressive nation was the 'Democratic Programme'. It proclaimed that in Ireland the rights of private property 'must be subordinated to the public right and welfare' and that 'no child shall suffer hunger or cold from lack of food, clothing, or shelter'. Agreed only at the last minute, it represented an acknowledgement of the martyrdom of the Marxist theoretician James Connolly in the 1916 Rising and the worldwide tide towards social reform, but more practically the hope that Irish Labour Party delegates at the upcoming conference of the Socialist International in Berne could achieve recognition for the republic by convincing delegates that Ireland would be a voice for international laws to improve the lot of the working classes. The session continued for two hours. It had been, as one participant remarked, 'dull but for us believers electric'. When it finished, the writer George Moore, from whom Lord French had commissioned a personal account of the proceedings, was satisfied that the gathering represented 'the general feeling in the country'.

That evening a reception and dinner was held in honour of the visiting journalists, a sign of just how much the whole event had been about publicity and a portent of how much the struggle to come would be about appearances, impressions and public relations. The censor, Lord Decies, prided himself on making sure that the Sinn Féin message reached the Irish public 'in diluted form', although the election result suggested that the watered-down version was no less persuasive. Thus, the newspapers were instructed not to publish the 'Democratic Programme', the 'Declaration of Independence' or speeches proposing and seconding the Declaration. But the 'Message to the Free Nations' and the 'Constitution of the Dáil' were passed for publication, as well as some minor speeches. The truncated reports might account for the apathy noted by Father Michael Maher when he sat down to write up his journal in the presbytery in Thurles. The opening of the Dáil seemed to have no effect, he observed, with no demonstrations 'nor any sign of rejoicing at our new born liberty, in fact there was as much quiet that night as if no political change was taking place'. Not far from his presbytery more radical members of the Irish republican movement were equally unimpressed by the political quietism that descended on the nation. They had already decided to do something about it.

4

'Where Tipperary Leads Ireland Follows'

On 4 July 1918 the Irish tenor John McCormack was President Wilson's guest aboard the presidential yacht, the *Mayflower*. It sailed down the Potomac to George Washington's plantation at Mount Vernon, where thousands of people had gathered on the lawn to celebrate Independence Day. As wreaths were laid on Washington's tomb, McCormack, standing by the president, sang 'The Battle Hymn of the Republic'. To those listening, McCormack would have been as much of a star as the president. In a few years, his American agent had turned a virtuoso opera singer into a box-office phenomenon whose concert tours across the US sold out months in advance. He owned an apartment in New York and a farm by the Connecticut coast, where he relaxed after his arduous tours by admiring his prize herd of pedigree cattle and indulging his passion for buying ever larger sailing boats. His life story, a hurriedly assembled celebrity biography, had just been published to cash in on his popularity with the American soldiers heading to Europe. His renditions of 'Keep the Home Fires Burning' and 'God Be with Our Boys in Picardy Tonight' had led the Red Cross to describe him as 'America's unofficial heartsease'. But his signature recording had been made in November 1914, long before the United States had joined the war. Composed overnight for a bet by a

Birmingham music-hall entertainer of Irish ancestry in 1912, 'It's a Long Way to Tipperary' quickly caught the imagination of soldiers marching to the front.

By the end of 1914, the lament of a lonely Irish emigrant in London pining for his sweetheart in Tipperary was the melody of patriotism. Ten thousand copies of the sheet music were already being sold every day. Newly enlisted soldiers sang it on their way to London railway stations as they embarked for the front. In Dublin crowds seeing off the first detachment of volunteers from the Irish Rugby Football Union to join the Royal Dublin Fusiliers stood by the train with Union Jacks draped over the carriage doors to give a rousing rendition of 'Tipperary'. An American journalist attending a performance of the musical *Tommy Atkins* at the Lyceum Theatre in London noted with astonishment that it was the only song to stir the patriotic feelings in the audience. In the trenches it was as popular with French soldiers as with their British allies. A senior French member of parliament, welcoming a delegation of Irish MPs to Paris to celebrate Ireland's commitment to the Allied cause, attempted to decode the meaning of the song. Was Tipperary 'the Promised Land', he wondered, 'where Paddy would find peace and happiness'?

During Christmas 1914, the London weekly *The Sphere* sent a photographer to Tipperary town to portray the real place whose name in song evoked the deepest longings and fears of men going off to war. The two-page spread, published in the first week of January, showed respectable men in suits on the pavements of a wide and not very busy main street and a photo of a woman driving a donkey and cart on a deserted road on the edge of town (the caption noted that donkeys and carts were rarely seen in Ireland these days but nonetheless added that the image was 'a characteristic glimpse of Irish life'). Inadvertently, the photo essay also captured the ambiguity of Tipperary's role in the war effort. To the left and right of the donkey and cart were images of two solid monuments commemorating popular Fenians: the local novelist Charles Kickham and the three men known as the 'Manchester Martyrs', hanged in 1867 for killing a police officer while attempting to rescue Fenian prisoners in that city (the caption diplomatically referred to 'certain ill-judged executions of three Irishmen'). Above and below the images of the monuments were shots of new recruits to Lord Kitchener's army. Soldiers from the local garrison had been familiar, domesticated figures in the towns of Tipperary, welcome customers for the local shopkeepers and traders and romantic targets for young women. As the war went on the fame of the eponymous music-hall favourite was not the only reminder of a local connection with the western front. Thousands of recruits had joined up and, especially in the towns, many people would have known families who had lost sons or fathers or seen wounded men in khaki hobbling along the street. For four years, long trains crowded with soldiers and their saddled horses shunted through the countryside, stopping for water and food in the town stations.

One of those who would have watched the trains go by was Dan Breen, who had been working as a linesman for Great Southern Railways since 1913. Breen cared little for the war effort, regarding the fight for the rights of small nations as mere cant. Most people in Ireland who cheered and waved as the soldiers passed by or sang 'Tipperary' were, to Breen's mind, suffering a very bad case of what would later be called false consciousness. Ireland was fighting Britain's war when it should have been fighting its own struggle for independence. He and his friends made a point of showing that they were above the war sentiment that had touched their more gullible compatriots by refusing to contribute to collections for wounded soldiers. At night they continued to drill with the minority of Irish Volunteers who had rejected John Redmond's call for Irishmen to enlist.

In the spring of 1918 the British government helped to make Dan Breen a less isolated figure by announcing that it would conscript all Irishmen over the age of eighteen. As nationalists of all stripes united to oppose conscription, the idea took hold that the country was on the brink of a war of its own. There were rumours that Gurkha troops would be sent to force men to join up, that British planes would bomb cities and that demonstrators would be mown down by machine-guns. Suddenly the anti-war Volunteers, the men Breen drilled with under police surveillance, put themselves forward as the troops to defend the Irish nation. Thousands of young men horrified by the idea of being forced to fight the Germans joined up to take classes in first aid, handling explosives and signalling, so that they could take on the British. They scouted for caves to hide food and arms, and planned for pitched battles with the police and the British army, a state of war in which bridges and buildings would be blown up, towns occupied and the whole country turned into a battlefield. Cathal Brugha, the first chairman of Dáil Éireann, devised a plan to assassinate members of the British cabinet. For Dan Breen this was an opportunity to unite the nation in a glorious cause, erasing ugly divisions over factions, ideology and class. Even if half the population of the entire island – two and a quarter million – was to die in a conflagration to compare with the worst horrors of the western front, he believed it would be a sacrifice worth paying because at least the survivors would be united.

The war that Breen longed for never came because circumstances on the western front improved and the British government held back from conscripting Irishmen. The great confrontation, which one ordinary Volunteer in Tipperary had looked forward to as a 'purification', dissolved into nothing. The eager new recruits drifted away and Breen and his friends were left parading and drilling a dwindling bunch of acolytes in isolated fields, trailed dutifully by note-taking constables on bicycles. Breen despised the men who had joined his unit only briefly in the hope that they could avoid shedding blood in France, but even those who stayed on he regarded as just children playing at revolution. Confrontations they provoked with the police over flying tricolours on lampposts were passé, merely cheap stunts. Breen and his closest friends really meant to fight for independence and they continued to craft for themselves an even more sharply defined outlaw lifestyle, living in discrete and remote rural cottages or outhouses where they made crude grenades, sleeping under hay and old newspapers, eating boiled rice and maintaining a distant relationship with their neighbours. It is easy to imagine a story he tells in his memoirs – in which, returning from a well with a can of water, he sees their hideout blown sky high by their home-made munitions – as a scene in a western in which he plays the principal outlaw.

The election in December of 1918 brought Breen and his friends down from the hills. They cycled the countryside painting walls with slogans urging voters to 'Rally to Sinn Féin', 'Vote for the Republic' or 'Stand by the Men of 1916'. The people voted to repudiate British authority but to Breen this popular mobilisation was just as much a disappointment as the anti-conscription campaign because victory led many of the Volunteers to put their faith in politics rather than soldiering. The country would have to be returned to a war footing, he thought. Around Christmas 1918, Breen, his friend Sean Treacy and Seamus Robinson – the commander of their unit of Volunteers – discussed making an attempt to seize gelignite that was often transported to a local quarry under the protection of RIC constables. They assembled nine men to hold up the horse and cart, chose the best location to spring the ambush and began to spend several hours each day waiting for the little convoy to pass.

On 21 January, a cold, wet, misty morning, Patrick Flynn, an employee of Tipperary County Council, readied the horse and cart to carry the boxes of gelignite from the military barracks in Tipperary town to the quarry at Soloheadbeg, three miles away, where it was to be used for blasting stone. The gelignite, weighing 160 pounds, was loaded on the cart behind the driver, Edward Godfrey. Two RIC constables, James MacDonnell and Patrick O'Connell, joined them. At first MacDonnell sat on the cart as it rumbled along the country road; then he jumped down and walked as they got closer to the quarry. They passed a man mending a bicycle puncture on the side of the road; they were not to know that he was a scout for the men waiting to spring an ambush. Later Patrick Flynn told how, when the gang of masked men shouted 'Hands up!', he and Godfrey took cover behind the cart but soon realised that the ambushers were paying them no attention; they seemed interested only in the two constables. They heard shots and saw the two policemen fall on the road. This was the opportunity to run away. As they glanced back they saw one of the masked men get up on the cart and whip the horse so that it bolted along the road.

It was Sean Treacy who had fired his rifle from behind the hedge, hitting Constable MacDonnell in the temple and killing him instantly. Another member of the ambush party shot Constable O'Connell in the back. Seamus Robinson recalled many years later how Treacy had performed a little dance after he had fired, kissing his rifle and exclaiming 'that was a comfortable place to fire from'. Afterwards, the ambushers said that instead of obeying the order to raise their hands, the two constables had levelled their rifles to fire, so they had shot them in self-defence. But more than thirty years later Dan Breen told interviewers from the Bureau of Military History that he and Treacy had always intended to kill the policemen and had decided to shoot them without telling Robinson, their commander. Breen said Treacy had told him that the only way of starting a war was to kill someone. 'The only regret we had, following the ambush,' Breen told the interviewers, 'was that there were only two policemen in it instead of the six we expected, because we felt that six dead policemen would have impressed the country more than a mere two.'

The local reaction against the ambush was strong; it certainly was not received by a jubilant population as a strike against oppression. At the inquest, Flynn collapsed and had to be taken to hospital for treatment as he told the story of what had happened. Constable MacDonnell's son asked whether his father had been given 'a dog's chance' for survival. The coroner remarked how both constables were decent, quiet men who had lived a long time in Tipperary and been very popular. It was sad, he said, to see them being shot down while doing their public duty and 'not doing anything that would injure anybody'. The local Catholic archbishop told his congregation that the death of the policemen was 'a crime against God'. And Monsignor Arthur Ryan followed Constable MacDonnell's son by saying that the assassins had treated the police at Soloheadbeg as if they 'were dogs not men', denying them the opportunity even convicted murderers received to prepare themselves for a Christian death. It used to be said, Monsignor Ryan recalled, that 'where Tipperary leads Ireland follows', but 'God help poor Ireland if she follows that lead of blood'.

It might be a mistake, of course, to read popular reaction reliably from the comments of senior churchmen. But Dan Breen himself wrote of how as they went on the run in the days after Soloheadbeg they were aware not only of clerical censure but of condemnation by 'the public', such that they felt betrayed by the people who had voted for a republic a few weeks previously. In a sign that at least some ordinary people responded in the same way as the clergy, a woman who met Robinson shortly after the ambush asked him what he would say in confession. People who they thought they could count on refused them shelter and would not even consent to letting them sleep with their cattle. In a house where they were allowed to stay a servant upbraided her employer for sheltering 'three murderers'.

Breen and his friends could not even be certain that the leadership of their own movement did not also regard them as murderers. Confirming Breen's poor estimate of the reliability of politicians, several members of the Dáil repudiated the ambush, assuring reporters of their shock and disapproval of the killings. The leadership of the Volunteers, the military wing of the movement for independence and committed to 'ruthless warfare' to defend Ireland from conscription, according to an article just published in their in-house newspaper, was strikingly ambivalent. Some weeks after the ambush Breen, Robinson and Treacy made their way to Dublin to meet Richard Mulcahy, the chief of staff of the Volunteers. Reserved, meticulous and cautious, Mulcahy was the antithesis of Breen, reluctant to risk the lives of Volunteers or inflict casualties on policemen if they could be avoided. He urged them to go to the United States; if they stayed in Ireland they would be disowned. An offer of money only further incensed Breen because in his eyes it would make them paid murderers.

This withholding of endorsement was partly tactical. Shooting policemen might produce an even more efficient repressive response from the authorities, which would be enough to suppress the whole movement before it had time to fight from a position of strength. And such an openly aggressive policy might also alienate a majority of the people supporting Sinn Féin. Mulcahy believed that 'the people had to be educated and led gently into open war'. At this early stage, as throughout the next eighteen months, the calculations were about how to enlist the majority of ordinary citizens. Violence had to be politically acceptable and be likely to produce results. This was not just about calculating effect; a moral feeling – ambiguous, often unarticulated – was also at work. In early January, while Breen and Treacy were planning their ambush, another company of Volunteers in Tipperary was told by a local farmer who was an important figure in the movement that it was not justified to shoot a man just because he wore a uniform – no excuse would condone shooting a policeman from behind a ditch unless some grave charge was proved against him.

Someone who had shot a couple of policemen in defiance of all that hesitancy and caution, someone who had taken seriously what others would only talk about, was likely to see himself as one of the elect. Rejection by superiors and peers only sharpened the commitment of Breen, Treacy and Robinson. In Breen's words, they would be vindicated 'when the scales fell from people's eyes'. Isolated in their cocoon of self-belief, the Tipperary hard men set about creating their own myth that would make themselves heroes among less bold Volunteers and inspire some to emulate them. They patented the glamour of being on the run, cycling vast distances, sleeping in houses where they were welcome and well fed (Breen's memoir is full of appreciation for good cooks), liberated from friends and family. The wandering was itself part of their growth as self-sufficient heroes and connected them with the stories of historic rebels who took to the mountains. Breen's book is a guidebook to the sites of great deeds of the past where Irish rebels had defied British occupiers.

Living on the run restored their own sense of a mission that they had been chosen to carry out. Breen revelled in his fearlessness and the cultivation of an outward coolness towards risk. They developed a heightened sense of how far in advance they were of their meek or more restrained comrades, who were often thought to be harmless. They considered themselves to be superior judges of character, deciding whether others had the qualities needed for the fight. Constantly at odds with their nominal superiors in Dublin, they were certain that they knew better than people playing at being staff officers. The newspaper accounts of the ambush, avidly consulted as soon as possible, were, of course, 'absolutely wrong', according to Breen.

Much of this was the colloquial professional disdain for head office by workers in the field. However, the experience of living their own myth, and publicising it, not only created a strong sense of comradeship but made a cult of strong personalities a key feature of the whole movement. To Breen anything less than a glorious death would be an insult, as he revealed in his account of crashing into another bicycle while descending a hill at speed in the early hours of the morning: 'To be killed in action by an enemy bullet was a fate I did not at all dread; but I strongly objected to be killed by the handle-bars of an ordinary, inoffensive push-bicycle.'

Grandiose visions of glory were not the only characteristic of the inner life of Breen and his comrades as they evaded the police and soldiers flooding into Tipperary after the killings. The prodigious cycle rides from one house to the next were also a boyish adventure, and delight in such thrills would become the hallmark of many IRA volunteers over the next two years. Sean Treacy was fondly remembered by Breen as a laconic comedian, remarking as they raced along in the horse and cart with the load of gelignite after the ambush at Soloheadbeg, 'Do you remember, Dan, when we were reading about explosives? The book says that they are dangerous if frozen, or if they get jolted?' They loved making the police appear as fools. Both Treacy and Breen relate stories of their audacity in requesting assistance from unalert policemen to mend punctures or being helped through roadblocks by gullible soldiers. And though they delighted in their image as desperados – Breen relished being called the 'Prince of the Assassins', with a £10,000 reward offered for his capture – they were still, like errant schoolboys, subject to the chiding of women. On the fifth day of fruitless waiting for the gelignite to pass at Soloheadbeg, Breen's mother sneered as she laid a breakfast before him at 4 a.m.: 'If you don't do something today you can get your own breakfast tomorrow.' A kindly priest's housekeeper called Molly ordered Breen to bed and was, he confessed, both a mother and a dictator.

Although in the months after the ambush they lived in an underground world – fugitive ghostly cyclists crossing the landscape by night, protected by priests' housekeepers as they slept by day – they were all the time aware that the real impact of what they had done would come from the retelling of their deeds in the public domain. They were less clear about what they hoped to achieve. By their example they aspired to goad or inspire their comrades into action and, more vaguely, to 'stir the country'. They also wished to 'bring Ireland's name before the world', animating international admiration for a fight for freedom against the odds. In the short term none of this appeared to be happening, as attested by the timidity of the other Volunteers, the denunciation by priests and bishops before church congregations and the evasive and hostile behaviour of people they might have relied on to give them shelter. But this antagonism was itself limited by the popular rejection of British rule and the historically sanctioned sympathy for rebels and outlaws.

Other Volunteers might not be prepared to shoot policemen themselves, but they would not readily disown Breen and his friends. They might not be as brave but they could derive a vicarious thrill from the adventures of the perpetrators of the Soloheadbeg ambush. The 'civilian' supporters of Sinn Féin or other nationalists might be horrified by the shooting of the policemen but their revulsion would not turn them into informers. Many might recoil at finding themselves acting like collaborators; others might fear censure from their neighbours or, worse, physical retaliation from the Volunteers. They could be inhibited for all three reasons.

The 'Wanted' poster circulated after the Soloheadbeg ambush is a good indication of the distance between the authorities and the people they hoped would assist them in capturing Dan Breen. It offered a reward of £1,000 for information that might lead to the arrest of a man 'wanted for murder in Ireland', as if addressed to a foreign audience.

Breen appears in a suit and tie in one photo and his Volunteer uniform in the other, looking like a respectable clerk who might have been recruited to the British army. He certainly does not display the 'sulky bulldog appearance' suggested by the poster, nor does he look 'rather like a blacksmith coming from work', a condescending description unlikely to appeal to a rural population where blacksmiths were hardly regarded as riff-raff. If the poster was intended to push civilians from their ambiguous allegiances, through the lure of money or by turning an outlaw into an outcast, it failed. In 1919 many people could not escape being ambiguous, having their loyalties torn in half. How to express your moral reservations about shooting policemen and still support Irish independence? Would rejecting one type of violence force you to side with another? The acts of the war that would develop over the next two years between guerrillas, policemen and soldiers would essentially be about exploiting that ambiguity. And the next shooting of a policeman in Tipperary would show just how malleable that equivocation could be.

On Monday, 23 June, crowds gathered in the market town of Thurles for the annual summer race meeting. At the racecourse, a mile and a half from the centre of town, Detective Inspector Michael Hunt was on duty. He had worked his way up through the ranks, after twenty-six years in the Royal Irish Constabulary, to become a dedicated and even feared policeman. As he made his way through the crowds in the stands and watched the horses parade in the paddock he did not notice that he was being watched and followed by six men who were intent on killing him. Each time one of them thought of drawing a revolver and opening fire on Hunt he hesitated because the density of the crowd would not allow for a quick getaway.

When the racing finished, the crowds streamed back into the town, and DI Hunt, conspicuous in his bottle-green uniform, walked along among them. Three of the men who had been shadowing him at the racecourse all afternoon had given up their pursuit, but three others were still behind him as he approached the town square. At around 5.30 p.m. DI Hunt stood outside a local pub to watch the racegoers surge around him at the bottleneck where the main street met the square. Suddenly, three revolver shots rang out and he fell on the street. The crowd scattered in panic. A local doctor who bent down to assist Hunt discovered he had been hit twice in the back. For ten minutes, as the doctor tried to help him, the policeman moaned heavily and his breathing became more laboured. A priest arrived and administered the last rites. When DI Hunt died they carried his body to a local news-agent's shop and waited for his wife to arrive. On the street, among the fleeing crowds, another doctor came across a man helping a small boy with a bullet wound in his knee. The doctor arranged for him to be taken to Dublin for an X-ray.

The men who had followed DI Hunt from the racecourse had not been disguised and had melted away in the crowd. Yet when he condemned this 'shocking crime', the Catholic Archbishop of Cashel said the man who had fired the shots must clearly have been a stranger, an outsider who had stained the reputation of the town. Astonishingly, he argued that there was no proof that it was a political crime. Switching from denouncing Hunt's killer to blaming the government for provoking violence and unrest, especially in Tipperary, he thundered with full prelatial pomp, 'Let the military domination of Ireland cease at once.' Any member of the congregation carefully reading the archbishop's statement for guidance on what attitude they should take towards Hunt's killing would have been struck by the implicit ambiguity that might have reflected their own ambivalence. And there was a further, openly acknowledged, complication.

Detective Inspector Hunt, the father of three children, one of whom had been wounded in the leg while serving in the First World War, was an unpopular policeman. Unlike the unequivocal tributes to the constables shot at Soloheadbeg, condemnations of Hunt's killing recognised that it was common knowledge that he had been antagonistic to Sinn Féin. A local priest, Reverend Michael Ryan, described DI Hunt as an upright and honest man 'who may not have studied the art of winning popularity'. There was no excuse for his violent death, though 'some people thought they had a grievance against him, whether real or imaginary'.

The local members of Sinn Féin and the Volunteers certainly had a grievance against him. Belying the image of the RIC as cowards that Dan Breen and others propagated, Hunt had shot and wounded the quartermaster of the local Volunteers a year earlier, when a bicycle patrol of policemen had confronted a group of cycling Volunteers on a country road. The Detective Inspector seemed to relish stopping meetings, searching houses and leading baton charges against protesting Sinn Féiners. The Volunteers feared him because he was also effective. In the obverse of Dan Breen's belief that his example would encourage other Volunteers to be bold, they hoped that killing Hunt would deter other policemen from being so diligent. Here it is worth recalling the statement of the prosperous farmer who told a company of Volunteers in January that there was no excuse for killing a man in uniform unless some grave charge was proven against him.

Hunt's unpopularity opened the way for an incremental advance to more brutal methods. The response of the crowd coming from the races on hearing the gunshots and watching Hunt collapse on the street was revealing. Some fled in panic and horror; some assisted other policemen in tending to the Detective Inspector as he lay dying on the pavement; but others, to the consternation of the police arriving on the scene, were jeering and laughing at what had happened.

The shooting of Hunt in broad daylight on a crowded street was the subject of much comment and discussion. The following Saturday Rosamond Jacob enjoyed a wonderful dinner in Waterford at the house of her friends the Dowleys. She was delighted with the fresh strawberries and chocolate biscuits. The shooting in Thurles came up in conversation and its brutality and the objections to it were mulled over. 'We agreed that killing Hunt was very excusable,' Rosamond noted in her diary later, the righteous smugness not entirely concealing the sense that the shooting was seen as an exceptional occurrence requiring justification and that each subsequent act would have to be weighed in the same way.

After Hunt's assassination Lord French informed the cabinet that Sinn Féin was an organised club for the murder of policemen and should be suppressed. In July, Sinn Féin, the Irish Volunteers, Cumann na mBan and the Gaelic League were proclaimed illegal organisations. The idea that putting pressure on the whole community would undermine support for the extremists still held sway in Dublin Castle. But it was more likely that this pressure would strain or sever the web of communal affiliations, personal attachments and moral hesitations that were holding back outright polarisation between the gunmen and the police. The Volunteers were becoming bolder and less restrained by conventional scruples. At the end of March, a resident magistrate in Westport, County Mayo, J. C. Milling, who had been notably assiduous in sending

Volunteers to prison, was shot through the window of his drawing room as he was adjusting his clock to summer time. He died the following day. In May six men arrived at a hospital in Cork seeking out a Volunteer who had been injured in an explosion at a home-made-bomb factory. In response to a challenge from medical students the men pulled out revolvers and brushed past. A doctor who ran to the telephone found two men guarding it. 'You have no authority to be here,' he told them. 'We have our authority in our pockets,' they replied and drew their revolvers. The doctor turned around to see the wounded bomber being escorted from the hospital dressed in a greatcoat – his escorts apologised to the doctor for the intrusion. The two men guarding the telephone stayed to ensure that nobody called the police and then left, carrying the wounded man's possessions, including a book lent to him by another patient.

This was the kind of spirit Dan Breen had meant to encourage. In Dublin, Michael Collins – himself nonchalantly ambivalent about the ambush in Tipperary – began to assemble a team of Volunteers skilful and ruthless enough to assassinate G-men, the most knowledgeable detectives tasked with harassing the Sinn Féin movement. To his surprise, several candidates interested in joining his special unit withdrew when they discovered they would have to shoot policemen. There was still some way to go before the police were to become seen by all separatists as legitimate targets.

5

Over a Policeman's Body

In 1893, District Inspector George Edwin Dagg of the Royal Irish Constabulary published a book that he had every reason to hope would be a roaring success. In the introduction he boasted that his painstakingly assembled guide – *Devia Hibernia, The Road and Route Guide to Ireland* – contained information on 'nearly every turn, every hill and every cross-road' in the country. Compiled with the assistance of RIC constables in towns and villages all across the island it would be ideal for 'the overcoat pocket or the handbag of the tourist'. Its motto, printed on the title page in Irish, was 'Let us wander around Ireland', and it included historical and archaeological notes on each location, as well as helpful practical information such as the opening times for post offices. Its unique selling point was the detailed knowledge of every road and by-road in the country, whether stretches were uphill or downhill, in good condition or bad. The routes all radiated from police stations and the precisely calibrated distances from one staging post to another were, the author boasted, 'the careful estimates of intelligent men, familiar, by their daily and nightly duty of patrolling these very roads'.

The book was a testament to the idea of the police force as the purest form of public service, a body of men devoted to their country and uniquely but benignly knowledgeable about their localities, men who not only kept the peace but who were also well informed about the standard of accommodation in hotels and the quality of food for sale (all part of their official duties). In an era of a marked decline in violent crime the police were now revealed as an untapped resource for increasing people's pleasurable engagement with the riches of Ireland.

The generation born at the time the guidebook was published would be taught by their parents to treat these men with respect. When the young Ernie O'Malley came across a carriage full of constables from the Royal Irish Constabulary, his eyes feasted sensually on the details of their appearance. Their uniform, blue-black with a touch of green, was 'the colour of the cheap ink we used at school' and made their faces appear darker and swarthier. The only touches of colour were a small patch of red cloth behind the band on their caps, a crown resting on a harp and the chevrons on the sleeve of the sergeant's coat, which, O'Malley noted, were 'salted-butter yellow'. They carried batons in leather cases and carbines with bayonets attached. At an angle across their chest they gripped their neatly folded greatcoats. The policemen exuded solidity and strength, their stillness projecting authority 'as if they wore an extra skin'. He had been aware of these men since childhood, when his family lived across the street from a police barracks. The constables would touch their caps to his father. As he grew up, the young O'Malley was invited into the barracks and shown 'carbines clipped in arms racks, blue-black revolvers, the steel of bayonets, and heavy-padded helmets'.

His sense of reverence had been shared by others who would in their youth also become revolutionaries and eventually implacable enemies of the RIC. For Seán Ó Faoláin, the son of a police constable in Cork, the symbols of authority and respectability that O'Malley admired from a distance were on daily display inside his home. When Ó Faoláin came to describe his father in his memoirs – 'a modest, pious trusting man, upright, honest as daylight, and absolutely loyal to the Empire as only a born hero-worshipper can be' – it was, he remembered, the uniform, truncheon case and black boots that transformed him into a figure of substance for his son. As he prepared to go on night patrol along the streets of Cork city, fortified by a special supper of chops, potatoes and strong tea, his father would look 'very big, powerful and handsome' in his long overcoat and domed helmet. He retired before the 1916 Rising, avoiding a direct confrontation between father and son. But Seán Ó Faoláin was sure his father would have stubbornly resisted the revolutionaries. And not because he would have conscientiously weighed up his competing loyalties to Ireland or the British Empire, but because it was the job that provided for his family.

The conflicting identities of the RIC – Irishmen, fathers, neighbours, sometimes nationalists and also symbols of authority and empire – were to be dissolved in the polarisation of the war. The policeman was an intrinsic feature of Irish rural life in the early twentieth century. He was, typically, the son of a farmer dedicated to ensuring that his sons and daughters would better themselves through education, a member of the congregation at Mass on a Sunday and a regular at the local pub that evening. But for over a century he was also the most conspicuous symbol of British rule in Ireland. The uniform that made him the upright respected figure in the community would also enable him to be transformed into the 'eyes and ears' of a failing regime.

The RIC had been founded in 1822 to keep order in a country still not reconciled to the Act of Union. So from the start it had a military character and was equipped to deal with political protest as much as ordinary crime. Unlike their late-nineteenth-century counterparts in London, Irish constables were always armed, and though they became embedded in Irish life, performing the mundane tasks of keeping order, the force never quite lived up to the maxim of Sir Robert Peel that 'police are the public and the public are the police'. In Ireland there was always a question of where the balance lay between consent and coercion. Throughout the nineteenth century the officers were generally Protestant and the constables were rural Catholics. For the son of a Church of Ireland clergyman, becoming an inspector in the RIC was a route to social status without the expense and demands of a career in the army or the law. Once established in the force police officers were often followed by their sons. An example was Samuel Waters. His earliest memories were of summer days swimming in Ireland's largest river near the barracks in Carrick-on-Shannon where his father was stationed. At eighteen he became an RIC cadet and embarked on a successful career in which promotion and increased pay were secondary to his interest in hunting, shooting, fishing and playing tennis and cricket. There was little divide between his work and his sporting life and he would canter along country roads in full uniform swinging his polo stick. The rigid religious functionalism dividing Irish society gradually began to dissipate in the early twentieth century and many Catholics were promoted from the ranks. By 1914, any suspicion that a candidate harboured particularly strong sectarian feelings could bar him from the RIC. Constables strove to keep politics and religion out of conversations in order to keep the locality harmonious.

In times of peace the Irish policeman was the personification of officialdom, the instrument through which the modern state imposed its regulations on daily life. He made sure that the village pubs closed on time, the shopkeepers and mobile traders did not obstruct the footpaths with their merchandise and that farmers did not allow their cattle to wander the roads. He functioned as a one-man government agency, collecting statistics on animal disease and distributing leaflets advising on the best way to protect the potato crop from blight. Many hours were spent recording incidences of sheep killed by dogs or registering new owners of horses and motor cars. Occasionally his work rose above clerkship. Breaking up cock fights and, especially, battling with the producers of poteen – an extremely alcoholic illegal hooch distilled from potatoes and sugar over turf fires in the mountains – would merit a write-up in the local papers. Only rarely might a policeman have to deal with actual violence; farmers fighting at fairs or political factions squaring up to each other at election time were the most serious public-order issues in normal times. Policemen were often unwitting social workers in communities underequipped to deal with social problems. The sergeant was just as likely to be confided in by families as the local curate. One policeman recalled how an orphan, whose parents were killed in an eviction during the nineteenth-century land war, was adopted by constables and lived in the barracks. Permanently traumatised by his loss, he rambled the roads as an adult, stopping at police stations to eat and pretend to conduct an inspection. They nicknamed him 'the colonel' and would humour him by noting in the logbook that he had inspected the barracks and found it satisfactory.

Police training at the depot in the Phoenix Park in Dublin (near the Viceregal Lodge) was an arduous immersion in a regime of Victorian discipline, endless drilling in the yard, rote learning of arithmetic and memorising government statutes.

The food was terrible – low-grade corned beef, tasteless jam – and for country boys accustomed to being spoiled by their mothers there was rarely enough of it. Guinness stout was on sale in the canteen but it was difficult to get a pass to venture into the big city. When the new graduate finally escaped the training depot he was posted to a rural station far from the county of his birth, where he took his place at the bottom of a rigid hierarchy. Constables paid one shilling a week from their wages for the privilege of sleeping together in a dormitory in the barracks (the sergeant, his wife – and a maximum of four children – had a separate bedroom and sitting room). They had to pay for their own bicycles; it might take two years before they could afford to acquire one. The barracks ran on a strict routine. In the morning a servant arrived to light the fire, make tea and clean the rooms before preparing meals for the single men and then washing and mending their clothes. There was no question of brightening up the drab decor officially mandated for the day room. Pictures, flowers or comfortable armchairs were strictly forbidden. As the clock ticked over the fireplace, the officer on duty would be absorbed scribbling entries in the many logbooks and ledgers that made infinite claims on his time and attention. If a district inspector arrived unannounced to conduct an inspection, there would be trouble if anything was awry.

For all its tedium, employment as a police constable was a major step up for the sons of small farmers. It required less education and examination grinds than the route to the civil service but delivered status, stability and a pension. The constable in his clean uniform gliding by the hedgerows on his new bicycle was the envy of his restless peers watching from the fields and condemned to a life of manual labour. Moreover, although it might take him three years to save enough money to buy a suit, a presentable constable was seen as a good catch. Marriage would trigger a transfer as constables were not allowed to serve in a county where their wives had close relatives.

This could make for a peripatetic lifestyle, which itself was a marker of the distance between the constabulary and the people they served. No matter how much they were inscribed in the life of parishes and small towns it was never entirely forgotten that the policeman represented a force with paramilitary trappings controlled from Dublin Castle and that his uniform was provided by the War Office. Unlike their counterparts in an English shire, RIC constables were taught how to use rifles, machine-guns and bombs to prepare them for the probability that they would be roused from their administrative torpor to repress challenges to British rule. Maintaining good relations with the locals was not just about generating trust; it also enabled the RIC to find out what was going on. Beneath the bonhomie there was a sense that the police were always watching, knowing and recording. Surveillance was the prelude to regulation. Police reports were a daily anthropological study of their surroundings in which the people they met were anatomised in character sketches with flourishes sometimes worthy of an observant novelist. They noted who was working for whom, the complications of family quarrels and the gradations of class and respectability; their files and insights amounted to a pointillist character reference for an entire community. This intelligence was invaluable in dealing with political upheaval when it came, and the complicated personal and social motivations and rivalries that accompanied it.

When Ireland became 'disturbed', in the parlance of the British officials in London who read the RIC's crime statistics, the legitimacy of the police force came under strain. During the conflict between landlords and tenants in the 1870s and 1880s, the police did not take part in evictions but they protected the bailiffs who carried them out. One officer complained that landlords were wont to regard policemen as their personal servants. Popular opinion was anti-landlord even it meant condoning attacks on animals and property, which in normal times would be regarded as crimes. In 1880, the viceroy remarked to the British cabinet that for the law to be respected the majority of the population had to be against the criminal; in the 'disturbed areas' of Ireland the truth was the reverse. For visiting British journalists at this time the RIC barracks represented a redoubt of civilisation in hostile territory and the colonial overtones in their reports were not accidental. At the end of the nineteenth century the RIC came to be regarded as the model that colonial police forces should emulate, and governors around the empire were demanding that recruits to their own constabularies be trained in Ireland. By 1907, the colonial office mandated that all officers in colonial police forces would have to complete their training at the RIC depot in the Phoenix Park.

The tension between the ingrained familiarity of the RIC and its fundamental loyalty to the Crown deepened after the 1916 Rising. Reports from district inspectors charted a gradual deterioration in relations between the people and the police. Constables had to implement government bans on drilling, the wearing of Volunteer uniforms and the carrying of hurleys, and arrest people for singing rebel songs or attaching tricolours to lamp-posts. Volunteers became more menacing and insolent. It became harder to gather evidence or persuade people to be witnesses for political prosecutions. More ominously the idea was taking hold that the RIC was an alien force. In Mallow, County Cork, in November 1917, a policeman tried to force a farmer to shake hands in a pub, shouting, 'I'm just as good an Irishman as you.' The threat of conscription and the prospect of the police going from house to house rounding up eligible young males made the situation far worse. Several priests warned that it would be a mortal sin for the RIC to enforce conscription. At a public meeting in 1918 in Castletownbere on the south-west coast, Mary Mac-Swiney, the sister of the future Lord Mayor of Cork, shocked the constables taking notes by describing them as worms – 'no decent girl would walk on the same side of the road with one of them'. Among the anti-conscription campaigners plans were drawn up to ostracise the police. Neighbours who once helped out with work in the barracks vegetable patch stayed away. People with cars refused lifts to policemen.

The irony was that many policemen were sympathetic to the national revulsion against conscription, and not just because they knew that compiling lists of men eligible to be drafted into the army would expose them to retribution. Their loyalty was even seriously doubted by the British authorities and many of the younger constables thought of resigning. Even as the tension mounted they could not quite believe that they would be cast out by their own people, derided as false Irishmen. Duty required them to monitor the Volunteers and Sinn Féin, to make arrests and to disperse crowds. But even as this antagonism sharpened, many policemen believed that at some level it was a formal game and that both sides would draw back before it became an irreparable breach. John Regan, a policeman in Bantry, County Cork, resented orders to carry out searches – it would be much easier to get information 'if neither side appeared particularly active'. Patrick Shea, the son of an RIC sergeant, remembered his first experience of political prisoners held in his father's barracks in Athlone. During their few days of incarceration, half-a-dozen farmers' sons sang Irish songs, played handball and sat chatting with the constables. One night, musicians came, the girlfriends of the prisoners were invited in and police and prisoners danced jigs on the tiled floor of the barracks kitchen.

During a two-day meeting of the Dáil in April 1919, the president of the new cabinet, Eamon de Valera, formally instigated the social ostracism of the police, anathemising them as 'spies in our midst' who were 'the main instruments of British rule'. To another deputy the constables who knelt by their neighbours in the pew at Sunday Mass were now 'lost souls who have sold themselves to the devil', Irishmen who had betrayed their country. That month Cumann na mBan published a leaflet forbidding members to share a church pew with a policeman and boycott notices were posted near churches. The word was handed down that nobody should let out a garden plot to a policeman. There were many reports of children of policemen being teased, shunned, called names or pelted with stones. The boycott was ostensibly about ideology but it became intimately bound up with private rather than public passions. Striking a blow against the instruments of British rule could be an acceptable cover for acts motivated by personal feuds and romantic jealousies. A Protestant constable recalled the hostility he attracted from young men at dances when he went out with a Catholic teacher at a convent in Tipperary: 'Some of them were, like, nasty enough, and with a bit of jealousy would be sort of rough with it.'

Revealingly he and his girl continued to socialise – a pointer that the boycott was hesitant, uneven and ambivalent. Often there was no boycott in areas where the IRA was marginal. A policeman might resign because he could not bear to be a social outcast in one locality and discover that there was no boycott when he moved back to his home county. When in March 1919 the Gaelic Athletic Association authorities in Meath debated a resolution that policemen should be banned from hurling and football grounds, it was narrowly defeated. Speaking against those who denounced the police were delegates who pointed out that many members of the GAA had brothers and fathers in the RIC. Who, they wondered, would be prepared to stop a policeman from coming into a GAA field to watch a football match? Rosamond Jacob came up from Waterford to the Sinn Féin convention in Dublin that same month. She was scornful of the righteous passion of those who railed against the RIC. One priest was particularly vituperative about 'these ruffians', fulminating that the clergy should refuse donations from policemen. 'I'd like to see them [turn down donations],' Rosamond noted contemptuously in her diary, and recorded her preference for another priest who spoke 'rather sensibly' about the difficulty of a boycott when policemen were closely related to so many people. Many revolutionaries were in favour of softer methods. Sinn Féin asked members to form local deputations that would lobby relatives and offer help to policemen who resigned to find other jobs.

Whatever method was employed cleared the way for a direct fight between the Volunteers – by 1919 increasingly better known as the Irish Republican Army, the IRA – and the RIC. Before long a policeman had to worry about being shot as much as being shunned. James Gilmer, the son of an RIC man, had joined up in 1919 to escape the tedium of working on the family farm in County Monaghan. One day during his training in the Phoenix Park he received a threatening letter from the IRA. He shrugged it off until he heard that a friend had also received a similar letter and had immediately emigrated to America. When his training finished he went home for a short holiday before receiving his new posting. A neighbour came to the house warning him that he should leave because gunmen were coming to get him that very night. 'I laughed at the idea of it [but] he was serious, you know, he wouldn't like to see anything happen to me. He wasn't one of the fellows that would go for trouble and he persuaded and persuaded and in the end I went down to my uncle, who drove me to the railway station. They went to my house and they went to my uncle too, looking for me, yes. They meant [business] that time.' It was obvious to the public that the police had become fearful. Emily Horsley Ussher, an English-woman who had moved with her Irish husband to his family estate in County Waterford in 1914, was exploring the small town of Carrick-on-Suir late one summer night and was shocked to observe a policeman jump nervously when she and her husband unexpectedly walked up the street behind him. '"War" was already being waged upon the RIC,' she wrote in her journal. Patrick Shea remembered how the days of hand-ball and dancing with Sinn Féin prisoners in his father's barracks suddenly ended. He was forbidden to bring his friends into the barrack yard, the back door that led to the riverbank was padlocked and the windows looking onto the street were bricked up. 'The feeling of an approaching siege grew; as security tightened we became more isolated from the townspeople.'

The isolation prepared the way for attacks on police stations, initially the small rural outposts staffed by a hand-ful of constables. Generally, they were let go once their weapons and stations were captured, but their barracks and living quarters were burned. The evacuation of these small stations began in November 1919. Constables were moved into larger barracks in towns, a process called 'concentration'. Barracks were issued with sandbags, barbed wire, steel shutters and grenades. Cut off from his friends in Athlone, Patrick Shea made the acquaintance of many new constables who had transferred from small stations that were closed down. The handball alley was in use all day long. Often the family of a sergeant who had been 'concentrated' would continue to stay in their living quarters in the small abandoned barracks. Emily Horsley Ussher was friendly with the wives of two local sergeants in County Waterford – one Protestant, one Catholic – who were moved out. The women were nervous about being left alone but could hardly countenance the idea that anybody would bear them ill will. Mrs Johnson, the wife of the Protestant sergeant, had made the tea at the local agricultural show for five years running and 'could not believe that anyone would find it in their heart to do anything to her home'. Mrs O'Connor was also certain that nobody held any grudge against herself or her husband.

One night the Horsley Usshers were woken by a metallic rattle at their back door. They had just recognised the squeak of the old pram in which Mrs Johnson pushed her disabled daughter when they heard the child crying. When they ran downstairs they found Mrs Johnson and her daughter accompanied by two men. Her son came up behind with two others. 'Will you be all right now?' the men said to her. Mrs Johnson and the Horsley Usshers pleaded with them not to burn down the barracks – it was her home. They would spare her possessions, they told Mrs Johnson, but they were under orders. Before leaving they warned the Horsley Usshers not to try to alert the military; their house was surrounded by armed men. Emily looked towards the bushes outside and saw the flicker of matches as smokers lit up. Taking the Johnsons inside, they all stood at the window and soon saw tongues of flame rising above the line of fir trees between the house and the little barracks. Mrs Johnson and her son stood speechless for several minutes. 'They are burning our quarters now,' she said when she finally spoke. 'What a pity I left those two loaves on the kitchen table. They would have done for breakfast.' The job was quickly finished and the men moved off to set fire to another barracks before daybreak. Later, Mrs O'Connor's home was also burned out. She managed to save a bottle of Wincarnis, a tonic wine heavily advertised in the newspapers at the time for those with weak nerves who were 'listless, low-spirited and weary of everything'. Both women were bewildered as to why the world had turned against them. 'Neither of these poor things was able to realise that they were the victims of concerted policy,' Emily Horsley Ussher noted in her journal, 'and that probably, when the inevitable day came for it to be carried out, the deed would be done by people from afar, knowing nothing about them.'

The swift corrosion of their shared understanding with people among whom they lived and worked was greeted with dismay and incomprehension by the police. A sergeant evacuated from a village in County Mayo returned daily, often not bothering to carry his revolver. He still called everybody by their first names. Occasionally somebody would say, 'Are you not afraid we would shoot you some night going home?' but he would treat the question as a joke. Placed in an impossible position, pilloried and attacked, subjected to insults and assaults from people they knew well, it was hardly a surprise that the latent sympathy of many policemen for nationalism curdled to resentment and even hatred. As they became outcasts, their loyalty to each other became even more important than their loyalty to the Crown. Dissatisfaction over low pay, lack of promotion and poor conditions had been growing for some time (the Treasury refused to install phones in barracks). They saw men they had risked their lives to arrest being set free from gaol when the government decided to humour Sinn Féin. The viciousness of their eventual response to being shot and assaulted was motivated by a sense of betrayal, both by their employers and their fellow Irishmen. Many could not bring themselves to imagine that they would be the objects of premeditated murder. 'If you thought about being targets sure you wouldn't be able to live,' one policeman recalled. 'You tried to put that to the back of your mind.' Ireland was, after all, a Catholic country where such a campaign would be unthinkable. Patrick Shea remembers a sense of 'incredulity and fear and horror' in his father's barracks in Athlone when news came of the shootings at Soloheadbeg. The two constables had been known to some of the men in the barracks and responses veered from anger to nervousness. Patrick Shea realised that his own father was now doing a dangerous job. 'If father was late coming home we lay awake and listened for the sound of his step. He became the centre of all our thoughts; we were frightened and sorry for him. We knew that he was not made of the stuff of fighting men but we also knew that he was not likely to come to any sort of compromise with what he believed to be wrong.' Being forced to endure such anxiety about a person he loved who seemed just as Irish as anyone else left the young Shea embittered about a cause he might otherwise have endorsed: 'I was filled with a fierce anger towards everyone associated with the new patriotism.'

Some policemen decided to act on their anger when their colleagues were shot, rushing into the streets at night, firing through shop windows and calling on Sinn Féiners to come out and fight. They were especially distressed and enraged by the sight of the violated bodies of their colleagues. In Tipperary one of three policemen killed in an ambush was found lying in the middle of the road, 'both eyes blown away and the lower part of his forehead – brain matter scattered on the road and a large pool of blood'. Young men were pulled from the nearby creamery, beaten and forced to kneel in the blood, kiss the road and say, 'The Lord have mercy on the souls of the men we murdered this morning.'

The English journalist Hugh Martin, who was sympathetic to Sinn Féin, concluded in August 1919 that the war that was developing would be 'fought over a policeman's body'. 'Over thousands of square miles of country there is active hatred between police and public. Each side "gets its own back" at every opportunity. Blood feuds persist and multiply. And this is a state of things that suits certain people at both ends of the political scale, though it poisons and degrades the life of the countryside.' Even the Sinn Féin propagandist Erskine Childers described the war with the police as 'a fratricidal vendetta', although he blamed Britain for arming the Irish nation against itself.

There were some 1,400 police stations dotted around Ireland at the beginning of the First World War. By the summer of 1920 almost one-third lay abandoned and burned. Fifty-five policemen had been shot dead since the ambush at Soloheadbeg; another fifty-five would be killed in the following six months. In a new edition of *The Road and Route Guide to Ireland* the charred ruins of police barracks would merit inclusion as features of the landscape. Home from Cambridge for the summer vacation in July 1920, Denis Johnston set out with two friends on a cycle tour that took them west from Dublin and then south on a loop through Tipperary before returning along the east coast. After a lunch of chops and tea they passed a burnt-out police station in County Meath. On day four they reached Kinvara in south Galway, where they stopped again for chops, lemonade and tea. 'Note police barracks burned and I[rish] R[epublican] flag erected,' Denis scribbled in his diary. On the afternoon of 25 July they crossed into Tipperary and passed through a village that Denis thought was 'delightful . . . or might be if it was clean'. After tea at a hotel they cycled late into the evening. Pedalling at dusk by the demesne wall of Woodruff House they noticed some figures on the road in the distance. '9.48,' Denis noted precisely in his diary, 'pass two fairly large crowds of men at an interval of about a mile. Probably out to raid some police barracks.'

6

Ancient Faiths

In November 1919, ten years after leaving Egypt to train as a doctor in England, Ibrahim Rashad embarked on a tour of Ireland with the intention of writing an account of the intense spirit of national revival that might hold lessons for his own country. Setting out from Dublin with an Irish companion on a cold, wet morning in a car with an unreliable engine, they headed south for Wexford along slippery roads shrouded in mist. Their first stop was a Catholic boarding school in Gorey where the Benedictine monks grew tobacco plants from Belgian seeds, drying the leaves to make cigars, cigarettes and pipe tobacco. Being invited to light up a cigarette put Ibrahim in an awkward spot: 'In spite of the great regard I feel for our Irish friends, I cannot say I enjoyed smoking it; perhaps being Egyptian and hence considered, rightly or wrongly, a connoisseur in the social art of smoking, I am rather difficult to please in this matter.' The Irish tobacco was too strong and stung his nostrils. He politely told his hosts that one might acquire a taste for it over time. Still, he was impressed by the school and its farm; if Egypt encouraged new industries and rigorous education like this, it would create a new kind of citizen who would work to strengthen national identity. As he travelled the country he stopped at creameries to watch farmers delivering milk on carts pulled by mules and donkeys.

He wrote admiringly of progressive landowners who started small woollen mills to provide local employment, or who practised and spread knowledge of advanced farming techniques promoted by the co-operative movement. Despite his religious aversion to pork, he ventured inside a co-operative bacon factory, noting down in detail the procedure for killing pigs and curing bacon 'for sake of those who enjoy "Bacon and Eggs" in the morning, after a plate of hot porridge'.

The Irish weather was more of a challenge. Sometimes, as he slumped in the back seat of the car, wrapped in a heavy coat and covered in rugs, the watery sunshine coming through the window reminded him of the Egyptian winter. Mostly he shivered with the cold, summoning memories of radiant sunshine for consolation. One evening, after a day driving through the mountains of Kerry, he finally managed to warm himself in an armchair by the fireplace in the Lake Hotel in Killarney. He was enjoying an Egyptian cigarette and a cup of Turkish coffee when his peace was disturbed by 'a trivial incident'. In the book he published later he set down no detail of what occurred, beyond disclosing that he witnessed an exhibition of 'the arrogance and haughtiness of the aristocracy' which made a profound impression on him: 'I was exceedingly angered, and for the first time in my life I felt a Bolshevik.'

A few days later his revolutionary impulses returned when he was taken to Adare Manor, the ancestral home of Lord Dunraven, the Lord Lieutenant for County Limerick and a powerful figure in southern Irish unionism. As he was guided through the Tudor mansion, Rashad observed an army of servants preparing for the arrival of Lord Dunraven and a party of guests for the hunting season. Here they were on their knees polishing the dance floor; there they were dusting pictures or cleaning silver. People were busy making sure that guns, fishing tackle and golf clubs were in good order; others were consumed with fixing the chandeliers equipped with electric light bulbs. The sight of all this effort to ensure that Lord Dunraven and his guests could enjoy themselves in the best of comfort moved him to anger: 'A social order which is responsible for poverty amongst the masses, while the rich are lapped in luxury, cannot endure, and unless practical steps are taken to abolish the prevailing inequalities and to reform the abuses of capitalism and landlordism, a revolution will convulse what is called the civilised world, and will destroy our present society. Revolutionary methods are being adopted in the East of Europe, while evolutionary ones are working in the West, and both for the same purpose.'

However it might have appeared to Ibrahim Rashad, the power of Ireland's landowners was already draining away. By the end of the First World War the political status of the Protestant gentry in most of Ireland was ornamental. Decades of democratic changes in the United Kingdom had all but dismantled the powers and privileges that had enabled them to become collectively known as the 'ascendancy'. Their church was no longer the state church. Adult male suffrage and the secret ballot had given the Catholic majority the power to send its own representatives to Westminster. Dublin Castle might be a last redoubt of the old order but this concealed the significant retreat from power everywhere except in the north-east. Since the reforms of the system of local government introduced in 1898, all the local bodies previously reliant on the leadership and patronage of local squires were now run by elected politicians, many of them from Sinn Féin.

But even this loss of political control was eclipsed by the solution to the land war, the bitter conflict between landlords and tenants that had raged for three decades. In the ten years before the First World War the British government instigated an ambitious scheme to buy out the Irish landlords, offering cash and extremely attractive terms to induce them to sell their land to their tenants, who would now pay an annuity to the state on much more favourable terms than the rent they used to pay to the landlord. More than 12 million acres were transferred from landlords to their tenants, creating a new class of farmers who would become the backbone of the Irish state. Instead of launching an all-out class war to hold onto the land that was the foundation of their wealth and status, the Irish aristocracy did a deal with the British state to relinquish most of it peacefully. It allowed many to retain substantial holdings – estates became merely demesnes – while enjoying a windfall that could be invested in Argentine railways or (unwisely as it turned out) Russian stocks. For some it brought a reprieve from anxiety and decline and funded an Indian summer of lavish spending. However, there was no escape from the rapidly expanding British state; the government had prodded and tempted them into giving up their land and status and now it was pursuing them for death duties and inheritance taxes. The British connection, once a guarantee of supremacy, was now as demanding as the rising Catholic majority.

And yet it was the one remaining source of prestige for the former 'ascendancy'. Military service in the empire increasingly compensated for the aggravations of rebellious tenants. Mounting costs turned the Anglo-Irish into imperial cosmopolitans, overlords of vast swathes of India and Africa. The landed families sent their sons to public schools in England, where they could enter the networks needed to get on in the military. Becoming an officer in one of the better regiments was not only glamorous but remunerative; it was cheaper to live overseas in the grand manner than depend on the crumbling and uncertain familial fortunes at home. Cash from the sale of land to tenants financed their ascent of the British military hierarchy. The high proportion of the sons of Irish landed families who fought and died between 1914 and 1918 had as much to do with this tradition of service as patriotic enthusiasm. The scale of their fatalities on the battlefield almost matched that of Old Etonians; as many as one in four of those enlisting was killed in the war. Although by no means an entire generation was wiped out, the losses among a small group were such that most Irish Protestants knew personally someone who had died. The effect was less demographic than psychological. The sense of an irrevocable blow to morale was captured by one of the few Catholic members of the landed elite, Lady Fingall, in a memoir written in the 1920s: 'I used to think and say, during the War, that if ever that list of Dead and Wounded could cease, I would never mind anything or grumble at anything again. But when the Armistice came at last, we seemed drained of all feeling. And one felt nothing. We took up our lives again, or tried to take them up. The world we had known had vanished. We hunted again, but ghosts rode with us. We sat at table, and there were absent faces.'

Gloomy and fatalistic, the Irish landed gentry retreated to the cavernous rooms of their Big Houses, the ancestral homes whose stature measured the distance between themselves and the mass of the population in cottages and cabins outside their estate walls. Although birthplace and local affections had always been important for Irish landed families, the Big House was now more than ever central to their identity. It represented solidity, elegance and distinction. If the glories of past days could not be re-enacted, they could be imagined with nostalgia: the crunch of carriage wheels on the gravel, the maids and footmen receiving guests in the glow of the hallway light, the excitement and bustle of a summer ball. The Big House was an economy in itself, sustained by socialising and hospitality. There were servants to light lamps, polish silverware and draw heavy curtains. (One of the compensations of working in one of the more forward-thinking Big Houses was the opportunity to dry stockings on the central heating.) When the young German economist Moritz Bonn visited Ireland to study the land question at the turn of the twentieth century, he glimpsed a world he had never seen before and that he thought he was unlikely to see again. The landowners he encountered knew they were doomed, but their lives were full of fun: 'There was always a bed for a guest and always lots of food, though usually a little monotonous.' He might have been unlucky here; the inventory of a grocer in the midlands who prospered supplying the local gentry included several varieties of curry paste and powder, figs, caviar, saffron, pistachio kernels and chow-chow preserve.

Some landowners were able to prolong the high life; for many selling out was not enough to cover debts and taxes and they were forced to divest themselves of family heirlooms that had preserved the veneer of grandeur. By the time the Troubles began in Ireland, precious Rembrandts, Chippendale furniture and rare books were being put on the market to enable the owners of Big Houses to survive. Cycling the country roads on his mission to train farmers to be guerrilla fighters, Ernie O'Malley took note of the broken-down demesne walls and was heartened by the signs of decrepitude: 'The Big House might be spruce, or gaunt in decay; weeds on the avenue and families without issue. Virtue and strength was going from the leeches who had sucked life from the people.'

The decay and rot of the Big House is a famous metaphor of innumerable novels charting the decline of the Anglo-Irish, in which the grotesque disintegration of roofs and foundations passes unnoticed by wilfully ignorant gentry determined not to recognise catastrophe. But it was a conceit based on reality. Many visitors to Ireland at this time noted once majestic mansions shut and boarded up and were fascinated to observe the madcap stoicism of a class facing ruin. Moritz Bonn recalled an evening with a large party in a Norman castle: 'All of us were in full evening dress. After dinner we ascended the great staircase leading to the drawing room. Unfortunately it started to rain, and like many things in Ireland, the roof was leaky, so we ascended, each gentleman holding an umbrella over his lady.' The spectacle of misfortune being met with a sporting insouciance was also a clue to how much consolation was to be found in amusement and playful risk. Beyond the walled gardens, the stables and the dog kennels there was still fox-hunting, horse-breeding and sailing. Most of this socialising was carried out within a small, tight circle. 'Nothing counted for about three miles on any side of us,' the journalist Lionel Fleming wrote of his childhood before the First World War, 'because there were no Protestants until then.'

Invariably, the Protestants three miles away would be other members of the landed aristocracy. But there were many other Protestants in Ireland whose existence was not so self-contained and aloof, whose livelihoods depended far more on daily contact with their Catholic neighbours. The landed gentry did not represent all of Protestant Ireland; their notoriety and the brilliance of their most talented progeny disguised the fact that they were an elite within a minority. Most of the 300,000 Protestants who lived outside the north-east of Ireland were not wealthy or grand but 'smalltime stock', as the writer William Trevor has described the background of his parents. Both his mother and father, a provincial bank manager who moved from town to town in the 1930s and 1940s, had grown up on small farms in circumstances that were anything but privileged. And there were many prosperous Protestant farmers whose homes were not Big Houses. Most Protestants lived in towns and cities and had little acquaintance with the county set. In Dublin there were some ten thousand Protestants who could be described as working class or lower middle class: clerks, shopkeepers and schoolteachers. It was still true that it was an advantage to be Protestant if you wanted to follow a profession or the more desirable white-collar jobs. Excluding the north-east, Protestants made up roughly 10 per cent of the population of Ireland but they accounted for nearly half the lawyers and three-quarters of the bankers and were also over-represented among insurance brokers, commercial travellers, auctioneers, civil engineers and in the top ranks of the police force. Firms in Dublin would advertise vacancies stipulating that they would consider only Protestant applicants. Nonetheless, times were changing and the easy equation between Protestantism and exclusionary privilege no longer held.

The Methodist grandparents of Jasper Wolfe, Crown solicitor for Cork city and county, had been tenant farmers and shopkeepers impoverished during the Famine of the 1840s. Rescued by an uncle who ran a successful milling and corn business, they opened a bakery in Skibbereen, a market town and fishing port in west Cork, from where the editor of the local newspaper, the *Eagle*, issued his famous warnings to the Tsar and the Kaiser that he was watching them. Jasper Wolfe was born in 1872 above the family bakery. He grew up with servants who were Catholics, but his father – who spoke Irish and lent money to farmers – refused to send his children to England for their education. Instead, Jasper was sent to a Catholic school dedicated to preparing boys for the examinations to enter higher education or take professional qualifications. His teachers were nationalists. In the classroom he sat with boys from ambitious Catholic families set on guiding their sons into the professions and poor farmers' sons picked out as potential priests. Although being a Methodist placed him at an angle to his fellow Protestant landowners, who were mostly adherents to the Church of Ireland, his path through life was eased by the fact that his religion placed him 'on the inner circuit of power'. After qualifying as a solicitor he slid easily into positions of influence, becoming a member of the governing body of University College Cork and a director of the *Eagle*. But he was a Protestant who no longer believed that Ireland should be run by an oligarchy. He won a seat on the local town council and supported home rule. At a meeting in London he shared a platform with George Bernard Shaw and spoke out against claims that self-government for Ireland would lead to papist tyranny. Catholics were not intolerant, he told his audience, and Irish Protestants should not fear the rise of the majority.

Wolfe was acknowledging a change that was already well under way in his own domain. The professions and the civil service had expanded hugely in the early twentieth century and Catholics were making inroads in spheres previously dominated by Protestants. In 1913 a pass in Irish was made essential for entry to the colleges of the National University of Ireland and the number of Protestant students dropped dramatically. There was increased competition for places at the traditional Protestant university, Trinity College, where Irish was not required; many others headed for universities in Britain. Some argued that compulsory Irish was a ruse to exclude Protestants and a portent of the systematic discrimination that would follow if Ireland was granted home rule. This was scaremongering, but Protestants who thought Catholics were out to displace them were not wrong. Leading spokesmen of the rising Catholic middle class openly proclaimed that their time had come and sought to organise their fellow strivers into networks and pressure groups. One prominent advocate of Catholic organisations wrote, 'Well, then, what do we want? In down-right terms we want to get on top.'

The most flamboyant exponent of rising Catholicism was the journalist D. P. Moran, who invariably referred to Protestants as 'sourfaces'. In his newspaper the *Leader*, which was popular with up-and-coming young nationalists, lay and clerical, he campaigned against Protestant discrimination in explicitly racial terms: 'There is something very distinctive about the face of the average loyalist, it is characteristic in its way as that of a Jew. They all understand one another especially when employment is to be given.' Catholics in the Irish equivalent of the English public schools thought they were well placed for the battle over respectable jobs. Arthur Clery, a nationalist lawyer and contemporary of James Joyce, wrote in the magazine of Clongowes Wood College that 'the first contest after Home Rule [will] be one in which our big Catholic schools are particularly fitted to take part – a social contest'. Just as the British state had facilitated the transfer of land to Irish tenant farmers, its rapid expansion was creating good jobs for their sons and daughters. 'They desert the country for the town,' *The Times* noted in 1913. 'They prefer to be clerks, civil servants, schoolmasters, journalists rather than farmers or curates.' The establishment of big departments such as the Land Commission and the Congested Districts Board to administer the death rites of landlordism meant more vacancies. In fifty years, the number of civil-service jobs had jumped from under a thousand to nearly ten thousand. Increasingly these jobs were filled by Catholics. These rapid and peaceful social changes were a signal to Protestants that they would have to adjust to a new dispensation.

Generally, relations between Catholics and Protestants were characterised by mutual tolerance in public and curious incomprehension in private. Many conversations were devoted to the mystery of practices and beliefs on the other side. A Protestant woman told Rosamond Jacob (who as a Quaker and a supporter of Sinn Féin occupied a rarefied position) of her incredulity when she read in a Catholic school catechism that lying was regarded as a sin. Perhaps, she suggested, this book was intended for consumption by non-Catholics and the opposite was really taught in the classroom? Jacob was affronted by her prejudice: 'Once people have got a name for deceitfulness, like Catholics, any appearance of decency on their part can be explained as more deception.' But she herself was aghast to discover from Catholic friends that friars terrified their congregations by informing them that unrepentant souls were sent to hell at a rate of four per second or that a priest had told a woman in confession that she had committed a sin by attending a mixed teacher-training college. 'My God what bigots they are,' she noted in her diary. Some Protestant evangelicals spread a fantastic story of a priest trying to anoint and thus convert a Protestant preacher beaten to near death by a Catholic mob. Many Catholics believed it was a sin to enter a Protestant church or that your soul would be damned for ever if you married a Protestant. Emily Horsley Ussher had to explain to Catholic friends that for Protestants renouncing work and play on Sundays was as important as fasting on Fridays for Catholics.

Such stories point to how Protestants and Catholics lived parallel lives. Mutual avoidance had to do with the intricacies of class as much as religious incomprehension. One Protestant woman remembered her mother's fear that she might end up playing with undesirable children when they moved house in Dublin. They might be vulgar, 'and a few might even be Roman Catholics'. The racecourse was one venue where all classes mingled. Liberal or well-connected Protestants in Dublin might encounter leaders of Sinn Féin or nationalist professors at social evenings. And in small towns such as Skibbereen, children playing together in the streets connected with innocent ribaldry. Jasper Wolfe ritually exchanged insults with boys his own age. Greeted with 'Proddy waddy greenguts, never said a prayer/Catch him by the long legs, and throw him down the stair', he would reply, 'Catholic, Catholic, go to Mass/Riding upon your old jackass'.

Once the IRA started shooting policemen the context for all these exchanges was transformed. With Dáil Éireann proclaiming that it had usurped the authority of the British government and the IRA shooting policemen, everyday loyalism, an unthinking attachment to the existing order, was suddenly rendered suspect. Dutiful respect for the authorities could now be perceived as treason. Many accounts of the experiences of Protestants during the revolutionary period exude bewilderment as the world shifted beneath their feet. The prized isolation of the landed gentry, once a badge of superiority, now left them physically vulnerable. When the police were evacuated from rural stations their sense of being protected vanished. Some landowners demanded that, rather than being vacated, the isolated police stations needed to be strengthened. Their houses were targets for arms raids because it was well known that they kept guns for hunting or as souvenirs from military adventures overseas. The disturbed state of the country severely restricted their social life. Men came at night to commandeer cars or weapons. Periodic military bans on motoring or the trenching of roads by the IRA made circulating between Big Houses stressful and tiresome. In any case, once carefree social events were now suffused with tension. Much of the excitement at balls and tennis parties was provided by gallant young officers from the local garrison flirting with eligible daughters (or mischievous spouses). Now it could seem like a provocation to fill your house with soldiers even if they were off duty.

And of course owners of the Big Houses usually had much stronger connections with the military than merely providing entertainment: many were retired army officers ready to consent to having their grounds requisitioned to accommodate soldiers pouring in to areas where the IRA had been active. Others held appointments as magistrates or county lieutenants, jobs and titles now deemed redundant by the republican state. Early in 1920 notice was given of what might happen to those who were too tenacious in their loyalty.

At 10 p.m. on the first Wednesday in February the servants at the residence of a Colonel Rowley in Summerhill, County Meath, were alarmed by a loud knock on the front door. The colonel had been living in England for several months, so they could be sure this was not a social caller oblivious to the lateness of the hour. The butler called all the servants together to decide if they should answer. They agreed to stay put, knowing they could escape through a concealed passage if the house was being raided. When they heard the crash of the back door being broken open they fled to the outhouses. From there they could make out thirty or forty men going from room to room, splashing gallons of petrol all over the floors. And they watched as the flames took hold. The police arrived too late; some constables used their rifles to shoot holes in a water tank at the top of the house, but it made no difference to the fire. The rumour locally was that Colonel Rowley had been in correspondence with the military authorities and his letters had been intercepted by the IRA. In April another landowner told of how he had rushed to the landing and picked up a rifle when forty men with revolvers, axes and guns broke into his house. He was lucky that they left after he fired and wounded one of them. There were no police for fifteen miles and many respectable people, he said, had kept quiet about raids on their property because they were afraid to report them.

Between January 1919 and July 1921 seventy-six Big Houses were burned out in the territory that became the Irish Free State. Since some of the most intense IRA and military activity occurred in County Cork, Big Houses were attacked there more than anywhere else. A retired Irish Guards officer, Colonel Mountifort J. C. Longfield, was on a holiday with his family in Rome when his mansion at Castle Mary, three miles from Midleton, was burned down in September 1920. He had spent thousands of pounds renovating the house over the previous two decades, constructing a tower, designing a smoking room and installing electric lighting. It was assumed that his refusal to resign his post as deputy lord lieutenant had made him a target, in the expectation that exemplary punishment would intimidate others who might have thought of making a stand. In December 1920 Timoleague House and the adjacent thirteenth-century Norman castle were destroyed in west Cork. Soldiers had occupied the castle over the summer after three policemen had been killed near by in an IRA ambush, using it as a base to patrol the roads and raid houses. They were blamed for desecrating graves in the local abbey in August; it was said that lids had been torn off coffins and human remains exposed. Less than two months after they moved out, the castle was blown up and the mansion of the owner, Robert Travers, burned to the ground.

Protestants who did not own large estates and Big Houses faced the same dilemmas. Jasper Wolfe's appointment as Crown solicitor for Cork city and county in 1916 was universally welcomed. It was noted that he was popular with all classes; he styled himself 'the people's solicitor'. He was admired for working his way up on merit and for expending as much attention on a minor case as on one in which thousands of pounds were at stake. His Catholic colleagues in the legal profession recalled how he had gone to England to rebut accusations that Catholics were intolerant. It was a prestigious job with a good salary and pension. There was little crime, so he could look forward to dabbling in business and settling in as a pillar of the local community. Instead, he found himself prosecuting Irish Volunteers, appearing in military and civil courts on behalf of the Crown and defending the police at inquests, most notoriously in the case of Tomás Mac Curtain, the IRA commander in Cork widely believed to have been killed by an unofficial police death squad in March 1920.

It was not necessary to be implicated in British rule to attract attention. The owner of a car dealership in Tipperary had been friendly with a district inspector of the RIC who was assassinated in August 1920. After the shooting his business was boycotted. Later that month forty armed and masked men arrived at his showroom and announced that they had orders to put out all loyalists. His proper place, they said, was in the north. Protestants even in the quietest parts of Ireland read the newspapers with alarm. Rosamond Jacob took tea at the end of March 1920 with a schoolmistress friend in Wexford. Miss Rowe dressed all in black and 'looked thinner than ever'. Her conversation was all about 'what was the country coming to and were we all going to be murdered'. Rosamond thought she spoke 'just as any uncivilized country Protestant might have', except for her 'superior amused manner'. Many Protestants who were insurance brokers, auctioneers or shopkeepers had stayed away from politics and wanted good relations with their Catholic neighbours. But they did have an interest in order. Their livelihoods suffered from broken railway lines, the fear of ambushes and military raids. A director of the Munster and Leinster Bank looked forward to the day when people would have 'a chance of settling down and making money'. In the meantime they laid low and embraced the self-effacement that some of their more vociferous Catholic opponents had demanded.

No visitor to Ireland in the early twentieth century left in any doubt about the influence of the Catholic Church. The countryside was dotted with churches and cathedrals, many of them built in the past few decades. On his journey through Ireland in the autumn of 1919, Ibrahim Rashad would some-times of an afternoon step inside a Catholic church for a quiet moment of rest. ('It was a house of God, and to me it mattered not whether it was a church, synagogue, or mosque.') He was much taken by the Gothic architecture and the stained-glass windows. And there were always children coming in on their way home from school, bowing their heads and making the sign of the cross over their chests, lighting candles in aid of some private intention, stepping into confession boxes to divulge their sins and receive the priest's absolution. 'Watching the children performing these religious duties, and looking at the holy scenes depicted on the stained-glass windows, I felt about me a religious atmosphere Eastern in its character.' Believing that a nation that drifted away from religion risked moral corruption, Rashad approved of this intense early cultivation of conscience and a religious sense that would inform all the worldly concerns of Irish Catholics. 'From childhood to old age their lives and their religion are one.' In his travels he had been struck by the involvement of priests in every facet of life. But he noticed that they were not just leaders and figures of authority; they studied the people and sympathised with them as much as they directed them.

A British army intelligence officer who was stationed in the midlands and the west of Ireland during the war had reached the same conclusion. 'The clergy', he wrote in 1916, 'live by the people, come from the people, and in many cases seem to guide where really they are led.' This could seem counter-intuitive at a moment when the Catholic Church was at the height of its power. In two generations since the devastation of the Famine, the bishops and the priests, financed by the richer class of farmers who had survived, turned a shrunken population of unobservant Catholics into a disciplined flock devoted to the rituals of worship. The new churches that sprung up all over the country were full on Sundays and families gathered in many kitchens at night to say the Rosary. On feast days in the summer priests in white capes singing hymns led long processions through small country towns under tasselled banners of the Virgin Mary and wafting puffs of incense. There was one priest for every thousand people.

To respectable families a child in the priesthood was prized more than a job in the civil service. Every year 600 new priests graduated from the national seminary at Maynooth. One alumnus suggested that savvy communists with designs on Ireland would do well first to destroy the college. Fondly remembering his days as a seminarian, he imagined an endless line of priests heading out of the college chapel 'into the four provinces of Ireland [across] the seas into neighbouring England and Scotland, and the greater seas into the Americas and Australia, and Africa and China; it covers the whole earth; it goes wherever man has gone, into the remotest regions of the world; it is unbroken, it is ever renewing itself . . .'

This sense of the British Empire as merely a conduit through which Irish missionaries spread the Roman faith, making full use of the English language, which had displaced Irish, shows how, for the Church, its own survival superseded questions of nationalism and imperialism. It had managed to force the British government to cede control of education in Ireland and withheld support from home rule until satisfied that this arrangement would not be threatened by the new native rulers. At the same time the Church presented itself as the defender of a people once persecuted by the Protestant British state because of their faith. Its spokesmen could even claim to have inspired the bodies promoting self-help and a new sense of national identity, such as the Gaelic League and the co-operative movement in the early twentieth century. 'We have marked the recovery of Ireland in the fields of education, of literature, of economic organisation and of industry,' wrote a contributor to a Jesuit publication in 1921. 'The close observer has been aware that the nation's progress has been accompanied, if not caused by, a deepened loyalty to its ancient faith.'

It was hardly a surprise then that political idealism was popularised in the language of Catholicism. In the 1916 Rising even the Marxist James Connolly had used religious symbolism to inspire his followers. The executed leaders, now martyrs, were commemorated in Masses and memorialised like saints. For most of the bishops, who valued the British connection, this popular reaction to 1916 was an embarrassment, though they thought it prudent to remain silent. Cardinal Logue praised a detachment of Irish-Canadian soldiers who arrived in Dublin in 1917 to promote recruitment because they were defending 'the centre of the empire'. Talk of an 'Irish Republic' sounded to the bishops very like the Bolshevik Republic recently established in Russia. Besides, the word had unhappy historical connotations for the Catholic Church. Republics, they pointed out in a statement, 'have been and are associated with the worst forms of civil tyranny and religious persecution'.

But like the ageing politicians in John Redmond's party, the bishops were facing a generational challenge. Many of the younger clergy were intoxicated by the Sinn Féin movement. Patrick Gaynor left Maynooth to start his life as a priest – 'quite happy under my tall hat and very conscious of my new dignity' – a convinced supporter of Sinn Féin at twenty-four: 'I believed that Ireland free, would be Ireland splendid – splendid in manhood, in culture, in virtue and in piety – and was ready to fight her battles on either point with the weapons that came to my hands as a priest.' His understanding was that in temporal affairs the Church 'was the child of the Irish people in each generation'. The bishops were losing touch but his generation was determined to keep in step with public opinion. This meant canvassing for Sinn Féin candidates and speaking at election meetings (he was elected to the party executive). When conservative bishops tried to control their young priests by preventing them from travelling around the country they failed. Gradually and reluctantly they had to come to terms with the nationalist movement that was sweeping the country or risk damaging their claim to be at one with their flock.

For much the same reason, Sinn Féin needed the bishops. And since most of its leaders and followers were devout Catholics it was not just strategic calculation that made them anxious to seek approval, or at least neutrality, from their spiritual mentors. Campaigning in County Clare in 1917, Eamon de Valera tried hard to impress on audiences at his election meetings that just because he was a radical in politics it did not mean he was a bad Catholic. He reassured them that he had been associated with priests all his life, that the priests knew him and trusted him, and that they were behind him in the election. Dealing with the bishops as politicians he combined warning with flattery. While campaigning, he seized the opportunity of the sudden death of the bishop most sympathetic to Sinn Féin to memorialise him as an example for other bishops to emulate, especially those 'who wish to win the heart of their flocks'. As long as there were bishops like him, de Valera told an election meeting in Tipperary, there would never be anti-clericalism in Ireland. Like everyone else, he would always defer to the authority of the bishops as 'spiritual shepherds', but they needed to do their duty to the nation as citizens and 'men of importance'.

A year later, in a sign of how the bishops were getting the message, Sinn Féin could risk distributing a by-election leaflet promising, in the popular advertising idiom of the times, 'Irish Bishops recommend Sinn Féin.' By 1919 bishops who had opposed Sinn Féin a few months previously were now convinced that the party posed no threat to their power and influence. One bishop assured another that he was certain that Sinn Féiners 'are not different from the rest of the people as Catholics. They are quite good and practical Catholics. They are not anti-clerical, [and] have many clerical adherents.' Another had discovered that the members of Sinn Féin in his diocese were 'the very reverse of anti-clerical or anti-religious'. And a third one-time sceptic was delighted to observe that they were 'most exemplary in attending to their Christian religious duties and living good Christian lives'. Here was a movement that had won the trust of the people and whose leaders were going out of their way to show how much they respected the Church. But as the assassination of policemen became commonplace in 1919 and 1920, a new problem arose: what position should the Church take on violence?

The Catholic Church in Ireland was opposed to violent revolution in principle. It held that the existing government was legitimate until it was peacefully replaced by some form of self-rule. For decades the bishops had also condemned secret revolutionary societies such as the Irish Republican Brotherhood. It is no surprise then to find that in the early stages of the IRA's campaign many priests and bishops were outspoken in their denunciation of violence. The columns of local and national newspapers were filled with hundreds of vehement statements fulminating that assassinations would draw down God's punishment on those involved. After a farmer was shot dead in County Galway in March 1920 the Archbishop of Tuam, Thomas Gilmartin, preached a sermon in the dead man's parish warning the congregation that any one of them might suddenly hear the accusatory voice of God at any moment. '"Where is Martin Cullinane, whose blood crieth to me from the hearthstone where he fell on Thursday night?" If the man who fired the shot which deprived a young wife of her husband and left four young children without a father should answer callously, as Cain did: "I know not; am I my brother's keeper?" the voice which cursed Cain might resound in his ears now: "Therefore cursed shalt thou be upon the earth."' Some bishops went beyond verbal censure. Following the shooting of a police sergeant on his way to Mass in County Cork, the local bishop decreed that men who took part in any further ambushes and assassinations would be excommunicated. Several priests tried to stop IRA attacks when they were being planned, sometimes informing the police if they heard of the specific location of an ambush.

But the Church never spoke with just one voice. Many priests sympathised with the IRA and thought its campaign was morally justified. Some were prepared to carry messages, give shelter to men on the run or hear the confessions of men who had taken part in ambushes. Priests were even prepared to conceal weapons in churches. The clerk of a chapel in Tipperary hid a weapon in a statue of St Joseph, and explained how to find it: 'Put your hand up his hole and you'll find a revolver. Then go over to the Blessed Virgin's hole and you'll find 400 rounds of .45 ammunition.' Even where priests might have felt ambivalent, they were so central to Irish rural life that they automatically identified with their parishioners either out of fellow feeling or because they feared losing their authority or being accused of deserting their flock. So priests opened their churches for the funerals of IRA men and allowed uniformed firing parties to discharge volleys of shots over their graves.

The tension between the bishops and priests who were sympathetic to the IRA strained the cohesion of the Catholic Church. As the IRA campaign continued, the frequency of the jeremiads against IRA attacks diminished and their tone moderated. To press the matter, to condemn political violence consistently, risked an open schism in the Church. It was clear that the denunciations and thundering sermons were being largely ignored. Outrage and condemnation seemed pointless when the most determined IRA men seemed immune to clerical censure despite being ardent Catholics and the general congregation was either passively sympathetic or cowed into silence. As early as June 1919 a priest told a police sergeant, 'There are a class of men going about who don't care for priests or anybody else. They think it is no sin to shoot a policeman.' Over time bishops and priests learned to close their eyes to the worst violence while accommodating themselves to the reality that Sinn Féin was now the de facto government.

7
The Virtual Republic

Just before 8.30 a.m. on the grey and drizzly morning of Sunday, 15 June 1919, an Australian soldier on honeymoon in the Railway Hotel in Clifden, County Galway, on the west coast of Ireland, detected the noise of an aircraft descending over the town. The congregation at early Mass noticed it too. The streets of Clifden seemed deserted to Arthur Whitten Brown and John Alcock from the vantage point of their cockpit. Then as their converted Vickers Vimy bomber dipped further they could see people running out, waving. Brown fired off two red flares in celebration. They had just crossed the Atlantic Ocean in one continuous flight, nearly 1,900 miles in just a few minutes under sixteen hours. Instead of flying home to England they had realised they could land on the west coast of Ireland and still claim the £10,000 prize put up by the *Daily Mail* for the first non-stop transatlantic flight: the rules had stipulated that the crew could land anywhere in the British Isles. To their right they saw the tall masts of the Marconi wireless station. As they flew over it they noticed a strip of green grass where they could put down safely. Men ran out of the buildings below to signal to them and they waved back. They cut the engines and glided onto the green strip, the wheels sending up a spray of mud as they hit the ground. The plane came to a sudden stop, the nose plunged into the sludge and the tail jerked upwards. They had come down in a bog – the men on the ground had been warning them to stay away. A hundred people came running towards them, some in uniform, others in pyjamas and overcoats. 'Where are you from?' someone cried. 'America,' Alcock shouted back. 'Yesterday we were in America.'

They had inadvertently chosen the perfect spot to broadcast their achievement. The Marconi station had been built in 1907 to provide the first commercial transatlantic wireless service to Nova Scotia. Powered by its own generating plant, it was now maintained by 150 permanent staff, who lived in a collection of trim bungalows spreading out under steel masts that rose 200 feet into the air. At night, from the houses in the surrounding countryside, dimly lit by oil lamps and candles, the station seemed ablaze with light, constantly sending and receiving messages, connecting the world. News of Alcock's and Brown's arrival was flashed within minutes to the *Daily Mail* in London and a few hours later a *Mail* reporter arrived with a photographer from Galway. The two pioneers were feted at a reception in the Railway Hotel in Clifden. Eddie King, the chairman of the local council, proclaimed it was only right that the first flyers from America should land in Clifden, since thousands had emigrated from the shores of Connemara during the Famine. Then the man from the *Daily Mail* put Alcock and Brown in his car to drive them to Galway. Crowds had turned out in villages along the way waving the tricolour; the driver suspected that they thought the car was carrying de Valera. The drone of the aircraft engines still resounding faintly in his ears, Brown slipped into a reverie. The twisting roads reminded him of Newfoundland; the crowds of people on the roadside seemed like extras in a film scene.

In the main square in Galway, people pressed against their car, thrusting slips of paper through the windows for an autograph. A message of congratulations from the king awaited them when they finally made it to their hotel. More followed from Woodrow Wilson and Lloyd George, and a Hollywood producer promised $50,000 if they would attempt a trans-Pacific flight. They were already worldwide celebrities when they boarded a train for Dublin the next day. Well-wishers waited at every station to greet them. In Athlone, a child fell onto the track from the edge of the crowded platform. At Mullingar, an army band played 'Hail the Conquering Hero Comes' as their train pulled in and Alcock and Brown disembarked to inspect British troops lined up in parade formation. On their last night in Ireland they were guests of the chief secretary for Ireland, Ian McPherson, at his official mansion in the Phoenix Park. Their names and faces were displayed on news-stands in London, New York and Paris, where they pushed the peace conference off the front page. A French delegate hailed them as 'a beacon fire' on the road to progress. Lord Northcliffe, the proprietor of the *Daily Mail* and *The Times*, looked forward to the time when London newspapers would be selling in New York in the evening and American evening papers in London the next day.

Many shared the view that the world had become a smaller place as a consequence of the news from Ireland. Air travel epitomised the limitless possibilities of the age. H. G. Wells was exhilarated by a trip in an aeroplane over Slovakia, marvelling as he passed little puffs of white cloud how flight opened up a view of 'the sunlit clearness and brightness of the outspread world'. He was convinced that air travel was an experience that could enlarge each person's sense of themselves. As more people took to the skies they would realise that they no longer needed to be constrained by 'a patchwork of various sized internment camps called Independent Sovereign States'. The obliteration of conventional notions of distance by the speed and reach of aeroplanes would, Wells believed, make the British Empire obsolete and hasten progress towards global government: 'It is part of the fantastic nationalism that still plays so astonishing a role in the political life of the world, to hold that every definable region of the earth's surface belongs, from sky to centre, to the inhabitants it supports.' It did not occur to him that national airspace would be perfectly compatible with a worldwide web of connecting flights; that nationalism, far from being an unlikely holdover from a bygone era, would flourish in an interconnected world. Nothing demonstrated this more than the peace conference convened in Paris to rebuild the world shattered by the war.

In the first half of 1919 miracles were expected from the statesmen and diplomats who had assembled in Paris. Well over a thousand delegates were deciding the fate of Germany and its colonies, anointing new nations and founding international organisations to foster world peace. The city was the centre of worldwide attention. American soldiers played baseball on the Champs-Élysées; delegates enjoyed Saturday-night dancing at the Hotel Majestic and cocktails at the Ritz. An unshaven Marcel Proust demanded to know from a British delegate the minutest details of what the diplomats said in their endless committee meetings. The official representative of Dáil Éireann, Sean T. O'Kelly, arrived in Paris on 8 February after a tiring journey from Dublin. There had been no porters available at a bitterly cold Euston station in London so he and his wife had to carry two big suitcases for nearly a mile through the snow to a hotel in Holborn. At reception, they were told there were no vacancies but they struck up a conversation with the head porter, who turned out to be from the west of Ireland and somehow found them a room. The following morning they made their way to the ferry. In Paris, they checked into the Grand Hotel, which they discovered was anything but grand.

O'Kelly was thirty-seven, small and slight, cheery and affable. He had spent most of his career in local politics in Dublin and had been imprisoned eight times for his Sinn Féin activities. But he had never been to France before, although he had some knowledge of French. On arrival he immediately sent a memo to the leaders of the peace conference informing them that he was the representative of the Provisional Government of the Irish Republic and requesting that Ireland be given a seat at the new League of Nations. There was no reply. Accompanied by an Irishman who was an ex-member of the French Foreign Legion and another who had worked for several years as a journalist in Paris, O'Kelly began making contacts with influential French intellectuals and politicians. Their lobbying did not go well. Professors at the Sorbonne were not readily impressed by Ireland's claims, complaining that Ireland had stabbed France in the back in 1916. Others appeared more sympathetic, happily accepting invitations to lunch and listening carefully to the Irish case. Until, that is, O'Kelly's assistant, Victor Collins, the ex-journalist, under the influence of a few glasses of wine, would blurt out his virulently pro-German views.

Trudging back to his shabby hotel after these disastrous lunches, O'Kelly must have envied the luxury and ease enjoyed by the main players at the conference. The Americans had taken over the Hotel Crillon, adding a barbershop to make themselves feel thoroughly at home. The British, who had brought more than four hundred officials, advisers, clerks and typists to support Lloyd George, occupied five hotels near the Arc de Triomphe. It must have galled O'Kelly to discover that at the Hotel Majestic representatives of the dominions and India were entitled to free drinks. What would have worried him even more was the obvious rapport between the British and American delegations, who had set up secure telephone lines to connect their hotels. By contrast O'Kelly worked in the wilderness. He called a press conference, but only a few journalists came to hear the representative of the Irish Republic. Short paragraphs appeared in the English-language papers, but nobody seemed to notice except the French security police, the Sûreté. Each time O'Kelly stepped out of the lift there was a detective in the lobby watching him.

The Sûreté was busy keeping an eye on all the exotic figures who had arrived in Paris. One of particular interest was another slim agitator, the son of a nationalistic civil servant from a colony that had also experienced an uprising in 1916, led by rebels who flirted with the idea of a German alliance. This young man had distributed a petition entitled 'The Demands of the Vietnamese People' to newspapers and conference delegates. 'All subject peoples are filled with hope by the prospect that an era of right and justice is opening to them . . . in the struggle of civilisation against barbarism,' it proclaimed optimistically. It was signed by Nguyen Ai Quoc ('Nguyen the Patriot'). Like O'Kelly, Nguyen Ai Quoc – later better known as Ho Chi Minh – was living out of a suitcase, moving from one cheap hotel to another, supported by contacts among the 50,000 Vietnamese living in France. He was twenty-nine but looked younger in his suit and tie. A French socialist likened him to Charlie Chaplin, by turns 'sad and comic'. The detectives tailing him discovered he was consorting with Korean and Chinese nationalists who had come to press their claims and, also to their surprise, the Irish. Nguyen Ai Quoc would later claim that he had joined demonstrations in favour of Irish independence in London when he had worked as a trainee chef at the Carlton Hotel. Nguyen entertained the hope that Woodrow Wilson would give him a fair hearing and sent him his petition. So optimistic was he of a summons to meet the American president that he hired a morning coat so as to make a good impression. But all that came back was a polite acknowledgement that the president had received his petition.

Sean T. O'Kelly's stream of letters to Wilson did not even merit an acknowledgement before the president returned to the United States in mid-February. O'Kelly now spent all his time trying to interest journalists in Ireland's claim to independence. Here he had some success. One French publication published an attack on Britain for excluding the Irish representatives from the peace conference and not realising that 'among crucified nations, Ireland occupies the foremost place'. But each little publicity victory was won at a substantial cost in wine and good food, and O'Kelly had to appeal to Dublin for thousands of pounds to continue entertaining the journalists. He soon grew tired of competing with the world's supplicant nations for the attention of the great powers. 'It seems', he confided bitterly to an American journalist, 'that the blacks and yellows, all colours and races, may be heard before the Conference except the Irish.'

Having failed at the peace conference, how was the reality of the Irish republic to be sustained? It helped when three well-known Irish Americans lobbying for the cause in Paris were cleared to go to Ireland by Lloyd George. Under the guise of a fact-finding mission they toured the country promising it would not be long before the Irish Republic was recognised. They addressed a meeting of Dáil Éireann in Dublin, arriving at the Mansion House in taxis adorned with the tricolour and the stars and stripes, as if on a state visit. Police and soldiers had tried to block them entering but retreated before an angry crowd. The visit, which horrified Dublin Castle, was symptomatic of the uncertainty of the British response to the nascent rebel government. Lloyd George was consumed by the peace conference. The administration in Dublin veered from ordering raids and arrests to allowing the Dáil to meet freely, displaying all the formality of a legal assembly. Members arriving to hear the Irish-American delegation wore evening dress.

The independence movement was also pulled in two directions on the question of how to respond to the indifference of the world and the inattention of the British government. It could continue the violent assaults on the police in order to make Ireland ungovernable, as the more extreme wing of the movement argued. Or, as those who believed in passive resistance urged, it could extend the reach of the Dáil so that it would seem, both to people in Ireland as well as to visitors, less like a theatrical gesture and more like a functioning government. Despite his reputation as a guerrilla mastermind, Michael Collins believed in both strategies. While some men lay in fields behind ditches waiting to shoot policemen, others were typing memos and instructions about the correct procedures for conducting business in Dáil Éireann or carefully filling ledgers and account books with the figures on income and expenditure by Dáil departments. Collins lavished as much attention on recruiting accountants, lawyers, typists and clerks as he did on finding hitmen. Candidates for civil-service posts had to sit examinations just like their British counterparts after replying to advertisements concealing the true nature of the position offered.

Far more people came to know the revolution by banal encounters with its civil side than ever came face to face with an IRA ambush. The business of what the Sinn Féin propagandists called 'constructive work' was carried out in offices and private houses, bars, hotels and village halls all over the country. In Dublin, on any given day, messengers could locate Arthur Griffith, the leader of Sinn Féin, sipping from a glass of whiskey in the Bailey pub in Duke Street, or, failing that, in the Ship in Abbey Street. Other men, less well known than Griffith, walked the streets of the city in bowler hats and sober suits and ties carrying thousands of pounds to pay the salaries of the Dáil officials; one of them was known as 'the walking bank'. The president received a salary of £500 and ministers £350; members of Dáil Éireann were paid hotel and travelling expenses. At the height of its activities the Dáil was employing 300 people – a fraction of the 12,000 employees of Dublin Castle, but a sign of how bureaucratic validity was as important to these orderly agitators as revolutionary elan.

Much of this work had to be pursued covertly because of the danger of arrest and disruption. Even when the Dáil was tolerated its officers knew that their mail was censored and kept secret cupboards at the back of Sinn Féin's office in Harcourt Street to protect sensitive paperwork from being confiscated. After the Dáil was declared illegal in September 1919, its members convened in private houses around Dublin. Officials of the departments of state the assembly had established – fisheries, home affairs, local government, trade and commerce – worked in rooms all over the city, rented under cover names. Many departments were run from offices on the quays, overlooking the River Liffey. As they clattered downstairs and stepped into the misty winter evenings to make their way home like so many Prufrocks, the civil servants of the underground government were likely to catch sight of one of their ministers passing by on his bicycle. After coming from Wexford to watch the inaugural session of the Dáil, Maire Comerford had stayed on to work for the revolution. She now possessed an encyclopaedic knowledge of these ministerial bicycles. Michael Collins rode a large-framed Lucania; if she saw a green Pierce leaning against the wall in a hallway she would know that the minister for defence, Cathal Brugha, was in the building; and if in the murky evening she caught sight of a piece of string dangling from the rear rack of a bicycle whooshing by she could be almost certain that it was Desmond Fitzgerald, minister for propaganda. Even a French journalist, probably tutored by Fitzgerald, learned to recognise 'a cheerfully juvenile figure which flits past on a muddy bicycle in a faded waterproof and a little cleft hat dripping under the pelting rain' as a revolutionary minister.

If visiting French journalists could spot members of the underground Irish government spinning through Dublin's streets, it is inconceivable that the British could not do so as well. In some cases they left the revolutionaries to get on with their business because it suited them. Griffith, for instance, was regarded as a moderate, somebody whom they might have to negotiate with, so he was largely left to sip his whiskey unmolested. He was even able to plant a ceremonial tree on the day designated by the Dáil as National Arbour Day on 29 November 1919. Officers of the Dublin Metropolitan Police sympathised with the revolutionaries and allowed them to pass unhindered. But they had also devised elaborate procedures to evade arrest and conceal their papers and networks. When rural deputies were required in Dublin for a meeting of Dáil Éireann, a letter would be sent to a girl who knew them, apparently from a boyfriend, inviting her to Dublin for an assignation on the chosen date.

What was remarkable was how much business Dáil Éireann was allowed to carry out in plain sight, enhancing its appearance to the public as the de facto government of Ireland. Griffith's planting of the tree was the culmination of a public campaign to restore Ireland's forestry. In addition to a series of lectures, thousands of leaflets were circulated urging every farmer to plant a tree for each man executed in 1916. A captured memorandum from Griffith arguing that the British government had failed to develop Irish fisheries prompted the commander of British forces, General Macready, to suggest to the government in London that it should start a new programme that 'would cut the ground from under these people's feet'. This was just one example of the chronic indecision about whether to compete with the revolutionaries or suppress them. Griffith – who had always supported the idea of creating a parallel civil service as the nucleus of an alternative state – assembled forty-nine businessmen, professors and scientists to travel the country taking evidence on what could be done to stimulate Ireland's industries and natural resources. Their first public hearings were disrupted by the police but after a public outcry over the suppression of such an obviously well-intentioned undertaking they were permitted to hear submissions for an entire week when they reassembled in Dublin City Hall. Irish newspapers were forbidden to report the hearings but British and foreign journalists were allowed to publicise the earnest work of the committee. The following month the inquiry moved to Cork, its proceedings were banned and the whole cycle of tolerance and repression began again. Another institution of the Dáil that was harassed but not suppressed was the Land Bank, which lent money to tenant farmers seeking to buy out landlords who were ready to sell. It was a legally constituted company that raised £325,000 (much of it from the United States) held in the bank accounts of English co-operatives. Prospective depositors were soberly informed that not only would they be acting patriotically but that their money would be safe in the hands of reasonable men who would put it to good use, not only in the interest of the country, but to provide 'a good return and first class security for yourself'. When soldiers arrived to search the offices of the Land Bank, the manager, Lionel Smith Gordon, played cards with the officer in charge while accountants inspected the books (only one account was closed down). Smith Gordon – a promoter of co-operatives and an Oxford graduate who was an example of how Dáil Éireann was able to co-opt progressive members of the ascendancy class – believed the bank survived because there was 'something in English psychology which inspires a respect for financial institutions'.

The Land Bank had been financed by the spectacular success of a campaign to fund the activities of the Dáil by issuing 'republican bonds'. The bond issue – itself the mark of a real modern state – was advertised in newspapers, on flyers handed out at church gates and through slogans painted on walls all over the country. Sinn Féin organisers were sent from house to house to persuade – or threaten – people to buy the bonds (although their diligence was variable and Michael Collins confessed that trying to manage them almost broke his heart). Newspapers carrying information about the bonds risked being shut down, so the Dáil prepared its own propaganda film. A showing of Charlie Chaplin's latest feature might be interrupted by Irish Volunteers, who had ordered the reel operator to halt the film. The cinemagoers were then invited to watch a short film advertising the republican bonds. A smiling Michael Collins, in a suit and tie, was shown receiving cheques and signing bonds on a block of wood reputedly used to behead the nineteenth-century patriot rebel Robert Emmet. The camera lingered on a letter of support from a Catholic bishop pledging £100. Then the mother of Patrick Pearse led a procession of widows of fallen martyrs and members of the Dáil to buy the bonds from Collins and his assistant, who looked like a pair of friendly bank clerks drumming up business at a fete. After seven minutes the reels were changed and the Chaplin film resumed; in the meantime, Michael Collins was imprinted on the public mind. In Ireland the campaign collected nearly £372,000, 50 per cent more than its target. Small farmers subscribed in large numbers. Some unionists invested in the bonds, possibly as an insurance policy to protect themselves from intimidation or, in some cases, out of sympathy and the conviction that they might receive a good return. The loan drive impressed visiting journalists, the *Daily Herald* concluding that despite all the attempts to suppress the Dáil the underground government 'commands the unforced obedience of the Irish people'.

But the most visible sinews of the republican state began to appear towards the end of 1919 with the establishment of the Dáil courts. The notion of ignoring the regular courts and launching a system of parallel justice based on arbitration and popular goodwill instead of archaic procedures had long been part of Sinn Féin policy. Repudiation of British justice became a commonplace as republicans in the dock 'refused to recognize the court'. In some areas arbitration courts had already appeared to settle land disputes in which owners were threatened and cattle driven from fields onto the roads. Now Dáil officials realised that the burned-out police stations marking large swathes of rural Ireland signified not just the gradual defeat and retreat of the RIC but a vacuum of authority: courts of some kind were a necessity to prevent the spread of law-lessness. The extension of the Dáil courts across the country turned out to be hugely popular because they were a credible guarantee of order. Hearings were held in halls or schools in towns or in creameries, farmhouses and even outhouses and barns in the countryside. Crimes prosecuted included petty theft, sheep rustling and desertion by husbands of their wives. In Kildare two men who stole cattle belonging to the British government were banished from the county for nine months and three months. A Protestant in Longford brought a neighbour before a republican court 'for malicious injury to his hat which the neighbour had struck with an ash plant'. The defendant was ordered to buy a new hat of the plaintiff's choosing. In Roscommon a wealthy Irish-American farmer was successfully sued by his niece for seven-and-a-half years' pay for her work as a housekeeper. A packed house in Cork City Hall watched a case in which a priest was charged with slander; his accuser prevailed and was awarded damages of one shilling.

There was no law against arbitration hearings but when the courts styled themselves as a fully-fledged judiciary of the republic, trying criminal cases with a high court, supreme court and a whole apparatus of judges, clerks and registrars serving arrest warrants and summonses, they were declared illegal and the police and military set out to suppress them. Elaborate precautions were taken to enable clandestine sit-tings. One judge had a reputation for convening his court at midnight, relishing the power to force witnesses out of their beds as much as evading the police. Kevin O'Shiel, a barrister who became a key figure in the courts system, travelled the country posing as a salesman for a heat-rub ointment that would treat all ailments. (His alias, 'Robert E. Seale', was chosen so that if a policeman asked if he was O'Shiel he could say he was mistaken.) Another judge deposited his case notes on loose leaves with his mother in case he was arrested and searched. The courts called on IRA Volunteers to enforce their judgments and arrest suspects. Without recourse to prisons, offenders were held in outhouses or threatened with violence unless they left the locality. In Kilkenny two men were held for a burglary at the residence of a retired British army major and released only after returning most of the stolen goods. A man convicted of stealing mailbags and assaulting his father was forced to spend a week on a farm spreading manure. Some prisoners reported that they were treated well and supplied with good food, cigarettes and newspapers. The head of the republican police force later recalled that he had asked his superiors for permission to flog 'incorrigible criminals' but was turned down because it was considered barbarous. As they gained confidence the courts and the Volunteers took pride in punishing crimes the police had failed to solve. The new regime also indulged its puritanical streak: pubs that kept lax hours were shut down, bookmakers were escorted from GAA grounds, people caught smoking foreign cigarettes had their clothing slashed.

Swiftly the traditional court network was immobilised. Magistrates arrived at courthouses to find no defendants and no prosecution cases prepared. Lawyers who should have appeared before them were now defending their clients in the republican courts. When Sinn Féin took control of a majority of local councils in the elections of 1920 official business was also transferred to the underground courts. Republican judges now heard applications to commit people to asylums or were asked to deliver judgments against citizens defaulting on their local taxes. One county council closed all courthouse buildings and instructed Volunteers not to allow judges to enter them. This represented the benign end of a campaign to enforce a boycott of the British system. A notice appeared on a courthouse door in a town in Kerry warning that anybody entering would be shot. None of the sixty-three people who had been summoned to appear turned up. Judges were refused hotel rooms in some towns. In Skibbereen, Jasper Wolfe became a marked man because he continued to act as crown prosecutor. His brother Willie, a justice of the peace, had his shop boycotted and notices were pinned to his door warning him to resign or face the consequences. Many courthouses, which were once the scene of witty legal theatrics, were now uninviting fortresses protected by sandbags, barbed wire and machine-guns. Throughout the summer of 1920 hundreds of magistrates resigned and by the autumn the system had virtually collapsed. Lord Justice O'Connor told a grand jury in County Clare that failure to obtain evidence was 'an extraordinary and anomalous state of affairs without parallel among any other of the white races inhabiting the British Empire'.

Even unionists and opponents of Sinn Féin were finding the republican courts effective. Landowners were delighted to find that the courts would order intruders to clear off their estates. Substantial farmers who found the police too preoccupied to track down their stolen cattle discovered that the personnel of the underground courts were able to secure the return of their livestock. The fairness of the procedures and judgments in the courts was praised by Irish peers in the House of Lords and letters to the newspapers. During his cycling tour of Ireland in 1920, when he noted the burnt police stations dotting the landscape, Denis Johnston and his friends also observed that the areas that seemed to be most peaceful and ordered were those without a military presence. In County Clare they received a good reception; 'every country-man had a pleasant nod or a cheery word for us'. The only sign of trouble came from the convoys of soldiers passing them on the country roads or filling the streets of the towns. 'I personally noted a very great difference in their noisy demeanour from the quiet geniality of the people,' he noted in his diary. 'And the fact of the matter is, they do no good at all. The Irish Republic is virtually established and if anyone wants justice or protection the only place he can get it from is from the Sinn Féin Authorities and he does get it from them.'

The success of the courts was an opportunity to turn around the image of a lawless regime that the British government had promoted. Foreign journalists were invited to observe court sessions. They watched sober and punctilious shopkeepers and teachers preside over orderly hearings in village halls and schoolrooms. Aggrieved farmers, repentant drunks and angry young men accused of assault and burglary told their stories before enthralled spectators who often had brushed their hair and freshened up after a day's work as if they were going out for an evening at the theatre. The improvised procedures impressed many visiting journalists. The courts seemed to retain their authority without pomp and arcane legal language. More importantly, their work was clearly accepted; 'the people's own law', as one man told an American journalist.

The overall impression created by the courts was that Dáil Éireann was not just a make-believe government but was capable of dealing in facts as much as dreams. The most basic practical functions of government – catching burglars, making the pubs close on time – were now being performed by Sinn Féin, not the British administration. 'The Sinn Féin tribunals are jostling British law into oblivion as a fast motor-car jostles foot-passengers off the road,' was the verdict of the *Irish Times*. Much as Irish perceptions mattered, demonstrating the reality of the Irish Republic to a British audience was even more important. In July 1920 the *Daily Mail* had jeered that 'Sinn Féin sets up law courts to keep the peace while policemen are being murdered'. But just over a month later the paper's correspondent concluded that 'the futility of trying to govern a people against its will is demonstrated by what happens at the Sinn Féin courts'. The reasoning here was compelling: if Irish nationalists were no longer waiting for permission to govern themselves, then the British government was faced with the choice of either acknowledging the new state or destroying it.

8

'Would You Shoot a Man?'

In late August 1920, Dublin prepared itself for the showpiece event in the city's social calendar, the annual Horse Show. For the elite and the fashionable, the parade and judging of the country's finest equine stock and the jumping competitions, for which there was a record number of entries that year, were the occasion for intensive socialising. Horse Show Week enjoyed an international reputation, drawing visitors from America, France and Belgium, and the elegant parties defined the city's reputation for combining grandeur with easeful amusement by the sea. British officers who might otherwise have chosen to escape Dublin for grouse shooting in the Scottish highlands stayed on to enjoy the delights of the season. The city streets were spruced up and the hotels and boarding houses were full, charging double for the rare suddenly vacated room. Theatres and music-halls were looking forward to filling every seat and a motor show was planned for Kildare Street featuring the latest American import, the Dodge Brothers' Roadster, with its split folding windshield. So this seemed a propitious moment for a new entertainment venue to rise out of the rubble of Easter Week 1916.

On Friday, 20 August, a cinema opened its doors on Princes Street North, across from the ruins of the General Post Office, which had been destroyed by the British bombardment of the rebel headquarters. La Scala was designed to emulate the advanced modern cinema complexes that had become hugely popular across the Atlántic. To call La Scala a mere cinema would be to do it an injustice; it was a pleasure palace. It housed tearooms, bars, smoking rooms and a ground-floor restaurant – all finished in luxurious style – and a ballroom with mock-Greek pillars, palm trees and the latest in American technology, a sprung floor that returned energy to tired dancing feet. The theatre itself boasted 3,200 seats, engineered for comfort, and 32 boxes for the more discerning clientele. Patrons would be entertained twice a day by a tenor and a symphony orchestra. The opening film programme featured *Parentage*, a parable about how an honest small-town upbringing guaranteed success in business; *When Love Was Blind* (a blind woman falls back in love with a married man who deceived her); and a travel feature on Japan, *In the Land of Madam Butterfly*.

Other evidence on screen might suggest that investing so much money in attracting people to the city centre was pure folly. When the newsreels flickered into life they revealed Dublin as a city under siege. Soldiers rolled out coils of barbed wire to protect official buildings from attack. Panicked crowds scattered jerkily along the streets fleeing the scene of the latest daylight assassination. Even the organisers of the Horse Show could not hide the fact that the viceroy, whose presence was usually the imprimatur of glamour, was staying away this year. 'His attendance there would have made everyone rightly nervous,' as one correspondent regretfully concluded. A curfew was in force and the streets had to be clear by midnight. Military lorries growled around the darkened city, suddenly swinging the beams of their powerful searchlights down side streets and into doorways. A British

soldier who arrived around this time, after service suppress-
ing riots in India, decided within a few days that Dublin was
'a rotten place to be in, people hurry along the streets,
armoured cars dash up and down, bristling with machine
guns'. Even the chips were inedible, potatoes so disgusting
that he thought they must have been fried 'in olive oil or else
wagon grease'.

He would have been surprised to discover that during the
eighteenth century his hellish posting had been regarded as
the second city of the empire. It retained a certain global
cachet. The Guinness brewery was still the most famous in
the world. Dublin had electric trams before any British city.
But the wide generous avenues and graceful Georgian mansions only partially concealed some of the worst slums in the
United Kingdom. Within walking distance of La Scala,
elegant mansions built for a family and their servants were
now inhabited by up to forty people sharing one toilet. In
these streets most families occupied a single room that often
overlooked back-alley slaughterhouses where animals were
butchered day and night. Every so often the walls of these
crumbling buildings collapsed into the street. Death rates in
Dublin were much higher than in British cities with infamous
reputations for slum housing, such as Liverpool or Glasgow.
Infant mortality for the city's professional classes ran at 7 per
thousand; for unskilled workers at 120 per thousand. The
state of the Dublin slums was acknowledged as a public
scandal, but it was an affront that failed to provoke any sense
of urgency in a largely rural nation. Officially, slum clearance
was a priority for the city authorities but many of the worst
landlords were nationalist councillors. Writing in 1919, a
campaigning Jesuit priest despaired that Irish people had
come to regard the Dublin slums as normal and inevitable;

they affected 'a general impression of horror' without knowing enough to spur them to indignant protest. Members of Dublin's professional and business class had long deserted the heart of the city for the comfort of stucco houses and detached villas to the south, wealthy suburbs that they ran as well-regulated townships while leaving the raucous city to be administered by Dublin Corporation. Living close to the clean air of the mountains and the sea, which glittered in summertime like the Amalfi coast, they found their main worry was that all the good servant girls were leaving for America.

A casual visitor might find it difficult to notice this segregation. Civil servants, lawyers and stockbrokers worked, shopped and socialised in the same densely concentrated city centre alongside tailors, candlemakers and the drivers steering dray horses pulling carts laden with barrels of Guinness. Within a few minutes' walk of the River Liffey, where unemployed men propped themselves against the embankment wall, were some of the most fashionable shops in Europe. Sampling the elegance of the city was a popular pastime that everyone could indulge. A clerk living in one of the new lower-middle-class suburbs on the north side could take a tram to Sackville Street, alighting at Nelson's Pillar, and then stroll across the River Liffey, along Westmoreland Street and up Grafton Street to St Stephen's Green, where nannies amused their children by throwing pieces of bread to ducks in the pond. Along the way he might linger to gaze at a furrier's – 'white fox and ermine cleaned by a special process' – or the window of O'Callaghan and Hill Millinery Specialists – 'smart hats at reasonable prices' – or be amused by the sign at Mr Steyn's dental practice promising that teeth would be extracted 'without the slightest twinge of pain' and boasting that his dentures featured the latest American improvements in materials and finish, giving an 'extremely life-like appearance, comfort and durability'.

British soldiers in uniform were often seen promenading along Grafton Street, a girl (or two) on their arms. Some still felt the pull of Dublin's recreational charm, even though they were realising that, from a professional point of view, the city could be their enemy. 'It is a maze of narrow streets and alleys set in no order,' an officer wrote. 'There is little definite residential area, slums and tenement houses are found everywhere, and in the older part of the city there are many ramifications of underground cellars in which men, munitions and munitions factories can be hidden. There are innumerable small shops and comparatively few large stores. It is, in fact, an ideal town for guerrilla operations.' Dublin had made exactly the same impression on Sean Treacy during his visits to the big city from Tipperary. He lectured his friends about how the streets, alleyways, bridges and shopfronts would provide continuous possibilities for concealment to a man on the run. Still evading capture after the shootings at Soloheadbeg, Treacy, Dan Breen, Séamus Robinson and Sean Hogan arrived in Dublin in the summer of 1919. Treacy passed the time playing draughts and reading books on military theory, itching to put the city's geography to use in a new campaign. Although lying low, they offered to help in the formation of a team of gunmen to attack the small band of dogged political detectives who had developed an expert knowledge of the underground movement.

They also planned a spectacular operation of their own: an attempt to assassinate the viceroy, Lord French. After several abortive attempts, when their quarry failed to show, they were finally presented with an opportunity a week before Christmas 1919. They cycled to a pub near Ashtown railway station in the north-west of the city to await Lord French's return from a trip to the country. It was a short journey from the station to the Viceregal Lodge through the gate of the Phoenix Park. As the convoy of cars carrying French and his military escorts left the train station, the ambush party rained bullets and grenades on the second vehicle, believing that the viceroy was inside. Soldiers from the following open-top car opened up with a machine-gun and rifles, one standing up on the back seat to take aim, killing one Volunteer and badly wounding Dan Breen in the leg. They continued blazing away as their car sped into the park. Leaving the dead Volunteer in the pub, the ambushers fled on their bicycles, Breen supported in his saddle by the man riding alongside him, until they got to a safe house in the north of the city. As darkness fell that afternoon paperboys in their printed aprons hurried through the rush-hour crowds to proclaim the news: 'Attack on the Lord Lieutenant – Sensational Fight at Ashtown – One of the Attackers shot dead!' It was only then that the IRA unit discovered that Lord French had survived: he had been travelling in the first car. Later that week, Robinson and Treacy sat in a darkened cinema and watched the newsreel of their own exploits, 'Scene of the Ashtown Ambush'.

Many of the revolutionary leaders, politicians and soldiers alike, were wary of violent conflict and resisted the aggressive restlessness of the men from Tipperary. Even after the Dáil was suppressed in September 1919 they preferred to keep the movement alive by dodging raids and evading capture, protesting to the rest of the world about the suppression of democracy in Ireland. But without ever breaking with his colleagues, and summoning his authority as an indefatigable organiser, the minister for finance, Michael Collins – who was also director of intelligence for the Volunteers – pushed for letting the young gunmen have their heads. Appeals to the Paris peace conference and Washington had failed, so Collins argued that it was time for assertive action rather than passive resistance. Creating a state of disorder in Ireland would force the British government to pay attention to Sinn Féin's demands. He courted people such as Breen and Treacy, complaining that the moderates in the government were holding out against a full-scale war and how it would take time before he could wear them down. But to his cabinet colleagues he argued that violence would be like flicking a switch: once it had served its purpose it could be turned off. The obvious targets of assertive violence were the G-men, the detectives from the division of Dublin Metropolitan Police tasked with investigating political crime. They made it their business to know who was in the IRA; they stood on platforms watching who was getting on and off trains, and they identified houses for military raids. A handful of the most assiduous were well known to the IRA men, intimate enemies conferred with nicknames, whose relentless pressure provoked an antagonism that was as much personal as political. By the nature of their work the G-men were likely to be loners and obsessives, anonymous toilers in plain clothes, isolated from the familiarity and popularity of the ordinary constables in the Dublin Metropolitan Police. To shoot them would show that the underground state meant business without risking the popular revulsion that might be aroused by the assassination of ordinary decent policemen.

Even so, there was still remarkable reluctance to take this step. Most of the Volunteers who expressed interest in joining the assassination team that came to be known as the Squad recoiled when they discovered that the job required them to shoot policemen. At first only eight reliable Volunteers were chosen, although several others eventually joined. Before they started work, the pool of targets was further reduced. Several detectives were warned that continued devotion to their duty would ensure their names were on the hit list. The Squad was forbidden to shoot policemen indiscriminately; assassination was by order only. Several detectives who might have been obvious targets had been recruited as spies for Michael Collins. One of them, Ned Broy, had even arranged for Collins to make a nocturnal visit to Dublin Castle to inspect G division's intelligence files by candlelight. Most remarkable of all, the men recruited to the Squad were told that if they were captured they would be disowned. The IRA chief of staff, Richard Mulcahy, who maintained a very distant relationship with the Squad, told them they were not to leave as much as a laundry mark on their clothing that might identify them. These were deeds the army of the Republic could not yet stand over.

Once it began, the campaign developed its own momentum. On 30 July 1919 Detective Sergeant Patrick Smyth – known to his assailants as 'The Dog' – was shot at close range after he got off the tram not far from his house on the north side of the city. He had refused to heed a warning to be less punctilious in his work, telling a neighbour who brought him the message, 'I'm not letting any young scuts tell me how to do my duty.' Three men from the Squad had been waiting a week before they were able to corner him. Unarmed and unable to defend himself, he outran his attackers almost to his front door, even though he was wounded in the leg. Nobody responded to his cries for help until two of his seven children, a teenage son and daughter, ran into the street to assist him. Smyth lived until 8 September, when he died in hospital. Four days later the Dáil was declared illegal and Detective Sergeant Daniel Hoey took part in a raid on Sinn Féin offices in Harcourt Street. Collins was in an office upstairs but managed to get out before Hoey could identify him. Word of his narrow escape was passed to the Squad. Later that day, Hoey was shot in the neck at point-blank range near the Palace cinema, as he returned from a break to Great Brunswick Street police station.

Their next target was Detective Sergeant John Barton, a genial Kerryman who had just uncovered an IRA arms dump. For Vinny Byrne, a nineteen-year-old cabinetmaker working in Crow Street, a short walk from Dublin Castle, this would be the first of many missions for the Squad. He had fought in the 1916 Rising, when his company had been jeered by people from a tenement near their post at Jacob's biscuit factory. They were, in Vinny's eyes, 'imperialistic people' and he watched a comrade shoot a man who had tried to grab his rifle. In November 1919 he was sitting around the fire at the house of Mick McDonnell, the first leader of the Squad, when McDonnell turned to him.

'"Would you shoot a man, Byrne?"'

'"It's all according to who he was."'

'"What about Johnnie Barton?"'

'"Oh," I said: "I wouldn't mind" – as he had raided my house.

'"That settles it. You may have a chance."'

A few days later he met McDonnell after work in front of Trinity College and was told that Barton had been spotted on Grafton Street. As he walked up the right side of Grafton Street with his comrade Jimmy Slattery, Vinny pointed out Barton on the other side. They kept their eyes on him as he walked along, unnerved by the detective's habit of stopping every few yards to look into a shop window and then glancing quickly across at their side of the street. It was as if he was conscious of being followed. At the top of Grafton Street, Barton stopped outside a bookshop and then, apparently unaware of their presence, crossed the street towards them and walked back down the street, pausing again among the crowds leaving work to stare in shop windows.

They tried to stay well behind him but still keep him in view. But at the bottom of Grafton Street they briefly lost sight of him, looking around anxiously until he reappeared behind them and crossed the street again. As they followed him along the wall of Trinity College, with the evening traffic roaring by, they recognised three other members of the Squad in the distance and realised that they too were hunting Barton. The office workers and newsboys in the rush-hour traffic were oblivious to the race between two different teams of assassins to shoot the detective. As one pair got close enough to draw a revolver, bodies in the swelling crowd of pedestrians came between them and Barton. The second pair marched past trying and failing to get a clear shot. This pursuit continued in the semi-circle around Trinity College, until Barton stepped off the pavement to cross the street by a monument with three fountains known as the 'Water Baby'. Byrne heard shots and saw the detective fall on his side. He had been shot by a third party of pursuers. He heard Barton shout, 'Oh God, what did I do to deserve this?' and watched him pull out his gun and fire ineffectually down the street. A policeman tried to block Vinny as he ran away but he drew his gun and threatened him and the constable let him go. Detective Sergeant Barton died in hospital later that evening.

At the beginning of 1920 the police stepped up their efforts to trace subscriptions to the Dáil national loan, raiding hundreds of premises. A seventy-year-old former magistrate and senior police officer, Alan Bell, was brought out of retirement to supervise the investigation. He ordered several bank managers to submit themselves for questioning about the source of their deposits. Collins could not be sure that the bank managers would protect the confidentiality of their customers. He obtained a photo of Bell from a sympathetic journalist and the Squad identified his home in Monkstown, a pleasant suburb by the coast on the south side of the city. They observed that a detective escorted him to his tram every morning, but that he then travelled alone until he reached the city centre, where he met another detective who would accompany him to his office. On Friday, 26 March, two members of the Squad watched Bell get on his tram at 9.30 a.m. and followed on their bicycles, pedalling furiously until the tram stopped at Aylesbury Road, where they signalled to the waiting hit team that their quarry was on board. Five men got on the tram; two went upstairs to prevent an unexpected intervention from the top deck. Bell was reading his newspaper on the lower deck when the man who had just sat in the seat behind tapped him on the shoulder. 'Are you Mr Bell?' Fellow passengers said the judge looked with 'blank astonishment' at his questioner. 'Come on, Mr Bell, your time has come,' another said. They stopped the tram but Bell still sat immobile, even though he had a revolver in his pocket. Rising from their seats the men growled impatiently, 'Ah, come on', and dragged him onto the pavement. The passengers sat still as they heard the pop of three shots. When they dared to look up they saw the body of the man who a few moments earlier had been sitting among them reading the newspaper, lying by the railings of the Royal Dublin Society showgrounds, shot in the wrist, the groin and behind the ear.

A civil servant who regularly saw Alan Bell catch the tram was on the top deck, smoking a cigarette and browsing his paper when the attack began. Afterwards, he swore to the police that he had no recollection of the men who had climbed the stairs. Like everybody else, he said, he heard a shot, looked down and saw the body slumped against the railings. Many visitors to Dublin remarked on the passivity of the public, how a man could be shot in the street but the traffic policeman would continue directing cars while the victim bled out on the pavement. The city was a theatre of war in a sense that was rare in the rest of the country. Shootings, arrests and frantic pursuits were carried on in full view of a vast audience of pedestrians, bystanders and tram passengers. A colleague of Alan Bell expressed his contempt for the people who watched him being dragged off the tram, branding them as cowards or sympathisers. Others suggested that witnesses to assassination had become callous and indifferent. It was likely that people experienced a constantly changing combination of all of these feelings as well as a sense of helplessness.

One day, the Australian journalist Joice Nankivell was walking across a canal bridge when she noticed a line of men, women and children leaning over the balustrade. They were staring at a large oil drum bobbing in the water. A tricolour was attached to the top and below it was a placard that read 'Spies and Informers beware!' By the middle of 1920 it was the talk of the town that the British were recruiting a new wave of undercover agents to replace the G-men. On the pavements there were always men and women watching and looking and standing with their backs to the street observing the reflection of someone behind them. A British agent with whom Joice Nankivell's husband, Sydney Loch, had become friendly was scornful that many of the new recruits were easily identified as the best-dressed men in Dublin: 'Men with eyeglasses appear suddenly to sell bookblacking. Men in spats turn up to explain they hold an agency in condensed milk. These people fill the lounges of the best hotels, drink together and talk confidently together.' Clerks in the telegraph offices and the railway stations passed information to the IRA. Lily Mernin, a typist for a British army major and one of Michael Collins's most invaluable sources, would walk down Dame Street and Grafton Street window-shopping arm in arm with a member of the Squad to identify British agents in plain clothes. Uniformed soldiers now avoided the risk of being surprised while patrolling on foot by travelling in lorries, packed together in their tin hats, moving at speed. Lookouts at the front and rear, instructed to be suspicious of 'harmless-looking parties of civilians', scanned the streets, rifles and revolvers at the ready. When they were sent to a house identified for a raid, the soldiers would cordon off the street with strands of barbed wire stretched between lamp-posts or the front door of a house. Crowds of spectators – many of them errand boys and beggars – gathered to watch residents being ordered to keep their doors and windows shut to prevent sniping. All adult males were brought outside and lined up on the pavement to be searched and questioned by intelligence officers while soldiers went through the house from the cellar upwards.

From early 1920, Dublin was placed under curfew from midnight. Night workers at newspapers, telegraph offices and bakeries were allowed special permits to be in the city during curfew, but theatres, cinemas and restaurants closed early. The last train to the southern suburbs left at 10.30 p.m. An hour later the lamp lights would be extinguished and cab drivers whipped their horses to speed up and bring their fares home before midnight, passing soldiers who had just been dropped off for sentry duty on the main bridges crossing the

Liffey. By midnight the city was dark save for the beams of the military lorries scouting for curfew breakers. Within hours they would have rounded up homeless men, drunken cab drivers and prostitutes. A British private recalled chasing a woman down the quays who cursed and kicked him. Patrolling the curfew inspired technical innovation. Three lorries were equipped with especially large and powerful lights that when suddenly illuminated would dazzle and blind anyone caught in their glare; a Lewis gun was attached directly to one of the lights so that fire could be directed at the space lit up by the beam.

One night Denis Johnston and one of his girlfriends were walking arm in arm in Ballsbridge ten minutes after curfew when they 'heard a great rattle of a car coming into town' and suddenly 'two big headlights set wide apart flashed into view'. They ran across the bridge, hoping to duck down a side street, but realising there was no time left to get out of sight they walked steadily, readying themselves to halt when called on. When the car drew level they saw it was an empty charabanc. Having left his girlfriend at her house, Denis was approaching his own home when 'a thing with searchlights came out along the main road from town – a pretty close shave'. Later that night he heard shots and ran to the window. Armoured cars rumbled somewhere close by and every so often the sky would be lit by flares. But the curfew had its compensations for Denis and his friends. In the Christmas holidays they would gather at one house until eight thirty and then move to another house well before curfew time, piling their coats in a bedroom and dancing until five in the morning with fires blazing in the grates of the rooms (they drank no alcohol, only coffee and soft drinks). The young people would flirt at the top of the stairs and engage in 'some unspectacular petting'. In the summertime there was an added thrill in taking a girl home during curfew, walking along the railway lines to avoid the armoured cars, risking exposure when they had to climb over level-crossing gates. The journey provided 'endless opportunities to hide in gardens, taking cover lying on the grass locked in each other's arms and stifling one's giggles with a hiss'.

Many people devised rules for navigating the city so as to avoid the risk of being caught in crossfire or an ambush. Wilmot Irwin was a twenty-year-old bookkeeper in the offices of the stockbrokers Dagg and Dawson in Foster Place, just off College Green. His work was sometimes interrupted when old Mr Dagg, a bearded man in his eighties, collapsed in a fainting fit, or else by two rings of an electric bell, the signal of a summons to the desk of young Mr Dagg, a tall, reedy figure in his forties, stooped by the pain of chronic arthritis, who spent much of the day silently staring out at the busy traffic on Dame Street. Wilmot realised that his workplace, despite this Dickensian torpor, was in a dangerous location. It was like having 'a seat in the grandstand' when an ambush or military raid erupted outside. (He was not to know that in another office above a printshop five minutes' walk away, in-telligence agents working for Michael Collins spent their days analysing and collating messages they had intercepted under the guise of working as 'manufacturing agents'.) The office manager, the errand boy and the typist were all fellow Protes-tants, so Wilmot felt he could speak his mind freely at work. Stepping outside, he had to be prepared for anything. Calcu-lating that a tramcar would be the most deadly place to be caught in an ambush, he spent an hour walking home most evenings in a carefully chosen route from College Green to his terraced house in Glasnevin on the north side. But he was not going to allow his caution to interfere with his socialising. Not even the risk of getting caught after curfew would stop him from going to the cinema three or four times a week.

The cinema business surmounted all the difficulties created by political upheaval. Five picture-houses were destroyed during the shelling of the General Post Office in 1916. But four new cinemas were opened in the city centre between 1920 and 1922. Almost all the films they exhibited were American. The major production companies that were to dominate the twentieth century – Warner Brothers, Universal, Fox – were consolidated at the end of the war. Film actors emerged from anonymity to become highly paid stars and the objects of public fascination. Dublin audiences sought out Charlie Chaplin, Mary Pickford, Rudolph Valentino and Douglas Fairbanks. (An IRA man who disguised himself in heavy goggles and a small moustache as he set out to burn down a police station in Cork heard a youth remark, 'Charlie Chaplin is going into the barracks.') Like everyone else, Rosamond Jacob often stepped into the cinema with little idea of the programme, often catching only a portion of some films. She laughed at Felix the Cat and Mutt and Jeff, and delighted in incident and sensation, noting in her diary a breathless account of random films she saw in an afternoon or evening: 'a French film with plague and a jealous husband and a family reconciliation at a shrine in a church and part of the *Brass Bullet* which was much more interesting, especially the trial scene and where the road bridge was burned and the motor was preparing to jump it'. She found it delightful that American films introduced the viewer to the hero's bedroom and found a scene of a fancy-dress banquet where all the men exhibited bare arms and shoulders 'a pleasing novelty', confirming the observation of her friend Hannah from her time in the United

States that 'American men who go in for social life usually keep their arms and legs shaved as well as their faces'.

At the cinema, families from the overcrowded tenements mixed with the people from the genteel suburbs even if they occupied differently priced seats. Denis Johnston was settling into La Scala one afternoon when he was struck by a peculiar smell. As his eyes became accustomed to the light he made out 'rows and rows of white spots shining in the dark'. He was seeing the collars of hundreds of children from the industrial school run by the Christian Brothers in Artane on their annual outing to the pictures. When the comedy films began they broke with their regimented discipline and shrieked with laughter. Going to the pictures was a such a popular pastime with the poor of Dublin that an enterprising fifteen-year-old boy from Summerhill, a north-side slum of once grand Georgian buildings, told the police who arrested him for using stolen money to buy magic lanterns and slides from a stationery shop that he was going to start his own picture-house and charge two pence for admission to his friends.

It took nerve and confidence to open a new cinema, especially one as lavish as La Scala. Cinema owners worried that the curfew and the possibility of a random street battle might deter customers altogether. In late 1920 they gave their employees notice that their jobs were secure only from one week to the next. Still, the crowds kept coming. All over the city music-halls, dance halls, pubs and cafes survived the terror of war. Wilmot Irwin was too young to be put off enjoying the city to the full. If he did not go to the theatre or the cinema two or three times a week it was because there was a party invitation or a dance at the parochial hall by a junction in the north inner city, renowned as 'one of the most deadly ambush spots'. Here, as a three-piece band belted out the melody, he and his friends would roar out the chorus of 'Ain't We Got Fun' (a Tin Pan Alley song that became a favourite of the Great Gatsby):

> Every morning, every evening
> Ain't we got fun!
> Times are sad and getting sadder,
> Still we got fun.

9

Bolshevism in the Air

In John Buchan's novel, *The Three Hostages*, published in 1924, the dashing hero of *The Thirty Nine Steps*, Richard Hannay, is reluctantly drawn out of retirement to take on the evil mastermind behind a frightening worldwide crime syndicate. The villain's gang had just kidnapped the daughter of the richest man in the world, a well-known young aristocrat studying at Oxford, and the ten-year-old son of an English war hero. Hannay realises his attempt to pursue a quiet life as a gentleman farmer is about to come to an end when his old friend Macgillivray of Scotland Yard arrives unannounced at his Oxfordshire manor house. Brushing aside Hannay's warning that he had come on a fool's errand, the detective, a lean-faced northern Irish Protestant, invites himself to lunch and sets about trying to persuade his friend to lend a hand in foiling the hostage plot. Macgillivray gravely explains that the shattering of civilisation under the impact of the war had spawned opportunistic criminal conspiracies determined to undermine efforts to restore balance to the world. The colossal confusions of the war had enabled moral imbeciles to flourish all over the world: 'Cruel, humourless, hard, utterly wanting in sense of proportion, but often full of a perverted poetry and drunk with rhetoric – a hideous, untameable breed had been engendered. You found it among the young Bolshevik

Jews, among the young gentry of the wilder Communist sects and very notably among the sullen murderous hobbledehoys in Ireland.' All the revolutions and upheavals across the globe were connected, Macgillivray revealed to a disbelieving Hannay. The fanatics who led them were themselves unwitting puppets of clever men who manipulated currency markets and engineered strikes for personal gain. The police forces of the entire civilised world – especially in America – were closing in on the most notorious of these gangs; this was why they had taken the three hostages. If they were not foiled within a few months, the stability of Italy and the United States, and the possibility of a settlement in Ireland, would be at risk. Naturally, Hannay is perturbed, though still determined to resist involvement. He sends the detective on his way protesting that he cannot possibly help. It takes a tearful appeal by the father of the ten-year-old boy before Hannay is moved to abandon his bucolic retreat, allowing the story of his hunt for the evil genius behind the kidnappings to begin.

Buchan was a politician as well as a writer and the menacing post-war scene he describes is an accurate reflection of how the world appeared to the soldiers and statesmen who had helped Britain to win the war. Many believed that Bolshevism would rule the globe in less than a century and there was a need to buy off the workers. In its *Survey of Revolutionary Feeling*, published in 1919, the Home Office provided an early sketch of the turmoil that Richard Hannay had turned his back on by hunkering down in the Oxfordshire countryside. Remarkably, it conceded it made perfect sense that revolution might be popular; profiteering, bad housing and unemployment were all contributing to a loss of faith in capitalism. The well-to-do and those who had profited from the war and the post-war boom were their own worst enemies.

Growing class tension was only sharpened by 'the foolish and dangerous ostentation of the rich', who boasted about their large dividends. In this climate, the Home Office assessment continued, it was no surprise that the propaganda of Labour education colleges and newspapers and the rhetoric of extremist trade-union leaders found a ready audience. And then there were external influences: 'Russia, Ireland, Egypt, India'. Only the popularity of the royal family and the mass enthusiasm for sport were preventing the bonds of the established order from snapping. Fresh from his triumph at Versailles, the prime minister himself endorsed the idea that the deteriorating situation in Ireland was contributing to the pervasive sense of instability. Playing Macgillivray to his cabinet colleagues in August 1919, Lloyd George told them that 'the Irish question . . . had more to do with the existing industrial unrest in Britain than the great majority of people imagined'.

Sitting in the Viceregal Lodge in the Phoenix Park, Lord French would have certainly concurred with this Buchanesque reading of the post-war world. On arrival in Dublin in 1918 to take up his appointment as Lord Lieutenant he had been advised that 'Bolshevism was in the air' and that Sinn Féin – the party of 'the troublesome uneducated' – was heavily tinged with Leninist spirit. The impressive strikes that plunged Belfast into darkness in January 1919 made him worry that syndicalism might be an even bigger threat than nationalism. One frightening possibility was that unionist and nationalist workers would dissolve their differences and come together in revolutionary action. The only way to stop the Bolsheviks who had allied themselves with the radical wing of Sinn Féin, he told the cabinet early in 1919, was to release all the Sinn Féin leaders gaoled during the conscription crisis in the hope that the moderate leaders would regain control of the movement. Lord French would have been sure to be further alarmed if he read accounts of a packed meeting at the Abbey Theatre in Dublin later that spring to hear Sylvia Pankhurst, the famous anti-war suffragist who had visited Moscow the previous year at Lenin's personal invitation, debate with a leader of the Social Revolutionary Party, which had broken with the Bolsheviks. The house was almost wholly in favour of Pankhurst's passionate case for the glorious Soviet experiment and insults were hurled at the Russian when he gave an anti-Bolshevik speech. How could they have been expected to listen to him politely, one member of the audience explained, when Bolshevism was the force they were counting on to complete the destruction of the British Empire, which was already crumbling before their eyes?

At that moment it was tempting to believe that this might, indeed, be true. In his bestselling book, anatomising the anxious post-war chaos, *The Economic Consequences of the Peace*, published at the end in 1919, John Maynard Keynes summarised how the Russian Revolution had subverted every concept treasured by the British elite – property rights, religion, the hierarchy of classes. It was easy for Keynes's readers to dismiss his confidence that such terrifying upheaval would not be repeated in Britain, and read industrial unrest and armed revolt across the Irish Sea as the prelude to an uprising of the masses. What would once have been obscure industrial disputes were now magnified by participants and observers alike into battles in a universal struggle. Tailors who occupied a workshop in Dublin and collectively supplied drapery shops in the city announced they had set up a soviet. In County Monaghan, a little-known union organiser called Peadar O'Donnell (who later became a celebrated literary figure in Dublin and one of the best-known republican socialists) was approached by warders at the local asylum when their three-week strike reached the point of collapse because the management was bringing in replacement staff under police protection. They proposed to cut off the asylum's food supply. 'Good God, you can't cut off lunatics from food,' O'Donnell advised them, 'even if I could I wouldn't.' Instead, he led all eighty-three of them through the gates of the asylum under the pretence of returning to work. Expelling the superintendent and his assistant, O'Donnell declared the establishment of a soviet, and, with a red flag fluttering above the roof, ran the asylum until they achieved an improved wage settlement twelve days later. White-collar workers were equally eager to cast aside the restraints of respectability. Law clerks and shop assistants were talking up workers' power, writing pamphlets and news-sheets in the syndicalist style. A bulletin put out in Limerick during a strike by employees at a local department store proclaimed that the city was 'rapidly becoming a vast reservoir of resentment, embitterment, but above all – and thank God for it – of class consciousness'. The newspaper of the clerical workers' union proudly reminded everyone that Lenin too had been a clerk before his rise to global notoriety. And *Watchword of Labour*, official organ of the Irish Transport and General Workers' Union, regularly carried stories on the seizure of the Fiat factory in Italy and workers' co-operatives in Finland. On May Day 1919, in small country towns all over Ireland, parading workers waved red flags in defiance of a warning by the police that such displays were illegal. A visiting Swiss journalist predicted that the spread of Bolshevism in Ireland would have a greater impact in Britain than faraway events, 'in what English workers consider the half fairyland of eastern Europe'.

This surge of labour militancy had less to do with Moscow than the post-war boom. The abolition of the final wartime restrictions set off a demand for furniture, clothes, cars and all the new branded goods that had been out of reach during the war. Foreign visitors remarked that Ireland seemed to be awash with money, the shops in Dublin's premier shopping area, Grafton Street, crammed with the latest expensive luxuries. But although wages for labourers, skilled workers and clerical employees had doubled and sometimes trebled during the war, they had still not kept up with inflation. Food prices continued to rise in the summer of 1919. The Irish Transport and General Workers' Union was having no trouble with recruitment: its membership soared from 5,000 in 1916 to 120,000 by 1920. Barmen, waiters and creamery workers pressed their demands with newly discovered confidence. Although couched in the revolutionary rhetoric that was now universal, they were seeking improved conditions, not political transformation; soviets dissolved when wage rises were conceded. Labour leaders also talked up their admiration for Bolshevism but in practice they were moderate and conciliatory. The leader of the Irish Labour Party, Thomas Johnson, would not deny to the Swiss journalist investigating conditions in Ireland that he was a Bolshevik, praising the Russian soviets as a perfect form of government. And then in the next breath he reassured the journalist that Irish labour leaders were not doctrinaire. The Swiss correspondent shrewdly drew the conclusion that Johnson, possessing the 'urbane manner of a Catholic prelate', was no firebrand. Irish labour leaders were usually intent on defusing militancy, not encouraging it. However, to the authorities, acts of industrial sabotage – the dynamiting of roads by striking roadmenders, the draining of a reservoir by council workers – could appear indistinguishable from political violence. And since many trade unionists were also republicans, the struggle for independence and workers' self-assertion would sometimes coalesce spectacularly.

In April 1919, Robert Byrne, a well-known IRA prisoner in Limerick who had been on hunger strike for several weeks, was badly wounded during a desperate attempt by twenty-four of his comrades to rescue him from a local infirmary during visiting hours on a Sunday afternoon. As a policeman lay dying after an exchange of fire that terrified patients in the second-floor ward, Byrne was helped down the stairs and bundled into a pony and trap. It took him to a labourer's cottage a few miles away where he too died later that evening. Ten thousand mourners followed his coffin through the streets of Limerick, many marching in military formation. The next day the city was put under military control and the authorities gave notice that troops would be deployed on the bridges over the River Shannon and nobody allowed to enter or leave without a special permit. Businesses would be cut off from their suppliers in the surrounding countryside, and thousands of workers who lived outside the city limits compelled to present themselves at military checkpoints several times a day. On Sunday, 13 April, a general strike was called in protest and by the following morning the strike committee had taken control of the city. Warehouses, factories and shops were closed. Only bakers and grocers were allowed to open for three hours in the afternoon to sell food at prices set by the committee and displayed on posters around the city. Men wearing red badges patrolled the streets to ensure no businesses without permits had opened and to keep order in the queues for bread and provisions. At night, street lights were turned off and the pubs were shut, but cinemas remained open. When supplies dwindled food was smuggled into the city, concealed in boats and, sometimes, in funeral hearses.

The transformation of Limerick was witnessed by dozens of foreign journalists who had arrived to report on the first attempt to win the *Daily Mail* prize for transatlantic flight, later so triumphantly won by Alcock and Brown. On the fourth day of the strike, hundreds of people headed for a landing strip outside the city in anticipation of the arrival from England of Major J. C. P. Wood, who intended to fill his plane with fuel and take off for Newfoundland. As dozens of cinema newsreel cameramen and photographers tried to find the best vantage point, a military aeroplane swooped low over the crowd. The excitement dissipated when word came that Wood had ditched his plane off the Welsh coast. Now the journalists would have time on their hands to write about what had become known as the 'Limerick Soviet'.

'I have witnessed many strikes in England but never one bearing any resemblance to this,' a *Daily Express* reporter cabled from Limerick. No crime or looting was reported. The strike committee held daily press conferences and invited journalists to their headquarters at the Mechanics Institute to observe officials preparing sheaves of permits in a display of efficiency redolent of the Smolny Institute, the Bolsheviks' headquarters in revolutionary Petrograd. To counter the shortage of money the soviet issued its own currency – 'backed by the national feeling', according to Thomas Johnson – in notes bordered with the inscription 'General Strike against British Militarism 1919'. The leader of the soviet claimed that an entire Scots regiment had been sent home for betraying its sympathy with the strike by allowing workers to move in and out of the city without passes. Observers soon realised, however, that this was no incipient proletarian dictatorship. The American journalist Ruth Russell noticed how the guards wearing red badges appointed by the strike committee stood up and blessed themselves when the chapel bell rang at 6 p.m. for the Angelus. The mayor of Limerick, a member of Sinn Féin, told her there was no prospect of any support for communism: 'There can't be. The people here are Catholics.' And a local bishop agreed that the Catholic Church had nothing to fear from the soviet. Long before the Bolsheviks, he explained, the Irish had practised their own brand of socialism, back in the time of St Patrick in the fifth century. Independence would bring a modern form of this ancient Irish state. He smiled when she told of the red-badged guards dutifully rising for the Angelus: 'Isn't it well that communism is to be Christianized?'

The combined pressure of the clergy and local business leaders and the reluctance of the national trade-union leadership to escalate the strike in Limerick into a national confrontation led to the dissolution of the soviet after two weeks (in return for a slight easing of the military regime). The underground government also preferred to see labour following its lead rather than striking out on its own. A perfect illustration of the revolutionary movement's view of the proper role for the labour movement was the general strike called in April 1920 to support ninety prisoners who were refusing food in Mountjoy Prison in Dublin in pursuit of their claim for political status. All over Ireland (except, of course, for the north-east) trains stopped running, schools closed and taxis and jaunting cars stayed idle. Local trades councils running the strike styled themselves soviets, in imitation of Limerick. Railway workers marched through the centre of Dublin. Swelling crowds assembled each day outside Mountjoy Prison on the north side, eventually peaking at 20,000, so that the gaol was virtually cut off. Troop reinforcements could not pass through side streets dense with people. Military aeroplanes were deployed to monitor and control the crowds; one flew along a broad street below the eaves of the houses. The dense mass of people surged towards the prison, tearing aside barricades erected by the soldiers. Even tanks would not stop them and troops were on the verge of being overwhelmed or opening fire on unarmed men and women. IRA men joined the crowd with revolvers in their pockets ready to return fire if the crowd was attacked.

Discovering the state of the city when she arrived in Kingstown from a trip to London, Lady Gregory bought a loaf of bread, a box of dates and two oranges and left them at the Abbey Theatre in case she needed to take refuge there if the staff at the Gresham Hotel joined the strike. Even though shops were closed she found the streets crowded and tense, everyone looking out for the next 'stop-press' editions of the papers for news on the condition of the prisoners. At the Abbey she tried to listen to the runthrough of a new play, but was distracted by the rumbling of the aeroplanes overhead. They seemed to her like vultures, waiting for death. To her relief, the Gresham was open. In the stillness of her room she could hear the 'constant quiet tramping of feet on the pavement of people heading for Mountjoy', the shouting of the newsboys and the buzz of the aeroplanes. When she remarked to one of the hotel maids that the strike might force the government to give in, the young woman was pessimistic: 'The military are very cruel.' It was an overestimation of Lord French's resolve. To defuse the crisis, the ninety prisoners were set free in return for a verbal pledge to behave themselves.

The trade unions had helped to inflict a deeply demoralising defeat on Dublin Castle. But most members of Sinn Féin and the IRA saw agitation for higher wages or better treatment, let alone pretensions to a workers' republic, as a sideshow to the main struggle for independence. Many of the men trained and led by Ernie O'Malley in Volunteer fighting units were wage earners but he paid no attention to their class interests. 'The Volunteer spirit in essentials was hostile to Labour,' he recalled in his memoirs, 'afraid that any attention to its needs or direction would weaken the one-sided thrust of force.' It was alarming then when a violent conflict developed in rural areas between labourers and farmers that had all the appearance of a class war.

Agricultural labourers were a dwindling sector of the Irish workforce but there were still some fifty thousand of them. In the past, their lives had been abject and peripatetic, but thanks to the burgeoning British welfare state many had settled in newly built cottages, which had become a feature of the rural landscape. Backed by the Irish Transport and General Workers' Union, they were emboldened to improve their wages and conditions in the knowledge that farmers had done well when food prices rose between 1914 and 1918. Their campaign was as much about status as wages. Labourers were hired and fired when it suited the farmers and were not entitled to claim unemployment insurance. On hiring days labourers would gather in the square of a small town to be appraised by farmers in much the same way as they might size up bullocks at a cattle fair. Arms were squeezed to test muscles and bodies prodded for signs of illness or injury. Servants were often demeaned by their employers, grown men and women referred to as 'the boy' or 'the girl'. At harvest time, a form of segregation was practised at the dinner table, neighbouring farmers who were helping out directed to one room and labourers to another. A list of demands presented during one local dispute listed 'no distinction at table' along-side a six-day week and a nine-hour day.

It would be hard to overestimate the poisonous impact of this agitation in rural Ireland. Because relations between farmers and labourers were so intimate and personal, the self-assertion of previously biddable farmhands, joined together in militant defiance, and egged on by a trade-union organiser, seemed to be a particularly aggressive form of betrayal. As relations in the countryside polarised, labourers drew on all the tools of intimidation used by farmers themselves during the land wars of the late nineteenth century: anonymous threatening letters, boycotts and violent assaults. Conflict erupted across the countryside in 1919. At the end of April the intervention of a priest prevented a bloody confrontation between farmers armed with pikes and labourers brandishing sticks in a village in County Kerry. In the north-west, farmers carried guns to protect workers they had hired to cross picket lines; they shot and wounded four strikers. In retaliation hay was set on fire. In County Cork a farmer's son was fired on and his mule was killed. Hundreds of striking labourers and creamery workers marched behind a banner emblazoned 'Workers of the World Unite'. At a railway station in Limerick suppliers of coal to a local creamery were stoned by strikers, the horses cut loose from their harnesses and the carts overturned and smashed. Dockers in Dublin refused to load cattle for export to England from farms where there was a wage dispute. When the farmers tried to ship their livestock to Belfast on a train in the middle of the night it was derailed after fifteen feet of track were torn up. Only one horse escaped alive from the wreckage of more than forty wagons. By midsummer, some 2,500 labourers were on strike. Pickets patrolled the roads and railway stations to prevent the

movement of goods. Cattle fairs and auctions were abandoned, telegraph poles felled and left lying across the road,
crops destroyed and hay left to rot in the fields because there
was nobody to save it.

Bitter though they had been, the strikes were successful.
The more aggression shown by the labourers, the more the
farmers settled on generous terms. As well as winning significant wage rises the ITGWU won agreements giving the union
a say in hiring and firing. Labourers in Cork were not only
among the most militant but also the best paid in the country.
It was a tactic ripe for emulation. The *Watchword of Labour*
reported in August 1920 that 'red commandants' were
preparing for a fight against the farmers in County Carlow.
'The experience of last year's land strikes', the paper advised,
'has proved that if the proletariat of the land are to win
against the organised farmers, victory only comes through
organised aggression, not organised passivity. Terrorism is the
most potent of Labour's weapons . . . it is on the Red Terror
that our greatest reliance is placed.' Farmers prepared to respond in kind. The farmers' union tried to recruit ex-soldiers
as strike-breakers but very few were prepared to take up the
offer. In Wexford farmers called for the establishment of their
own paramilitary unit, a 'Farmers Freedom Force' that would
serve as 'a national bulwark against Labour, Socialism and
Bolshevism'.

The strikers noted that bearing weapons to fight for an Irish
Republic was treated by the authorities as a crime, 'but any
farmer may keep a gun for potting the Transport Union
officials'. Farmers supporting Sinn Féin chose to show their
contempt for British rule by ignoring the rates set by the
government wages board, to the detriment of agricultural
labourers. Terence MacSwiney, a member of the Dáil and later

Lord Mayor of Cork, was appalled by the divisive impact of tensions between farmers and labourers. Strikes were an urban phenomenon, not something he associated with the country-side, the source of the nation's food, but also its self-image. In an important strand of Sinn Féin thinking, rural Ireland was not merely the country's breadbasket, but was idealised as the essence of the nation the revolutionaries were striving to create: frugal, patriotic and spiritual. Class conflict belonged in materialist Britain, not pastoral Ireland. 'No man had a right', MacSwiney was reported as telling farmers and labourers in Cork, without any apparent sense of irony, 'to advocate force on the part of one body of Irishmen against another.'

An even bigger challenge was developing in the west. The government scheme to buy up large estates and redistribute the land to tenant farmers had been suspended during the war to save money. This left over 100,000 tenants, who had been waiting for a decade to occupy their own plots, still blocked from their dream of ownership. A further 400,000 impover-ished farmers lived on holdings deemed 'uneconomic', too small to make a decent living. This problem was particularly acute in the west, where thousands of young men with no land, who would normally have gone abroad to look for work, were prevented from emigrating during the war. Land that should have been transferred was rented out to the 'ranchers', wealthy farmers who bought up cattle from their impoverished neighbours and then fattened them up for export to the lucrative British meat market. The retreat of the police and the paralysis of the crown courts gave thousands of tenant farmers the opportunity to vent their frustration by refusing to pay rent. Even farmers who had received land found that they could get away without paying the annuities they owed to the government. They eyed up the lush fields of grass controlled by the ranchers, former landlords and their wealthier neighbours, and decided to carry out their own land-redistribution scheme.

In 1920 conflicts over land raged all along the western seaboard. A Dáil minister worried that it might not be long before the taste for violent seizures of property would spread to the rest of the country and turn into a full-scale civil war. The police, consumed by their struggle with the IRA, reported that the countryside had descended into 'utter lawlessness'. It was common in many areas for several farmers to band together to confront a landowner and demand that he sell his property at whatever price they offered him. Many of these coercive sales were financed by generous loans from bank managers. A rancher who refused to sell would be sent warning letters from 'the IRA' or 'Sinn Féin', illustrated with crude drawings of a gun or the skull and crossbones. A stubborn landholder might wake up to find a grave had been dug outside his front door. One Protestant landowner was forced by several men to sit at a table on his lawn and sign over his land. When he at first declined to pick up the pen, two of them held revolvers to his head while the others began to dig a grave a few feet away. A common tactic of harassment was to drive livestock off the land. Walls, hedges and gates were torn down and animals chased onto the roads. They often ran for miles until they were exhausted and hungry. A local newspaper estimated that 20,000 head of cattle and sheep had been driven from their pasture in County Galway.

When threats failed, violence was the next option. One day, Godfrey Hardy, a Protestant whose family farmed 140 acres in County Clare, was waylaid by a gang of armed and masked men who demanded that he turn over his farm to them within two weeks. The assault had come out of the blue; he maintained friendly relations with all his neighbours and had no inkling that anybody coveted his land. Unnerved by the experience, he sent a message to the men offering to sell 40 acres. They replied that it would have to be 'the whole place or nothing'. Shortly after this exchange he was set on by twenty men with blackened faces as he walked along the road. Beating and kicking him, they forced him to go down on his knees and swear to give up his farm. When he refused he was blindfolded, his hands and legs bound and revolvers thrust in his stomach and back. His sister ran to his rescue and the men fired on her before making off. Boycott notices were posted on the boundaries of his land warning local people to steer clear of the Hardy family. The campaign of intimidation often extended well beyond the original target. Shots were fired into the houses of labourers who continued to work for the Hardys; his foreman resigned out of fear. In County Mayo two tenants were stoned and beaten to death when they refused to take part in the boycott of an estate; in County Tipperary a herdsman who ignored an order to stop working for a landlord met the same fate. At the root of many of these cases was a sense of historic grievance, a raw memory of a past injustice now brought alive by troubled times. Farmers tried to reclaim plots from which they had been evicted half a century before. Sometimes this involved the revival of a slight or betrayal that had happened within families. In Galway, two brothers sent threatening letters and opened a grave in their uncle's field in an attempt to make him give up his land.

It was not merely a case of individuals taking advantage of the political upheaval to grab land. In the west of Ireland, where Sinn Féin drew much of its support from the sons of small farmers, the coming of the Republic was equated with the fulfilment of an entitlement to reclaim the land from the colonisers of three or four centuries before. Prominent members of Sinn Féin led crowds of local people to drive away livestock and take possession of estates. Placards were erected in fields declaring that the land had been 'Occupied by order of the Irish Republic'. Sheep liberated from the fields of one Anglo-Irish landowner wandered the roads with their wool daubed in the green, white and orange of the tricolour. But in some places it was members of Sinn Féin who tried to dampen the popular clamour for the seizure of property, attempting to turn back crowds preparing to march onto a grazier's land. Instructions were given to the Volunteers to keep their distance: the passions aroused were an even bigger threat to the unity of the movement than the labour disputes.

The authority of the revolutionary government was also at stake. Embattled landowners, exhausted by weeks of sleepless nights fretting that noises in the dark might signal the arrival of an execution party, arrived in Dublin to petition the Dáil to protect them. In one sense this was a flattering tribute to the success of the revolutionaries in undermining British rule; appealing to the crown courts or the police was futile. But it also posed a frightening challenge: if the Dáil could not control incipient anarchy in the countryside, what use was its claim to be the legitimate government of Ireland? The minister for agriculture, Art O'Connor, and Kevin O'Shiel were sent to the west to find out what could be done. They decided that if they could provide arbitration for land disputes, in the same way as the underground courts were dealing with petty crime, they might be able to impose order on the chaos.

The emissaries from Dublin, armed with the authority of the Dáil, quickly realised that when it came to land, mere moral authority was worthless. At the first land-court hearing in May 1920, they found in favour of two farmers whose fields had been occupied. Instead of complying with an order to quit, the claimants stormed out, denouncing O'Shiel and his colleagues as worse than the British. They refused to move off the occupied farm and boasted at cattle fairs of how they had defied the Dáil. On his return to Dublin, O'Shiel sought an urgent interview with the minister for defence, Cathal Brugha. Such open contempt for his ruling, O'Shiel argued, would render the land courts powerless. Brugha listened in silence, writing down the details of the case, then curtly informed O'Shiel that he had no interest in courts. A few days afterwards, four of the most prominent violators of the court's decree were taken away by armed men in the middle of the night to a lake island. They were released only a week later when they promised to end their occupation. The local IRA commander had been reluctant to carry out the order to detain the land agitators: all of his men, the sons of small farmers, were sympathetic to their claim and some were blood relations. But everybody now knew that the land courts were backed up by the IRA. In July, O'Shiel made an order at his court in Ennis that if there was any further interference with the County Clare farmers, Godfrey and Violet Hardy, the offenders would be 'dealt with in a prompt and summary manner'.

Going west exposed O'Shiel to the huge social divide running through the Irish countryside. In the towns where he held his court sessions the smell of money hung over each dispute. Hotels were packed with lawyers, land valuers and litigants and hundreds of people turned up to give evidence or watch the proceedings. Sometimes the cases would continue past midnight. Land, O'Shiel realised, was 'like black gold' and it was not just dispossessed men who were desperate to get hold of it. Many of the farmers prepared to break the law to extend their holdings were already wealthy. In contrast, travelling through the west revealed to him a hidden Ireland of rural poverty that he had never dreamed existed. His eye was usually drawn to the pleasing warmth of neat whitewashed cottages, the cosy homesteads that provided the image of a national idyll. So it was a shock to be confronted with the degradation of a rural slum: 'You came upon it suddenly without any warning . . . It seemed to be hiding itself for shame of its misery.' Here, ten or more families might share four or five acres between them, grazing their cattle in the winter, planting cabbages and potatoes in the spring. In the autumn the men would go to the Scottish lowlands to work as hired hands for the harvest. Ragged and barefoot children ran away at the approach of a stranger. O'Shiel took in the densely packed low houses, weeds growing from the thatched roofs. Urine trickled out of the front doors and hens pecked on the earthen floors. At night, there was the consolation of a modern touch: 'With the advent of John D. Rockefeller and the American oil companies, the candle had been replaced by the paraffin oil lamp, an ugly, oily, smelly but quite serviceable utensil, exceedingly cheap to run, whose double wicks gave forth a light surprisingly strong and mellow.'

10

A Crowd of Unknown Men

In the playground of St Ignatius College secondary school in Galway in 1920, a precocious, untidy, fourteen-year-old boy named William Joyce regularly subjected his fellow pupils to speeches warning of the deadly dangers of communism. A contemporary recalled that the teenage prophet, who had been born in New York, 'bubbled over with self-importance'. It had been seven years since William Joyce's family had returned to Ireland from Brooklyn. His father, Michael, the son of a small tenant farmer in County Mayo, had made enough money in the building trade in America to establish himself as a landlord in the city of Galway, where his properties included, appropriately, the local RIC barracks. Michael Joyce had developed a deep distaste for the violence and disorder he had seen at first hand growing up in County Mayo during the Land War of the nineteenth century. The Joyce family had wholeheartedly supported the war against Germany, and the local police regarded Michael as 'one of the most respectable, law-abiding and loyal men in the locality'. William was brought up to revere England and the British Empire in an atmosphere of such patriotic intensity that English people he met would find his imperial convictions excessive to the point of parody. He loved military ritual; if there had been a troop of Baden-Powell's Boy Scouts in Galway he would have joined it. Instead, he made do with getting hold of a khaki scout shirt and a badge, which he pinned to the lapel of his coat. It was not a style likely to court popularity. He once fought a boy who called him an Orangeman. The broken nose he received in this fight permanently altered the tone of William's voice, enabling him, in later life, to enunciate an exaggeratedly upper-class version of a BBC announcer's delivery.

In 1920 William had found a new outlet for his imperial patriotism and love of uniforms. At the beginning of the year, the British government began to recruit ex-servicemen to reinforce the Royal Irish Constabulary, and in the summer it established a separate unit to fight the IRA, the Auxiliary Division, composed entirely of ex-officers. When members of this new force set themselves up at Lenaboy Castle, a Tudor Gothic estate house on the outskirts of Galway, William Joyce was intensely curious to make their acquaintance and he gradually became a regular (and often irritatingly persistent) visitor to their temporary barracks. He made no attempt to conceal his affinity for these mysterious gendarmes in black leather jackets who were loud and flamboyant and flaunted their revolvers. He seemed proud to be noticed riding with them as they sped along the country roads in Crossley Tenders, the small lorries built for the Royal Flying Corps during the war. A schoolfriend remembered how Joyce had stepped forward from a crowd watching the funeral of a British officer to give an elaborate salute, holding himself rigid, the tips of his fingers straining at his temple for several minutes, as people stared in amazement or disgust.

Over a quarter of a century later, William Joyce, now known throughout the world as Lord Haw-Haw, the nasal-toned radio propagandist of Nazi Germany (who had a following among Irish nationalists), was convicted of treason at the Old Bailey and hanged at Wandsworth Prison in 1946. Rebecca West, who covered his trial for *The New Yorker*, thought he looked like a comic gangster. Joyce tried to invoke his youthful patriotism as a defence by claiming implausibly that he had fought with the Crown forces in Ireland to preserve the British Empire. His lawyers produced a letter he had written to the secretary of the Committee for Military Education at London University when he was sixteen: 'I have served with the irregular forces of the Crown in an Intelligence capacity, against the Irish guerrillas.' This was a gross exaggeration but his infatuation with a hastily assembled collection of paramilitary fighters was the first step on a journey that brought him from Galway to Berlin, via a career as a Mosleyite street fighter in London. When he broke up communist meetings in the East End he spoke of his opponents with 'real horror', West noted, just as he might have regarded Sinn Féiners as a teenager: 'There was working in him nostalgia for the Irish situation.' In 1920, W. B. Yeats had made the connection between Ireland and the breakdown of the old European order in a letter to Lady Gregory, who was dealing with paramilitary violence practically on her doorstep. 'The trouble is that there is world wide reaction owing mainly to Russia & everywhere governments & military power are let do much what they like,' Yeats wrote, placing events on a plane Lady Gregory found somewhat removed from her own immediate concerns about her neighbour's welfare. 'People speak quite calmly of a large part of Europe sinking back into barbarism & compare it to the break up of civilization at the fall of the Roman Empire. They cling to any authority.'

The idea that ex-servicemen be sent to Ireland was first suggested by Walter Long, the First Lord of the Admiralty and, from October 1919, chairman of the cabinet's Irish committee.

Visiting Ireland in May 1919, Long was affronted that, in order to travel safely from Dublin to the races at the Curragh, less than thirty miles away, he had to be accompanied by five armed detectives and trailed by a car full of soldiers. He thought Ireland should be treated like a British colony in the West Indies until Sinn Féin agreed to home rule on Westminster's terms. This would mean 'ruthless' policies, which the Irish police on their own seemed incapable of carrying out; Long thought ex-servicemen would be just the men to raise the game. It was the worry over the ability of the RIC to stay the course that was the main problem. Part of the rationale for introducing English recruits with hardly any experience of Ireland was an attempt to overcome the vulnerability of the Catholic and Irish constables to pressure from their neighbours. By contrast, men from outside were likely to be merciless without compunction.

Moreover, there were pressing reasons to find enticing work for the stream of returning soldiers. The chief of the Imperial General Staff, Sir Henry Wilson, revealingly dismissed the ex-servicemen sent to Ireland as '8,000 scallywags', a 'crowd of unknown men'. They were no more anonymous than the millions of others who had died on the western front. But in a curious inversion of the sentiment behind the Tomb of the Unknown Soldier, Wilson was worried that once reliable soldiers could become treacherous in the new unstable post-war climate. Ex-servicemen were regarded in Whitehall as a potential threat to the British state. Organisations representing them had been under surveillance since 1918. Some had moved beyond talking about better pensions and homes fit for heroes to proposing radical ideas for restructuring society. During the entire period of the Irish revolution, as Britain lurched from boom to bust and labour militancy increased, there was a constant fear that ex-servicemen could turn into revolutionaries as former soldiers had done elsewhere in Europe. In June 1920 the British Ministry of Labour reported 167,000 fit ex-servicemen receiving unemployment benefits in Britain – 52,000 in London alone. Demobilised soldiers clashed with police in Whitehall and occupied vacant homes and buildings. Intelligence reports warned that 'next to the coal question, the grievances of the ex-servicemen are the most serious troubles of the moment'. The minister for labour told the cabinet that if ex-soldiers began to lead unemployment marches they would not 'stick at trifles' to advance their cause. In September 1920, the head of the Special Branch, Basil Thomson, a consistent alarmist about revolutionary upheaval and a trusted voice on British security policy in Ireland, reported unemployed ex-servicemen were 'in an ugly mood' and warned that if they turned to rioting 'for the first time in history, the rioters will be better trained than the troops'. So when Dorothy McArdle wrote in 1937 in *The Irish Republic*, the canonical nationalist account of the war, that sending ex-servicemen to Ireland 'helped to relieve England of a very dangerous type of unemployable men of low mentality whose more primitive instincts had been aroused by the war and who were difficult to control', she was half right. The authorities were worried about how to control these men but they were not necessarily of 'low mentality' and their 'primitive instincts' had been no more aroused by the war than those of any other soldier.

The demobilisation of 200,000 ex-officers at the end of the First World War had created an entirely unforeseen problem. The length of the conflict and the scale of the casualties had quickly exhausted the traditional demographic pool from which the officer class was drawn – the landed and professional elite regarded as 'gentlemen'. From 1916 onwards, men who would never have dreamed of becoming officers were promoted from the ranks. So by the end of the war more than half of the officers demobilised were from the middle and lower middle class; men who had been junior civil servants, bank clerks, commercial travellers and even shop assistants in 1914. On the assumption that officers were gentlemen of means, unlikely ever to have recourse to labour exchanges, they were excluded from unemployment insurance. Thousands of men promoted from the ranks found themselves denied support to re-establish themselves in civilian life when they were demobilised in the summer of 1919.

The down-at-heel ex-officer, returning from the battlefield to find himself cast aside by a society in which war profiteers and trade unionists seemed to prosper, was the object of middle-class sympathy. *The Times* published a stream of hard-luck letters signed 'Fed-up', 'Ex-Major' or 'Disappointed'. Men who had gone to minor public schools took jobs as bus conductors or coalminers. The journalist Philip Gibbs knew a lieutenant-colonel who was reduced to earning his living as a door-to-door salesman, hawking copies of *A History of the Great War*. Not only had these men lost good salaries when they hung up their officer's uniforms; they also lost the acquired status that had given them a sense of being persons of consequence. Instead of being praised for their valour and success they were mocked for their delusions of grandeur. The term 'temporary gentlemen' was applied with snobbish derision to the pretensions of lower-class officers who, it was whispered, had to be advised not to eat with their knives when they took their place at table in the messroom.

One tempting opportunity opening up for those with a taste for action was to continue to get paid for fighting. There were many armies around the world seeking battle-hardened veterans. One man who ended up in Ireland recalled that some of his fellow officers were recruited by one of the factions in the Mexican Civil War with the rank of colonel and a scarcely believable salary of a thousand pounds a year. When twenty-three-year-old Raymond Cafferata and his friend were considering their prospects while waiting for de-mobilisation in France, the non-combatant world held little appeal. If he had to fill out a form to make his case to an em-ployer, Raymond realised it would have to say 'qualifications for civil employment nil' as he had been in the army since he was seventeen. What were the alternatives? Life as a clerk behind a soot-smudged windowpane? Neither he nor his friend had any time for 'pen pushing' and the war had left them 'loathing inaction'. The most alluring possibilities – and the only tangible offers – arose because the end of the war did not mean the end of soldiering. They were invited to join the new Polish army, but judged the recruiter too smooth to be trusted. They were asked to join the French Foreign Legion, but the pay and the five-year contract held little appeal for them. One evening, while socialising after a hockey match, they were told about a new force being recruited in Ireland, the Auxiliary Division of the RIC. The pay was very attrac-tive – a pound a day, at a time when a respectable clerk in Barclays Bank could expect less than £200 a year. It was the best on offer for any police work and there was the prospect that temporary cadets could become permanent officers in the RIC or another constabulary when the job in Ireland was done. They did not take long to decide. A week later Cafferata and his friend were stationed at the military camp at the Curragh in County Kildare, near the famous racecourse where Walter Long had been burdened by an armed escort.

The first impression made by the ex-servicemen sent to Ireland was visual. Many people noticed that they looked different from the RIC constable or the familiar normal British soldier. On St Patrick's Day 1920, a police patrol parading towards a barracks in strange attire was the subject of much comment in Tipperary. They wore the normal constabulary caps and heavy overcoats of very dark bottle green, but their trousers and tunics were khaki. Such irregular dress was merely the result of a shortage of police uniforms (possibly caused because tailors were boycotting the RIC) but it was to become the signature of their notoriety once an anonymous wit referred to them as the Black and Tans, the name of a well-known Limerick hunt. The nickname circulated throughout the country and eventually became the generic term for both the ordinary police recruits – 'temporary constables' – and the ex-officers of the Auxiliary Division, who were designated 'temporary cadets'. When he published his account of the Spanish Civil War in 1938, George Orwell could refer to how 'the poorer classes in Barcelona looked upon the Civil Guards as something rather resembling the Black and Tans' and be sure that his readers would require no further explanation or context to understand that he was describing a police force out of control.

In the case of the new recruits to the RIC, style was substance. Their botched and random turnout revealed much about the haste and desperation of their origins, the sense that they were being bolted onto a failing institution. And in the case of the Auxiliaries, who began to arrive in Ireland in July 1920, dress became a telling emblem of the kind of image they wanted to project. The only constant was a Balmoral beret, flat on the top and rising to a peak at the side. Other than that, personalised combinations of army or Royal Air Force breeches, tunics and leggings, leather coats and scarves and their habit of wearing their Webley revolvers strapped to their thighs marked them out as careless and strutting desperados.

The public could look at them from a safe distance; the policemen of the Royal Irish Constabulary had to work, and often live, alongside them. It was an uncomfortable mix, the arrival of these English and Scottish ex-soldiers with their strange accents and urban ways into crowded barracks that ran on punctilious routine and were now more isolated than ever behind steel shutters and doors reinforced with sandbags and heavy shell boxes. Most of the new recruits to the police force were shorter than their Irish colleagues; why is not clear, but the discrepancy would have confirmed the suspicions of those who had been worrying since the Boer War that British military supremacy was being undermined by the decline of the racial stock. They were most likely to be young, working-class Protestant men from London or the south-east of England who had previously been casual labourers or train drivers or had held jobs that made them urban exotics to their Irish colleagues: actors, musicians, jockeys, professional boxers.

Policemen's recollections of the new recruits are not universally damning but even the most equable references to them are coy and wary. They were the kind of men whom the sons of Irish farmers found vulgar and unseemly, although their worldliness could also induce pangs of inferiority; Irish policemen might have been taller, but they could be made to feel small. One policeman recalled how the new recruits refused to tolerate dried bread for breakfast: 'They weren't going to be like these people from the bogs of Ireland that put up with anything.' (He was right; several resigned because of the poor conditions.) Compared with the older policemen, they had little training in constabulary routines and were not disposed to take seriously the painstaking work of detection or to be reverent about paperwork. Arriving at the rate of 250 per week by the autumn of 1920, they were sent for preparation to the former air-force base at Gormanston, 30 miles north of Dublin, where the hangars were still full of disused military aeroplanes. Nearly 1,200 men were crammed into accommodation for half that number and, after a lecture course lasting only two or three weeks, they were sent out to patrol a restive country they had never visited before. It was, perhaps, over-optimistic to hope that they would absorb the principles of policing set out in the form of a professional catechism:

Q: What qualification is made indispensable for you
     as a policeman?
A: Perfect command of temper; never suffering myself
     to be moved in the slightest degree by threats or
     irritating language.
Q: How should you behave towards the people generally
     amongst whom you are stationed?
A: I should always be good-humoured, civil and
     courteous with them, ready to oblige or do any
     little service or favour in my power consistent
     with my duty as a policeman.
Q: To whom specially should you be kind, gentle and
     considerate?
A: To the poor, the helpless women and children.

Some of them, as one Irish policeman conceded, were 'fine fellows'. A Dutchman who had been a medical officer with the Black Watch during the war made a good impression on local people in a village in County Offaly by helping a mid-wife with a difficult delivery when the local doctor was away. But mostly their colleagues regarded them as unreliable, given to 'dodging and scrounging' or associating with 'low company' (i.e. loose women). On a raid of a shop they might put a wedge of bacon in their big coat pockets. In one station a Black and Tan levelled a revolver at the sergeant after he had relieved a drunken colleague of his gun. 'They were on their own; hurt one and you hurt them all,' concluded the Irish Protestant policeman who stepped in to defuse the row. Indeed, rather than just the IRA alone being responsible for the legend of the Black and Tans as the scum of England's gaols, there is enough in the policemen's descriptions of their conduct to suggest that it was members of the RIC who helped to popularise this notion. To Patrick Shea, whose father was a head constable, the new recruits were at once 'a revelation and a plague and a Godsend'. Their behaviour 'frightened even those they had come to help'. If the recruits to the RIC itself were frightening to their colleagues, they were at least nominally subject to the organisational discipline of a traditional police force. But the men recruited to the Auxiliary Division were a law unto themselves, organised into companies of a hundred men, mobile units ready for despatch to 'disturbed areas'. The only direction they were given was to take the war to the IRA. How this was to be done, the rules and discipline that should apply and the methods they should use were hazily defined. From the beginning they were conceived as 'a counter-murder association', which would use the same methods as the IRA against Sinn Féin.

It was Winston Churchill who crystallised the cabinet discussions about sending ex-servicemen to Ireland, inspired by his sense of a world in crisis and his belief in robust practices for keeping the peace in more distant colonies. Like a modern manager trying to impress on a company away day, Churchill was prone to blue-sky thinking about how to impose a version of shock and awe on the Irish rebels. He suggested using aeroplanes to machine-gun or bomb Volunteers drilling in fields (in the same way he was deploying the RAF in Iraq). His most fantastical idea was to recruit 30,000 unionists from the north to uphold law and order throughout Ireland, which would likely have provoked the sectarian civil war that the Irish had so far avoided. He was particularly impressed by how the Bolsheviks were using summary justice to put down opposition to the revolution in Russia and thought it might be worth sending three or four judges or generals to tour Ireland, trying and convicting anybody accused of murder within a week of the incident that led to their capture. But clearly he was looking west for solutions as well; in his history of the period, *The World Crisis*, he defended the Black and Tans on the grounds that they had merely used the same freedom that the police in New York and Chicago permitted themselves in dealing with gangsters.

Churchill was in tune with the post-war *zeitgeist* in another significant sense. In Germany and other countries in central Europe paramilitary forces were decisive in restoring order after attempted revolutions. At the moment the Auxiliaries were established, the Spanish government was recruiting a special unit of hardened volunteers to put down the campaign of the Berbers for an independent republic in northern Morocco. This force (which made a celebrity out of a major called Francisco Franco) would be paid far above the wages of ordinary soldiers and gain a reputation as 'a motley band of desperados, misfits and criminals' prone to indiscipline and specialising in atrocities (though, to put the brutality of the

Auxiliaries in perspective, the Spanish legion regularly exhibited the heads of decapitated prisoners as trophies). Churchill had become a fan of recruiting paramilitary militias, and not just for Ireland. Worried about 'attempted revolution' by British trade unions and socialists, he wanted to use the Territorial Army as strike-breakers but was rebuffed by his cabinet colleagues, who feared it would be an unpopular tactic. He was able to revive the idea through an old friend he had recommended for appointment as police adviser to Dublin Castle.

Major General Henry Tudor began his military career when he was seventeen and became an accomplished gunner, serving in South Africa (where he was badly wounded), India and Egypt. He had first met Churchill in Bangalore in 1895 and they became firm friends. Although his artillery expertise led to his rapid promotion from captain during the First World War, there is little to suggest that he had any aptitude for police operations. But he seems to have possessed the imperial grit that Churchill desired: a diehard admirer, generally caustic about the weakness of British military leadership in Ireland, reported that Tudor was exempt from disrespect and was regarded as 'a real white man'. As his deputies Tudor chose two soldiers who were also familiar with keeping order in the colonies. Brigadier General F. P. Crozier was born in Bermuda but brought up in Ireland, where his grandfather was a resident magistrate in County Galway. Diverted from his ambitions to be a tea planter in Ceylon, he enlisted to fight in the Boer War and later served in campaigns in Nigeria. The second of Tudor's deputies, Brigadier General E. A. Wood, was a veteran of the South African police force, also renowned for his courage; his obituary described how he was wounded five times, gassed and buried. It was hardly a coincidence that the men running the Auxiliaries were friends of Winston Churchill and veterans of imperial policing. Churchill told an audience in London in the autumn of 1920 that 'the Irish murder gang' was part of a great conspiracy of the 'rascals and rapscallions of the world' to deprive Britain of its global dominance.

The Auxiliaries took time to establish a reputation for themselves as aggressive, efficient and dangerous fighters. The early days of the new recruits were marked by boredom and frustration. Bill Munro recalls spending much of his time at his company's base in Macroom Castle in County Cork hunting rabbits and game or shooting at bottles they threw into the river, until the locals complained that ricocheting bullets were breaking windows. After dark, the evenings dragged slowly to a close and the only consolation was poker, roulette and drink. They explored the countryside but poor intelligence meant that they often arrived at the scene of IRA ambushes long after they had finished. But what seemed to Munro to be purposeless expeditions through Irish farmland left a different impression on those who were watching them.

By the springtime of 1920 the local IRA had established its dominance around Macroom. The police had given up and in May even army units had been withdrawn from patrols in the hills after three officers were killed in ambushes. IRA Volunteers could then patrol the country roads without fear of interference. Once the Auxiliaries became established, however, this impunity disappeared. From behind ditches IRA scouts observed the new, strangely attired and insouciant commandos regularly passing in their noisy lorries. They patrolled aggressively and regularly so that Volunteers who had once walked these roads and fields with proprietorial assurance could no longer be certain that they would not meet a heavily armed convoy coming around a bend. Even more shocking for the Volunteers, whose self-regard was based on being younger, tougher and fitter than the much ridiculed policemen, the Auxiliaries thought nothing of giving chase, in daylight or darkness. They jumped walls with their rifles in their hands and the IRA men had to use all their strength to outrun them. By the end of October 1920 the local police inspector noted in a report to his superiors that Macroom was 'now about the quietest part of the County'.

It was not only in Cork that the IRA became afraid of the Auxiliaries. In many areas operations were paralysed as word circulated that engaging these newcomers was not the same experience as smoking a few policemen out of a barracks. In Westport in County Mayo there was panic when news spread that the Auxiliaries were coming to town; although only three showed up, sauntering down the street 'swinging their guns', their reputation, like Calvera's bandits in *The Magnificent Seven*, was enough to make all the men associated with Sinn Féin and the IRA leave their homes before they arrived.

Their caution was not misplaced. The Auxiliaries were prepared to fire on anyone they considered an enemy. They burned Sinn Féin parish halls and the houses of Sinn Féiners; they set fire to hay, turf, oats and straw. Young republican women were dragged from their beds and their hair sheared. They torched creameries and looted shops. And they left messages to amplify their menace. The owner of a drapery shop ransacked and looted in Galway found a note on a shroud that read: 'You are a doomed man.' After shooting out a window of the jewellery shop of a republican sympathiser in Leitrim they chalked a skull and crossbones on the wall and scrawled a notice: 'Three lives for one of ours. Take heed, Sinn Féin. Up the Black and Tans.' In October 1920, the journalist Hugh Martin investigated the deaths of two young members of the IRA in Tipperary. They had been pulled out of bed and shot dead. Witnesses gave the same description of the men who had killed them. One, who appeared to be in command, wore a cap and had a khaki-coloured muffler tied round the lower part of his face. The others were dressed in long coats similar to those worn by the police, and soft hats. They were wearing 'white masks and handkerchiefs fastened so as to conceal every feature but the eyes'.

It was not just IRA fighters who experienced the aggression of the Auxiliaries and the Black and Tans. In August 1920 an Englishman living in County Clare wrote to the liberal London weekly *The Nation* to describe his experience of watching an armoured car and two open lorries full of policemen driving through the streets of Limerick one busy Friday evening as the shops were closing. The policemen were jeering, waving their revolvers and firing their rifles in the air: he counted at least a dozen shots and watched as a policeman trained his revolver on the pedestrians in O'Connell Street. If he had been told about a scene like this, he confessed, he probably would not have believed it. The Auxiliaries showed no deference when they were determined to be menacing. The unionist MP and eminent surgeon Sir Robert Woods was riding in a Dublin tramcar when the Auxiliaries boarded to search it. Woods was driven to protest when one of them walked through the tram shouting at women and children and waving his pistol recklessly. 'You ought to be more careful, young man, that thing might go off.' 'That's all right, old man,' the Auxiliary replied. 'I can soon reload it.'

Above all, the Auxiliaries and the Black and Tans seemed to take enormous pleasure in their swagger and indulged a taunting contempt for their enemies. Regular British soldiers

regarded them as a breed apart. 'The men who style themselves as Black and Tans walk about like miniature arsenals,
a brace of revolvers on each hip, bandoliers of ammunition
slung around [their chests],' wrote Private J. P. Swindlehurst
in his diary. 'To hear them talk one would think this trouble
was made especially to amuse them and the[m] alone.' They
scrawled 'Reprisals Galore' on the side of their lorries and
delighted in trailing tricolours in muddy streets. On Christmas
Eve 1920 Denis Johnston thought it noteworthy enough to
write in his diary that he saw Black and Tans buying balloons
and streamers in Woolworths in Grafton Street. The night
before, one of his Catholic girlfriends had been complaining
to him how they would grin and leer at girls in the streets.
Not everyone found the Black and Tans so repulsive. Rosamond Jacob listened with horror to her friend Helen's stories
of her encounters with them when they stopped and searched
people at random on the streets of Dublin. Her reaction
turned to dismay when Helen confessed that she found many
of them very good looking and that she virtually flirted with
them while they searched her.

Throughout the autumn of 1920 the Black and Tans and
the Auxiliaries carried out a series of reprisals in towns when
policemen were assassinated by the IRA. Although they
would often seek out known members of the IRA or Sinn
Féin, the object was collective punishment of the entire population. Shops and houses were set on fire and businesses
looted. The destruction wrought on 20 September in Balbriggan, a town of just over 2,000 people 20 miles north of
Dublin, attracted worldwide newspaper coverage. In the early
evening two IRA men had shot and killed Head Constable
Peter Burke in a local pub. Just before midnight four lorries
arrived from the Black and Tan training camp at Gormanston.

A dozen policemen walked down the main street, breaking windows and firing shots in the air. They broke into a pub owned by a republican, forced the family out of their upstairs living quarters and set it on fire. They went on to burn sixteen other houses in the same street. Entire families fled in their nightclothes, hiding behind haystacks in the fields near by, watching their town burn. The Black and Tans, one woman said, were yelling 'like dirty wild Indians' as they went about their work. The following morning, as women and children crowded onto trains heading into Dublin, twenty-five houses lay in ruins, as well as four pubs, two groceries, a newsagent's and the local hosiery factory, which gave direct and indirect employment to more than 400 people. Two local republicans were taken to the police barracks and asked to name the killer of the head constable. The next morning their bodies were found with bayonet wounds on a street ten yards from the barracks.

'Reprisals are wrong,' admitted the *Weekly Summary*, a propaganda sheet produced in Dublin Castle and distributed to all police barracks in Ireland, 'but reprisals do not happen wholly by accident.' The Irish policeman was in the same position as 'the honest German soldier' during the Franco-Prussian War of 1870–71 who became justifiably enraged at being surrounded by seemingly inoffensive French peasants, any one of whom could have been the sharpshooter who had just killed one of their comrades. 'The German authorities . . . had nothing for it but to punish the parishes where outrages against German soldiers [occurred] by burning down one or two houses.' It was an unfortunate choice of comparison for the publicist of a nation flush from a victory over 'Prussian barbarism'. And it appeared to acknowledge a policy rather than excuse an aberration. Furthermore, reprisals and attacks on the local population were not even always connected to police fatalities. At her home in Coole Park, County Galway, through the autumn of 1920, Lady Gregory filled her diaries with a catalogue of atrocities committed by the Black and Tans practically on her doorstep.

In early October, a local doctor told her of how a party of Black and Tans had raced through a village, firing indiscriminately, and then downed eleven glasses of whiskey in a pub and thrown a shilling on the counter as payment. They dragged three men out of a house and shot them. 'I used not to believe the stories of English savagery whether written or told,' the doctor told her. 'I thought they were made up by factions, but now I see that they are true.' Only the intervention of the regular RIC had prevented the Black and Tans from burning Gregory's local town, Gort. Women and girls leaving church ran at the sight of them. Her bank manager told her people were depositing money they would usually keep at home for fear it would be stolen by the Black and Tans.

In early November, Ellen Quinn, the young wife of a local farmer who rented land on Lady Gregory's estate, was killed as she sat on a wall cradling her child by a shot fired by Black and Tans passing in their lorry. People said the same men had earlier been firing into houses and killing fowl along the road. When Malachi Quinn came to see Lady Gregory a few days later he could hardly speak at first, 'looking dreadfully worn and changed and his nerves broken'. He was certain they had shot his wife on purpose because they had driven so close to her. The fondness with which he spoke of her was heartbreaking. 'She could play every musical instrument.'

At the end of November, Patrick Loughnane and his brother Harry, president and secretary of the Sinn Féin club in a village near Gort, were arrested (Patrick was also an active member of the IRA). A few days afterwards the Auxiliaries told their mother that her boys had escaped. But the local suspicion, Lady Gregory noted, was that they had been 'done away with'. The Auxiliaries who arrested them had stopped in a local shop to buy a rope, and had taken a bottle of whiskey as well. The shopkeeper who dared to ask for payment had a revolver thrust in his face. On 5 December the bodies of the Loughnane brothers were found naked in a pond; they appeared to have been choked. People who saw the bodies after they were retrieved said 'the flesh had been torn off the bones' from being dragged behind lorries.

The day before the discovery of the bodies Lady Gregory had come across an appeal that Henry James had written on behalf of Belgian refugees from the German occupation during the First World War. He referred to the testimony of thousands of people who had been 'surprised by sudden ruffians, murderers or thieves in the dead of night, and marched out terrified and half clad, snatching at the few scant household goods nearest at hand, into a darkness mitigated by the flaring incendiary torches . . .' The similarity struck her immediately. 'Is not this just what I have been hearing of from the crossroads . . .?' By then she could barely control her feelings of disgust. 'When I pray "God Save Ireland" the words come thrusting through "Gott strafe England",' she confided, 'in spite of my desire not to give into hatred.'

11

The Stigma of Race

Standing on a terrace overlooking Dublin Bay on a beautiful summer afternoon, the writer George Moore had once observed that the calm sea below appeared like 'a cup of blue water', enclosed by hazy mountaintops covered in heather and scattered with the white sails of pleasure boats. Naples, he thought, could hardly be more beautiful than this. The view was just as arresting for passengers arriving on the early mailboat from the Welsh port of Holyhead on a summer morning. Green hills appeared out of the dissolving mists, and the white-walled villas of Dalkey and Sorrento caught the first sunbeams. Although, in one view, the steam ferries had 'made the islands of Ireland and England one island', the emotional response to the crossing could equally be the opposite. Denis Johnston made the journey every few months while he was at Cambridge, and that first sight of the coastline was always an invigorating evocation of his attachment to a different place: 'Every hill, every valley . . . calls up associations and memories. It's MY country; they're my own hills and I love them.' Their first glimpse of land could also confirm for many new arrivals that Ireland was foreign, even exotic. 'Ireland is a small but insuppressible island half an hour nearer the sunset than Great Britain,' the home-rule politician Tom Kettle wrote in 1909, imagining how a modern geography text might begin. 'From Great Britain it is separated by the Irish Sea, the Act of Union and the perorations of the Tory party.'

As the war in Ireland intensified, the Irish Sea came to seem more like a barrier than a bridge. In addition to the conversational staples about the state of the evening train from Euston (crowded or empty) and the quality of 'the crossing' itself (calm or choppy) travellers now expounded on the chaotic searches of cases and trunks on the quayside at 2.30 a.m. The boats were often crowded with Auxiliaries and Black and Tans. 'Determined [to think] they were nasty men,' Denis noted after one calm crossing on the mailboat, 'until I got involved in talk with some of them and found them really nice fellows. Can they really be the other murder gang?'

At least the journey itself was no longer hazardous. On the morning of 10 October 1918 the Royal Mail steamer the *Leinster* was attacked by a German submarine an hour after it had left Kingstown with 771 passengers on board. Soldiers sitting on deck thought the first torpedo was a porpoise or a whale as it sped past the bows. But the second missile tore through the mailroom, where postal workers were sorting hundreds of bags of letters and parcels. And the third, which hit just as the passengers were assembling to evacuate the listing ship, set off a huge explosion. A lifeboat carrying 70 people was blown to bits as it was being lowered into the water. More than 500 people were lost, among them Lord Northcliffe's fifteen-year-old nephew and the brother-in-law of the Irish tenor John McCormack, who immediately offered to help the fund set up to care for the orphaned children. 'This most cold-blooded murder has brought home to me', the singer told the press, 'that this is a holy war to save the world from slavery.' Public outrage intensified when it was revealed that, only three days before the attack, Germany had approached President Wilson seeking peace terms. 'At the very moment that the German Government approaches the Government of the United States with proposals of peace,' Wilson thundered, 'its submarines are engaged in sinking passenger ships at sea.' What the public did not know was that the vast majority of passengers on board the *Leinster* were military personnel – troops from Ireland, Britain, New Zealand, Canada, Australia and the United States. Two of the survivors were Sergeant T. F. Denny of the US Chemical Warfare School and Captain Hutch Cone, the head of the US Naval Aviation Forces in Europe returning from an inspection of US bases in Ireland. He had been in the smoking room reading the *Saturday Evening Post* when the torpedo struck.

By the summer of 1918 there were US naval stations all around the Irish coast. Nearly 70 warships were stationed at Queenstown, most of them American. Their job was to protect the vast transfer of American troops to the European battlefield; between March and November 2 million soldiers crossed the Atlantic. The Irish bases were also essential for escorting the convoys of merchant ships delivering supplies from the United States to British ports. The vulnerability of the Irish Sea to German submarines was a jolt to those who regarded it as a safe secluded lake. The idea that the waters around Ireland were essential for British security was not merely the product of circumstance; it was central to the nascent discipline of geopolitics, based on the idea that geography shaped international relations. For the originator of this new discipline, Halford Mackinder, command of the sea was key to Britain's success in building an empire. Now that the world was interconnected, the once impregnable British Isles were under threat from newly powerful land powers. The founder of geography as a university subject and a

Conservative MP, Mackinder dreamed of a reformed British Empire run by an imperial parliament and allied to the United States. The Irish Sea, in Mackinder's eyes, was 'a British Mediterranean', the 'private sea chamber' of the world's greatest maritime power. The notion that the island at the other side of this inland waterway could be a sovereign state outside the British Empire, and so be free to consort with any power hostile to Britain, was inconceivable.

Thousands of schoolchildren would have read Mackinder's bestselling primer, *Our Own Islands*. Many in Britain unacquainted with his more elaborate geopolitical theories instinctively shared his assumption that the British Isles was a political unit determined by physical reality. One means of challenging the role assigned to Ireland in Mackinder's political geography was to present the case for independence in a setting far removed from the constricting intimacy of the two islands. And there was no better way of putting a cause on the map in 1919 than taking it to the United States. 'America in a very literal sense is truly the world state,' said Will Hays, the Republican politician who became the first president of the Motion Picture Producers and Distributors of America. 'All races, all creeds, all men are to be found here.'

One evening in June, eight months after the sinking of the *Leinster*, the president of the Irish Republic, Eamon de Valera, stepped aboard a ferry from Kingstown to Holyhead to begin a perilous journey to New York. To the dismay of his colleagues in the Dáil cabinet, de Valera had decided to go to the United States to appeal to the American people 'above the head of President Wilson'. That evening he was legally entitled only to cross the Irish Sea; without a passport he could not travel in the style a president making his first visit to the US might expect. Reaching Liverpool, he was smuggled aboard the White Star Line's passenger ship, SS *Lapland*, by sympathetic Irish crew members. He spent the first day of his journey to New York in the hold at the bottom of the ship, where rats gnawed through his jacket in pursuit of a cheese sandwich. For the next seven days he hid in the lamplighter's cabin, locking the door from the inside during the day, and, after a debilitating bout of seasickness, confining himself to a diet of Bovril. On 11 June he stepped off the ship in New York disguised as a member of the crew.

It was a week before Harry Boland, the Dáil's representative in the United States, announced that 'Eamon de Valera, President of the Irish Republic, is in his native city . . . as the direct representative of the people of Ireland to the people of America.' The president was certain, Boland told the press, 'that America will insist upon her war aims being enforced' and would not allow 'the people of Ireland to be the only white people in Europe, or in the world, condemned to slavery'. The distinction was important because de Valera was not the only leader of a subject nation to take his case for independence to the United States. A large delegation from the Philippines, then ruled by an American governor-general, had taken up residence at a hotel in Washington to campaign for the fulfilment of the promise the US had made after the Spanish–American War to grant independence to the archipelago. Their campaign of speeches and publicity in San Francisco, Boston and New York aimed 'to advertise an entire people' and dispel the impression that Filipinos were 'a mere coterie of savage or semi-civilised tribes devoid of any sense of nationality'. To emphasise his own status in the competition for nationhood, de Valera took a suite in one of the most famous hotels in the world, the Waldorf Astoria on Fifth Avenue, which prided itself on being 'tremendously international'.

Patrons could avail themselves of a drugstore, a barbershop, a beauty parlour and Turkish baths in the basement, a resident doctor and dentist, and the hotel's own squad of detectives for the protection of guests, led by a former employee of Scotland Yard. The world's newspapers were displayed in the reading room off the huge foyer, where a twelve-foot-high clock with four faces displayed the time in New York, London, Paris and Madrid. Afternoon tea was served to the accompaniment of an orchestra. It was here, transformed by tailors from a workman to a statesman, that the president of the Irish Republic announced himself to the world at a news conference on 23 June.

De Valera's obvious audience was the huge Irish diaspora that had become a powerful voting bloc in American politics. In the previous century almost 5 million Irish people had emigrated to the United States. Now established in most major cities, Irish Americans had developed a strong exile nationalism that was not only an expression of a sentimental attachment to the country they had left but a dynamic mobilising force in their adopted homeland. Their gift for organisation and political manoeuvring had made them the envy of other immigrant groups. In a despatch from America, the British journalist A. G. Gardiner explained to readers back home that the power of the Irish Americans came not from their numbers but because as a political group they were 'a compact mass' driving forward a single idea. 'The most brilliant writers on the Press are Irish. Nearly every political caucus is under Irish control. Most of the great cities have an Irish mayor. The police are almost invariably Irish . . . The Irish vote is the crucial element in every election.' For de Valera, Irish Americans were a rich source of financial support for the revolution. Before his arrival the Irish Victory Fund had already amassed more than a million dollars and the campaign he launched to sell bonds issued by the not yet legally established Irish Republic would eventually raise more than $5 million in subscriptions. But Irish American politics was riven by factionalism, feuds and personality clashes. More importantly, the fierce commitment of its ageing leadership to isolationism and their hostility to American involvement in foreign conflicts reflected the degree to which their nationalistic priorities were American first and only secondarily Irish. They regarded de Valera not as their president but as a rival. If he was to make good his authority to speak for the Irish nation, de Valera would have to win recognition as an international figure of stature from Americans with only the vaguest idea of the Irish struggle.

A grand tour of America captured in print and on camera had become the ticket to universal fame for European leaders aiming to connect with a mass audience. De Valera's time in America coincided with a seven-week official visit by King Albert of Belgium and his wife Queen Elisabeth. Their democratic tastes were appreciated at the Waldorf: they had gamely insisted that the same standard of luxury enjoyed by wealthy Americans would be good enough for them. Even greater public interest was aroused by the arrival of the twenty-five-year-old Prince of Wales, the future Edward VIII. The prototype of the British royal with mass appeal, his right palm was swollen from shaking hands with the huge crowds that turned out to see him as he made his way around America. Everyone was enthralled that someone so exalted could possess 'the personal touch', the quality now most prized in a public figure. The prince's publicity emphasised his normality – a modest, likeable young man holding views no different from the average Englishman, a democrat beneath the regal aura. This was the standard that the president of the Irish Republic would have to meet if he was to make a similar impression on American public life and the media that shaped it. Practically unknown before his audience with reporters at the Waldorf, his name and Brooklyn origins promised an intriguing back story that might give him more appeal in the United States than most Irish nationalists possessed. A mathematician who cheated a firing squad in 1916, escaped from a British gaol and was smuggled to New York disguised as a seaman had enough biographical drama to arouse the anticipation of a press fixated on personality. Harry Boland, transformed from Ireland's representative in the US to de Valera's 'valet, shepherd and manager', cultivated excellent relations with journalists. De Valera himself gratified reporters by praising them as his conduit to the people. For their convenience his speeches were circulated in typescript well before he appeared to deliver them.

Advance publicity was the keynote of de Valera's journey across America. Planned by a supporter with experience of presidential campaigns, its photocalls, motorcades, receptions and walkabouts appeared to the public as a mirror image of a royal tour. The train taking him from New York to Boston was mobbed at stations along the route. Fifty thousand people were waiting for him in Fenway Park, the baseball stadium of the Boston Red Sox. At Wrigley Field in Chicago before a crowd of 40,000 waving the stars and stripes and the tricolour, de Valera was carried onto the stage on the shoulders of his bodyguards, American war veterans in uniform. Then he waited nearly half an hour for the cheering to die down before he could begin his speech. In San Francisco thousands of people were crammed into the lobby of his hotel when he arrived in a car pulled through the streets from the train station by members of the Ancient Order of Hibernians. The night he appeared in Philadelphia a torch-lit procession accompanied him as he made his way to the Metropolitan Opera House. Schoolchildren chanted: 'One, two, three, four. Whom are we for? De Valera, de Valera. Rah, rah, rah.' In October he visited a Native American reservation in Spooner, Wisconsin, where a famous photograph was snapped of a po-faced de Valera in a Chippewa war bonnet. Although de Valera was often tired and lonely, Boland loved being on the road. 'It is a treat to travel thousands of miles through this land and not to see a high wall with broken glass on the top to keep out the plain people,' he wrote in a letter home. 'It's grand, to let the eye wander round to the very horizon, unimproved by any relic of feudalism.' He was thrilled by American mass culture: going to the movies, gambling in Atlantic City, taking a tourist bus to Coney Island. Leaving Louisville, Kentucky, he remembered 'dark and bloody soil, lovely women, fast horses, strong whiskey'.

It was to America's sense of its own success rather than to a narrow Irish American audience that de Valera appealed in his speeches: 'You Americans, who were looked down upon, are the cream of the earth today.' Many in the US were drawing their own conclusions about how to capitalise on their exceptional good fortune. It was possible to be powerful but not entangled in world affairs. The mood was turning against Wilson's moral crusade, the Versailles peace settlement and especially the League of Nations. De Valera still tried to flatter his audiences by telling them that the United States was the only power standing that was fit to give the world moral leadership: 'We in Ireland recognize that if the wrong turning is now taken, if violence be re-established in its former supremacy as the final sanction, humanity is faced with a

period of misery for which history hitherto has no parallel
. . . a whole series of irregular wars vastly more terrible than
the huge organized conflict now ended.' All of mankind was
counting on America to save democracy and especially the
Irish, though not, de Valera emphasised, because of their
own selfish interest in independence but because they were 'a
spiritual people with interests second to none in humanity's
future'.

De Valera's criss-crossing of America over eighteen months
certainly brought him notice. Some idea of the impact he
made can be measured by his appearance in Sinclair Lewis's
bestselling satire on American conformism, *Babbitt*, published in 1922. The eponymous hero – real-estate broker,
Republican and 'pious motorist' – finds de Valera's name as
he scans the headlines of the newspaper that lands each
morning on the front lawn of his home in an immaculately
homogenous Midwest suburb. According to the *Advocate
Times*, a mass meeting in Birmingham, Alabama, where de
Valera was due to speak, had demanded his deportation.
Drawing on his first cigar of the day, Babbitt finds the hostility shown in Alabama towards 'this Mick agitator' just as
satisfying as the news that college boys had stepped in to
break a strike by elevator runners in New York. '"Dead right,
by golly! All these agitators paid with German gold anyway,"
Babbitt thought puffing smoke. "And we got no business
interfering with the Irish or any other foreign government.
Keep our hands strictly off."' Lewis had drawn on a real
incident in de Valera's tour to provoke the fictional Babbitt
during his almost sacred daily perusal of the paper. Opposition to de Valera's presence in Birmingham had prompted the
city authorities to ban a parade organised to welcome him to
the city. The meeting reported in Babbitt's newspaper had

been attended by over a thousand people who condemned de Valera because he represented 'an element in Ireland that. stands before the world as notorious traitors, slackers and pro-Germans'. Babbitt's response is a reminder that, beyond the audience of Irish Americans, de Valera's high-minded affirmations of Ireland's spiritual gifts to the world met with hostility or indifference from those who maintained neat backyards, loved baseball, drank home-brewed beer while endorsing prohibition and were suspicious of all things 'un-American'.

The wartime panic over German infiltration (sauerkraut became 'victory cabbage' and frankfurters were renamed 'liberty dogs') was transferred in 1919 to the peril of Bolshevism. In response to hundreds of bitter and violent strikes in steel-works and coalmines the US attorney general, A. Mitchell Palmer, warned that revolution was spreading across the United States 'like a prairie fire', the red menace 'eating its way into the homes of the American workmen . . . licking the altars of the churches, leaping into the belfry of the school'. Immigrants were suspected of poisoning American minds with revolutionary doctrines. A senator in New York State established hearings to investigate 'Alien Anarchy in America'. Newspapers stoked paranoia. The US Congress considered imposing a prison term on anyone caught waving a red flag. Immigrant schoolteachers, intellectual 'hyphenated Americans' capable of plotting in their native European language, were screened by vigilance committees. Just before de Valera's arrival, in June 1919, bombs had exploded in eight American cities. The attorney general's own home in Washington was a target, but the man carrying the bomb tripped on the steps up to Palmer's front door and blew himself up. The new chief of the Justice Department's Bureau of Investigation, twenty-four-year-old J. Edgar Hoover, compiled files on tens of thousands of Americans and instigated raids and arrests that eventually put 10,000 people in gaol.

The red scare also had a racial dimension, a direct result of America's intervention in the First World War. President Wilson worried that the returning black soldiers would be 'the greatest medium in conveying Bolshevism to America'. To white supremacists the experience of the war had made black Americans dangerously confident and assertive, and they were outraged by stories of black soldiers consorting with French women. They listened with horror to a new generation of radical black leaders celebrating the military achievements of black soldiers who had displayed 'nerves of steel' on European battlefields, and would now return home to fight for their own rights. 'We new negroes,' the black nationalist leader Marcus Garvey promised, 'we men who have returned from this war, will dispute every inch of the way until we win.'

The summer of de Valera's tour saw an upsurge in racial violence. Segregation was being challenged in the south and the great black migration northwards, which would see the black population of Chicago double in a decade, was already under way. Black war veterans were targets for attack; several of the 78 men lynched that year were wearing their army uniforms. Race riots erupted in 25 towns and cities, with over 100 people killed. In July, 2,000 federal troops were deployed in Washington DC after six people were killed in riots sparked by reports of sexual assaults by black men on white women. The violence played into a modish discussion among commentators on both sides of the Atlantic about how the world might be on the brink of a race war. Scores of articles in respectable journals were preoccupied with the end of the white man's ascendancy. 'Coloured' races outnumbered whites by three to one, it was argued. Their lands were overcrowded and they possessed more vitality than the pampered workers of the West. Japan's victory over Russia in 1904 presaged an Asiatic world empire that might make Americans slaves. An Indian uprising could cause the collapse of the British Empire. The humiliation of Muslims, now subject to European protectorates in the Middle East, might lead to a militant revival. The white race had compromised its prestige by enlisting 'coloured' peoples to kill white soldiers on European battlefields. The Bolsheviks would appeal for support from uncivilised peoples out to destroy those who had demonstrated racial and intellectual superiority. The American author Lothrop Stoddard, a Harvard historian and journalist, was one of the chief popularisers of this 'race consciousness'. His bestselling book, *The Rising Tide of Color Against White World-Supremacy*, raised the spectre of 'a pan-Coloured alliance for the universal overthrow of the white hegemony at a single stroke, a nightmare of race-war beside which the late struggle in Europe would seem the veriest child's play'. White southerners in the United States hoped that the need to hold the colour line would force the rest of the civilised world to realise that segregation was a modern, efficient model of how to solve the race question. In 1921 President Warren Harding, who had succeeded Wilson, told whites in Birmingham, Alabama, that 'the time has passed when you are entitled to assume that this problem of the races is peculiarly . . . your problem. The "southern problem" is becoming a problem of the north . . . the problem of Africa, of South America, of the Pacific, of the South East.'

The red scare and the fears over race made a direct impact on de Valera's attempt to appeal to the American public. On the west coast his appearances drew protests from the American Legion denouncing his whole campaign as 'unAmerican'. In Portland, Oregon, the police confiscated tricolours from supporters attending de Valera's rally. The *Los Angeles Times* accused members of Sinn Féin of assaulting American soldiers during the war. The protests against de Valera in Birmingham were also organised by the American Legion and encouraged by the Ku Klux Klan. Once a fringe secret society, the KKK was now enjoying an extraordinary surge in popularity in towns and cities all over America. Klan candidates won state elections by excoriating elite politicians, promising to fight crime, enforce prohibition and ban suggestive dancing and immodest dress, all the while anathematising Blacks, Jews and Catholics. In Birmingham, the KKK overlapped with vigilance groups such as the 'True Americans' agitating for local businesses to fire Catholic employees.

De Valera had even bigger problems than his Catholicism or suspicions of his pro-German sympathies. One of the most prominent of the new black leaders, Marcus Garvey, had explicitly modelled his quest for black 'self-determination' on Sinn Féin. In the post-war peace settlement, Garvey argued, the former German colonies in Africa should be given to African Americans: 'As the Irishman is struggling and fighting for the fatherland of Ireland so must the new negro of the world fight for the fatherland of Africa.' In August 1920 Garvey convened the first International Conference of the Negro Peoples of the World in Madison Square Garden in New York. It opened with a parade through Harlem of brass bands, massed choirs and Black Cross nurses carrying banners inscribed 'Down with Lynching' and 'The Negro has no Fear'. To the noisy approval of 25,000 delegates, Garvey read out a telegram he had sent to de Valera: 'We believe

Ireland should be free even as Africa shall be free for the Negroes of the world.'

Earlier in the year, as de Valera prepared to address a mass meeting in New York, a small African American boy stepped up to present him with a bouquet of flowers. The symbolism of this photo opportunity was not strained. De Valera admired Abraham Lincoln throughout his life and equated the liberation of the slaves with Ireland's long fight for freedom. In cosmopolitan New York, Irish-independence activists consorted with Indian and Egyptian anti-colonialists and black civil-rights campaigners, addressing each other's meetings. The Gaelic League had a branch in Harlem. But the image of de Valera accepting the floral tribute from a black child in New York would not have served him well when he toured eight southern states in the spring of 1920. Here, as his adviser Liam Mellows briefed him before his appearance in New Orleans, he would have to negotiate lingering southern resentment that some 150,000 Irish Americans had fought for Lincoln's army during the Civil War. The solution, Mellows suggested, was to remind his audiences that one of the most steadfast supporters of the Confederacy had been John Mitchel, a celebrated nineteenth-century Irish nationalist who, after escaping from penal servitude in Australia, became a champion of slavery when he settled in Virginia. Theatrical display helped drive home this message. On stage at the Grand Theatre in Augusta, Georgia, de Valera was joined by veteran Confederate soldiers in their rebel uniforms. His rally in Birmingham, Alabama, went ahead in spite of the protests that Babbitt had read about so approvingly. De Valera wooed his audience by returning to the theme that Ireland 'was the only white nation on earth still in the bonds of political slavery'.

It was odd then that, at the same time he was emphasising Ireland's entitlement to sovereignty in terms of the new understanding of racial privilege, de Valera should generate most controversy during his time in America by drawing comparisons between Ireland and Cuba. To counter the arguments of anglophile Americans that an independent Ireland might align itself with Britain's enemies, de Valera suggested in a newspaper interview that independent Ireland could adopt the same relationship to Britain as Cuba had established with the United States after the Spanish–American War of 1898. The Irish Republic could sign a treaty with Britain giving up any right to an alliance with a rival power, just as Cuba had agreed with the United States. 'Why doesn't Britain declare a Monroe Doctrine for the two neighbouring islands?' de Valera asked, referring to the mid-nineteenth-century US edict to European powers that Latin America was within its sphere of influence. The suggestion accentuated de Valera's already deeply hostile relationship with the Irish American leaders. They accused him of preparing to compromise the struggle for Irish freedom and making Ireland an ally of Britain in what they believed would be an inevitable battle for naval supremacy with the United States.

Not long before, Irish nationalists had hailed Cuban independence and American support for it as a path Ireland should follow. When United States marines helped the Cubans expel their old colonial masters in the Spanish-American War, the campaign was followed with great interest in Ireland. During a tour of Ireland that summer the British journalist W. T. Stead discovered that the war in Cuba was a constant subject of conversation among ordinary people, many of whom had relatives fighting on the island: 'It affected them far more closely than anything that was going on in Westminster.

The whole petty fabric of domestic economy in a thousand homes was directly affected by the war. Passages had been given up. Remittances had been postponed.' This confirmed Stead's view that Britain had lost its moral hold on Ireland, which had developed 'a moral dependency on the United States'. The expulsion of the Spanish from Cuba also convinced him that a new crusading America was ready to extend its reach far beyond the western hemisphere: 'A new naval power had been born into the world and one which from its birth is disposed to regard its mission seriously as an avenger of the oppressed and a minister of the vengeance of Heaven.' Stead was not alone in noticing the implications of the American intervention in Cuba. Queen Victoria was underwhelmed by America's assertion of the right to be the world's policeman: 'No doubt Cuba was dreadfully governed,' she conceded, '[but] they might as well say we governed Ireland badly and they ought to take possession of it and free it.' This was precisely the possibility that aroused the interest of Irish nationalists. 'America had established a very important precedent,' the Irish MP Tim Healy suggested provocatively, 'that of interfering with arms on behalf of an oppressed nationality.' After Cuba it might be 'an island very much nearer to home'.

Cuban nationalists were not so convinced that they had experienced the deliverance dreamed of by the Irish. Although they had been fighting their own war of independence for three years, the Americans took all the credit for beating the Spaniards. They discovered that the US regarded Cuba much as Halford Mackinder viewed Ireland: a possible springboard for a hostile power eighty miles from the coast of Florida. For the future, according to Senator Orville H. Platt, Cuba would be bound to the United States 'by location, helplessness and . . . the sentiment of gratitude'. His infamous amendment to the new Cuban constitution, a condition for ending the American occupation, stipulated not only that the new republic was denied the right to sign treaties with foreign powers – as de Valera was aware – but that the US had the right to intervene in Cuba at any time. A sliver of Cuban territory was ceded to the United States so that it could establish the infamous naval base at Guantanamo Bay. Protests erupted when the Platt Amendment was passed in the Cuban national assembly by one vote. One veteran of the Cuban War of Independence declared that the destruction of the entire island would be preferable to subjugation to the Americans. 'Rather than living under the "humanitarian Saxon race" we prefer death, because death is preferable to humiliating slavery. We, the veterans of the independence struggle, who took to the fields of the revolution in order to defend the sacrosanct cause of Cuban liberty, should force the complete fulfilment of the program of the Revolution. Independence or death!'

So Queen Victoria's anxiety proved unfounded; the liberators of Cuba were shaping up to be consummate imperialists themselves. Rudyard Kipling saw the Spanish-American War, rather than a threat to British interests, as a sign that the United States was ready to share the white man's burden. Joseph Chamberlain believed that the next logical step was an Anglo-American alliance, since the United States was a 'powerful and generous nation, speaking our language, bred of our race, and having interests identical with ours'. What Irish nationalists hoped might lead to American intervention to secure Irish freedom was the beginning of the alliance of 'English-speaking peoples', in which London would accommodate American power and Washington would defer to the interests of the British Empire. As the American publisher George Putnam wrote in anticipation of the visit to the United

States by the Prince of Wales in 1919, 'The world must be made safe for democracy and the responsibility rests upon Englishmen and Americans of showing that democracy can secure a safe, wise and just rule for the world.'

De Valera was to discover what this meant when he failed in his attempt to win recognition for the Irish Republic from the US Congress, or even from the Republican and Democratic election campaigns. America presented the Irish cause with a stage from which to win world attention, but Ireland's claim for sovereignty still had to be resolved across the Irish Sea, not the Atlantic Ocean. Scarcely a month after de Valera had arrived in New York, Michael Collins had already reached this conclusion in Dublin. De Valera was making a terrific impression in America, he acknowledged in a letter to a colleague. 'Yet our hope is here and must be here,' he cautioned. 'The job will be to prevent eyes turning to Paris or New York as a substitute for London.' As de Valera prepared to return to Ireland at the end of 1920, Collins had a new plan for sending a message to London.

12

No Pity

Of the string of stylish cafes along Grafton Street in 1920, the most fashionable and eclectic was Café Cairo. An orchestra played daily from lunchtime. The Rose Room was advertised as the perfect place to read, write, rest or use the telephone. At a corner table in the long room on the second floor, writers and journalists with Sinn Féin sympathies met to discuss literature over serial cups of coffee. The Dublin branch of the Charles Dickens Fellowship gathered here to discuss the most villainous characters in the novelist's books. In the evening you could catch a jazz band featuring two black musicians. It was a favourite venue for company parties. Members of the Irish Association of Advertising Men gave a send-off to a colleague who had landed a new job at Selfridges in London. In November, Rosamond Jacob met her friend Helen at Café Cairo before going to the opera (not long afterwards she complained that it had become 'beastly dear'). Denis Johnston was also a frequent patron. One day visiting the Gents his eyes were drawn to the graffiti scrawled on the wall. 'Who are these Sinn Féiners anyway?' Moved to reply, he scribbled underneath, 'Sinn Féiners are patriots, prepared to die for their country.' The next time he dropped in for lunch he discovered that somebody had written below his words, 'For God's sake die then, and give your country a chance.'

A journey to death could, indeed, begin at Café Cairo. In March 1920, Frank Saurin and Vinny Byrne from the Squad met a clerk from British army headquarters called Molloy for tea in the cafe. Molloy had sent word that he could procure arms for the IRA, but Lily Mernin, the mole in the British army barracks, had identified him as a double agent. Vinny Byrne arranged to meet him again the following evening at the top of Grafton Street. He suggested they both pin flowers in their lapels so that they would be sure to spot one another in the rush-hour crowds. At 5.30 p.m. the next day, Vinny was joined by three comrades from the Squad near the rendez-vous point. They watched from a distance as the man with the buttonhole arrived and hung around for forty-five minutes, until he gave up waiting for his IRA contact and walked off down Grafton Street. As they followed him, they tried to close in to get a clear shot, but pedestrians kept getting in the way. Shortly after he turned left into Wicklow Street one of the gunmen swept aside a young woman and shot Molloy in the knee. Then Vinny Byrne and Jim Slattery stepped up and shot him in the abdomen and the right temple as he lay on the ground. Vinny was startled when people in the street started shouting, 'Stop them!' Civilians had never done this before. Vinny thought they must have taken the men from the Squad for plainclothes Auxiliaries.

The success of Michael Collins's assassins in killing the most effective Irish detectives, the G-men from the Castle, had forced the British to organise their own intelligence operation in Dublin. A training school for spies was established in the London suburb of Hounslow. Retired army officers were in-structed in the basic techniques of subterfuge and sent to Dublin, posing as railway porters, journalists or commercial travellers. By the autumn of 1920 there were almost a hundred intelligence agents in Dublin. In October, an American journalist, Carl Ackerman, was told by Basil Thomson's chief of staff, Colonel Carter, that the military in Ireland were 'getting' the Sinn Féin leaders: 'He [said] they were disappearing so fast that his friend in Dublin Castle told him he would give him a dinner in London on March first "and there would not be an assassin left in Ireland".'

The most remarkable fact about British agents in Dublin was that they were so visible. Many of them boarded in flats and hotels around the city alongside regular army officers. Colonel C. J. Woodcock had returned to London from serving with the British occupation forces on the Rhine thinking that he would be sent to India, when he was suddenly ordered to go to Dublin in May 1920. His wife began searching for a flat when she arrived in July. What the estate agents showed her was very disappointing. She kept thinking of her beautiful bathroom in Germany with tile-covered walls and floors and its sparkling variety of taps, showers and douches; even in well-appointed Dublin rentals there was often only one tap on the landing. Besides, there were so many military couples living outside barracks in Dublin that it was difficult to find any suitable rooms at all. The flat she finally chose, at 28 Upper Pembroke Street, was in a building where eight or nine suites of rooms were already occupied by military officers and their wives. They shared with each other their sense of being exposed, joking that the well-paid officials too afraid to set foot outside Dublin Castle would stay there until they were eligible for their pensions, and then leave by aeroplane. Four of the Woodcocks' neighbours in the house in Upper Pembroke Street were secret-service men who came in and went out at irregular hours. Mrs Woodcock knew them as 'the hush-hush men'. Although a regular soldier, her husband would announce after dinner that he was heading out on a job, and usually not return until morning. They were suspicious of the servants and constantly felt watched. The officers feared their wives might be targets of reprisals. Mrs Woodcock often noticed knots of young men at street corners who stared into her car as she passed. Walking along the pavement one day she saw a man step out into the street to note down the number plate of an official car as it disappeared down the street. She was told that the IRA kept lists of people they might attack and knew them by sight.

Mrs Woodcock was not being paranoid. Journalists who visited Dublin quickly developed a sense that they were being watched on trams, in theatres and in bars or followed by street loungers determined to eavesdrop on their conversations. The IRA had cultivated a network of well-placed spies in Dublin Castle and at British army headquarters who were able to reveal the contents of secret files or the timing of searches and round-ups. But to track the daily movements of the officers who occupied rooms in the Georgian townhouses on Dublin's south side or the suspicious commercial travellers who checked into hotels on Sackville Street they depended on cleaning women and barmen, telephone operators and porters, taxi drivers and doormen who each contributed tiny scraps of detail to the files: fragments of conversations overheard, crumpled pages of notes thoughtlessly tossed into bins, the clocking of exits and returns. Mrs Woodcock was right: there was a lengthening list of targets. Michael Collins called them 'the particular ones'. Some of those on the list liked to socialise among the Sinn Féin intellectuals, advertising executives and the jazz fans at the Café Cairo. These men became known as the Cairo Gang.

The designation was a sign that the enemy had taken shape and that a plan was coming to fruition. Word was passed down the ranks that the new arrivals in Dublin were the cream of British intelligence, men who had developed formidable reputations during the war in outposts of empire all across the world, characters straight out of a Buchan novel. It was decided to kill a large number of 'the particular ones' in simultaneous attacks on Sunday morning, 21 November 1920. The aim was to relieve pressure on the IRA by killing the men who were tracking down their fighters. And the scale of the attacks would also demonstrate that the Irish resistance was powerful, ruthless and could not be overcome. The assassinations in Dublin were to coincide with sabotage attacks on the Liverpool docks, a power plant in Manchester and timber yards in London (plans eventually aborted following their discovery in a raid). An operation of this scope would require the recruitment of many more men than the usual assassination squad – not only men prepared to shoot, but also assistants to stand guard, keep watch and patrol streets surrounding the targets. Many who took part were informed that they were required only the night before and were unclear about the precise nature of their duties the following morning. Those who realised what they were about to do were confronted by qualms they thought had been resolved: to shoot men barely roused from sleep, in the privacy of their bedrooms, required more reserves of pitiless will than picking off detectives going about their business. One man recalled the commanding officer advising those who took part that they would need to be at ease with their consciences in order to carry out the mission successfully. No country had scruples about shooting enemy spies in wartime but 'if any man had moral scruples about going on this operation he was at full liberty to withdraw and no one would think any the worse of him'.

Charlie Dalton, the intelligence officer of Dublin Brigade, met his group at five minutes before nine the following morning, a mild winter's day of weak sunshine. Church bells were ringing around the city and many people were on their way to Mass. Dalton had got to know the maid in the house where Mrs Woodcock lived. She had told him that Major Dowling, an officer of the Grenadier Guards, and Colonel Hugh Montgomery of the Royal Scots Regiment occupied adjacent rooms on the third floor of 28 Upper Pembroke Street. When Dalton and his men knocked on the door the porter was polishing the lino in the hallway. As he opened it, they pushed him backwards and pinned him to the wall, holding a revolver to his face. Several men went up the stairs; one made his way to the back of the house and two others stayed in the hall, savouring the aroma of fried breakfasts drifting from the kitchen.

On the second floor, Mrs Woodcock's husband was hurrying to get dressed for a ceremonial parade, while she struggled with fiddly buttons on her blouse. Standing at the window trying to fasten her cuff, just as her husband headed down for breakfast, she noticed a man jumping over the garden wall. For a second she watched him with no particular interest, surmising that he must be the sweetheart of one of the maids. It was when he pulled a revolver from his coat pocket that Mrs Woodstock called her husband back. He joined her at the window to watch the silent gunman in the garden. Then he rushed downstairs to warn their friends in the lower floors and make sure the hall doors were bolted.

On the floor above the Woodcocks, Charlie Dalton and three comrades had entered the rooms where Major Dowling and a man they thought was Colonel Montgomery (but who was actually Captain Leonard Price) were still in bed. They sat up in their pyjamas, startled. The men ordered them to get up and stand against the wall. One of the gunmen, Paddy Flannigan, shot both of them in the chest and they fell down. Dalton wanted to search the room for papers but Flannigan told him to get the hell out. He noticed that the British officers made gurgling noises as they lay on the floor.

Downstairs there was chaos. On his way to secure the door, Colonel Woodcock discovered that the hallway was full of armed men. A youth ordered him to put his hands up but he turned sharply to go back upstairs. The young man fired and the colonel fell on the floor with bullets in his back and shoulder. On the second floor Captain H. B. C. Keenlyside and his wife had come out onto the landing to be confronted by three armed men. They told Mrs Keenlyside to move aside but she clung to her husband and they had to drag her away so that they could shove him downstairs. In the hallway he saw that Colonel Montgomery had been captured after coming down from the first floor. To the IRA men in the hall it seemed that British officers were arriving from all directions. Lieutenant Murray from the Royal Scots Regiment was shot as he came down the stairs. Thundering down the steps from the third floor, Charlie Dalton could see two figures in pyjamas, with their hands raised, standing at the top of the staircase to the kitchen in the cellar. 'Who are you?' one of the panicked IRA men shouted at Dalton when he reached the hall. 'I'm an intelligence officer,' Dalton shouted. They fired at one of the men in pyjamas and he fell down the steps.

In her room on the second floor, Mrs Woodcock stood staring at the man in the garden below covering the back door with his revolver. She was certain he would be caught at any minute. Firing echoed around the house; she had counted six loud reports from the hallway. (Two shots wounded Colonel Montgomery so badly he would die three weeks later; four shots hit Captain Keenlyside in the arm and the jaw.) Even when her husband staggered through the door, his shoulder covered in blood, Mrs Woodcock could not take her eyes off the garden. Over the wall she could see a crowd of men running and cycling down the passageway. A servant with a key scurried out and opened the back gate and the gunman she had spent so long watching disappeared. Turning away, she finally took in her husband lying on the bed, the sheets soaked in blood. She ran downstairs to call for help. Blood was splashed on the walls, on the staircase and in the hallway, where splinters of plaster were scattered on the floor. The body of a man in bright blue pyjamas was slumped at the top of the kitchen stairs. She telephoned the barracks and asked for soldiers to be sent at once.

Similar scenes had been enacted at seven other locations in Dublin. Around the corner, twelve men had burst past the landlady at 92 Lower Baggot Street. Four of them ran upstairs to the flat Captain W. F. Newberry shared with a woman assumed to be his wife. She saw the guns in their hands as soon as she opened the living-room door and immediately tried unsuccessfully to shut it against them. She ran back to Captain Newberry in the bedroom and they were able to slam the door as the gunmen approached, throwing themselves against it. One IRA man wedged his foot between the jamb and the door. For several seconds both parties pushed ferociously from either side until a gunman fired through the door, wounding Captain Newberry. He ran back and made to climb out through an open window. Finally overcoming the resistance of the woman at the door, the gunmen rushed in past her and fired seven shots into Captain Newberry before he was able to jump to safety. They searched the room as his body lay straddled on the window frame.

At 119 Lower Baggot Street, men called, looking for Captain Bagelly, a courts-martial prosecutor who had lost a leg in the war. A maid pointed out his room. The door was unlocked and they entered to find a man lying in bed in his pyjamas.

'"Captain Bagelly?"

'"That's my name."

'"I suppose you know what we came for? We came for you."'

They fired one bullet through his left eye and three into his chest. They heard the maid screaming as they gathered up Captain Bagelly's papers and his camera.

Not all of the assassinations went to plan. Three men went to the Shelbourne Hotel but fired in panic at a shadow on the stairs, alerting their intended victim, who fled to a room on the top floor. At two other hotels the officers expected to be there were absent. In the Gresham Hotel on Sackville Street, men arrived and asked the doorman to bring them to rooms 14 and 24. Lieutenant Leonard Wilde was shot dead when he answered the door to room 14. Instead of going to room 24 they went to room 22 and found a man in bed reading a racing paper. They shot him in the neck, the wrist and the groin. This was Captain Patrick McCormack of the Royal Army Veterinary Corps, who had come to Dublin from Egypt to buy mules for the army.

At 22 Lower Mount Street some of the men who arrived went to the room of Lieutenant Peel. The others woke up Lieutenant H. McMahon and his roommate. They asked McMahon to show them where he kept his guns. He indicated a bag in the corner of the room. One of the men placed the bag on the table, ripped the locks off and took out three revolvers, shoving them into his pockets. Suddenly, they heard shots fired outside in the street and a noise from the hallway below, as if the front door was being smashed in. 'Are you all right there, boys?' came a voice from the landing. 'They're surrounding the house.' A maid screaming for help from the top-floor window had attracted the attention of a lorry load of passing Auxiliaries on their way to the train station. Some tried to break down the front door; others ran around the passageway to the back of the house. Two were sent to Beggars Bush barracks to fetch reinforcements. In Lieutenant McMahon's room the five men made to go, then swung around suddenly and fired at McMahon, who raised his arm to cover his face. His companion threw himself on the floor. In the room across the landing, Lieutenant Peel had piled furniture against his door and although seventeen shots were fired into his room he was uninjured. Some of the IRA men ran out of the front door firing their revolvers and got away. At the back of the house, Frank Teeling was shot in the ankle as he tried to escape and was captured. The two Auxiliaries who had been sent to raise the alarm ran into IRA lookouts and were shot dead in a residential garden.

There had been so many killings in bedrooms, hallways and back gardens within half an hour on a quiet winter Sunday that it was some time before the scale of the morning's events became public knowledge. After the doctors decided that Colonel Woodcock's wounds were not life-threatening, Mrs Woodcock accompanied her husband to the Military Hospital. People kept offering tea and brandy. Soldiers were standing guard outside the house on Pembroke Street when she returned to pack up and move to an army barracks. They had heard a rumour that Colonel Woodcock had died and men who had served with him in Malta, India and France approached her to express their anger. Inside, her orderly had prepared tea. He had scrubbed the hall and the staircase and tidied her room, leaving her husband's uniform soaking in the bath. They argued over the most effective agent for removing bloodstains. Salt would be best, the orderly said, but Mrs Woodcock insisted on Lux soap. It was only when she went back to the Military Hospital that she discovered that gunmen had visited many other houses that morning. The matron told her there were fourteen bodies in the hospital mortuary. Two of the dead officers had been to dinner with the Woodcocks the previous night when they entertained the American consul.

The commanding officer of the Auxiliaries, Brigadier General F. P. Crozier, went to the house on Lower Mount Street when he heard an IRA man had been captured. In the back garden he found Frank Teeling lying on the ground, his ankle smashed by a bullet. An Auxiliary was holding a revolver to his head, threatening to fire if Teeling did not give up the names of his accomplices by the count of ten. Crozier pulled up the revolver and gave orders for Teeling to be taken to hospital. Inside the house he found the body of Lieutenant McMahon. Across the landing, Lieutenant Peel was still hiding behind the furniture piled against his bullet-riddled door. Crozier persuaded him it was safe to come out. Reports of the shootings were trickling into Dublin Castle when Crozier returned in time for breakfast. He heard a soldier say that fifty officers had been shot. Nonetheless, he did not cancel his game of squash. After a hot bath he went to lunch at the Shelbourne Hotel with a Liberal MP over from London.

Pat McCrea, who had driven the getaway car for the men who shot Captain Bagelly, got back home to Dollymount, on the north side of the city, by 11 o'clock and found his family sitting down to breakfast. They wanted to know where he had been. Out fishing with the boys, he said, and then to Mass. 'Where are the fish?' his wife asked. He stuttered to answer. To escape further questions, he left the house, took a tram into town and went to the short 12 o'clock Mass at the Pro-Cathedral in Marlborough Street. He came home for lunch and went to sleep on the couch. At about four o'clock his wife woke him. She was crying, holding a special edition of the newspaper with headlines about the massacre that morning. Was this the fishing expedition you were on, she wanted to know. He decided to confess. 'Yes, and don't you see we had a good catch?' 'I don't care what you think,' his wife said. 'I think it's murder.' 'No, that is nonsense; I'd feel like going to the altar after that job this morning.'

Whatever consolation McCrea had found at Mass, his nerves were rattled as soon as he left the church and met some of the other men who had killed British officers that morning. They had all intended to go to Croke Park that afternoon to watch the Gaelic football match between Dublin and Tipperary. The proceeds from the ticket sales would be donated to dependants of IRA men killed or imprisoned. But now the Black and Tans seemed to be on the move all across the city. Turning up at Croke Park might mean trouble.

The military did have their eyes on the football match. The plan was to surround the ground as soon as the match started. Armoured cars would pull up at the main entrance and soldiers would guard all the exits and the railway line that ran behind the ground. Fifteen minutes before the end of the match, an intelligence officer with a megaphone intended to warn the crowd that all males leaving Croke Park would be stopped and searched when the game finished. Anyone trying to leave by routes other than the official exits would be shot.

They were right to assume they might be able to capture IRA men on the run, even some of the men who had taken part in the morning's shooting. Members of the Tipperary team had fought with British soldiers on board their train to Dublin the previous day. Two players, Mick Hogan and Tommy Ryan, heard that a major operation was planned for the following morning. That evening, Tommy Ryan helped to carry revolvers and ammunition to a hotel for collection by one of the assassination teams in the morning. There was some discussion among officers of the Dublin Brigade of the IRA about calling off the game but thousands of people had already bought tickets and were on their way into Croke Park by two o'clock.

The match got under way just before 3 p.m., the Dublin team in sky-blue jerseys, Tipperary in green and white. After ten minutes of play, an aeroplane flew over the ground and fired a red flare. Tipperary was on the attack when a Dublin player was penalised for a foul. Tommy Ryan was about to take the free kick when he heard a burst of machine-gun and rifle fire. Spectators began to run for cover and some players fled the pitch. Ryan, his teammate Mick Hogan and four of the Dublin players remembered their IRA training and threw themselves flat on the grass. Looking up, they could see sparks flying as bullets struck the wall at the railway end. People were rolling down the embankment as if they had been hit.

The firing appeared to be coming from the south-west corner of the ground at the canal end, from where policemen and Auxiliaries were running onto the field. Hundreds of spectators scaled a high wall to get away into the gardens of adjoining houses. An Auxiliary in plain clothes who had jumped over the turnstile ran through the crowd, chasing down young men and firing his revolver. The players lying on the field decided to make a run for the low fence surrounding the pitch. Mick Hogan fell, hit by a bullet. When Tommy Ryan reached him and tried to lift him up, blood was spurting from a wound in his back. His hands and jersey covered in blood, Ryan ran to the side line and jumped into the crowd. The Auxiliaries herded spectators into small clusters, ordered them to hold their hands up and searched them. Rifles and machine-guns were trained on them from the walls around the ground as they were searched. Players from both teams were lined up against the railway-embankment wall. The searches went on for more than an hour. Afterwards policemen who were present said that as their lorries pulled up outside the ground, several men standing there had sprinted towards the turnstiles, opening fire as they ran. But many witnesses – constables from the Dublin Metropolitan Police, a sports reporter covering the match and ex-British soldiers – testified that all the shooting had been unprovoked. A secret military inquiry later found that the security forces had fired 228 rounds from rifles and revolvers and at least 50 rounds from a machine-gun at one of the exits.

A member of the Dáil, Robert Brennan, was travelling into town from the north side on the open top deck of a tram when he saw crowds of people running away from Croke Park. Some of their faces were smeared with blood. Shoving and jostling they tried to board any passing tram. A sports writer who was an old friend of Brennan emerged at the top of the stairs to the top deck. The Black and Tans had driven into Croke Park and opened fire on the football crowd, he told Brennan. Players had been killed, along with many spectators.

At dusk that afternoon the journalists Joice Nankivell and Sydney Loch were also returning to the city after a day walking on Howth Head peninsula. The cold wind was making them shiver on the top deck. There was an ugly-looking crowd gathered at Nelson's Pillar in the city centre when the tram stopped. A military lorry passed with the boots of a dead man sticking out of the back and a murmur of anger rose from the people around them. Several more lorries and an armoured car drove by, turning down the quays towards the Castle. They could not make out what the newsboys were shouting as they darted among the crowd with bundles of the 'stop-press' edition of the paper under their arms. One passed close by and they bought the paper. It was covered in an enormous headline: 'BRITISH OFFICERS MURDERED IN BED'.

When they returned to their flat, the landlady came down the stairs as they closed the hall door. 'Have you heard the news?' she cried. 'Dreadful! Horrible! But I have no doubt they deserved it.'

'You don't approve of this?' they asked her.

'No, I don't approve of it. I don't approve of shooting at all; but you must remember how the Irish people are goaded.'

After tea they ventured outside. Rumours of the shootings at Croke Park were circulating but few people knew the details. The trams had stopped running and civilian motorists had been ordered not to take their cars out. Armoured cars and Crossley Tenders full of Black and Tans rolled through the streets.

Across the city, the wife of one of the British officers badly wounded that morning had taken refuge in an army barracks. She was anxious to visit her husband, who was being treated in a nursing home near their flat, but was afraid to make the journey by herself in a car full of soldiers. She asked Mrs Woodcock if she would come too. They climbed into the cab of an armoured lorry and as it drove along there seemed to be firing everywhere. The driver told them he was so angry about what had happened to their husbands and the other men shot in their pyjamas that he was ready to run someone over in the street. A soldier at the back fired on a car that failed to stop when challenged. It was driven by policemen, calling at hotels to collect survivors of the massacre who had been moved to the Castle. Mrs Woodcock saw some people falling to their knees on the pavement and putting their hands up as they drove past. 'I could feel no pity for them. I hated them.' Later in the evening, three prisoners being held by the Auxiliaries at Beggars Bush barracks – including Dick McKee, the commander of the Dublin Brigade of the IRA, who had been captured the previous night just after he had finished plans for the Bloody Sunday assassinations – were shot dead while allegedly attempting to escape.

Charlie Dalton couldn't get to sleep that night. He thought he could hear the noise he had heard in the moment of silence after they had shot the officers in the room on the third floor of 28 Pembroke Street – the burbling of blood rising in their throats. His friends reassured him that it was all in his imagination; there must be a tap running somewhere in the house. Finally, he fell asleep. Great crowds gathered along the quays the following Thursday to watch gun carriages carry the officers' coffins in a military procession to the ship that would take them across the Irish Sea. Rosamond Jacob's thought as she watched them was: 'Are there any more of your English dogs that you want to be slain?' She was furious at the men who meekly removed their hats as the cortège passed. Those who dared not to were noticed by the Black and Tans, who marched up roaring, 'Off with those hats.'

Fourteen officers were killed on Bloody Sunday; not all of them were intelligence agents but it has never been established definitively how many were in the secret service. In spite of the outrage in the newspaper headlines, the British government reacted in the hard-boiled style which had become the code for responding to the myriad threats all over the empire. 'Tragic as the events in Dublin were, they were of no importance,' was Lloyd George's view. 'These men were soldiers and took a soldier's risk.' Bloody Sunday appeared to curtail an ambitious effort to identify the most dangerous men in the IRA and eliminate them by arrest or assassination. The agents who survived or escaped were hidden away under guard, 'from where it was impracticable to do any useful work', as one agent put it. But the searches, roadblocks and curfews in the weeks following Bloody Sunday led to so many arrests that the prisons were overcrowded. The British had not given up hope that Ireland could be pacified.

13

Flying Columns

At midday on Tuesday, 25 January 1921, Mark Sturgis, a charming aristocratic official at Dublin Castle, arrived at the Four Courts on the banks of the River Liffey to watch the court martial of three men accused of killing an officer on Bloody Sunday. As his eyes wandered across the faces of the defendants in the dock he was surprised to find that one of them, Frank Teeling, who had been captured by the Auxiliaries in the back garden in Lower Mount Street, was 'not at all a bad looking type' but another was 'a miserable hang dog looking fellow'. None of them fully satisfied his idea of what a ruthless killer should look like. 'It's an amazing race,' Sturgis confided to his diary. 'None of the three looked capable of the cold blooded beastly murder of a defenceless man in bed.' After the court adjourned, Sturgis went down to the prosecution bench and picked up the revolver Teeling had used, savouring its 'good grip and balance'.

Such a cool appraisal of the weapon used to inflict the most notorious British casualties during the war in Ireland was typical of Sturgis's ironic detachment. He had arrived in Dublin the previous summer as one of a team of ultra-efficient civil servants from London sent to save the Castle regime from collapse. All of them were examples of the new breed of professional administrators who had thrived in the expansion of the state bureaucracy during the war. Young, liberal, pragmatic and convinced that they possessed more knowledge and better judgement than politicians, they mocked the post-war austerity regime being imposed on their colleagues in London, indulging themselves with fine hotels and first-class travel. John Anderson, from a middle-class background, had achieved first place in Britain in the civil-service entrance examinations and was running the national-insurance scheme. Andy Cope had been a customs-and-excise detective. Sturgis, an Old Etonian from a landed family, married to the daughter of an aristocrat, had worked as a special commissioner for income tax. Freed from the tedious detail of tax returns, he savoured the danger and intrigue attached to life as a British official in Ireland. He set off on car journeys into the countryside using a false name. At lunchtime he practised firing a Colt 45 revolver given to him by an officer who said it had belonged to Sean Treacy, who had been killed in a gun battle with British agents and Auxiliaries in October 1920. Inside Dublin Castle, surrounded by sandbags and barbed wire, he made light of the regular panics provoked by the sound of firing in the street and took sardonic pleasure in chronicling the competitive plotting and manoeuvring of his colleagues in the heightened atmosphere of an administration under siege. Sturgis joked about persuading the bureaucrats in London that the Crown's representatives lived like monks in the besieged castle. But he never missed an opportunity for hunting or going to the races and far from being bleak and solitary his evenings were often taken up with dinners and dances at the Viceregal Lodge, where the commander of British forces in Ireland, Nevil Macready, would recite 'Gunga Din', Kipling's poem about the travails of the British soldier in India.

Like a fan watching a football match, Sturgis followed the court martial of the Bloody Sunday assassins in a state of emotional excitement. Impressed by the bravery of a servant girl who had been at the scene of the shooting and with steady assurance refused the invitation of the defence team to doubt the certainty of her identification of the gunmen watching her from the dock, Sturgis made a mental note to make sure that she would not come to harm. What most pleased him was his impression that the defence lawyers were amazed by how much the prosecution knew about the workings of the IRA. Then, just as it seemed the trial was going well, the momentum of the Crown case was undermined by incompetence: instead of waiting outside the courtroom door to take his place on the stand, their star witness, an officer who had pretended to be dead after the shooting started, was discovered to be at some unknown location in England. And, on Thursday, 27 January, the court martial of another four Bloody Sunday defendants was adjourned owing to procedural errors by the prosecution. 'Wonder what the next hitch will be,' Sturgis remarked acidly.

This combination of hope and frustration summed up the British effort to hold Ireland. Taking advantage of the extra powers given to them by the Restoration of Order in Ireland Act passed in 1920, the military had responded to Bloody Sunday with a massive sweep of arrests and searches. Then, a week later, seventeen Auxiliaries were killed in an ambush near the village of Kilmichael in west Cork. Planned and led by Tom Barry, it became the most celebrated IRA operation of the war (and, many years later, the most controversial because of allegations that Barry had concocted a story about survivors of the initial assault opening fire after pretending to surrender, which justified their immediate execution). Another successful ambush on 11 December in Cork city provoked the Auxiliaries from 'K' company to embark on a drink-fuelled orgy of burning and looting in the main commercial district that destroyed City Hall and the Carnegie Library, as well as many of the city's major shops. In the following weeks hundreds of people were arrested and sent to internment camps in the north, on naval stations at Spike Island and Bere Island in the south and at the British military base in the Curragh. In rural areas soldiers would set out on foot at dawn, encircling a wide area of countryside and searching farmhouses and cottages as they converged to trap IRA Volunteers. In the cities raids and house searches became more frequent and intense. Officials of the underground government were surprised in their anonymous offices, yielding valuable caches of documents and memos revealing that Michael Collins had spies in Dublin Castle. Planes were sent to fly low over farmland and photograph suspected sites of weapons dumps. To counter ambushes on the ground, the number of lorries available for carrying troops was doubled and they travelled in much bigger convoys protected by armoured cars. The new spy chief, Colonel Ormonde Winter, was given a £10,000 budget to recruit informers. He sent intelligence officers to establish themselves in nine towns and cities and share the information gathered by their agents with the army and the police. There even seemed to be signs that people were prepared to help the authorities.

The final hope for turning around the war in Ireland was the introduction of martial law in the counties in the south where the IRA was most active. It was an admission that they were dealing with a revolt and not a crime spree, but they hoped that the lawful discharge of harsh justice would be both effective and more justifiable than random shooting and burning. By the beginning of 1921 all of Munster was under military rule. Any gathering of more than six people was forbidden; even loitering could provoke immediate arrest. Cars could not travel at night or for more than twenty miles from where they were registered. Bicycles were forbidden in a martial-law area. Households were forced to have a list of occupants inside the door ready for inspection by any military patrol. The first proclamation issued under the new dispensation was that all guns and rifles be handed over. Anyone found in possession of a firearm would be brought before a court martial of three British officers, who had the power to impose the death penalty. The first IRA Volunteer sentenced to death for carrying a gun, Con Murphy, was executed four weeks after his arrest. Reprisals, so often denied or disowned, now had official sanction. When the IRA carried out an ambush in the martial-law area, the local brigadier was empowered to destroy the property of anybody he considered implicated 'owing to their proximity to the outrage or their known political tendencies'. Lorry loads of troops would draw up outside a farmhouse chosen for demolition and family members were given an hour to remove what they could (except furniture) before standing and watching as their house was blown up. In towns and villages where a terraced house was selected for reprisal, tables, chairs and dressers were piled up in the street and burned. As well as these spectacles of licensed retaliation, repeated more than thirty times a month, being a deterrent to aiding and abetting the IRA, British officers hoped that they would restore discipline by sating the nervous anger of the British forces in Ireland. But like the despairing Mark Sturgis, the officers running the British campaign were frustrated. The prized notion that the military would now make all the decisions proved elusive. Martial law applied to only a portion of the country; Dublin, the site of constant IRA activity, was still excluded. The military courts were not the ultimate arbiters of the fate of captured IRA men. Death sentences were still subject to challenge in the courts, judged by the scruples of lawyers rather than the brutal efficiency of soldiers.

For all its frustrations, the more aggressive British approach building since the late summer of 1920 succeeded in putting real pressure on the IRA, not least in widening the gulf that already existed between the most committed gunmen and the part-time Volunteer, between the men who would shoot a policeman on his way to church and those whose most vivid experience of the struggle was blocking a road while an abandoned police barracks was burned down in the middle of the night. Many local companies were led by officers for whom military operations were a pastime, necessarily taking second place to milking cows or working in an office. Young men who entertained ideas of fighting for Ireland's freedom could still be browbeaten by their fearful parents. One Volunteer recalled knocking on the window of a friend late at night to bring him off on an operation and being suddenly confronted by his enraged mother. 'Wait till I meet your mother, calling people out of their beds to commit murder and get killed yourselves. Well if you have nothing else to do Martin has. Clear off.' Others were still too respectful of their neighbours and dissuaded by a strong rebuke. The Anglo-Irish writer Hubert Butler remembered his mother being furious with two men who arrived at their doorstep asking for money for the republican cause. 'I know who you are,' she barked at one of them. 'Take your cigarette out of your mouth when you're talking to me.' The would-be guerrilla obligingly removed the cigarette and the men slunk away.

In the new, more oppressive environment the dedicated fighters now had to leave their homes to evade capture, forced into adopting the lifestyle that Dan Breen had pioneered. It was much more dangerous to be a man 'on the run' but all the more exhilarating because it meant casting aside the constraints of demanding parents or the oppressive conformity of small-town life. Instead of taking orders from mother or being measured by the opinion of their respectable betters, the fugitives now kept company with their exalted peers and were judged on whether they were daring, courageous and tough. They went from house to house eating well for nothing, attracting the admiring solicitude of those who sympathised with the cause and the cowed deference of the scandalised or indifferent. If this scattering of their toughest and most skilled fighters was not to dissipate the struggle, the strategists at IRA headquarters needed to figure out how best to make use of them.

The idea of flying columns gradually emerged: disciplined bands of professional guerrilla fighters who roamed the countryside preparing themselves to launch carefully planned ambushes and sabotage operations. A flying column could vary from ten to a hundred men who camped in woods or derelict farmhouses, rising early to practise tactical formations, drills and intensive exercise to keep them fit for their long, gruelling night marches across the fields so as to avoid the main roads. Like any elite force, durability and stamina were prized and some dropped out because the physical exertion was too severe. Local Volunteers, unwilling or unfit for the demands of the flying columns, were now reduced to acting as their support staff, guiding them through unknown terrain, helping to organise food deliveries to encampments, acting as scouts and guarding them from surprise attack at night.

The flying column developed as a self-chosen band of brothers. One officer told the men in his company that there was nothing to be gained from joining the column but an early death and no man would be looked down on for deciding against it. He scraped a line along the ground and asked volunteers for the column to step over it. Crossing the line meant privilege and prestige as well as danger and hardship. Their less adventurous comrades would pay a levy to support the column. Clothing and boots were supplied by drapers and shopkeepers. Days of privation would be leavened by feasting on sheep or cattle bought or commandeered from local farmers. 'The sky looks good' was their private in-joke when stepping into a safe house with enticing sides of bacon dangling from the rafters.

Ernie O'Malley depicted a relaxed but respectfully distant relationship between the itinerant fighters and their hosts. 'After night-fall the neighbours came in one by one for a chat around the fire. The latch door rattled, a voice would say "God save!" and there was an answering chorus of "God save you!" from the fire. They talked of the day's news; most of them now had read the daily paper. They passed comments on the fighting, as reported, and talked of rumours and stray bits of information they had gathered at the creamery or in Tipp. They discussed foreign politics in detail and their judgements were shrewd enough. If they were in a difficulty about geography or history someone would say "ask himself". That meant me.'

Hospitality meant music and dancing as well as bed and board, these self-possessed, weather-beaten young men dipping into laughter and flirtation but all the time conscious of their status as being one of 'the boys'. The formation of the columns was another stage in the continuous process by which the most dedicated Volunteers took control of the movement. The initiative passed from cautious, hesitant amateurs bound closely to their neighbours to men for whom revolution was a vocation and whose compass was set by other revolutionaries exalted beyond mundane concerns. For Tom Barry these men represented 'the highest expression of our Nationhood, the Flying Column of the Army of the People'. They never numbered more than about two thousand men and although they carried out some spectacular ambushes, they spent most of their time evading capture or blowing up roads and bridges. One successful attack such as Kilmichael would make a significant public and psychological impact but the response – more Crown forces in the area, intense searches and raids – was likely to curtail any more operations for months. It was the very existence of the flying columns that was the major threat.

In 1921 the war in Ireland crystallised into a ferocious contest between the flying columns and British troops. In the spring of that year the British deployed their own flying columns, who would camp out, carrying their own field kitchens and travelling by bicycle at night. As British intelligence improved they were able to identify individual IRA men and their families for arrest and harsh treatment. Stories circulated of men who were pistol-whipped in prison, stripped naked and doused with cold water, had pins shoved into their flesh, their teeth pulled with pliers or were subjected to mock execution. The British began to carry IRA hostages on their convoys. A public notice posted in Fermoy on 1 January 1921 by the local brigadier general proclaimed that 'all motor lorries and vehicles in this area carrying His Majesty's troops will also carry one or more officers or leaders of the so-called "Irish Republican Army"'. IRA units were reluctant to attack convoys carrying their own men. Sean Moylan, an IRA commander, described waiting to ambush a British patrol in Cork:

'We soon heard the sound of approaching lorries [then] immediately they were in sight. They were crowded with men in civilian dress and these seemed to outnumber the soldiers they carried . . . Had there been no hostages there would have been slaughter . . . Where I lay half a dozen British Tommies were five yards away . . . Yet I could not blow the whistle. I could not condemn those unarmed, handcuffed men to death that would surely be theirs if the fight started.' Ernie O'Malley recalled: 'A bitterness and ferocity came from . . . extravagant killing or torturing by the British. I cursed blindly for hours when I heard that a man in East Limerick had been tied behind a lorry and dragged until the life burst from him, and when I read a Kilkenny report of a hostage during a fight being made to stand up whilst a Lewis gun resting on his shoulder sprayed a column of our men. Such happenings relit old race hatred, but it would die down again. I could see it work in the men. They faced their task squarely. They were fighting ruthlessness and they did not want to give mercy.'

As the official reprisals targeted the homes occupied by the families of men in flying columns, the IRA retaliated by burning down the mansions of the Protestant gentry. Almost forty Big Houses were destroyed between April and July 1921, most of them in County Cork. Leaders of the IRA's Southern Division sought permission from General Headquarters in Dublin to destroy the property of 'active enemies' but did not wait for approval before local units began identifying landed families as hostile civilians. IRA men who broke into the early-nineteenth-century house of the Third Earl of Listowel waited for his niece to come downstairs, then handed her a notice from their commander addressed to her elderly absent uncle: 'You being an aggressively anti-Irish person, and your residence being in the battalion area of enemy reprisals, I have hereby ordered that [the] same be destroyed as part of our counter-reprisals.' All rooms but the servants' quarters were gutted and the earl's antique furniture and art collection was reduced to ashes. Following the demolition by the British army of four houses in Cork in May, armed and masked men entered the residence of a well-known unionist businessman in the middle of the night, forced him and his family to dress, locked them in the stables with their servants, and then marched from room to room splashing petrol and paraffin on carpets and furniture. When the family was released two hours later they saw 'their home . . . burning furiously in all parts'. Before the flames consumed the hall door they were able to make out a card fixed to it announcing that the fire was a reprisal for the destruction of the four houses in Cork. Worried by the sectarian connotations of this selective arson the official endorsement of the tactic issued in June carefully advised that 'no persons shall be regarded as enemies of Ireland, whether they may be described locally as Unionist[s], Orangemen, etc., unless they are actively anti-Irish in their actions'. IRA leaders in Cork had calculated that the sheer audacity of destroying some of the finest country houses in Ireland would shock British commanders into curtailing reprisals. Instead they promised to set fire to three 'Sinn Féin dwellings' for every two loyalist houses destroyed and to increase the ratio if the arson attacks continued.

Avoiding being singled out for attack by steering clear of politics was no longer a guarantee of escaping the violence. The chances of being caught up in ferocious exchanges between the IRA and the British military while going about your daily business increased in 1921. After road convoys were strengthened by adding more and better-protected lorries, IRA units switched their attention to soldiers travelling on trains. To deter ambushes soldiers were ordered not to sit together but to spread themselves among the other passengers. In April fifty IRA men seized Upton station about fifteen miles south-west of Cork and took positions at each side of the line to await the arrival at 10.30 of a passenger train travelling from Cork to Bandon with forty soldiers on board. When the soldiers engaged the attackers, passengers threw themselves on the floors of the carriages as hails of bullets shattered the windows and doors. When the firing stopped only one soldier and one IRA man had been killed but six civilians lay dead in the train compartments, three of them commercial travellers on their way to appointments to sell tea and shoes. Two women were among the wounded, as well as a ticket collector and a signalman working at the station. For civilians the war was 'like a fever chart, away up today, smooth enough tomorrow, blazing here, happily quiet there, every day unpredictable . . .' Motorists and cyclists ran the risk of coming across an ambush, colliding with a military vehicle or crashing into deep trenches recently gouged in the roadway. Trees by the roadside could be obstacles just removed by the military or material for a barricade that would be erected during the night. The writer Wilfrid Ewart came across a barrier consisting of four heavy beech trunks covered with branches and boughs at a point where the road curved round the flank of a hill and was shaded by trees. It was not dissimilar, he thought, to a Grand National fence at Aintree, though far more substantial. At any moment lorry loads of Auxiliaries, shouting and singing, might come careering around a bend, exulting in their speed and the roar of revving engines. They fired shots to scare horses or over the heads of children bathing in a river. In June 1921 a crowd of people outside a rural pub started to run when they saw a military vehicle approaching. The soldiers called on them to halt; some did but others kept running. From the back of the lorry the troops opened fire and a sixty-year-old farmer fell dead by the roadside. It was not just that they were trigger-happy. Any occupants of a military vehicle had to be prepared for a sudden ambush. After being arrested while snooping around a police barracks in Mallow, Wilfrid Ewart was driven through the Cork countryside at sunset in an army tender, with a party of soldiers following behind. At every corner the young officer sitting beside Ewart tightened his grip on his revolver and looked back to make sure that the lorry full of soldiers was keeping its distance. When the little convoy passed civilians on the roadside, women and children gathering flowers, the soldiers raised their rifles.

A dramatic incident could intrude on the quietest moments. One Sunday, Emily Horsley Ussher and her family were sitting down to lunch when they heard a succession of fifteen to twenty-five shots. The servants, who had just returned from Mass, crept down the driveway and saw three lorry loads of soldiers at the crossroads. A man dashed through their neighbour's house and then ran across their turnip field, leaving behind a trail of blood sprinkled on the stalks. When he vaulted the hedge he turned and emptied his revolver at the soldiers pursuing him. They threw themselves flat in the field and he got away. After this incident their neighbour, Mrs Clancy, lived in fear that the police or soldiers might suddenly return. For days she would refuse to get out of bed. Not long afterwards she died. 'This kind of casualty is often overlooked', Emily Horsley Ussher noted in her diary, 'by those who arrange periods of kidnapping, shooting and sorrow.'

In Dublin tossing improvised grenades into military trucks as they passed through busy streets became such a popular tactic in 1921 that the lorries were covered in cages of wire netting. Sudden explosions provoked stampedes of pedestrians. Walking across O'Connell Bridge one Saturday afternoon with his girlfriend, Denis Johnston 'got mixed up in one of the daily shooting affrays. A lorry of Black and Tans just down Eden Quay were blazing away at something and others were shooting in Abbey St. I never saw a street clear quicker in all my born days. I wouldn't have minded it so much if it hadn't been for Olive – who was merely calmly interested throughout – and we went up the steps of the Picture House and tried to get in . . . but a mob . . . inside . . . had just barred the door so we stood on the sidewalk a few minutes – the sole solitary figures in the street watching the Back and Tans charge round and then we walked on and into La Scala.'

The new British measures were deliberately intended to shrink the space for ambivalence, although making it difficult to stay neutral risked alienating waverers. Many who disapproved of the IRA were so appalled by the Black and Tans that they ended up hostile towards the security forces rather than supportive of them. But the policy of official reprisals did impose a real cost for showing sympathy for 'the boys' or merely toleration of their activities or even being acquainted with them. The presence of a flying column could expose a whole district to military reprisals. When two IRA officers in County Clare went to live in a secret dugout they had prepared in a field for emergencies after their houses were blown up, they found it had been destroyed by previously friendly local people in a panic that their complicity might lead to their own homes being destroyed by the military. Men hurried to drink their tea in houses where they had previously been entertained lavishly but where now they were unwanted, an atmosphere of guilty fear that stopped just short of hostility.

The more ruthless IRA leaders lost patience with people not prepared to suffer for the cause. They were exasperated by civilians who allowed themselves to be dragooned by the military into repairing roads. The same people were often forced to dig trenches by the IRA and later ordered to fill them in by the army. Some people went to the police because they were repeatedly inconvenienced by sabotage of roads or railway lines. In March 1921 an officer of a flying column became so frustrated by the lack of cooperation from people in south Galway, where he was preparing an ambush that he rounded up everybody passing the road and held them as prisoners in the gate lodge of a nearby landed estate. He concluded that there was a need for 'a wholesale wiping out policy for people associating with the enemy'. Depending on the locality, support for the IRA could vary from being very strong to practically non-existent. Town dwellers in particular were suspected of being soft on the cause. One IRA man said Wicklow town would never be any good until they burned it and blamed it on the Tans. In Tipperary, Sean Treacy had advised a colleague to 'deport all in favour of the enemy'.

As the war became more polarised and deadly, acts of opposition to the IRA might have fatal consequences. Giving away an ambush position or a hideout could result in a flying column being wiped out by a swift counterstrike. The most notorious case was Mrs Mary Lindsay, a Protestant widow who noticed an IRA party preparing an ambush in Cork in January 1921 and informed the police. The ambush party was surrounded by British troops, who killed two men and captured five others who were executed after a court martial. Mrs Lindsay and her chauffeur were kidnapped and later killed. A general order sanctioning the execution of informers had been issued in April 1920. But suspected spies were not always shot. Some were tied up, some were told to leave the area and not come back. For informing the RIC about a barricade on the road a man could be fined £50. An old woman in Sligo was taken from her bed, forced to walk two miles and then tied to a telegraph pole on which was pinned a notice, 'Long tongues beware.' Women who took up with soldiers immediately raised suspicion but they were also a public affront to the IRA's view of national honour. A woman followed by IRA men after she was suspected of passing information to the authorities was discovered to be meeting a soldier in a field favoured by courting couples. The soldier was beaten up and the young woman's plaits were snipped with sheep shears; she was told to go home to her mother. Regular raids on mail trains and post offices or the robbery of a postman's bag were often the trigger for executions after letters were read by the IRA. Many who passed on information thought that committing it to print in a sealed envelope was sufficient for discretion. People who came under suspicion as informers were often passed details about fictional IRA activity so that if the Crown forces acted on it, this would prove their guilt.

It was after Bloody Sunday that the fear of spies, real and imagined, escalated. Seventy-three bodies were recovered with placards attached identifying the victim as 'Traitor – Shot by the IRA' in the first four months of 1921. In theory no suspect could be condemned without approval from headquarters but in the last months of the war even junior officers were making life-and-death decisions often on the basis of very little evidence. There were real British agents scouring the country to identify IRA men, and when they were discovered they were dealt with brutally. Two British officers on leave and in civilian clothes disappeared while travelling on a motorcycle and sidecar from Fermoy to Killarney. Another intelligence officer last seen riding his motorcycle was found dead in a field, blindfolded and shot several times. Agents posed as commercial travellers or members of the IRA. Some had a less than firm grasp of spycraft. One British intelligence officer disguised himself as the humble owner of a donkey and cart as he went about seeking information in an English accent. He never captured a Sinn Féiner of any importance but he feared afterwards that his inexperience might have led others who dealt with him to their deaths. There were IRA men who claimed they could identify British agents by their walk and demeanour. Martin Corry, an IRA commander in Cork who later enjoyed a long career as a member of parliament, said he once shot a tramp whose cigarette case and monogrammed silk underwear revealed his true identity.

In these circumstances it was easy to see how ex-soldiers, former policemen, eccentrics and down-and-outs fell under suspicion. In spring of 1921 East Clare Brigade ordered: 'All strangers walking or cycling through any part of the Brigade must be placed under arrest and held until they can prove who and what they are satisfactorily.' One Tipperary Volunteer remembered an order to treat all beggars as spies. In Offaly a man who attracted suspicion by going into houses for a glass of milk was taken away and killed after a priest heard his confession. A middle-aged Protestant woman who scraped a living making the illegal spirit poteen went to the police to denounce her competitors. She was later found dead by the roadside, covered with a card warning 'Spies and Informers Beware. Tried convicted and executed by the IRA.' She had shared a small cabin on a few acres by a mountainside with her senile parents and disabled brother. A local IRA man dismissed her as 'scarcely normal and not sufficiently

1 Boarding up a window broken by the Black and Tans in Templemore, County Tipperary.

2 Funeral of a police constable in Dublin. More than fifty policemen had been killed by the IRA by the summer of 1920 when ex-servicemen began to arrive in large numbers to reinforce the RIC.

3 and 4 A car is searched on a country road and a man leads his horse and jaunting car over a temporarily repaired road. 'The Troubles were like a fever chart,' Seán Ó Faoláin wrote, 'away up today, smooth enough tomorrow, blazing here, happily quiet there, every day unpredictable . . .'

5 Citizen soldiers: military intelligence photograph of suspected IRA members taken at Bandon barracks, County Cork.

6 Auxiliaries and Black and Tans outside the London and North Western Hotel in Dublin after an attack by the IRA in April 1921. 'To hear them talk one would think this trouble was made especially to amuse them,' a regular soldier wrote.

7 Night-time view of the destruction caused by Auxiliaries and Black and Tans in the centre of Cork, December 1920. City Hall, the Carnegie Library and nearly sixty business premises were burned and looted.

8 The aftermath of an official reprisal in County Cork in January 1921. Collective punishment of people living close to the site of IRA attacks was also meant to curb impulsive acts of retaliation.

9 The remains of Harry Loughnane, one of two brothers tortured and burned by Auxiliaries in Galway in November 1920. The photograph was taken during their wake, held in a haybarn to escape detection.

10 The body of Private Fielding, a British soldier from the East Lancashire Regiment shot by the IRA in County Cork in April 1921 on suspicion of being an intelligence agent.

11 A republican prisoner being escorted by Free State troops during the civil war. Despite the bitterness of the split, there were also many former comrades in the independence struggle who were reluctant to fight each other.

12 Dublin's main thoroughfare after the street fighting at the beginning of the civil war, July 1922. Winston Churchill expressed admiration that the Provisional Government was prepared to destroy historic property worth millions of pounds to crush resistance to the Anglo-Irish Treaty.

13 General Richard Mulcahy being interviewed by Pathé News. 'Ireland was one of the world's sores,' wrote one of the many foreign correspondents who came to Dublin.

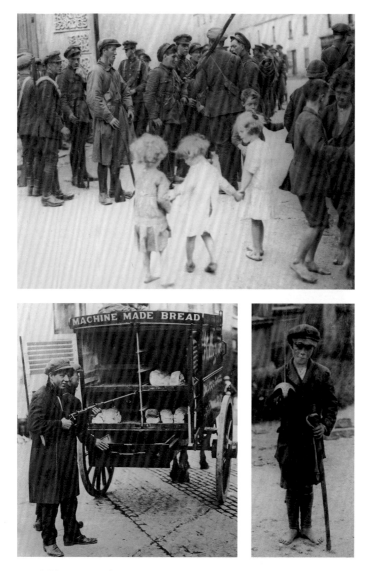

14 Children in a southern town. As Free State troops advanced in the summer of 1922 people became almost indifferent to seeing soldiers fill the streets.

15 Boys with rifles.

16 Displaying a sword plundered from a barracks in Cork.

17 Michael Collins arriving at the Pro-Cathedral in Dublin for the funeral service of Arthur Griffith.

intelligent to cloak her activities'. The loyalty of Protestants to British rule was taken as read, so they became more vulnerable as the conflict deepened, regardless of whether they had any valuable information for the police or how aloof they kept themselves. Even those bitterly opposed to the IRA dared not speak openly, even to those sympathetic to their isolation. Wilfrid Ewart's experience of calling at the house of a Protestant clergyman in Cork is telling:

> Two knocks and a long interval of waiting brought a maid-servant.
>
> 'What do you want?'
>
> 'Can I see Canon – ?'
>
> 'He's engaged.'
>
> ' – when he's disengaged.'
>
> Undisguisedly suspicious, she went to report to her master. Presently the Canon himself appeared.
>
> An unmistakable look came into his face when I asked if he could oblige me with his views on local conditions?
>
> 'My views! Impossible, my dear sir. Why it would be more than my life's worth. There's many a poor lad in these parts been laid under the sod for less than that.'
>
> 'Perhaps I haven't made myself clear? I'm –'
>
> 'I don't think you have.'
>
> The door slammed and there was an end of it.

Most informers were far more likely to be from the same community and even the same families as the IRA fighters. One man killed in Cork on suspicion of being a paid spy was the brother of a local IRA Volunteer. Without the local knowledge possessed by the RIC, the Black and Tans, Auxiliaries and regular troops had a particular need for guides and informants. Some cooperated out of conviction, others because they needed money or drink or because they were afraid or in some way vulnerable. Fear of spies and informers kindled a state of paranoia in some areas. Entire units of the IRA devoted most of their time to watching people they thought were spies or might turn into informers. In February 1921 seven civilians were shot dead by the IRA in Cork city, two of them prominent Protestant businessmen. The escalating rate of executions worried staff officers in General Headquarters in Dublin. They began to reinforce the rule that these decisions must have sanction from the top and demanded definite evidence for convictions.

One tactic for confirming suspicions about informers was for IRA men to disguise themselves as policemen or pass themselves off as intelligence agents to solicit information. Men in south Roscommon dressed like soldiers in order to draw out two men they later executed. This subterfuge worked because it was often difficult to tell whether a man in breeches and leggings with a leather bandolier and a slouch hat was an Auxiliary or a member of an IRA flying column. Many IRA fighters had stories about being mistaken for policemen in the middle of a firefight. The Black and Tans stole Volunteer uniforms for future use. Civilians could never be certain whom they were dealing with. As he led his men through a village in the hills one evening at twilight Ernie O'Malley noticed men and women scampering into their cabins. Through a half-open door they heard the cries of a frightened girl. 'They saw our tin hats – they think we're Tommies on a raiding party,' said one of O'Malley's men. The column began to sing an Irish marching song made famous in 1916. But the people were not reassured and the doors stayed closed.

On a Sunday evening in mid-April 1921 an RIC sergeant and two constables in County Clare with a few hours' free time decided to cycle across the county boundary to the Shannon Hotel in Castleconnell, a small village by the side of Ireland's biggest river. They changed out of their uniforms so that they would not present themselves as targets for an IRA ambush but brought their revolvers. Arriving safely at the hotel they parked their bicycles, went to the bar and ordered drinks. At eight o'clock an Auxiliary officer led fourteen of his men into the hotel and spoke to the receptionist. They were searching for any suspicious characters who might be lurking around the neighbourhood and wondered who owned the three bicycles leaning by the door. They were told these had been left by three strangers who had gone into the bar. The Auxiliaries marched into the bar with revolvers drawn and ordered the three men chatting to the proprietor to put their hands up. Believing they were about to be shot by the IRA the three policemen pulled out their revolvers and opened fire. A ferocious gunfight erupted. The sergeant, one of his constables, an Auxiliary and the proprietor of the hotel were all dead before either side realised whom they were fighting. In Britain the story of this extraordinary affray provided further evidence to the government's critics that the war in Ireland was a disaster.

14
Frightfulness

Early one damp morning in December 1920, a tall handsome young Englishman, a veteran of the Battle of the Somme, stepped off the mailboat at Kingstown harbour and took the train into the centre of Dublin. George Mallory taught English and History at Charterhouse public school in Sussex; he was also, at the age of thirty-four, one of the best-known English mountaineers of his day. He had already scaled Mont Blanc and would soon be invited to take part in the first attempt to climb Mount Everest. Mallory was a representative figure of his age. A graduate of Oxford, a friend of the Bloomsbury set, his war experiences had prompted him to renounce the values of his class. 'I want to lose all harshness of jagged nerves, to be above all gentle,' he wrote to his wife the day after the armistice. 'I feel we have achieved victory for that almost more than anything – to be able to cultivate gentleness.' He became a supporter of the Labour Party, and, after scaling Everest, planned a future as a social evangeliser, maybe even as an MP. As his schoolfriend Robert Graves recounted in *Goodbye to All That*, George Mallory had 'tired of trying to teach gentlemen to be gentlemen'.

In the summer of 1920 he had written to Gilbert Murray, Regius Professor of Greek at Oxford University, one of the most renowned liberal intellectuals in Britain and a leading figure in the League of Nations Union, explaining that the war had convinced him of the need to develop a sense of world citizenship: 'Perhaps the most important thing about me I ought to tell you is that I think and feel passionately about international politics.' Mallory asked Murray if there was any work he could do to further the aims of the League of Nations Union. It is likely that Mallory's journey to Dublin during his Christmas vacation was prompted by a request from Murray to provide him with a personal account of what had become known in British liberal circles as 'the terror in Ireland'. Making contact with Conor O'Brien, a fellow climber and yachtsman who had helped to land guns for the Irish Volunteers in 1914, Mallory arranged an introduction to Desmond Fitzgerald, the director of publicity for Dáil Éireann. On the back of a photograph of Mallory presented to him Fitzgerald wrote, 'Mr G. Mallory is anxious to have first-hand information as to acts of oppression and terror. I shall be glad if he can be assisted.'

Dublin was calm when he arrived that Sunday but Mallory soon found the atmosphere intolerable. At lunch in a restaurant he was spooked by the lack of chatter at the tables around him. 'I often felt there was but one subject to be talked about, and in public no one dared to talk about it.' He made sure to conceal his letters and notes before leaving his room, kept his hands out of his pockets as he walked about the city, and curbed his inclination to run for fear that he might appear to be somebody attempting to escape. One night he was awoken at 1.30 a.m. by a visitor with a flashlight in one hand and a revolver in the other. 'Who are you? What's your name? Where were you born? Are you a Protestant?' Mallory replied that his father was a Church of England clergyman and his interrogator withdrew without searching the room. He was taken into the countryside, where he met the families of dead republicans and heard stories of summary executions by the Black and Tans. Although he was fully aware that violence was not the preserve of one side, he identified a crucial difference between the Crown forces and the IRA. 'There has been wrong on both sides,' Mallory wrote of his visit, 'but national aspirations, a passionate idealism, are to be found only on one side. It is to this fact that Irishmen appeal when they exclaim "If only people in England knew! If only they would come and see!" They believe in the truth of their idealism. But how are they to project a message from this spirit to penetrate English apathy?'

In fact, Mallory's presence in Dublin was in itself an illustration that, far from being ignored, the Irish conflict now attracted world attention. Nothing illustrated how much Ireland's troubles had become a global issue than the attention commanded by the slow death by hunger strike of the Lord Mayor of Cork and IRA commandant, Terence MacSwiney, in Brixton Prison in London. Shortly before MacSwiney died on 25 October 1920, after refusing food for 74 days, Marcel Proust dismissed a visitor eager to discuss the latest instalment of *Remembrance of Things Past*. 'Don't speak to me about *Le Côté de Guermantes*', Proust interjected brusquely, 'but about the Lord Mayor of Cork, that will be very interesting.' The great French novelist was not alone in his fascination with MacSwiney's self-sacrifice in pursuit of an idea. 'You could not see the face of that man in his coffin, looking like the face of a starved child of 10, without feeling the most awful moral wrong had been done,' a friend of Lady Gregory had written to her after MacSwiney's funeral procession through London.

It was not as if hunger strikes were a novelty in the news columns. Workers in Berlin had stopped eating towards the end of the war to protest against food shortages. In 1919 a hunger strike by sixty-eight communists interned on Ellis Island collapsed in the face of an indifferent public and they gratefully seized prunes and bread coated in ersatz butter from the hands of prison guards. And in August 1920, at the same time as Terence MacSwiney had started to refuse food in Brixton, a black prisoner in Pennsylvania serving seven years for robbery and attempted murder died after 43 days without eating. None of these protests succeeded in provoking sympathy and compassion to equal MacSwiney's because they remained snippets of news, marooned in their own inconsequence, lacking a compelling narrative of struggle and suffering. For Virginia Woolf, MacSwiney's ordeal, his 'shriek of agony' was enthralling because it was daily retold with all the detail of a great novel.

For this achievement the Irish revolutionaries owed a debt to British suffragists. They had adopted the hunger strike as a tactic of defiance from the Russian revolutionaries in Siberian prisons, whose plight had aroused British liberals to campaign against the brutality of the tsar. When the British government decided to force feed the women rather than let them die in prison, the suffragists publicised the brutality of the procedure: women pinned down by warders while doctors shoved fifty centimetres of plastic tube through their nostrils. They hit on a new genre of prison literature, a day-by-day account of suffering and endurance, each scene all the more vivid for being rendered in prose stripped of emotion and all the more sinister because doctors were supposedly the epitome of a benign state increasingly identified with public welfare.

There was no better protagonist for a story of endurance and suffering than Terence MacSwiney. On his election as Lord Mayor of Cork he had told his fellow councillors that 'it is not they who can inflict most but they who can suffer most can conquer . . . Those whose faith is strong will endure to the end and triumph.' Arrested while presiding over an IRA meeting in the city hall, he was convicted by a court martial of possession of a secret police telegram. Sentenced to two years' hard labour, MacSwiney was transferred to Brixton Prison on 18 August and shortly afterwards was admitted to the prison hospital. Despite advice from the medical officer that MacSwiney was a personality who would not fit the government's efforts to portray Irish revolutionaries as mere criminals, the home secretary decided to make him an example of the government's resolve and refused to consider any solution that would involve letting him go. Nobody had expected that a hunger strike could last so long. Details of the agony of his final decline and approaching death were released each day to the press. He entered a stage of delirium and screaming; his body had to be constantly turned to prevent bedsores. He was given morphine, milk and dextrose to prolong his life. Accounts of the distress MacSwiney was prepared to endure to establish the principle that he should be treated as a political prisoner and not a criminal were no longer just directed at the British government. They appealed to a new and influential humanitarian strain of public opinion around the world. By the time many people heard of Mac-Swiney, they might well have forgotten the precise purpose of his hunger strike but they were captivated by the idea of a Christ-like martyr for idealism. As his brother Peter Mac-Swiney insisted, 'He is dying to bring all these atrocities before the people of the world.' MacSwiney's journey from Brixton to the train at Euston station that would take his coffin to the ferry for Ireland was carefully prepared; paper handkerchiefs imprinted with the programme of events were distributed to the public. The funeral procession drew huge crowds onto the streets of central London. Along the route green, white and orange Sinn Féin flags were draped from high windows. Hawkers sold mourning cards and republican rosettes to the people lining the streets. Foreign correspondents were astonished at how the city was awash with the flags and uniforms of a guerrilla army at war with Britain and how the public treated the whole demonstration with respect.

Many of these journalists were already avid readers of the *Irish Bulletin*, the stencilled news-sheet of the revolutionary movement that circulated among politicians and diplomats in London and European capitals. Largely written in the restrained, neutral tone of the news itself, the *Bulletin* offered a readily usable catalogue of arrests and shootings by the British forces in Ireland. Its coverage also prompted journalists to go to Ireland in search of the same experiences George Mallory sought. They were assisted by a revolutionary publicity operation that devoted the same care to dealing with potentially sympathetic correspondents as it did to the scripting of MacSwiney's sacrificial death. Visitors wanting an explanation of the causes of Irish disaffection were directed to meet captivating personalities who belied the British stereotype of the Irish revolutionaries as a savage murder gang.

An American journalist arriving for an appointment with Maud Gonne MacBride at her house overlooking St Stephen's Green in the centre of Dublin was immediately awed by the modernity of the brilliant wall colouring and the sense of superior taste conveyed by the Japanese screens and figurines of ancient curved madonnas. Then she caught sight of Yeats's muse, once renowned as the most beautiful woman in Europe. Tall and slim in the black gown signifying her deep state of mourning for her husband, John MacBride, who was executed in 1916, her widow's bonnet made her look like a Red Cross worker. She approached her visitor, trailed by two enormous Airedale terriers bounding up the hallway. Maud Gonne bent down to take the head of one of the dogs in her hands. 'They won't let anyone arrest me again, will they?' Her seventeen-year-old son Seán entered breathlessly with the news that troops had surrounded the Mansion House, where Dáil Éireann was about to receive the Irish American delegation that had arrived from the peace conference in Paris. Accompanied by the visiting British suffragist Sylvia Pankhurst they raced across St Stephen's Green and pushed their way through a double line of soldiers and policemen blocking entry to Dawson Street with bayonets and batons. 'Wars for democracy and small nations!' Seán MacBride sneered at the military cordon. 'And that's the only way they can keep us in the British Empire – brute force. Nice exhibition for the American journalists in town.' Regarding the crowd that had gathered in the street, Sylvia Pankhurst, from atop a low wall, with a puzzled frown, demanded to know why everybody was smiling; suffragists would be driven to fury by such oppression. 'You forget. We're very used to this,' replied Seán MacBride, affecting an air of tolerant forbearance beyond his years. The crowd sang 'The Soldiers' Song' and shouted 'Up the Americans!' as the car carrying the delegates arrived flying the tricolour and the stars and stripes.

Another famous figure, Countess Markievicz, the first woman elected to the House of Commons, appeared in a green tweed suit rubbing her hands in glee: 'Excellent propaganda! Excellent propaganda!' After a brief, friendly exchange between the police chief and the Americans, the soldiers and policemen withdrew and the delegates' car drove towards the Mansion House. In the reception room the

American delegates were 'filled with boyish glee' by their triumph. 'Look! Out there by the portrait of Queen Victoria,' their leader exclaimed, pointing to a cluster of Sinn Féin leaders, 'see that man in a green uniform. That's Michael Collins of the Irish Volunteers and minister of finance of the Irish Republic. The very man they're after.' Many visiting journalists stayed in the Shelbourne Hotel overlooking St Stephen's Green, a Dublin landmark and the apogee of Anglo-Irish style. In 1916 British troops had smuggled a machine-gun onto the roof to fire on rebels who had massed in the Green and during the week-long siege guests slept in corridors and tore up bed linen to bandage the wounded. Relishing its central role in history, within walking distance of most of the city's great public buildings and the shops it boasted were the equal of those of London or Paris, the Shelbourne delighted in combining traditional hospitality with the most advanced modern conveniences. The table d'hôte dinner was offered at 6.30 p.m. to accommodate those planning to catch the mail train to Euston at 7.45 from Westland Row around the cor-ner. Journalists had only to walk a minute to reach a telegraph office that stayed open until 8 p.m., and could avail them-selves of an on-site barbershop, cigar kiosk and bookstall when their despatches had been safely wired. Sauntering across the lobby they might encounter an official from Dublin Castle on his way to dinner with a colonel or request a light from a spy newly arrived from London. (The Squad had once made detailed plans to kidnap a British agent from the foyer of the Shelbourne; these were abandoned at the last minute before Bloody Sunday.) Other journalists might be rushing down the stairs to meet a courier sent by Eamon de Valera to drive them to a safe house for an interview with the fugitive president of the Republic. On at least one occasion, Michael

Collins himself had seen a journalist home to the door of the Shelbourne before riding off on his bicycle.

The revolutionaries relied on a network of sympathetic interpreters, eloquent explainers of Ireland's history and her cause. One of the favourite haunts of visiting journalists was the weekly Sunday-night soirée hosted by George Russell, the painter and mystic, universally known by his pen name 'Æ', who was editor of the journal of the Irish co-operative movement, the *Irish Homestead*. With his enormous head, brown beard and clear blue eyes, he embodied the mystical authority of a theosophist with a practical programme for creating a new, efficient Ireland driven by self-help and competent citizenship. Waving his pipe to emphasise his arguments, he held forth in the back room of his red-brick house while his guests sat on the floor and his wife passed around tea and scones. To Wilfrid Ewart he was 'the incarnation of an Irish bard' as he sat in front of the fire wearing a tie the colour of shamrock. The rank and file of the IRA, Russell explained to his guests, were 'inspired by a mystical passion of nationality', but if the government would declare a truce and offered Sinn Féin the same rights as Canada or Australia, the whole Sinn Féin movement might reconsider its demand for outright separation. How, Ewart wanted to know, could he account for the psychology of men prepared to kill their opponents in cold blood as on Bloody Sunday? 'Personally I am not in favour of violence,' Russell replied. 'But you fought in the war, didn't you? Well, the IRA men consider themselves to be fighting for their country's integrity and freedom just as much as you did during the war with Germany. As to the murders, you must have seen Germans shot in cold blood – prisoners, for instance? Such things happen in war and always will. People in England seem to forget or not to realise that a state of war prevails in this country.'

Just as the German high command persuaded themselves that the real cause of their defeat in the First World War was British propaganda, that they 'were hypnotized . . . as a rabbit by a snake', so it was later argued that Irish mastery of public relations had frustrated the British campaign to defeat the revolutionaries. In Buchan's novel *The Three Hostages*, one of the most sinister features of the villainous gang plotting to destroy world peace is their command of publicity, a diabolical skill newly available for exploitation by any group challenging the established powers. 'Look at the Irish,' the Ulster detective Macgillivray says to Richard Hannay to prove his point, 'They are the cleverest propagandists extant, and managed to persuade most people that they are a brave, generous, humorous, talented, warm-hearted race, cruelly yoked to a dull mercantile England, when God knows they were exactly the opposite.' Buchan, of course, wrote with supreme authority, having himself spent the war writing propaganda in Whitehall, ending up as director of information. His fictional detective distinguished between using publicity 'cleanly', as Britain had supposedly done in the war, and deploying it 'to poison and warp men's minds'.

Senior military figures longed for a Svengali figure such as Lord Northcliffe to do in Ireland what he had done for Britain during wartime (his propaganda was described by Hitler in *Mein Kampf*, with envious admiration, as 'an inspired work of genius'). Instead of a master manipulator of public taste they got Basil Clarke, 'a short clean-shaven man in glasses', a former *Daily Mail* war correspondent who faded into anonymity in the corridors of Dublin Castle. The seat of the Irish administration was not somewhere to find hospitable and mesmerising spokesmen. Journalists were taken through the courtyard past soldiers and officials, barbed wire, sandbags and armoured cars. The place reminded Ewart of a headquarters post in France during the war. In the press room during briefings younger reporters stood, deferring to their elderly colleagues, who occupied the chairs. All of them transcribed into shorthand notepads the words of a monotonous voice handing down the news – 'Crown Forces operating Thursday on the Kerry–Limerick border called upon three civilians at Knocktoosh to halt' – while the muffled metallic chiselling of typewriter keys penetrated the wall from the adjoining room. Reproduced daily in the newspapers under headlines announcing 'More Houses Destroyed' or 'Succession of Attacks on Irish Police', these communiqués had the opposite effect of that intended. Instead of creating an impression of outrage in need of suppression the cumulative message was that Ireland had slipped out of the government's control. The news portrayed a state of disorder that was ultimately the responsibility of the government, not of the guerrillas, 'the horrible condition into which the government has allowed Ireland to sink', as the *Manchester Guardian* put it.

Correspondents travelling around Ireland focused on the activities of the Black and Tans, describing scenes of random shootings of civilians, burnt-out creameries, wrecked streets and looted shops. Writers from Europe, the United States and beyond portrayed Ireland as the scene of imperial atrocities. Analogies were borrowed from the most notorious landmarks of the war just finished. The ruination of Cork reminded observers of Ypres or Amiens; the destruction of Balbriggan was compared to the sacking of Louvain by the Germans on their rampage through Belgium. The self-proclaimed tactic of *Schrecklichkeit*, 'frightfulness', which the Germans had employed to crush resistance in Belgium, had become the synonym for ruthless militarism entirely alien to the British way: 'Prussian frightfulness' was all that Britain stood against. Now, the phrase made famous by Lord Northcliffe's propagandists was regularly applied to British policy in Ireland. More galling still, the righteous rhetoric of the war against barbarism was satirised by foreign observers. Cartoons depicting British persecution of the Irish appeared in newspapers in New York, Zurich, Warsaw and, astonishingly, Berlin. 'That last gibe, the sneer of a nation whose tyranny we nearly ruined ourselves to destroy,' sighed a London columnist who surveyed the foreign press, 'was the unkindest cut of all.' One might despise these cartoons, Revd Duncan C. MacGregor, moderator of the Presbyterian Church of England, wrote in a letter to *The Times*; 'they are detestable: but the worst is, they are partly true'.

The crusading reporters were followed by English peace activists. A party of Quakers toured Ireland meeting civilian victims of police lawlessness in the autumn of 1920. In County Kerry women invited them into their homes to display the aftermath of a police raid – smashed ornaments and the splintered remains of a wardrobe. A plaster Virgin had been miraculously spared. In County Clare, the Quakers watched soldiers in helmets pass slowly through a seaside village, their fingers poised on triggers, their eyes darting from windows to doorways. A local man beckoned the Quakers down a passageway: 'We followed and there at the back of the houses in a low poor shed was a comparatively small chest covered with a white cloth, and on top a few flowers. "He was burned, sir, in one of the houses. He was a stranger; we don't know who he was."'

The feminist and socialist Ethel Snowden, the wife of Philip Snowden (shortly to become the first Labour Party chancellor of the exchequer), spent ten days in Ireland in January 1921.

As a well-travelled Englishwoman, she had grown used to being greeted with renditions of 'It's a Long Way to Tipperary' in foreign lands. In the real Tipperary she found 'ruin, misery, desolation and death'. Nervous children screamed in the dark; young women were afraid to undress for bed in case they were ordered out during the night by soldiers. She witnessed the destruction of two shops in an official reprisal in Cork and 'the blackened walls and twisted machinery of the gutted creameries'. An old man whose son had been shot was reluctant to speak to her, but relented when she assured him that his story would help put a stop to the violence. 'Well, ma'am, ye seem to have a kind heart,' she transcribed in her dubious effort to reproduce faithfully his native diction, 'an' if it's really wantin' to help sthop this koind av thing ye're afther Oi'll thry to tell ye.' Her own message to her Irish guests was reassurance. Ordinary men and women in England had a strong sense of justice; they just needed to be roused from their obsession with the sports news and salacious tales from the divorce courts.

Not very many people were paying attention to Ireland. For all the anxiety among the elite over Bolshevism and revolutionary disorder, there was a popular sense that Britain was fortunate in its post-war tranquillity compared with the crisis-torn continent. The desire to turn away from great public issues to private consumption was symbolised by popular excitement at the return of the *Daily Mail*'s Ideal Homes Exhibition. Fascination with new gadgets, such as the dishwasher, the electric towel rail and the milk steriliser, prepared the middle classes for life without servants. In this atmosphere it was painful to be reminded of the seamy business involved in preserving the victorious empire. A common reaction among politicians when the massacre of almost four hundred unarmed protestors in the Indian town of Amritsar in April 1919 finally became headline news almost a year later was that the atrocity was a grotesque aberration. Churchill could not emphasise this enough, describing Amritsar as 'an episode . . . without precedent . . . an extraordinary event, a monstrous event, an event which stands in singular and sinister isolation'. It was the exception that proved the rule. 'Frightfulness is not a remedy known to the British pharmacopoeia,' he concluded. But press coverage of events in Ireland suggested otherwise, highlighting more mundane practices of colonial policing usually kept carefully out of view.

A small band of MPs – the few remaining Irish nationalists, independent Liberals, Labour, some Conservatives – were prepared to challenge and question the government about the covert reprisals policy in Ireland. Among them was the twenty-four-year-old Conservative MP for Harrow, Oswald Mosley. He had been approached by a young man who had joined the Black and Tans because he was hard up but was disgusted by their predilection for mistreating prisoners. The disillusioned recruit gave Mosley details of how suspects were beaten with thin rods and had hot boiled eggs shoved under their armpits. Mosley had no sympathy with the Irish 'murder gang'; it was perfectly fair for British forces to shoot men who failed to put up their hands when ordered to do so. In other circumstances he might even have empathised with the daredevil bravado of the more honourable Black and Tans. But he regarded their tactics in Ireland as an egregious departure from the standards of soldierly conduct expected of Europeans, a descent into the kind of savagery indulged in by the lesser races. The British Empire, Mosley told parliament, had survived because it rested on the power of moral force and the tactics being used in Ireland were a 'gambler's expedient'.

Mosley became the secretary of the Peace with Ireland Council, a campaigning group of liberal activists, writers and politicians. Even the horror aroused by the assassinations on Bloody Sunday did not shake their conviction that the campaign in Ireland was indefensible. It was argued that the British officers who died had been sent to carry out a shameful mission and then left unprotected. The killings at Croke Park were likened to the massacre at Amritsar. A week after the shootings in Dublin, J. M. Keynes and thirty other Cambridge professors signed a letter to *The Nation*: 'We think that no words of reprobation can be too strong for the detestable series of murders and other outrages committed by the agents and adherents of Sinn Féin. But we feel at least an equal horror at the similar acts, of which the victims have often been admittedly innocent people, recently committed in Ireland by persons in the pay and service of the State, and at the omission of the members of the Government to condemn these atrocities with any force or sincerity, or even to allow an impartial investigation.' The most transparently insincere member of the government was the Irish secretary, Hamar Greenwood, a stolid Canadian lawyer who stood in the House of Commons and denied that any reprisals were taking place. According to Greenwood, photos of Irish civilians being flogged were faked and creameries were burned by IRA men dressed up in British uniforms. The discipline of the Crown forces was 'sternly maintained' and Ireland was slowly being returned to the state of tranquillity prevailing in rural Kent. 'It seemed to be agreed', Lord Hugh Cecil remarked of Greenwood's performances, 'that there are no such things as reprisals, but they are having a good effect.'

Watching all this from Ireland was demoralising for the troops. At a convivial dinner with the staff of the Kerry

Infantry Brigade, Wilfrid Ewart was treated to a litany of complaints about the lack of appreciation for the conditions their men had to face. 'People in England don't seem to realise what things are like over here,' the commanding officer told Ewart, 'or else they don't care. Most of the newspapers damn us or take sides with the other people.' A major volunteered that he would prefer to spend another two-and-a-half years in the trenches in France than serve the same amount of time in Ireland: 'How can you expect anything but reprisals when our pals and our men's pals are killed like this? If somebody you were fond of was murdered – murdered, mind you! – in cold blood, wouldn't you "see red"?' The commanding officer of British forces in Ireland, General Sir Nevil Macready, was certain that it was the effect of reading abuse of himself and his comrades in the newspaper columns that caused the ordinary soldier to 'see red'.

Exasperation with their mission sometimes turned to contempt for their enemies and the Irish race in general. Macready regarded many of the IRA fighters as degenerates and thought that their method of waging war was barbaric, 'such as would not be indulged in by the wildest savages in Central Africa'. Another British officer believed the Irish to be 'an extremely backward race', unfit for self-government. Their skulls, he observed, were of a similar shape to those of African negroes. Major Charles Howard Foulkes, the British government's adviser on chemical warfare who was appointed as director of propaganda in Dublin in 1921, thought it would be a good idea to emphasise that the best people in Ireland were of English or Scottish Protestant descent and that 'the native Irish are . . . the lazy, dirty element'. Even the urbane Sturgis could be driven to racial fury: 'I almost begin to believe that these mean, dishonest insufferably conceited

Irishmen *are* an inferior race and are only sufferable when they are whipped – like the Jews.' British propaganda directed at the IRA urged them to observe the sporting rules of war commonly accepted by white men. But the Irish were very aware that their skin colour was an advantage in defending their methods of guerrilla warfare. The deputy Lord Mayor of Cork, Barry Egan, pointed out to Wilfrid Ewart that the ambush was a legitimate tactic of war. And to the objection that the Irish did not fight in uniform, he countered that neither did the Boers, but they were recognised as legitimate combatants.

Ireland was spared methods of pacification deployed more easily in peripheral corners of the British Empire. The age of poison gas, aeroplanes and machine-guns opened up new possibilities for efficient and cost-effective means of controlling restless populations. Churchill devised a scheme that used the RAF to police Mesopotamia. (Far from being barred from the list of remedies for colonial unrest, as Churchill suggested, frightfulness 'in a more or less severe form' was acknowledged by the RAF to be the essence of air control: collective punishment of villages by indiscriminate bombing, for example.) However, what was good medicine for the desert tribes was not fit to be administered in Ireland. The chief of the Air Staff, Hugh Trenchard, opposed proposals to use aircraft to attack IRA ambush parties and street disturbances because the unavoidable deaths of innocent people would have immediate consequences: 'A great popular outcry will be created against the unfortunate pilots who are involved in the action, from which it will be impossible to shield them. Further a feeling of annoyance and exasperation at the reckless use of such a powerful arm, which once loosed in the air cannot be delicately controlled, will infallibly arise and engender great bitterness.'

In February 1921 *The Times* identified Ireland as 'a world problem' because through the mass migration of the nineteenth and early twentieth centuries the Irish had become 'an integral factor in modern civilisation'. Unwise British policy in Ireland was encouraging challenges to the empire and straining Britain's relationship with the United States: 'We cannot afford to face the uncertainties of world and Imperial politics with our own house divided against itself, and the Irish race abroad our embittered enemy . . .' At about the same time the British education secretary, H. A. L. Fisher, warned his cabinet colleagues that the longer the war went on, 'the more certain does it become that great bodies of opinion in this Country will swing over to the Republican side'. By May 1921, during a discussion of a possible truce, Churchill – the original champion of the Black and Tans – was advising that it was 'of great public importance to get a respite in Ireland' because the news from there was damaging 'the interests of this country all over the world; we are getting an odious reputation; poisoning our relations with the United States . . .' Fisher himself now estimated that the war was 'degrading to the moral life of the whole country', and even Balfour, arguing against concessions to Sinn Féin, accepted that 'naturally we should wish to end this uphill, sordid, unchivalrous, loathsome conflict – we are sick of it'.

This same sense of moral exhaustion also pervaded Dublin Castle. For all his worldly amusement the diaries of Mark Sturgis trace a private corrosion of will. 'I wish these lorry loads of police could be restrained from this idiotic blazing about as they drive along,' he wrote in his diary on 3 November. 'It can do no conceivable good and yesterday's case of a woman in Galway, shortly expecting child, shot in the stomach and now dead is beastly.' At the end of the year, on

Tuesday, 28 December, he examines his own mood: 'To-night I have black fit and am wrapped in gloom. I think it is not so much because there is an atmosphere of war but because there is an atmosphere of complete contentment with our methods of waging it . . . I think my desire for an early peace springs from an instinctive dislike of much of our method of warfare and I hate to feel that we are doing things, and profiting by them to which we cannot admit.' By March 1921 he thinks Cope and another colleague 'have allowed themselves to slip into an attitude of mind in which it seems to them that every charge of any sort or kind made against our soldiers or police *must* be true – every single unexplained outrage *must* be the work of "the Black and Tans" and every report of every single policeman *must* be lies from start to finish'. They had been stampeded into this state – 'all our nerves are wearing thin'. On an outing to the races in April he was experiencing a very bad day until his luck suddenly turned with his last bet: he put his money on Pacifist in the Leopardstown steeplechase, and the horse romped home.

15

A Republic of Their Own

In 1914 the British clothing firm Burberry was well positioned to have a good war. The company that had introduced the world to the gabardine overcoat possessed a special flair for celebrity marketing. It had supplied the polar explorers Roald Amundsen and Ernest Shackleton and displaced Mackintosh as the generic brand for waterproof coats. So when the First World War began it already had its eye on making sure British forces would wear Burberry while they sought to defend the rights of small nations. Lord Kitchener endorsed the Burberry waterproof as 'a most valuable addition to campaigning kit'.

The demands of industrial warfare could only improve it. Just as the relentless attrition of the trenches inspired mustard gas and the tank, it also accelerated scientific improvements to the military overcoat. Better to meet the often atrocious conditions on the western front, designers perfected a double-breasted, breathable gabardine lined with fleece that could be fastened up to the throat. It was spacious but with a belt that tightened it snugly around the waist. Large pockets could easily accommodate field maps and keep them dry, and cunningly placed flaps and vents allowed the air to carry away stale odours.

Competitors such as Aquascutum advertised its coats with glowing letters of recommendation from officers 'somewhere in Flanders', but in the public mind it was Burberry that was most associated with a new couture classic, the trenchcoat. It was too good an opportunity to miss; after the war Burberry set about making the trenchcoat aspirational for civilians. The advertisements pointed out that between 1914 and 1918 over half a million military Burberry overcoats were worn by officers in combat. Ideally suited for 'facing the Hun', in peacetime they were perfect for combating the worst weather. Smart and soldier-like, an outdoor man in a trenchcoat would be 'a civilian in uniform'.

The IRA really took to trenchcoats. Indeed, citizens in uniform was how they saw themselves, in an unintentional echo of Burberry's advertising. When he presided over the Dáil courts in small rural halls, Kevin O'Shiel thought it amusing to look down from his bench and see a dozen IRA men in trenchcoats and belts leaning against the walls on each side of the room, their hats and caps pulled over their heads at a variety of angles. Although policemen and Auxiliaries wore them too – and on several occasions they were the cause of misunderstandings – the trenchcoat became synonymous with the IRA, often with fatal consequences. A Volunteer stalking a party of Auxiliaries in a village in Tipperary gave himself away by crossing the moonlit street in his trenchcoat, attracting immediate fire. Ned Broy, the detective in Dublin Castle recruited as a spy by Michael Collins, was impressed by his first meeting with his chief, who wore 'a trenchcoat with all the usual buttons, belts and rings'. Eamon de Valera claimed to have made his own contribution to improving the design by sketching an outline of a trenchcoat with even bigger pockets to accommodate all the necessary field equipment. Far from being just a functional garment, the trenchcoat was the epitome of dash among the guerrillas. Robert Brennan recalled catching sight of Ernie O'Malley for the first time, marching jauntily into a house on St Stephen's Green, a trenchcoat draped over his arm to conceal a Parabellum pistol. As O'Malley joked about his exploits in the countryside, which had made him the subject of fascination among his audience, word came that the Black and Tans had arrived. 'Time for me to be off,' said O'Malley. And Brennan and his colleagues watched him walk straight to the cordon just formed in the street outside, conduct an apparently amusing conversation with a British officer, and then be waved through. (O'Malley said later he had made the officer laugh by saying the trenchcoat was covering a machine-gun.)

When a truce was declared in July 1921, IRA men could appear in their trenchcoats without fear of being shot or arrested. They drove around in Ford cars (often commandeered), made an entrance in pubs and dancehalls or swaggered down the street past impotent policemen. To a British officer they appeared 'rather a pallid, unwashed crowd who endeavoured to look important'. But to many others they were heroic and glamorous figures. The fact that they had been fugitives, often only glimpsed in half-light, increased their allure and mystery. A young Dublin student was shocked to see a badly nourished and unkempt youth from the slums in a Volunteer uniform: her imagining of an IRA man was a tall, dark, black-haired figure blessed with 'flashing eyes'. In Elizabeth Bowen's *The Last September*, eighteen-year-old Lois Farquar sees a figure in a trenchcoat hurrying across a shrubbery path at Danielstown and takes in 'a resolute profile, powerful as a thought'.

In the vintage summer after the truce, hundreds of young men who had been nowhere near a flying column affected the Burberry look, alongside the real fighters who had emerged from hiding. But the truce was an enigma. Was this victory? Surrender? Did it mean peace? Or an opportunity to prepare for renewed war? Ernie O'Malley was in the farmhouse kitchen in rural Tipperary, which had been his headquarters for the previous three months, when a despatch rider arrived. He carried orders from General Headquarters in Dublin that all hostilities would cease within forty-eight hours, at noon on Monday, 11 July. 'It was the first official intimation we had received and we did not understand it,' O'Malley recalled. 'Why had the truce been ordered? We were gaining ground, each day strengthened us and weakened our enemy; then why was it necessary to put a stop to hostilities?'

Although he was far away from the capital it is difficult to believe that O'Malley would have been oblivious to the signs that a ceasefire was imminent. The newspapers had carried large photographs of the expectant crowds who had gathered in sunshine the previous Monday outside the Mansion House – decorated in the stars and stripes for American Independence Day – to wait for news of de Valera's meeting with the leaders of the southern unionists and General Smuts to discuss peace terms. And the day before the despatch rider arrived with the ceasefire order – the hottest day of the year – an even bigger crowd had spent all day kneeling in the street to recite the Rosary in the hope that the conference inside would lead to peace. At six o'clock they were astonished to see the commander-in-chief of British forces General Nevil Macready arrive in an open-topped car. They cheered him as his driver slowly made a path through the crowd, a pained expression on his face. The announcement of a truce from the steps of the Mansion House by Eamonn Duggan, a member of the Dáil released from prison only the previous week, was greeted by cheering and repeated renditions of 'The Soldiers' Song'. The crowd had doubled when de Valera struggled through well-wishers to a waiting taxi an hour later. They roared with joy as he drove off, throwing hats in the air and waving tri-colours.

The truth that O'Malley possibly did not want to hear was that during the most vicious fighting there had been a parallel struggle for peace. Secret contacts and negotiations had been going on since the previous autumn. Patrick Moylett, a businessman who was an ally of Arthur Griffith, had seen H. A. L. Fisher, the British education secretary, and C. J. Phillips, an official at the Foreign Office. On the day of Terence Mac-Swiney's funeral, Moylett drove four IRA men to Southwark Cathedral, where they formed a guard of honour by the coffin during the funeral Mass, then walked in the procession to Euston station. That evening he was summoned to Downing Street by Phillips to discuss a possible peace conference. A few months previously Phillips had told an American journalist that, in three years, 'Ireland would be a republic in everything but name and in less time than that all the British troops would be out of Ireland'. Griffith himself had nearly had a secret meeting with the head of the civil service in Dublin Castle, Sir John Anderson, in a solicitor's office in Dublin. George Russell met Lloyd George, who told him that the British government would not concede a republic but would consider anything short of it. Republican leaders had also signalled a desire for compromise. As far back as July 1920 the Dáil's director of propaganda, Desmond Fitzgerald, had let it be known to British officials that if they accepted the Dáil as the legitimate representatives of Ireland ('to refuse to recognise the Dáil is as futile as to refuse to recognise the Soviet'), then 'any bona fide scheme of real self-determination would be earnestly considered'. Griffith suggested that Ireland

would not insist on its own navy or army and would allow
autonomy for the north as well as recognise British security
concerns. Even the military leaders were recognising that their
campaign could not go on for ever. 'It is too much to expect
that Irish physical force could combat successfully English
physical force for any length of time if the directors of the
latter could get a free hand for ruthlessness,' Michael Collins
told Griffith in December.

One of the new team of civil servants sent to Dublin Castle
in the summer of 1920 was the central figure in contacts
between the British government and the revolutionaries.
Alfred Cope, known to his colleagues as 'Andy', was the
forty-three-year-old son of a bottle merchant, and had joined
the civil service as a youth in the lowest rank of customs and
excise. Not so long before he was sent to Ireland he had been
a detective on the trail of smugglers and illegal distillers in
London. But it was his aptitude for administration that won
him a transfer to the Ministry of Pensions, where he impressed his superiors as the kind of modern civil servant lacking in Dublin. Obsessive about his work, driven to get on top
of whatever he was doing, Cope initially appeared too serious
to the carefree Sturgis, refusing invitations to dinner and hat-
ing cigars. But within weeks of his arrival, Cope was clear in
his own mind what needed to be done. 'I have met quite a
number of prominent Sinn Féiners and I feel that I have the
temper of the present position,' he wrote. The government
was wrong to insist on not negotiating unless the IRA called
off its campaign, Cope believed, because nobody in Ireland
trusted the British. He argued that Sinn Féin did not relish
violence but tolerated it because it was advancing their cause.
If a decent offer was made Sinn Féin might persuade the gunmen to halt, but 'the move must be with the government in

the first place'. Cope became the main point of contact for British peace feelers. He mingled with the crowd at the funeral procession for the officers killed on Bloody Sunday. When the Australian Archbishop Clune was accepted by Lloyd George as an intermediary it was Cope who met him at the Gresham Hotel and took him to Mountjoy Prison to meet Arthur Griffith, who had been briefly imprisoned. He was invited to the funeral of the Archbishop of Dublin and chatted with all the Sinn Féiners in the Gresham Hotel afterwards. When he went to secret meetings with his revolutionary contacts Cope had to elude British intelligence agents from Dublin Castle who suspected him of passing information to Sinn Féin. His enormous influence, which stretched to advising the cabinet, was resented by the military.

Access to the highest level of government did not mean his guidance was followed. The early contacts and discussions ended in failure when they were read in London as a sign that the IRA was about to collapse and that martial law might turn the tide. At a cabinet meeting in late January, Bonar Law argued against conciliation: 'Coercion was the only policy . . . the Irish were an inferior race.' But the vicious fighting that followed showed that an easy victory was impossible.

General Smuts, who returned to Britain for a meeting of colonial prime ministers, informed Lloyd George that the situation in Ireland was 'an unmeasured calamity', which was poisoning Britain's relations with its Commonwealth partners and the rest of the world. Reprisals were expensive, financially and morally, Smuts argued. Worse, they had failed. Days after Smuts visited Dublin the truce was announced.

At noon on Monday, 11 July, a few ships sounded their sirens in Dublin Bay to greet the end of hostilities. Five minutes later the owner of a yacht in Kingstown harbour ran a tricolour up his flagpole. Four British soldiers rowed out and hauled it down but were themselves overruled by an officer who arrived in a second boat and ran up the tricolour again. Some schools in the city gave their children a half-day holiday and some workmen took a holiday for themselves. The real sense of the truce emerged that evening with the end of the curfew. The streets of Dublin were thronged until midnight; many people stayed out until dawn. Bands of children from the slums marched around town trailing the tricolour. As darkness descended they lit bonfires which crackled in the side streets, and danced around them.

When Denis Johnston emerged from La Scala with his girl-friend after the late film he found the streets crammed. They travelled up and down Sackville Street twice on the top deck of a tram to watch the revelry. On the way home they passed a huge bonfire at Ballsbridge. In the following days the city pal-pably relaxed, and the sense of tension and wariness appeared to vanish. Even the Auxiliaries who now sauntered along the streets looked as if they were about to fraternise with civilians or chat up girls. Soldiers sprawled unarmed in their lorries. Crossley tenders still roared by, but now the Auxiliaries were heading for the seaside with towels around their necks. The writer Frank O'Connor – then a seventeen-year-old IRA Volunteer – remembered watching British armoured cars and tanks moving in formation along the streets of Cork. Small knots of people formed in the streets, wary that a round-up was imminent: 'Then as the Angelus rang out from the city churches, the barrack gates were thrown open and tanks, ar-moured cars, officers and men filed in. Here and there a man would turn and give a derisive hoot at the silent crowd. Then the barrack gates closed, and the crowd began to move away quietly with bewildered looks. Did it really mean that it was all over?'

The twenty-four-year-old French journalist Simone Téry drove across Ireland with the twenty-five-year-old leader of the IRA in Clare, Michael Brennan. He reminded her of the famous images of French revolutionary generals: 'He looks like a young war god. Whenever he goes down the street, heads turn to admire his vigorous physique, broad shoulders, and perfectly beautiful head.' Brennan took off his trenchcoat so that his green Volunteer uniform would be visible as they asked for guidance around trenched or broken roads. Boys jumped on the running board and the bonnet shouting directions in unison as they slowed to drive through villages. When they reached County Clare, she watched twenty of Brennan's men exercising in a square behind a ruined police barracks. Among his comrades from the flying column Brennan relaxed, joking, imitating a Dublin accent and joining in ballad singing: 'They acted like a bunch of boys back from a Sunday outing with only the problems of youth.' One of Brennan's men told her they were all ready to die for their renowned commander. 'Are there really countries where they haven't heard of our Mihall [Michael]?' he asked the young French journalist. She was invited to a village dance where the priest commended the brave young men to the girls who had turned out in their bright summer blouses. 'But the girls didn't seem to need that exhortation. Everyone got in place, and the violin attacked furiously those interesting Irish jigs and hornpipes, where groups cross and criss-cross, as light-footed and complicated as flies in the springtime.'

Téry concluded that her dancing guerrillas, far from being a gang of murderers, relished their peacetime pleasures more than the excitement of battle. But other IRA fighters were loath to give up soldiering. One member of a flying column feared the loss of status that would accompany its dissolution. 'We'll all wake up some morning to find ourselves members of the civil population,' he told a comrade, 'with peace made and our occupation and our power gone. Then I'll go back to the poorhouse, and I suppose you'll start selling collars again.' In Monaghan, one IRA commander reported that his men were disappointed because peace had come before they had achieved anything worthwhile. Another said his men were bewildered by the truce: 'In the mind of every soldier was a little republic of his own in which he was the hero.' The end of hostilities meant that 'the little hero was back at his plough'. The truce also unleashed all sorts of resentments bottled up during the desperate days on the run: personal jealousies, class antagonism, rivalry between families or long-harboured grievances over bad leadership, indolence and the lack of decent weaponry. Cliques, factions and intrigue flourished. A Dáil official described a drift towards anarchy in County Kerry; some fighters 'would wish to set up a Mexico here so that they may be free to continue the noble profession of arms'.

The desire to protect their status prompted some IRA men to become high-handed in their dealings with civilians. Police reported that IRA men commandeering cars and bicycles said they were 'entitled to some consideration for having fought for the Freedom of Ireland'. An IRA commander in County Clare told the county council that if his nominee for the job of rates collector were not accepted, 'anyone else who attempted to collect rates would be shot'. In some places the IRA was imposing levies or taxes on stout. The minister for defence, Cathal Brugha, issued an order that 'no pressure of any kind is to be used to make unwilling persons subscribe to our funds'. And the official Volunteer newspaper warned members of IRA units against adopting 'an aggressive or intolerant attitude towards civilians and the non-combatant elements of the nation'.

IRA men greeted as heroes when they emerged from life on the run enjoyed the attention. A disapproving officer looked askance at men who had once been disciplined fighters but had now 'gone soft', fond of being entertained in pubs, engrossed in conversation with 'gossipy girls'. It was easy for this adulation to translate into a sense of entitlement. One IRA officer described spending the day with fellow fighters drifting from pub to pub at a festival in County Cork: 'We felt very important and very conspicuous militarily, dressed as we were in column fashion – riding breeches and leggings, green shirt and collar, trenchcoat and Slouch hat.' At 11 p.m., closing time, local republican police arrived to clear the pub where they were drinking. When they refused to leave, other men demanded that the republican police force them out: 'I opened my overcoat, exposing to view my Sam Brown belt and holster complete with Colt, and quietly told them that myself and my companion were I.R.A. officers on active service in the district and that we were going to have a meal and intended to stay there that night.'

Such bravado also signalled a larger indifference to the complicated political negotiations that were now getting under way between Eamon de Valera and Lloyd George. The British prime minister had already told de Valera that there would be no question of conceding an Irish republic. But he wanted to persuade him of the value of being a member of the British Empire in a volatile world. Shortly before he began his exchange of letters with de Valera, Lloyd George had presided over the first imperial conference since the end of the war. 'The British Empire is a saving fact in a very distracted world.

It is the most hopeful experiment in human organization which the world has yet seen,' he told the delegates from the dominions and India. 'There was a time when Downing Street controlled the Empire. Today, the Empire is in charge of Downing Street.' The dominions were now acknowledged as full nations, equal partners with the United Kingdom: 'If there are any means by which that status can be rendered even clearer to their own communities and to the world at large we shall be glad to have them put forward . . .' This was the spirit in which he tried to overcome de Valera's insistence that Ireland was already a republic.

The careful formula that was eventually agreed as the basis for a conference, 'to ascertain how the association of Ireland with the community of nations known as the British Empire can best be reconciled with Irish national aspirations', was open to many different interpretations. Most of the fighting men were not interested in the subtlety of phrasing that fascinated de Valera (to the extent that Lloyd George compared negotiating with him to 'trying to pick up mercury with a fork'). Already the intense localism of IRA units had made them distrustful of the staff officers in headquarters, the men who seemed more preoccupied with detailed and well-presented reports free of typos than getting weapons into their hands. The gap now widened because the Dublin leadership was inevitably drawn further away from purely military considerations into the political judgements and nuanced positions necessary for managing peace negotiations.

These tensions between the leadership and the men in the field had an immediate focus in the implementation of the truce in each local area. The British authorities were determined to avoid acknowledging that the IRA had the status of an army. For the IRA the existence of a formal truce and the need for daily contact between British officers and IRA leaders to enforce it was itself recognition that they were the equal of their British counterparts. Tom Barry, the celebrated mastermind of the Kilmichael ambush, was appointed liaison officer for the IRA in the southern counties but British officers would not receive him in his Volunteer uniform. In his dealings with them he felt they passed up no opportunity 'to remind us that we are not the army of the Irish Republic, and that such an army does not exist'. To acquiesce, Barry argued, would be to accept that he and his men were murderers, not freedom fighters. When his patience ran out, Barry cut all communications with his British contacts. Michael Collins sympathised with Barry's anger. The British attitude, Collins agreed, was 'arrogant and provocative' and intended to demonstrate at all times that they were dealing with irresponsible gunmen rather than a disciplined army. But Collins and the IRA chief of staff Richard Mulcahy were preoccupied with larger concerns than hurt feelings. Any dispute that might endanger the truce or provoke even a local crisis or skirmish might also derail the peace negotiations. Mulcahy became increasingly irritated with Barry's belligerence towards the British liaison officers, accusing him of indulging his own vanity and petulance instead of doing everything possible to make sure that the truce was upheld. Barry was not the only junior officer tempted to use the truce to bait the enemy. Finally losing patience, Mulcahy issued a general order that all petty provocation must stop: 'We have either peace or war, and whoever by any want of discipline reopens war prematurely; will have to be held accountable for it.'

Ernie O'Malley and his colleagues thought the truce would last for two or three weeks. It would be an opportunity to stock up on home-made grenades and import badly needed guns and ammunition. He was worried about discipline, in particular that the IRA was becoming 'too popular'. Between July and December the ranks of the Volunteers were swollen by thousands of new recruits anxious to claim for themselves a share of the glamour and glory of fighting for Ireland. O'Malley despised these 'trucilleers' or 'sunshine soldiers'. He was focused on maintaining dedicated fighters in battle readiness for the inevitable moment when war resumed. At a castle in the Galtee Mountains in Tipperary he assembled seventy officers for a training camp, a tricolour flying from a flagstaff near the workmen's houses where they lived. Summoned to parade by a bugle call at 6 a.m., they ran across country before lectures on fieldcraft, bayonet practice and a game of hurling before their tea at 6 p.m. After full parade at sunset they read until they went to sleep. On Sundays they marched six miles to Mass in the local chapel, swinging along the road singing marching songs. Women from Cumann na mBan decorated the dormitories and placed bunches of fresh flowers in empty tin cans on tables at mealtimes. At a meeting before they dispersed, many officers said they wanted to break the truce.

But it would be wrong to think that it was only the IRA that was preparing for a renewal of hostilities. Any setback or breakdown in the settlement negotiations might equally trigger British military intervention. A week after the truce took effect, Lloyd George established an expert committee to examine the military and political implications of resuming the campaign in Ireland. The plan drawn up envisaged a rigorous regime of martial law, with the civil administration pushed to one side. Fears that the IRA was using the truce to regroup and rearm informed an estimation that it would require a massive military effort to subdue Ireland if peace talks broke down, requiring the blockade of rebel districts or the recruitment of loyalist militias. Less than a week before the truce was agreed, the Dublin Castle spy chief, Ormonde Winter, predicted in a memo that there would be no peace settlement. By the autumn he was advising that a very dirty war was imminent. The IRA had plans to kidnap loyalists so that for every guerrilla killed two loyalists would be shot. And 'when the majority of people in small towns are loyal, gas will be used, which is being manufactured in laboratories owned by the Christian Brothers and other like institutions'. Resentment that his views about the wisdom of the truce were not canvassed might have contributed to Winter's fantastical speculation about the Christian Brothers' talent for chemical warfare. But it was consistent with his constant attempts to throw doubt on Sinn Féin's commitment to peace. The alarmist reports of Winter's staff were augmented by countless individuals and groups in Ireland with connections to British establishment figures who were hostile to the negotiations and the concession of any form of independence to Ireland.

It was Cope and his urbane boss, John Anderson, who sustained the cabinet's faith in the bona fides of Sinn Féin. They wrote the weekly reports contradicting the doom-laden assessments of Winter, Macready, and Basil Thomson of the Special Branch. In reference to Winter's intrigues in particular, Cope advised his superiors that 'we have to keep a constant eye on these people for unless we do they run amok'. He consistently explained away public displays of intransigence by the Irish side. De Valera's 'fiery speeches', Cope explained, were for the benefit of the 'extremists' whose support de Valera needed before negotiations opened. Only a handful of members in the Dáil were opposed to compromise and few of them carried real weight in the movement. Sinn Féin was ready to climb down and call off the war.

16

Not Irish in the National Sense

It was a standard observation by travellers arriving in Belfast from Dublin in the early twentieth century that they felt they had left Ireland. The looming gantries of the Harland and Wolff shipyard, the smokestacks of the linen mills, the red-brick warehouses, the streets where everybody appeared to be hurried evoked comparisons to Liverpool and Glasgow. Belfast was modern and busy, wide awake, when Dublin seemed to be asleep. If you took a boat trip along Belfast Lough you would hear 'the rattle of thousands of hammers riveting' and the creaking of the swinging gantries. At 5.30 p.m. sirens and hooters signalling the end of the working day re-sounded across the city. Crowds of workmen in blue overalls and caps and collarless shirts emerged from the shipyards and boarded the trams marked 'Workers Only' that followed each other in procession down the High Street.

This busy metropolis seemed to have sprung from nowhere. A hundred years previously Belfast was just a small town; now it was the biggest city in Ireland. Linen, engineering and ship-building were thriving and its future was yoked to industrial Britain and the expanding empire. In a special supplement published in 1914, the *Financial Times* proclaimed Belfast the 'premier shipbuilding centre of the entire world' saluting its 'captains of industry' for their investment in technical education. Here was the world's largest shipyard, the biggest ropeworks and tobacco factories and the busiest linen-spinning mill. G. K. Chesterton compared Belfast to Berlin, both bursting with modern pride and 'a self-hypnotised superiority'. Douglas Goldring found a mixture of squalor and ostentatious consumption: 'One would guess that her people's chief idea of happiness lay in drink, football matches, and the hot gospel. Gin palaces glorying in a name which one imagined was a bitter joke of the middle nineteenth century jostle spirit lounges and pawnshops in its interminable thoroughfares. The town is neither grim nor is it smoke-laden, but to me at least it seemed mean with a meanness which defies description.'

Visitors from the south of Ireland found the north just as strange as did English travellers. A soldier in the British army from a small town in County Cork posted to a northern town in 1912 found it bizarre to see 'To Hell with the Pope' and 'No Rome Rule' whitewashed on the gable ends of houses in the poor quarters. It was impossible to dodge evangelical proselytisers and their tracts promising salvation: 'Our tunic fronts were often stuffed with them, and we found them on our beds on return to barracks . . . Uniformed women asked us in the streets if we were saved.' In a part of Ireland they associated with progress they found it odd that both Protestants and Catholics were in the grip of embittered sectarianism. The distinctiveness of the north had sharpened considerably in the previous thirty years. Here Protestants held tenaciously to power that was slipping away from their co-religionists in the south. Joe Devlin, the nationalist politician who dominated Catholic politics in Belfast, declared that since the mid-nineteenth century the north-east had become 'steadily more Protestant and less Irish'.

Arguably, it was the spread of democracy that had produced these sharper divisions. Irish Catholics had organised themselves into a formidable electoral machine to send a disciplined party to Westminster demanding home rule. By the 1880s the Irish MPs held the balance of power and had won over the Liberal Party. Faced with this threat to their dominance (and their liberty) Protestants in the north-east mobilised themselves. The Orange Order, previously looked down on by respectable Anglicans and Presbyterians as a rowdy working-class fraternity, was revitalised to unite Protestants of all denominations and classes to resist home rule. In 1905 this opposition crystallised into a political movement, the Ulster Unionist Council. The identity of 'unionists' and 'Protestants' took on a more clear-cut definition. Their sense of freedom, religious liberty and the right to the land their ancestors had settled in the seventeenth century was woven together. Protestantism was associated with science, progress, wealth, the glories of the British Empire and democracy. Evangelists saw themselves as the vanguard in a worldwide battle between Christian commerce and Catholic superstition. Their value to the empire as a minority could not be measured in numbers, the merchant Thomas Sinclair wrote in a letter to *The Times* in 1913. Protestants in the north of Ireland made a disproportionate contribution to the British national character by the strength of their 'sympathy with the world mission of the British Empire in the interest of civil and religious freedom'. Most northern Protestants believed a home-rule government in Dublin would mean oppression by the Catholic majority, subjection to the irrational dictates of priests and the ruin of Ireland's economy. In a speech in the House of Commons in 1912, William Moore, the MP for North Armagh, proclaimed his people 'West Britons' for whom the British Empire was an emblem of liberty: 'We have prospered under it and we will take nothing less. And instead of the sentimental humbug about Ireland's well-being . . . we maintain our own ideals because we are connected with Britain by ties of blood . . . religion and history; and we object to being swallowed up in the claim that . . . we should come into [Redmond's] fold because we live in Ireland.'

Geography need no longer determine their loyalty. In the period between the introduction of the third home-rule Bill in 1912 – now no longer subject to veto by the House of Lords – and the outbreak of the First World War in 1914, Ulster unionists essentially concluded that they could go it alone. They were backed by powerful figures in the Conservative Party, the upper reaches of the British military and judiciary and the landed aristocracy. For them Ulster's cause was a proxy for defence of the empire and resistance to the nascent welfare state and high taxation being introduced by the Liberal Party. The real impact of the movement led by captains of commerce and industry in Belfast was made by mass meetings and dramatic displays of loyalty and defiance, energised by apocalyptic oratory and evocative biblical imagery. In September 1912 nearly a quarter of a million people signed the Solemn League and Covenant, pledging to defend themselves against the conspiracy of their enemies to establish a home-rule parliament in Ireland. The promise to defy the will of the British parliament was backed up by an army, the Ulster Volunteer Force, which quickly signed up 100,000 members after its launch in 1913. When the home-rule Bill passed in the summer of 1914, the United Kingdom was faced with the prospect of civil war.

For all the Ulster movement's Old Testament rhetoric, its phenomenal success rested on very modern foundations: the idea of democratic sovereignty and the deployment of state-of-the-art methods of marketing and publicity. It was the 6th Marquess of Londonderry, the epitome of the landed political class, who best articulated the claims that this was a people's movement: 'Opposition to Home Rule in Ulster . . . has destroyed all differences between parties and classes. I doubt there are any more democratic organisations that those of the Ulster Unionist Council, the Unionist Clubs and the Orangemen . . . It is an uprising of the people against tyranny and coercion . . .' The leader of this cross-class revolt was well positioned to be fashioned into a popular icon. Edward Carson was a Dublin-born lawyer who had achieved celebrity in Britain for his brutal cross-examination of Oscar Wilde during his successful defence of the Marquess of Queensberry for criminal libel. Carson's image appeared on cigarette cards, tea-towels, badges and mementoes. The signing of the Covenant was filmed and shown in cinemas. Open-air meetings and marching displays by the UVF were carefully choreographed. The message was that Ulster's strength was its Protestant people – all of them, women and children included. Whether as loyal wives of prominent men or nurses preparing the field hospitals that would be needed if war erupted, women achieved unprecedented prominence, all captured on camera. Carson even changed his mind about votes for women, promising they would not be denied full rights of citizenship under the Provisional Government for Ulster that would be set up in opposition to a Dublin parliament. Schoolchildren were also caught up in the excitement. Long before *The Chronicles of Narnia*, the imagination of a ten-year-old C. S. Lewis in suburban Belfast was engaged in crafting schoolboy essays on the evils of home rule.

The projection of a new nation on the march was not accidental. The northern unionists were no longer fighting to save all of Ireland from home rule but to ensure that the north-east would be excluded from its reach, even if that meant abandoning their Protestant and unionist brethren in the rest of the country. Carson pointed out that the four most Protestant counties in the north-east had a population greater than New Zealand or Newfoundland. The outbreak of war in Europe allowed the British government to suspend the implementation of the home-rule Bill in Ireland and avoid a confrontation. Members of the Ulster Volunteer Force were recruited en masse into the 36th (Ulster) Division of Kitchener's New Army. A red hand, the symbol of the ancient province of Ulster, was stamped on their tin hats and the New Testaments they carried into battle. On the first two days of the offensive at the Somme in 1916 more than half the division was wiped out. The sacrifice reinforced the idea that a loyal corner of empire in the north of Ireland deserved special recognition.

This rapid embrace of their own version of self-determination by the unionists of Ulster was regarded with helpless horror by nationalists in the rest of Ireland. The cartographic image of the island as one nation was sacrosanct to them. 'We claim that Ireland is a nation, made up of many races,' John Redmond said. 'This idea of two nations in Ireland is to us revolting and hateful. The idea of us agreeing to the partition of our nation is unthinkable . . . and we would resist most violently as far as it is within our power to do so.' His decision to face up to reality and reluctantly accept what he hoped would be a temporary partition as the price of home rule contributed to his downfall. De Valera denied that a 'solid homogeneous Ulster' even existed. It was an invention of the British so that they could divide and rule the Irish people.

Once the British stood aside and set Ireland free, the Orangemen would realise that they had been pawns in a Machiavellian game and divisions among Irishmen would disappear.

This analysis, a core belief of Irish nationalists, sat oddly with de Valera's other comments describing the northern unionists as 'a foreign garrison' who were 'not Irish people'. At times he even suggested that if they continued to block the road to Irish freedom 'they would have to go under'. Rather than articulating alternative policies, de Valera's confusions merely revealed an abject failure to come to terms with an intractable problem. Mostly, Sinn Féin chose to ignore the problem of Irish unity, hoping that it would somehow resolve itself. Only very occasionally did a Sinn Féin spokesman address the implications of determined resistance in Ulster. In an article published just before the sons of Ulster went into battle on the Somme in 1916, Father Michael O'Flanagan, soon to be vice president of Sinn Féin, pointed out that while geography had worked hard to make Ireland one nation, history had conspired against it: 'The Unionists of Ulster have never transferred their love and allegiance to Ireland. They may be Irelanders, using Ireland as a geographical term, but they are not Irish in the national sense. They love the hills of Antrim in the same way as we love the plains of Roscommon, but the centre of their patriotic enthusiasm is London, whereas the centre of ours is Dublin.' Would it be sensible, he asked, for nationalists to compel the unionists to love Ireland by force?

However clear-sighted this might appear, merely conceding the right of northern Protestants to choose their nation would not solve Ireland's minority problem. One-third of the population in the area of the north likely to reject Dublin rule was Catholic. For these people a divided Ireland would be the ultimate disaster, consigning them to isolated submission to perpetual Protestant dominance. They already felt themselves a conquered people, swept off the best land by the seventeenth-century planters, denied a fair share of the twentieth-century industrial prosperity, an inferior caste now defined by poverty and disloyalty in the eyes of their neighbours. The poet Louis MacNeice, son of a Protestant clergyman who opposed sectarianism and refused to sign the Solemn League and Covenant, remembered the rare visits he made as a child to the slum he knew as 'the Irish Quarter' in his home town of Carrickfergus: 'I used to hold my breath till I got through it. There was a dense smell of poverty as of soot mixed with porter mixed with cheap fat frying mixed with festering scabs and rags that had never been washed. Many of the houses were mere cottages and you looked down over the half-door into a room below the level of the street, always dark but the glow of a grate might show up a mangy cat or a quizzical wrinkled face. The thatch on the roofs came down to within five feet of the street, was sometimes mottled with grass or moss, and was usually dripping.' In Belfast, where thousands of rural Catholics were drawn by the city's phenomenal expansion, Protestant workers dominated the skilled trades in the shipyards and engineering works. Catholic men found work as labourers, dockers or shoe-makers; Catholic women made up a large proportion of the unskilled workforce in the linen mills. Some Catholics managed to rise to respectability and financial security as butchers, shopkeepers or, especially, publicans.

Decades of sectarian rioting had enforced rigid lines of residential segregation. On the night before her visit to Belfast in 1849, Queen Victoria confided an aide-memoire to her diary: 'The Protestants and Roman Catholics are nearly equally divided in Belfast, and religious hatred and party feeling run very high.' The majority of Catholics lived in seven distinct neighbourhoods, the largest on the Falls Road in west Belfast, 'row upon row of newish brick tenement-houses, squalid shops, picture palaces innumerable'. It was one of the few places in Ireland where the old Irish Party had survived, in the person of Joe Devlin, the local MP since 1906, who presided over a political machine based on the Ancient Order of Hibernians, the Catholic counterpart to the Orange Order. The promise that the three-week general strike in 1919, when Protestant workers took their lead from a Catholic trade unionist, might mean class solidarity would finally obliterate sectarian and political divisions was short-lived. Some hundred thousand workers marched in the May Day parade but many were carrying Union Jacks as well as red flags. Within a year there was outrage that Catholics who had replaced Protestants fighting in the war still held jobs in the shipyards. Although Belfast Catholics identified with nationalists in the rest of Ireland, their politics was an intensely local struggle for incremental advantage, heavily influenced by the clergy for whom national aspirations took second place to local survival. 'The Protestants here are bigots,' a young shy priest told Wilfrid Ewart. 'We're living in a prison. If I walk down the street the children spit at the sight of me. Our letters are censored and our telephone tapped.'

In the eyes of Protestants, the overwhelming success of Sinn Féin in the 1918 election and the intensification of the IRA campaign in the rest of Ireland made the Catholic minority appear more than ever as 'the enemy in our midst'. In his tram journey across west Belfast, Ewart noted the names above the shops – Murphy, Ryan, Connor, Mahoney, Keogh, Molloy – and the slogans on the walls: 'Up Dublin!', 'Your hour is come!', and 'Up the rebels!' Recent developments had given substance to this sense of siege. Local elections using the system of proportional representation enabled candidates from the temporary alliance of nationalists and Sinn Féin to win control of several urban and district councils in areas where Catholics were numerous. The rhetoric of the victors was not conciliatory. 'Rest assured that mighty changes are coming in Ireland,' the local nationalist newspaper warned when unionists lost control of Derry Corporation in 1920. 'Do you Protestants wish to play a part in them? The Unionist position is no longer tenable . . . do you not see that Englishmen are prepared to sacrifice you if they can get the good will of the rest of Ireland?'

The sense of insecurity this was intended to arouse among Protestants was heightened by the countrywide evacuation of rural police stations in response to the IRA's campaign against the RIC. Sporadic IRA attacks in the north-east in the spring and summer of 1920 prompted the appearance of Protestant vigilante patrols. In a village in Fermanagh where the police barracks was attacked by IRA fighters, church bells rang out to summon the band of local defenders to repel them. British army officers attempting to disarm these patrols were told they were all fighting under the Union Jack. The landowner, Sandhurst graduate and war hero Captain Sir Basil Brooke, who assembled fourteen of his retainers to defend his demesne, wrote to the authorities in Dublin appealing for official recognition of the militias springing up across the north. The previous year Carson had warned at the great Orange parade in Belfast on 12 July 1919 that 'if any attempt were made to interfere with the rights and liberties of Ulster he would get the Ulster Volunteer Force into activity again', and this was the moment of its resurgence. After the IRA fought a four-hour gun battle with police in Derry in May 1920, masked men with blackened faces set up roadblocks in the city, asking pedestrians to declare their religion, beating up those who admitted to being Catholics. This set off two months of rioting: snipers fired into Catholic neighbourhoods from the old city walls, Protestants were burned out of their homes. Troops intervened and declared a curfew. But they openly aligned themselves with the Protestant paramilitaries; the UVF organiser in Derry reported to his superiors that the army commander deferred to him as if he was 'virtually the Governor of Derry'.

In this atmosphere, the deaths of Protestant members of the RIC from the north serving in the rest of Ireland were easily construed as proxy strikes at the heartland of unionism itself. The funerals of policemen cut down in the parts of Ireland where the IRA held sway were the occasion of displays of emotion redolent of the return of fallen soldiers from enemy territory. Coffins draped in Union Jacks were paraded on gun carriages in northern towns. The assassination of RIC Divisional Commissioner Colonel Gerald Brice Ferguson Smyth at the County Club in Cork coincided with the end of the annual holiday to celebrate the 12th of July. Workers returned to the Belfast shipyards fired up by Sir Edward Carson's declaration that it was time to 'take the matter into their own hands'. At a mass lunchtime meeting to denounce the killing of DC Smyth it was decided to expel all non-loyalists. Rumours that a mob was on the way had reached some Catholics at the Harland and Wolff yard by the time the sledgehammers began battering down the gates. The Protestant workers stormed through the yard, pulling off the shirts of any man they thought might be a Catholic to see if he was wearing a medal or rosary beads. They also sought out Protestants known to have socialist sympathies. Many men who tried to escape by jumping into the harbour were pelted with nuts, bolts, rivets and shards of steel as they attempted to swim to safety. By late afternoon there were no Catholics in the shipyards. At the Royal Victoria Hospital a stream of cars and taxis delivered men with bloodstained bandages wrapped around their heads. The following day there were similar mass expulsions at the city's main engineering works and linen mills.

A reaction had also begun. Protestants were run out of workplaces where they were a minority, such as the dock-yards. Trams taking Protestant workers from the shipyards were showered with paving stones and men were dragged off and beaten in the street. Rioting erupted between Catholic and Protestant mobs. Dozens of Catholic groceries selling alcohol were ransacked and looted; flour, sugar and broken glass were strewn on the streets and beer flowed in the gutters. Gunfire erupted after dark. A Catholic woman visiting her mother was shot dead by a policeman. In Banbridge, the home town of DC Smyth, crowds set fire to the shop of a Catholic newsagent who had refused to close during the funeral. Workers at the Banbridge Weaving Company demanded the removal of all 'Sinn Féin workers' and the manager shut down the factory. They then toured the other factories in the town, calling on Protestant workers to join them until all the main workplaces were closed. At night the streets were full of seething crowds who attacked public houses and off-licences owned by Catholics.

In August an IRA assassination team, led by Sean Culhane, an intelligence officer from Cork who had been one of the men involved in the shooting of DC Smyth, travelled to

Lisburn near Belfast to assassinate Detective Inspector Oswald Ross Swanzy as he walked through crowded streets after Sunday service (he had been blamed for killing the Lord Mayor of Cork, Tomás Mac Curtain, four months earlier). Lisburn's Catholic district was attacked and many houses set on fire, and the rioting spread to Belfast, where troops were already blocking off streets with barbed-wire cordons and walls of sandbags. Fires raged across the city and over the next few days thirty people died. Tramcar services were suspended and businesses shut. Armoured vehicles brought people to work.

Sniper fire was likely at any time – people mastered the art of 'running low'. There were stampedes in Belfast's most fashionable shopping streets when gunfire broke out in the afternoon. The city's trams were often the target of attacks. Drivers crouched down low behind the controls when passing dangerous side streets. At night the lights on board would be dimmed; passengers pressed their bodies to the floor. Most deaths were recorded where the Catholic and Protestant residential areas, rigorously segregated as a result of previous rioting, abutted. A man peering round a street corner was shot in the nose; a hundred-year-old woman was shot in the arm. The occupational status of the victims followed a recurring pattern: barman, policeman, labourer, ex-soldier. But proportionate to their population the death rate among Catholics was much higher than that of Protestants.

Publicists highlighting the plight of Catholics in northern Ireland compared their fate to Belgians under the German invasion in 1914. Appeals for charity were circulated around the world. In the House of Commons, Joe Devlin presented homeless families and weeping women and children: 'If that's what we get when they have not got their Parliament, what may we expect when they have that weapon with wealth and power strongly entrenched? What will we get when they are armed with Britain's rifles, when they have cast around them the Imperial garb, what mercy, what pity, much less justice or liberty will be conceded to us then?' Petitions were sent to the Dáil in Dublin urging a commercial boycott of the north to stop the 'war of extermination' against Catholics. The plan was rejected but as the rioting intensified support grew for the idea that Belfast should be taught that it depended on Ireland for its prosperity. At first the idea was to withdraw money from banks and insurance companies based in Belfast but over the next few months dozens of boycott committees sprang up in towns all over the south, drawing up lists of pro-scribed goods made in Belfast. Their job was also to police shopkeepers still doing business with northern suppliers and identify commercial travellers who were to be run out of town. Salesmen were intimidated, kidnapped or threatened at gunpoint. Their samples were burned, confiscated or, in the case of a carload of shoes, dumped in a lake. A Dublin rep-resentative of a Belfast drapery was doused in the canal and tied with a rope to a telegraph pole. The boycott became more systematic in 1921. The list of goods banned from sale was extended to include biscuits, boot polish, soap, margarine, paint brushes, chocolate and oatmeal. The IRA established patrols to monitor trains arriving from Belfast, destroying bread and newspapers and looting whiskey. A train that had slowed on its way up a hill was boarded by armed men who ordered the driver to stop. Demanding the invoices for the goods on board from the guard they went through the wagons, taking off drums of oil, boxes of tea, clothes and cartwheels. Few thought of distinguishing between Catholic and Pro-testant firms, so Catholic wholesalers of fruit, vegetables, groceries and shoes in Belfast watched their business dry up. One signatory of the original petition to the Dáil for a boycott was forced to close his bagpipe factory as shops in the south imported pipes from Britain rather than buy them from Belfast. Merchants who continued to stock products from the north had 'Belfast Goods Sold Here' daubed on their shopfronts. Local IRA units demanded that money owed to companies in the north be turned over to them.

The boycott had a severe effect on its original targets, the Belfast-based banks. Customers in the south closed their accounts or were poached by the Dublin banks. Branches of Ulster Bank – which lost £1 million in withdrawals of deposits in less than three months – and the Northern Bank were closed. Both were subject to rumours of insolvency. Belfast's role as the distributive centre for many of the British products sold throughout Ireland was undermined. The chocolate manufacturer J. S. Fry closed down its confectionery warehouses in Belfast; Dunlop tyres advised customers to order from Dublin or Birmingham.

Despite the hardship, unionist politicians dismissed the boycott as ineffective. Rather than being reminded of their dependence on the rest of Ireland as the architects of the boycott intended, they emphasised how the market for Belfast's most lucrative manufactures was the rest of the world: linen to America, battleships to the imperial fleet. 'It does not hit Ulster very hard,' an elderly flour importer called Hugh Pollock told Wilfrid Ewart in Belfast in May 1921. With his fierce, bearded face, bushy eyebrows and thrusting chin, Ewart felt he had never met a more uncompromising man. But the real significance of Mr Pollock was that Ewart had gone to interview him because he had been designated to be finance minister in the first government of the new state of

Northern Ireland. In its final attempt to disengage from the Irish Question the British government had passed the Better Government of Ireland Act in December 1920 establishing federal home-rule parliaments in Belfast and Dublin and imposing a border between the six north-eastern counties – to be known as Northern Ireland – and the other twenty-six, which would now form Southern Ireland.

The passage of the Act, which retained supreme power over Ireland for Westminster, was ignored by Sinn Féin but the northern unionists now had the opportunity to establish legally the provincial government they had previously threatened to inaugurate by *coup d'état*. Abandoning areas heavily populated by Protestants that now fell on the southern side of the new border (and which they had previously pledged to defend to the death against home rule for the entire island), the unionist leadership created an administrative unit in which they would have a secure and unchallengeable majority. They would also have the full support of the British government in protecting their supremacy. Even before the Government of Ireland Bill was passed, the British government had approved the establishment of the Ulster Special Constabulary, a locally recruited gendarmerie to back up the police. The force would consist of 2,000 full-time armed members – A Specials – ready for despatch to any location where there was trouble and 20,000 part-time voluntary members – the B Specials – serving in their own districts with their weapons stored in the local police barracks (a third category of C Specials was a reserve to be called out in an emergency). In Fermanagh, Sir Basil Brooke united the men from his estate and the other volunteer platoons so that the county had 2,200 B Specials within a few months. The Specials used Orange halls for training. Some RIC officers feared the new force would usurp their authority. In January 1921 the police fired on a platoon of Specials looting a pub, killing one of them. The commander of British forces in Ireland, General Macready, thought the new force would be ready to fight the British government if it suited them.

When Carson stood down in February, Sir James Craig, the Boer War veteran, stockbroker and MP who had crafted the publicity campaign that had made him a popular idol, became the new leader of the northern unionists. He was determined to prevent labour or any other kind of politics from distracting unionists from winning an overwhelming victory as a solid bloc in the elections to the new parliament. Only then would their position be absolutely secure. Craig believed 'the British government would let Ulster down tomorrow if it could get the smallest bit of political comfort out of it'. But with a huge popular mandate the unionists would be in control of their own destiny. The election was not a disappointment. The unionists won 40 of the 52 seats, leaving Sinn Féin and the nationalists six each.

On 22 June the king came to Belfast to open the new parliament. For weeks hundreds of workers had laboured to transform the Lord Mayor's seat in the council chamber of Belfast City Hall into a facsimile of the throne in the House of Lords, surmounted with the royal coat of arms and set with three steps to approach the monarch. *The Times* printed a special supplement to mark what it regarded as an episode of world history and delivered it to Belfast by aeroplane in time for breakfast. On his return journey the pilot carried photographic plates recording scenes of intense loyalty. A huge crowd crammed the pavements and every window overlooking the route of the royal procession as it began at midday. The king and queen passed in their state landau, pulled by four grey horses brought from London. At many points there were spontaneous renditions of 'God Save the King'. But sometimes the king was greeted by a verse of 'Derry's Walls', the Orange ballad commemorating the Siege of Derry. And it was noted that some sections of the crowd greeted the monarch with silence. Aeroplanes flew low over the city to search the roads for unauthorised spectators; nobody was allowed to watch from a rooftop. In addition to heavily armed police, soldiers in trench helmets with fixed bayonets stood at every corner. Car loads of Auxiliaries in plain clothes kept watch and an armoured car with a machine-gun turret paraded the route. The ceremony itself lasted barely a quarter of an hour. Sir James Craig, the new prime minister, bowed low before the king. Finally, self-determination had been realised in Ireland.

17

The Crown Close at Hand

If Michael Collins had taken the time to read the *Daily Mirror* on his first week in London as a member of the Irish delegation sent to negotiate a settlement with the British government, he would have seen that the historic talks were not the only events that were drawing the attention of newspaper readers. Astonishing results had been obtained from two experiments using radium to treat cancer. A pilot had flown passengers from Paris to Amsterdam and back without touching the controls, thanks to a new automatic stabilising device. Charlie Chaplin was pictured leaving for America on an ocean liner from Southampton; Alexander Kerensky arrived in London on a cross-Channel ferry. Nor could Collins have been in any doubt about the British public's fascination with the royal family. The day he arrived – Monday, 10 October 1921 – there were many photos on the *Mirror*'s front page of the king opening the new Royal Exchange in Manchester, where he spoke of his anxieties over rising unemployment. If he had cared to read carefully through the *Mirror*'s pages, Collins would have gathered that the post-war world was full of 'jangled nerves' and uncertainty. Modern youth was determined to observe 'no set rules of life and behaved just as it pleased. Girls are getting so accustomed to shouting at one another in buses, tube trains, at their games, in the noisy streets and in crowded restaurants where jazz bands make terrific "music", that they frequently forget to lower their voices when they converse in their own homes,' complained one *Mirror* correspondent. The Bishop of Guildford was worried that women were now adopting lower standards of behaviour than men. The *Mirror* thought he was right: 'The task before women today is rather to hold on to their old ideas, which demonstrated their real superiority, than to strive for equality with standards of freedom beneath them.'

By the end of the week Collins would realise that he too was part of this world. As the conference opened, the *Daily Express* boasted how its reporter had tracked down 'the Sinn Féin mystery man' who had been 'as elusive as in the days when a price was set on his head and thousands of detectives and policemen searched for him in vain'. Collins explained how he had crossed the Irish Sea and slipped away quietly from Euston station by adopting the same principles that had enabled him to evade arrest in Ireland: 'I always watch the other fellow instead of letting him watch me. I make a point of keeping the other fellow on the run, instead of being on the run myself.' He reminded the reporter that his paper had called him a murderer. But the paper's tone had changed; he was now 'this big, good-humoured Irishman with the rich brogue and the soft, yet decisive voice'. In the *Washington Post* he was portrayed as a man who slept for only three hours a night, working stenographers from seven in the morning until 'all three of his own girls [were] dropping from fatigue' and he had to borrow a secretary working for a less assiduous member of the delegation. 'Elusive Michael Collins – there he goes,' an Irish official remarked as a stout figure burst through the door of the house the delegation had rented in Kensington, and bounded down the front steps into a waiting motor car.

The Irish negotiators had arrived in two open-topped Rolls-Royce cars at 10 Downing Street, where a crowd of supporters cheered for the Republic. The reporters were looking out for the revolvers bulging the pockets of the men sitting beside the drivers. Collins's dash to the doorstep to avoid the photographers only made them more eager. On the front page of the *Mirror* his slightly sheepish image – trilby-covered head inclined downwards – appeared below a photograph of a carpenter from Hornsey who had received the first divorce decree of the new law term. It was reported that the Irish had brought their own waiters, and a 'Sinn Féin cook who is a potato specialist'.

Collins could not resist sending some of these cuttings to his fiancée, Kitty Kiernan. 'What do you think of the enclosed? Writing all bosh,' he protested with false modesty. 'I never said any of these things. Just a few remarks. Newspaper men are Inventions of the Devil.' Stepping into the limelight seemed at odds with his initial reluctance to join the negotiating team in London; he had told de Valera that he was a soldier not a diplomat, that he could turn his reputation to advantage by playing the reclusive hardliner in Dublin. The glamour surrounding Michael Collins gave the Irish delegation in London an exotic revolutionary profile; without it they would have appeared an altogether familiar political deputation in the capital to petition the government. However, raising Collins to the level of Kerensky and Charlie Chaplin had a cost too. His celebrity, useful though it was, was likely only to increase the tensions and rivalries already present among the Irish delegates. The team had been chosen by de Valera to represent a balance between the rival factions in the independence movement. Contrary to his reputation, de Valera judged Collins a pragmatist, just like his colleague Arthur

Griffith. Both were likely to draw the British negotiators to the limit of their generosity because of their inclination to accept a settlement that kept Ireland inside the British Empire. De Valera believed other members – Robert Barton, George Gavan Duffy and the secretary to the delegation, Erskine Childers – would hold out for the Republic. If the talks reached stalemate, de Valera could then step in from a position of strength in Dublin with an ingenious proposal that Ireland should remain outside but associated with the Commonwealth. His hands unstained by the dirty business of negotiation, de Valera thought he could convince purist republicans that his scheme was the nearest they could come to absolute independence.

By bowing to pressure from de Valera to go to London, Collins felt that, from the start, he was caught in a trap. Compromise was inevitable, he felt, but would be denounced as treachery and he would take the blame. This fundamental mistrust and uncertainty was at the root of other weaknesses in the Irish delegation. They carried credentials giving them full negotiating powers on behalf of 'Saorstát Éireann' – the Irish translation of 'Irish Republic' – but they were also required to refer back to their cabinet colleagues and de Valera in Dublin. They had no clear proposals to set the agenda for the talks. Disunity increased as the negotiations progressed, conflicts of personality and principle widening the gap between themselves and the cabinet in Dublin. Throughout they felt a crushing burden of responsibility, exacerbated by a sense of isolation.

It was not the right frame of mind for bargaining with the government of a victorious empire. 'We Irishmen were nervous and ill at ease, it was our first introduction to Diplomacy,' Robert Barton recalled of their first introduction to the round table in Downing Street. 'The English were at home and confident in surroundings where they had met and out-manoeuvred or intimidated their opponents in a hundred similar struggles.' Now he knew how John Redmond must have felt. Victory and the peace settlement appeared to have vindicated Pax Britannica. The empire had extended its reach in Africa, the Pacific and especially the Middle East, where control of new oil reserves would fuel the Royal Navy's dominance of the world's oceans. The restyled empire looked more attractive than ever to its white dominions in a threatening world. A month before the Irish delegation arrived in Downing Street, the Australian prime minister spoke of how 'its mighty navy, its flag on every sea, its strongholds on every continent, its power and glory shining and splendid' gave his country a voice it would otherwise never possess. 'With our hands on the lever of Empire we move the world, but casting this aside we are shorn of our strength and count for little or nothing.'

The global hegemon looked more powerful from Melbourne than it did from London. Managing this sprawling collection of nationalities was now an anxious challenge for Britain's imperial administrators in the democratic age. Squaring the newly expanded British electorate's expectations of 'homes fit for heroes' and strategic commitments on the other side of the world was impossible for a country in hock to Wall Street. The United States was now an equal, not an upstart power. While Lloyd George and his senior ministers were negotiating with Michael Collins and his team in Downing Street, Lord Balfour was conceding American naval dominance at the first ever conference of the world's great powers to convene in Washington. And for every leader of a white dominion enraptured by the shining power and glory of empire, there were millions in other territories loyal to leaders

fighting to escape its dominion. Throughout the Irish negotiations the viceroy of India was sending back ever more
alarming despatches on the growing strength of Gandhi's
passive-resistance movement in spite of thousands of arrests.
For all the boasts about a new commonwealth of equals, the
appearance of freedom would suffice as long as the ultimate
blow of independence was avoided. Churchill had organised
a rigged election in Iraq in 1921. As the Irish talks began,
Lloyd George passed on to his Indian ministers his assessment
of 'a very critical phase' for the empire: 'It will not survive
unless it shows now in the most unmistakable fashion that it
has the will and the power to . . . deal conclusively with any
who challenge its authority.' So the British negotiators knew
exactly what they wanted. Ireland would have to retain,
however tenuously, a link with the empire; otherwise it would
undermine Britain's position elsewhere and provoke a reactionary rebellion in parliament that would bring down Lloyd
George's government.

The other concern was more local. However much independence was finally conceded to Ireland, it was essential to
deny future enemy states the opportunity to use Irish ports to
attack Britain. As for Irish unity, British policy in that regard
was already determined by the northern unionists, who now
had their own parliament, devolved government and security
forces. Unless they suddenly changed their minds, partition
would be irrevocable. The British team started out thinking of
Michael Collins and his colleagues as 'anarchic gunmen',
people who had trafficked with Germany. 'He fancied he had
met and defeated the whole might of the Empire,' was Lloyd
George's assessment of Collins on first acquaintance. 'If
necessity came he would find out his mistake.' The judgement of
men who voluntarily wished to renounce British citizenship

must automatically be so suspect that their very fitness for self-government was questionable. Geography alone refuted their claims that Ireland was not British, even though they had succeeded in persuading much of the world they had a case. The fact that they were sitting across the table meant that the British negotiators had to acknowledge their success. But if they offered them the substance of freedom without conceding their republic, and the Irish rejected such a generous offer, the roles would be reversed and Britain would be on the right side of world opinion.

The Irish delegation knew this. So if talks were to break down they wanted the decisive issue to be partition. Their negotiating position was based on staying formally out of the empire and preserving the unity of Ireland, objectives that at this point were irreconcilable and a further sign of their blind spot as regards the feelings of Ulster Protestants. A sovereign, united Ireland was prepared to have a defined relationship with the Commonwealth (even recognising the king of England as its head), allow Britain to have naval bases on the Irish coast to meet its concerns about security and grant the north of Ireland home rule under an Irish government. If Ireland showed it was prepared to meet Britain's major concerns, world – and indeed British – opinion would not be sympathetic towards intransigent northern unionists standing in the way of a breakthrough. The Irish delegates negotiated from the premise that their country was not part of the worldwide British family but an ancient nation recovering its historic rights. A sovereign Irish republic would freely enter binding agreements with the British Empire on defence, trade and other areas of common interest. In Arthur Griffith's words, Ireland would be outside the empire but they would become 'permanent allies'.

To the British delegates these proposals suggested the Irish might be aiming to achieve a compromise based on an unimaginable polity, a republic that was also a member of the empire, with members of the Irish parliament pledging allegiance to their own written constitution, not to the king. This raised an issue that eventually dwarfed such apparently momentous questions as whether Ireland should have its own army or control its economy. As the talks moved to a climax, the fundamental British demand was 'Would Ireland accept allegiance to the Crown?' For the British, the Crown symbolised the invisible emotional bonds of empire, but it also made the imperial family of nations a worldly entity: 'It is the keystone of the arch in law as well as in sentiment . . . The Crown is the symbol of a common citizenship which makes all subjects of the King one in international law.' Repeatedly, in discussions and position papers, the Irish delegates tried to persuade their British counterparts that the symbolism of the Crown did not mean the same in Ireland as it did in other dominions. Historically the Crown represented oppression; retaining it would concentrate rather than dissipate generations of Anglophobia and energise republicans who opposed any pact with Britain. Further, as Erskine Childers argued, Ireland's proximity to Britain meant accepting the Crown would have consequences that would not apply in lands far distant from Britain's reach. What in Canada would be merely a symbol would in Ireland become an instrument to legitimise interference. 'The Crown thousands of miles away would never menace the Dominions with its powers,' a memorandum submitted by the Irish delegation argued. 'The Crown close at hand would prove a constant menace of this kind.' For all these reasons, the Irish delegates argued, recognising the king in his capacity as the head of an international association with which Ireland was in partnership was the limit to which they could prudently go. Voluntary acceptance of the Crown in any capacity was 'a momentous step for the Irish people in view of history and geography', Collins argued, 'and showed their sincere desire for a friendly and lasting settlement'.

That a symbol had now become the dominant issue at the peace conference was partly because the British failed to grasp the strength of Irish feeling about the Crown. Lloyd George remarked with irritation to C. P. Scott that even the fiercely anti-imperialist Boer War hero General Hertzog had taken the oath of allegiance without protest. But the contention that it was a technicality, a curious Irish obsession with form not substance, disguised the renewed importance the British themselves now attached to their head of state. In the democratic clamour of post-war Britain the monarchy seemed to be the only institution capable of rising above class warfare and demands for national rights in the empire. Fretful conservatives were delighted to discover that discarding the fiction of the divine right of kings, far from opening the door to revolution, merely made the royal family seem even more magical in the age of the film star and the popular press. The king was assigned a full-time press secretary in 1918. And it was at this time that George V's son, Albert (later George VI), characterised the monarchy as a 'firm', which, like any modern business, depended for its success on advertising and a ubiquitous public profile. As de Valera himself saw during his stay at the Waldorf, America was mesmerised by the Prince of Wales. And although H. G. Wells dismissed the prince's endless trips to the far corners of the empire as 'a propaganda of inanity unparalleled in the world's history', for the proponents of the rebranded empire the modern publicity-friendly royals were the best advertisement that it was here to stay.

This was why, in desperation, Lloyd George told the Irish delegates that any British government that proposed the abrogation of the Crown would be 'smashed to atoms'. He offered to write into the treaty any phrase they liked to make clear that the Crown would have no more influence on Irish business than it did in Canada or the other dominions. He was prepared to modify the oath of allegiance used in all the other dominions so that it gave the least possible offence to Irish sensibilities. And he went even further, promising that the king's representative in Ireland would be purely a token, chosen by the new Irish government, which would always have the final say in any dispute. In other words he was offering 'the Sterilisation of the Crown' if the Irish would accept it as a symbol. In addition, he promised to put pressure on the unionists in Northern Ireland to incorporate their provincial government into a united Ireland. If they refused and insisted on partition, a commission would reassess the boundary between north and south, an exercise that might transfer areas in which Catholics were the majority to the southern government. To Griffith this would put the unionists on the spot: they could come into a united Ireland or be left with an unviable state. At this stage both Collins and Griffith had become convinced of the merits of the British offer. For Collins, dominion status would be 'a stepping stone to complete independence'. Griffith was satisfied that Ireland would have practical control of its own affairs in return for acceptance of a mere symbol. The issue was how to sell the deal to their cabinet colleagues. 'Dublin is the real problem,' Collins noted in November. 'If we accept at all it will be inferred as a gross betrayal or a similar act of treachery.'

When the delegation returned to Dublin on the first weekend in December 1921 to brief the cabinet on the final British proposals there was vigorous discussion but no dramatic split along the lines some of them might have feared. Griffith's judgement was that no better terms could be obtained; the British offer was tantamount to recognising the Republic. Collins described the clauses on the oath and allegiance to the Crown as 'sugar coating to enable the English people to swallow the pill' of conceding Irish independence. To reject these terms would be a gamble: the British had the capability to resume the war in a week. Barton and Duffy argued that the British ministers were bluffing; a few small concessions and they could win recognition of a republic. Childers favoured rejection because the concession of naval bases undermined Irish sovereignty and would make Ireland a party to every future British war. Neither de Valera nor the defence minister Cathal Brugha were prepared to countenance the oath of allegiance as it stood. For them, acceptance of inclusion in the empire and an oath of allegiance to the king would also be to accept that the British monarch was the source of authority in Ireland. As the delegation left Dublin after seven hours of often confusing discussion, de Valera assumed nothing would be signed that pledged Ireland's allegiance to the king or membership of the empire.

The events of the next seventy-two hours, culminating in the signing of the 'Articles of Agreement for a Treaty Between Great Britain and Ireland' at 2.20 a.m. on Tuesday, 6 December, destroyed the carefully constructed unity of the Irish revolutionary movement. The treaty that was actually agreed was unexpected, its terms not readily understood, and susceptible to widely varying interpretations. The Irish negotiators had returned to London with no clear idea of what the Irish cabinet had agreed. The British pushed them hard for a final settlement on the terms already outlined. The negotiators allowed themselves to be bound by an artificial deadline to decide whether they would go for peace or war and neglected to consult their colleagues in Dublin, an omission that would be discussed ad nauseam in the years ahead. Under intense pressure, Griffith was induced to sign on the basis of an earlier undertaking he had made to Lloyd George. At the last minute the British threw in two major concessions, giving the Irish Free State full control of its economy and a national army. The final ultimatum was war within three days unless every member of the delegation signed the treaty.

When the moment arrived for individual delegates to sign or reject the treaty, the full depth of the bitterness and tensions that had built up in long weeks of stressful negotiations was exposed. In the final hours of ferocious discussions before the treaty was signed, Collins was pacing the dining room waiting for his colleagues, 'like a wild beast in a cage . . . morose, silent and sullen', according to one of his secretaries. Then he threw himself in a chair and appeared to fall into a profound sleep. 'As I gazed my heart ached with anguish at the thought of what his mental torture must be.' The pressure was unbearable. 'It was as if the world fell in pieces around us,' Barton later recalled. He was told he would be hanged from a lamp-post in Dublin if he refused to sign and brought down renewed war on Ireland.

News of the agreement filtered out slowly in Dublin, where the shops were alight with their seasonal window displays, the first Christmas without war in three years. The long truce had created a strong expectation of peace, although nobody had a clear idea of what constitutional arrangements for Ireland would eventually make this permanent. 'We heard tonight Ireland is a Free State and every English soldier to be out of Ireland in 6 months,' Celia Shaw, a university student, wrote in her diary. 'Not a flag, not a bonfire, not a hurrah.' De Valera, staying with friends in Limerick, refused to come to the telephone when the call came from London to inform him that a treaty had been agreed. The following evening he was getting ready to preside at an event in the Mansion House to commemorate the sexcentenary of Dante's death, when Eamonn Duggan, one of the first delegates to return, arrived with a copy of the treaty. 'What should I read it for?' de Valera said, ignoring the envelope proffered to him. Duggan told him it would be published in London and Dublin at 8 p.m. 'What?' de Valera exploded. 'To be published whether I have seen it or not? Whether I approve or not?' Duggan affected nonchalance. 'Oh well, that's the arrangement.' De Valera took the envelope, opened it and glanced at the contents. To his friend Austin Stack, the minister for home affairs, he looked a broken man.

Accusations of a sell-out were already in the air. Mary MacSwiney, the sister of Terence and a member of the Dáil, suggested that the plenipotentiaries should be arrested once they stepped off the mailboat. In the circumstances, the cabinet discussion when Collins and the others returned was remarkably orderly. The cabinet split 4–3 in favour of the treaty. Kevin O'Higgins and W. T. Cosgrave, who a few weeks earlier had stood with de Valera against an oath to the king, changed their minds and supported the decision of the negotiators.

De Valera immediately issued a statement making clear he could not accept the treaty. The near universal acclaim for the settlement that poured in from around the world, from supporters of the Irish cause in Britain and from the major Irish newspapers heightened the sense that he was fighting a losing battle. 'The British and Irish Press carried the people off their feet in favour of the "Treaty and Peace",' recalled Austin Stack, who backed de Valera in rejecting the treaty. But the more fundamental reality was that the revolutionaries were caught off guard. They were ill prepared for the process of making decisions about war or peace, of judging whether this was an opportunity to secure Ireland's freedom or a compromise that would render the whole struggle futile. For more than four years the movement had maintained its sense of purpose by gliding over fundamental differences about what freedom meant. This loose and fluid organisation was not robust enough to contain and manage the airing of these differences. The genuine and even pedantic attention to rules and procedures in Sinn Féin, the Dáil and at IRA headquarters concealed (sometimes out of necessity) a lack of real clarity about lines of authority and about real political differences. The many overlapping personas through which Michael Collins exercised his power was a striking example of this confusion. At every stage since the negotiations started there was doubt and uncertainty about who had the authority to accept or reject a settlement. Were the negotiators real plenipotentiaries, entitled to act on their own judgement, or were they subject to the cabinet in Dublin? Should the cabinet or the Dáil decide on the treaty? Was the IRA entitled to take its own view? Sinn Féin too? What say should the people have? There was awareness that the split on the treaty could provoke a civil war but no settled idea of how to avoid such a terrible outcome. Too much rested on individual judgements and personalities.

Many supporters of Sinn Féin were uncertain how to react to the treaty. Rosamond Jacob's first impression when she read the terms in the newspaper was that they seemed very poor. Then she met two friends who were 'pleased' and others who were 'displeased' so that, although her instinct was to reject it, she was not sure of her own mind. All the brigade commanders in the 1st Southern Division rejected the treaty. Six individual Catholic bishops made public statements welcoming it immediately and another four within a few days, so that half the Church hierarchy welcomed the treaty. One said it was marvellous and that the men who made it would be immortal.

It was in this atmosphere of uncertainty that the Dáil convened on 14 December in the senate chamber of University College Dublin on Earlsfort Terrace to debate the treaty. Two large, low-ceilinged rooms separated by folding doors had been prepared, one for the deputies and another to accommodate the press. At the back of the tightly packed crowd of journalists from around the world a tall black man and a Japanese reporter craned their necks to hear the speakers in the other room. The following day the Dáil began a series of private sessions before resuming public debates on 19 December. These early sessions were conducted with good humour, deputies smiling and exchanging greetings as they gathered. De Valera spoke almost casually, playing down the split in the cabinet as an ordinary political division.

The main argument advanced by supporters of the treaty was that rejecting it would mean a renewed war, which the IRA was in no position to fight. Most deputies who were senior officers in the IRA argued that it would be impossible to regain the momentum established before the truce. None of the cabinet believed that a military victory was possible: the IRA chief of staff, Richard Mulcahy, said they had no hope of driving the British into the sea. Besides, the only practical alternative to the treaty would be some other compromise on the ideal of a republic. The moment, back in the summer, when they had accepted Lloyd George's invitation to the talks was itself an immediate compromise. In the private sessions de Valera had admitted that some form of association with Britain was inevitable. He advanced his plan for 'external association' as a better alternative to the treaty. But Griffith and Collins were adamant that this was irrelevant as it had already been rejected by the British.

Collins said he had signed the treaty not because of threats but because he thought it the best thing to do. 'In my opinion it gives us freedom, not the ultimate freedom that all nations desire and develop to, but the freedom to achieve it.' Griffith emphasised what the treaty would gain: an end to military occupation and the freedom to determine Ireland's own economic policy. If it was interpreted smartly the treaty could expand these powers and, eventually, unify the country. Treaty supporters argued that it was time to address the country's economic and social problems. The most eloquent case on these lines was put by Piaras Béaslaí, the stage manager of the opening session of the Dáil back in 1919. Opponents of the treaty had become so immersed in struggle for its own sake, he argued, that they had lost sight of what they were fighting for. The Irish nation was not an abstraction but the hopes and desires of living people who would now be free to determine their future. The anti-treatyites, he concluded in a famous phrase, were throwing away nationhood for a formula.

Finally, many on the pro-treaty side argued that to reject the treaty would be to ignore the will of the Irish people. Collins had begun assassinating detectives in Dublin without seeking a mandate, but he now declared that only the people had the right to decide on peace or war. This went to the heart of the issue of authority in the revolutionary movement. Up to this point, IRA commanders and the dominant personalities in the political leadership had made the decisions about the war with little but the most formal consultation with the Dáil. Dáil members themselves were much more radical than the electorate; most of the new intake in the 1921 election was merely nominated since there were no electoral contests. Suddenly, they were being overwhelmed by expressions of public feeling on the treaty: resolutions from county councils, letters and telegrams from members of Sinn Féin and others, to say nothing of the commentary in the press, which was strongly pro-treaty. After the Dáil adjourned on 22 December, deputies returning to their constituencies were subjected to Christmas sermons reminding them of their moral duty to reflect the majority view when they voted on the treaty. Republicans felt there was an orchestrated campaign by the Church and the press to fix in the public mind an equation between the treaty and peace.

Opponents of the treaty felt that their arguments had been dismissed before they had even been heard. De Valera's position was that the treaty was flawed; it would bring neither freedom nor peace. A better deal (his plan) had been possible but the delegates had failed to refer back to Dublin before committing themselves under duress. The right thing to do, he urged the Dáil, was to reject the treaty and reopen negotiations. However, his previous admission that a republic (or an 'isolated republic' as he liked to call it) was unattainable left him open to ridicule; he was, his opponents charged, a fantasist, driven by vanity to reject a settlement that was not his own.

The members of the Dáil who held out against any compromise on the republican demand (including all six women deputies) were far more vehement than de Valera in accusing the negotiators of betrayal, provoking Collins to rap the table in front of him as he defended himself against those who called him a traitor. For treaty opponents it was not the verdict of the people that mattered but the view of the fighters. Seamus Robinson, who was assassinating policemen at Soloheadbeg when the first Dáil convened, demanded that the IRA should have a veto on any constitutional change since it was not a professional army but a political body that had been let down by its leaders. If the IRA was not allowed to call a general convention to decide what should happen – or if the treaty was approved – he predicted war.

In substance, opponents of the treaty argued that the republic proclaimed at the General Post Office in Dublin on the first day of the Easter Rising in 1916 had been ratified by Sinn Féin's success in the 1918 election. To abandon this republic now for the status of a dominion in the British Empire would be contrary to democratic principle. To supporters of the treaty who argued that the independence made possible by the treaty could eventually be peacefully transformed into the republic they all dreamed of, the anti-treatyites replied that the republic already existed; the treaty would disestablish it in response to a threat of war from Britain. Abandoning national independence like this, Erskine Childers argued, would be an unprecedented act in the history of democratic nations. In this passionate discussion of sovereignty, the fact that the treaty meant the partition of Ireland was all but forgotten.

The core of this debate turned on whether Irish nationalists needed to adapt to a radically changed world. Michael Collins pointed out that he had not signed an agreement with the British Empire that had crushed the Easter Rising in 1916 but with a new entity, 'the Community of Nations known as the British Empire'. This radical overhaul of the empire was formally acknowledged for the first time in the treaty. In this sense, Ireland had achieved a breakthrough, the first subject nation to force a readjustment of imperial relations. The Commonwealth was no longer a British venture but an international alliance, with power leaking from London to the dominions. With Ireland leading the way it would soon become a kind of anti-colonial club. When Childers raised the point he had made during the negotiations, that Ireland could not have true dominion status because Britain was too close, the pro-treatyites responded that the rest of the dominions would offer the protection that geography seemed to deny.

The republicans could not accept this account of a reformed empire. 'The British Empire stands to me in the same relationship as the devil stands to religion,' spat Liam Mellows, who had been one of de Valera's closest advisers on his American tour. It was not a commonwealth but 'that terrible thing that has spread its tentacles all over the earth, that has crushed the lives out of people and exploited its own when it could not exploit anybody else'. Several anti-treatyites argued that the disturbed state of the empire would make it too costly for Britain to renew the war in Ireland. Even if Britain attempted it, Mary MacSwiney argued, 'she will not be allowed to exterminate the people of Ireland, for the conscience of the world is awake . . .' And in the most ingenious twist on this theme, Seamus Robinson argued that Ireland could strike at the British Empire like no other people. Its relative poverty conferred an advantage in war: 'We have no debt and no great factories, comparatively speaking, and their destruction would mean comparatively little to us.' And its emigrants constituted a rival 'Irish Empire', to be feared 'because one thousand effective shots and one thousand effective fires in Britain would ruin England for ever'.

Opponents of the treaty were quickly characterised as puritanical and doctrinaire in their opposition to the oath of fidelity to the king that the treaty required. Mary MacSwiney believed that 'Ireland must choose extermination before dishonour'. This unbending refusal to accept the treaty was not entirely abstract. Instead it was fuelled by their conviction that the revolutionary years had made their country a powerful moral force in the world. Ireland had won global admiration, according to MacSwiney, because its fight had been 'essentially a spiritual fight . . . of right against wrong . . . a small people . . . against a mighty rapacious and material Empire'. To sign the treaty would be to dishonour the trust of the world. Liam Mellows suggested the world was looking to Ireland for a lead precisely because the revolutionaries did not seek to become materially prosperous like other countries but instead 'would rather have the people of Ireland eking out a poor existence on the soil; as long as they possessed their souls, their minds, and their honour'. In this way Ireland was 'a beacon' for all struggling peoples: 'This downtrodden, this miserable country, as some of you called it, was, during the last few years, the greatest country in God's earth.'

This same sense of Ireland's spiritual destiny was shared on the other side of the argument. Pro-treaty speakers such as Alex McCabe also talked of building an Irish state that would be a distinct civilisation. For Gearóid O'Sullivan, later a Free State general, the treaty gave Ireland the opportunity to stop being the slaves of other cultures and become the master in its own house. 'We believe that the Gaelic-Irish outlook of civilisation and culture should permeate and influence the life of every nation in the world.' Even the pragmatic W. T. Cosgrave, while stressing a partnership with Britain, suggested Ireland could bring about 'world improvements in problems that have never been solved and that are not even in the way of being solved'.

The vote to approve the treaty by 64 votes to 57 on 7 January 1922 put an end to these high-flown hopes. The tears and exchanges of insults as the debates ended presaged a split that rippled through all the organisations that the revolutionaries had built up since 1916. Engrossed by this struggle, they hardly paid attention to the gradual birth of a new state. The rest of the world assumed that the Irish question had been solved.

18

The Quietest Triumph

In July 1922 the American consulate in Dublin received a letter from the editors of a publication called the *American Paint and Oil Dealer*. They were organising a world symposium on the question, 'Is human nature universal as regards the average man's lack of credulity in confirming the veracity of signs marked "fresh paint"?' They wondered if the consul could provide 'an account of the Irish characteristic in respect of this trait' and helpfully accompany his interpretation with a photograph of a sign in Irish indicating that a glistening surface near by was sticky to the touch. Undoubtedly the editorial team at the *Paint and Oil Dealer* was better in its timing with this letter to Dublin than any of the other American diplomatic outposts around the world they spammed. In an extraordinarily swift reply, given that civil war had broken out in Ireland, an official at the consulate wrote back within two weeks informing them that it was only in recent times that Americans in Dublin had seen the words 'fresh paint' in Irish. Since the new Provisional Government had come to power under the Anglo-Irish Treaty, the red pillar boxes once owned by the British Post Office were being overlaid with a new green coating and a notice in Irish which advised that the new colour was 'fresh paint'. As to precisely how credible Irish people found the sign, the official was diplomatically evasive: 'As far as has been noticed the native of Ireland reacts to warnings of this kind in precisely the same manner that is usually observed in the United States.'

The postmaster general of the Provisional Government later boasted that changing the colour of the pillar boxes from red to green was a significant revolutionary act. To the trade publication for the American paint manufacturers the Irish Free State was just another country opening for business, a source of valuable copy for a public-relations stunt. The war, according to New York advertising executives, had annihilated time and space, and American businessmen now saw the world as their marketplace. Within a few days of the treaty being signed the Sinn Féin consul in New York was worried that the new power of the dollar might result in US control of the new state: 'Quite a number of these people imagine that the whole Irish race is pauperized and that we can do nothing for ourselves without Wall Street money,' he wrote to Michael Collins. From tyre companies in Texas to suppliers of typewriters and plumbing equipment in New York, the US consulate in Dublin was flooded with requests seeking contacts with dealers and distributors or opportunities to open factories. The Texan oil magnate Joseph Cullinan, founder of the company that became Texaco, was intrigued by the prospects for investment opened up by the new administrations in the north and south of Ireland. He sent a trusted lieutenant to meet government ministers and officials with a view to building an oil terminal and cornering the market in oil distribution in the Free State. For all their talk of developing native industries, Irish nationalists were by no means immune to the appeal of American business methods. One of the founders of the Dublin branch of the Rotary Club, Tom Grehan, had also been a member of the Gaelic League in

London at the same time as Michael Collins. As advertising manager for Ireland's most widely read newspaper, the *Irish Independent*, Grehan had heralded the 'Age of Advertising', when everyone would live in 'an atmosphere of restless push'. An avid golfer and founder of the Irish Association of Advertising Men, he invited ministers from the Provisional Government to its first dance in the ballroom of the DBC cafe on St Stephen's Green in February 1922. He might have pressed on them his belief that salesmanship was a vital modern science that must be taught in Irish universities. 'America's bounding prosperity is largely due to the extraordinary attention they give there to every aspect of salesmanship,' Grehan wrote at the time. It was advice that the new ministers might have heeded because from the beginning the Irish Free State was a colossal failure of salesmanship.

The best advertisement for Irish independence should have been the withdrawal of British forces and the transfer of power to new rulers. But there were no ceremonies of the kind that forty years later would announce 'freedom at midnight' for British colonies across the world. The handover of power in Ireland was accompanied by no independence celebrations, sonorous speeches or a single symbolic hauling down of the Union Jack. The transfer of the citadel of British power, Dublin Castle, was consummated in a private ceremony. Lord Fitzalan, who had replaced Lord French to become the last viceroy of Ireland, met Michael Collins in the Castle chamber, while the new ministers and officials of the old regime sat staring at each other in the room next door. The formalities completed, Fitzalan slipped away in a private car and the Irish ministers joined Collins around the table in the chamber before the civil servants were called in and introduced to their new bosses. Henry Robinson, vice president of the Local

Government Board, was struck by the youthful appearance of the new ministers. Most of them, he thought, 'seemed scarcely out of their teens, and all looked pale and anxious', except for Collins, who was 'cordiality itself', reaching out what the officials would have regarded as his bloodstained hands to grasp their own and shake them warmly. The event made little impression on the public. In Thurles, Father Maher confided to his diary that the takeover of Dublin Castle was 'the quietest triumph of all'. Suddenly, the synonym for British misrule had disappeared and yet 'the mighty metamorphosis for which we and our forefathers yearned passed off as if it were an everyday occurrence'.

Similarly, the evacuation of most British troops in Ireland, instead of being scripted as a historic retreat, appeared banal rather than momentous. The operation had been given the codeword 'Finis' and once the treaty was signed this was telegraphed to all commands in Ireland to signal that they should commence preparations for withdrawal. Within weeks most of the British troops had left the countryside to assemble in Dublin, Cork and the huge encampment at the Curragh in County Kildare, awaiting transport across the Irish Sea. In garrison towns across the country there were yard sales of billiard tables, cricket nets and harnesses as the barracks were emptied. Although the troops had been ritually denounced as an army of occupation, much comment focused on the loss of trade and income prompted by the departure of such reliable customers. Around the Curragh, where 7,000 troops were stationed in a camp that had all the appearances of a small town, including a cinema, it was estimated that up to £100,000 a month was spent by the military. In some villages practically every family depended on work at the garrison; farmers, market gardeners and local shopkeepers would be badly out of pocket. The dissolution of the Royal Irish Constabulary was equally swift. Half of the Auxiliaries left Ireland before the new Provisional Government took office and all had disappeared by the end of January 1922. It was the same with the Black and Tans, who headed for the Dublin ferries in cars sporting signs such as 'Sorry to leave you' and 'Good Luck to Ireland'. Regular constables were summarily withdrawn from their barracks to a holding centre near Dublin. Once again, there was no time for ceremonial leave-taking. One policeman returned to his station from a night shift at a Dublin hospital to find all his belongings piled in the square. Another recalled sitting on boxes in the street and watching the tricolour going up over his barracks. Within a couple of months of the signing of the treaty, there was no longer a functioning police force in most of Ireland.

The split had robbed the moment of any glory. Prisoners were released and returned with little fanfare. De Valera and the anti-treatyites took no part in any of the formalities in which the British administration relinquished power. Just as confusing was working out who was now in charge. Both the fictional and effective authority of the republican government and the legal but ignored authority of the British government were in suspension. A Provisional Government was to be established in Ireland in line with the arrangements set out in the treaty. But the Dáil still existed alongside a new entity called the Southern Irish Parliament. Some members of the Dáil were also Provisional Government ministers. From whom did they derive their authority? The Dáil was to be dissolved in March, a new election held in April and a constitution for the Irish Free State to be published in June. But would the final say on the constitution rest in Dublin or London? The most significant outcome of this confusion was that many of the evacuated military bases were taken over by anti-treaty IRA units. British officers who handed over the keys believed they were dealing with the army of the Provisional Government. The result was that except for the midlands, the west and parts of Dublin the barracks were in the hands of men who were not prepared to obey the new minister for defence, Richard Mulcahy. However worrying this was for the Provisional Government, ministers could not afford to admit to their British counterparts that Mulcahy was not in control of the Irish Republican Army.

They set about trying to incorporate loyal units into a new regular army. They looked like the old Volunteers in their dark-green uniforms but potential recruits with anti-treaty views were weeded out. Soon they became known as 'Government' troops, while the anti-treaty fighters were referred to as 'Republicans' or 'Irregulars'. The first battalion of the new army was the Dublin Guard, which occupied Beggars Bush barracks. It was led by men who had formed Collins's Squad during the days of street assassinations. Many of them were lukewarm about the treaty and reluctant to take orders from anyone except their old boss. And despite the efforts to ensure the loyalty of the new troops none of the new generals could be entirely sure that the men under their command were not secret allies of the anti-treaty IRA. Such was the uncertainty about allegiances that the adjutant general of the new force later admitted that he could trust nobody. 'At that [sic] time we were in Beggars Bush I did not know but the man in the next office would blow me up.'

The Provisional Government troops were in no position to challenge the anti-treaty fighters for control of the military bases around the country. The new recruits were raw, untrained and often unarmed. Even when equipped with guns, their lack of confidence meant that they often surrendered them when challenged by anti-treaty fighters. Others surrendered because they saw no point in putting their lives on the line for a government often unable to pay their wages. Small mutinies over the lack of pay or the distribution of ranks were frequent. In lieu of wages soldiers commandeered food and supplies from civilians who were now thoroughly sick of wartime norms. So when the new army finally took possession of the most important British base in Ireland at the Curragh the transition was chaotic. No ceremony had been planned, not even an exchange of pleasantries. As arranged, on seeing the Irish detachments moving towards the camp on a rainy Saturday in May 1922, most of the British soldiers marched off to the train station before their former enemies arrived. After officers from both sides completed an inspection of the perimeter, the two remaining British platoons lined up and the last post was sounded before they marched away. The Irish officers were pleasantly surprised to find that the mess rooms had been left in good order: fire grates blackened, billiard tables ironed and the cues tipped with chalk. But they then discovered that all the flagpoles had been cut down and it was midday before the tricolour was finally raised over the water tower as a line of drenched officers saluted, the rain pelting into their upturned eyes.

Those officers were fortunate that the anti-treaty fighters who controlled much of the country failed to press their advantage; instead of seizing the initiative they generally avoided open determined confrontation. In Limerick, a city that linked the west and the south-west, a stand-off developed between the government forces and the republicans that had as much to do with the rivalry between local guerrilla commanders as the principle of accepting or rejecting the treaty. Supporters of the treaty worried that if the anti-treaty fighters controlled Limerick, they would have a strong base to resist and even overthrow the Provisional Government. They were also aware that there was little they could do about it immediately because their own forces were too weak to mount a successful fight for the city.

The tension was defused by a compromise. Still reluctant to start an all-out civil war, the republicans clung to the hope that their strong position might force the Provisional Government to amend drastically or even abandon the treaty and re-establish a united anti-British front. They were supported by a large majority of IRA brigades and, most importantly, a majority of the most experienced combatants. Their strategy was to insist that the army should reassert the independent voice it enjoyed by default up to the truce. For reasons of sentiment, necessity and calculation, and in the face of opposition from some of his colleagues, the minister for defence, Richard Mulcahy, reluctantly agreed to allow them to hold a convention in March. In effect this would mean the IRA was autonomous and no longer subject to the authority of parliament. A week before the delegates were due to assemble, the government backtracked, declaring the convention illegal on the grounds that it would be the first step to establishing a military dictatorship. It was not an accusation that caused the anti-treatyites much embarrassment. At a press conference in Dublin their military leader, Rory O'Connor, claiming to represent 80 per cent of the IRA, pointed out that in many countries armies had been justified in overthrowing governments. 'If a Government goes wrong', he said plainly, 'it must take the consequences.' As guardians of the nation's political virtue, a majority in the army had the duty, he argued, as well as the means, to stop an election that was not in the country's best interests. Did this amount to a military dictatorship?

'You can take it that way if you like,' he told the journalist who had asked the question. The Provisional Government was too weak to enforce its own ban. The army convention went ahead, attended by over two hundred delegates from IRA brigades all over the country. However, rather than consolidating a united bloc with a clear strategy, the gathering revealed that the anti-treatyites were themselves split by the prospect of open war. Some pressed for a coup to stop the implementation of the treaty and push aside the politicians and staff officers prepared to compromise with the British. Others counselled restraint and a renewed attempt to find common ground to reconcile the movement. Outraged that details of this debate were published in an account of the convention that appeared in the *Freeman's Journal*, O'Connor ordered the destruction of the paper's printing press.

The public could now see that the movement that had led the country into a war or freedom was fatally divided. Two separate military organisations were forming, each with its own leaders and command structures, each claiming to be the rightful heirs to the independence struggle. The only thing the republicans lacked was a headquarters, a visible sign of their own legitimacy and coherence, a refutation of the charge that they were irregular. In a dramatic extension of the tense battle around former British outposts all over the country, anti-treaty fighters occupied the Four Courts and several other buildings in the centre of Dublin on the night of 13 April. Rising over the north quay of the Liffey, a fifteen-minute walk from Sackville Street, the Four Courts had been the centre of the Irish judicial system for more than a hundred years, its great green dome and Corinthian columns a city landmark. The occupation was not yet a declaration of war; even republican fighters struggled to divine what military advantage was gained by taking up a fixed position in the city where the government forces were strongest. It replicated the symbolism of the 1916 Rising, even though the sacrificial stand in the General Post Office came to be regarded as heroic folly by men who had fought during Easter Week and assumed the mantle of their martyred leaders.

From their new redoubt the republican leadership set out their conditions for avoiding civil war. The treaty should be abandoned, elections postponed, and the IRA established as an independent army not subject to political control. Having matched the Provisional Government by taking possession of one of the symbols of the old regime, the republicans now faced the problem of how to finance their own army. Until the army convention, anti-treaty IRA units were still funded by General Headquarters. The price of outright defiance of the government's authority was that their money was cut off. To keep the republican army intact, the leadership decided it was justified in the circumstances to hold up banks, post offices and mail trains. Newspapers were filled with accounts of armed robberies and the daily theft of cars. Provisional Government figures recorded 331 raids on post offices and 319 attacks on trains in March and April. On a single day at the beginning of May £50,000 was stolen in co-ordinated raids on branches of the National Bank. Other robberies, hold-ups and muggings on country roads were carried out by people with no connection to the IRA. There was scarcely any force with the authority to impose order. Recruiting had begun for a new police force to replace the RIC, but less than a thousand officers had been deployed when it was paralysed by mutinies and ill-discipline.

The RIC itself had almost ceased to function. Like the British soldiers, RIC constables were ordered to vacate their barracks and report to holding centres to await discharge. Unlike the situation for the soldiers there was no swift resolution of their status. Restive and anxious about what might happen to them after they gave up their uniforms, batons and rifles, separated from their wives and children, they felt incarcerated rather than liberated. 'Cannot something be done to hurry up R.I.C. disbandment?' an official at Dublin Castle wrote in March 1922. 'I hear complaints on all sides that the men are becoming discontented and moody, and that their impatience at the delay is telling seriously on their discipline. They are largely herded in concentration camps, and this in the case of the married men means separation from their wives and families, who in many cases have to face local ostracism and petty persecution unprotected . . . All fighting spirit has gone out of the men and . . . apathy and disloyalty are making inroads into their self-respect.' Although Churchill had insisted on a generous severance and pension package worth in total over a million pounds, the options for an unemployed RIC man were not enticing. Recruitment bans prompted by the public spending cuts in response to the slump left few opportunities to join a police force in Britain. Even when there were openings there were signs that the reputation of the Black and Tans had tainted any candidates from the RIC, not just in Britain but in other possible destinations such as Canada, Australia and New Zealand. There was one colonial outpost where a reputation for brutality seemed to be an advantage. Almost five hundred former RIC men, half of them Irish, joined the police force in the newly acquired British mandate in Palestine. The experience was not to everyone's taste – one recruit, finding the heat unbearable, quit after only thirteen months with lifelong memories of how some of his colleagues had 'knocked them Arabs about a bit . . . Oh, they were rough, yes.' Some of the more adventurous Black and Tans accepted generous grants to buy farms or establish a business in the US, Egypt or China. And although some Irish constables were helped to set themselves up as newsagents or tobacconists in provincial English towns, they could find it difficult to settle. The father of the literary critic Denis Donoghue took two months to find a job as an insurance agent in Chester but his life became impossible when a rumour circulated that he was a fugitive who had committed murder in Ireland. Defeated, he signed up with the new police force in Northern Ireland, despite being a Catholic, keeping his old RIC rank.

This was often the least worst option. Members of the old police force who might have imagined that relinquishing their duties would ensure their safety had discovered their mistake. Returning to Ireland as a civilian opened up the risk of being shot – more than twenty RIC men were killed in the six months after the treaty was signed. Others had narrow escapes. A sergeant imagined he would be protected because his brother was in the IRA but when he got home to Cork he was ordered to leave within twelve hours or be shot. One constable, looking forward to returning home to Donegal after demobilisation, received word from his brother that a girl had warned he should stay away. 'The man who was going to have to shoot me, him and I was pals, used to work on the next farm, and he said it was the toughest order ever he got to have to shoot me. That was why he tipped the girl to tip me off.'

Policemen were not alone in their vulnerability. On five successive nights at the end of April in County Cork, thirteen Protestant men were shot dead by anti-treaty units of the IRA, apparently in retaliation for the killing of an IRA commander during a raid on the house of a Protestant farmer. Some suggested the victims had been chosen because they had previously given information to the departing British forces or that their names had been surrendered by three British intelligence agents captured and killed by the IRA at the same time. Fearing a further massacre, hundreds of Protestants in west Cork took flight for the city or England. The attacks were unprecedented and shocking, particularly to nationalists who prided themselves on being non-sectarian. A local IRA commander issued a proclamation saying the IRA would do all in its power to protect 'all citizens irrespective of creed'. But in the power vacuum caused by the British withdrawal, the weakness of the Provisional Government and the enmity provoked by the treaty split it was not at all clear that any citizens could be guaranteed protection.

Violence or the threat of violence now accompanied the mass public meetings to debate the treaty. Rosamond Jacob noticed bands of IRA men in the big crowd assembled in Dublin to watch de Valera and others speak. On the pavement there was 'a fearful squash . . . some men apparently out to kill'. A few weeks later she watched a pro-treaty meeting in College Green. 'Collins was blasting away in his angriest style, hitting one hand with the other and loosening his hair but he didn't look half so horrid as his photos in the newspapers afterwards . . . There was a great crowd, nearly as big as the [anti-treaty] one but no IRA. They had the cheek to have Republican flags.' Roads were cut and railway lines torn up to prevent pro-treaty meetings around the country. Shots were fired while Collins gave speeches in Castlebar and Killarney. Hundreds of IRA men carrying rifles occupied Thurles when de Valera came to speak on St Patrick's Day. If the treaty was accepted, he said, the men around him would have to fight the government to defend the Republic. 'They would have to wade through Irish blood,' the newspapers reported him saying, 'through the blood of the soldiers of the Irish Government, and through, perhaps, the blood of some of the members of the Government in order to get Irish freedom.'

Remarkably, considering this charged language and the shadow of violence, many on both sides still clung to the hope that they could be reconciled. This was the sense in which de Valera could respond to accusations that he was inciting civil war by insisting that he was merely warning of the lurid consequences of division. Bloodthirsty rhetoric flourished alongside a horror of what Collins called 'fratricidal strife' and the final disintegration of a national movement in which young men had found intense camaraderie and an almost sacred purpose. Desperation to avoid an irrevocable split produced an extraordinary agreement between the two factions to prevent the election scheduled in June from becoming a referendum on the treaty or even a real contest. Under the terms of their pact, instead of competing against each other both sides would put forward a joint panel of candidates to the electorate so that the balance of pro- and anti-treaty members would not change in the new parliament. They would then form a coalition government, somehow setting aside their differences on the treaty. Parallel to the electoral pact, negotiations continued to try to reunify the army. The republican leaders in the Four Courts even agreed to stop commandeering cars and evacuate their followers from other buildings they had occupied in Dublin. Michael Collins declared that 'unity at home was more important than any treaty with the foreigner'. Whether sincere or manipulative, this note was intended to appeal to a lingering hope among anti-treatyites that the movement could come together again and defy the British government by conjuring a republic out of the treaty.

One tempting strategy for keeping the movement together was a joint front against the new administration in Northern Ireland. The signing of the treaty, with its provision for a review of the border between the six northern counties and the twenty-six counties of the Free State, raised fears among northern unionists that the territory where Protestants enjoyed a two-to-one majority might be dismembered. The Catholic minority, whose leaders had boycotted the new institutions in Belfast with the support of the government in Dublin, were subject to increased repression. At first, it appeared that the two administrations might reach an accommodation to defuse tensions. James Craig and Michael Collins met and agreed that Catholic workers expelled from the shipyards would be reinstated and the Belfast boycott ended. Encouraged by Winston Churchill, there were even optimistic hopes that these pragmatic negotiations might eventually lead to Irish reunification, as if the old nationalist idea that Irish people could settle their differences if Britain stood aside might be vindicated. But this was a mirage. Craig continued to consolidate his regime based on the B Specials and supported by the British government; Collins reached out to the anti-treaty IRA offering arms, training and financial support in a campaign to destabilise the northern state which included the kidnapping of forty-two unionists in an attempt to secure the release of IRA prisoners.

Since he indulged most of these schemes without informing his colleagues in the Provisional Government, the goal of his strategy was never entirely clear. Was it a ruse to prevent a final split in the independence movement? An attempt to overthrow the northern government and force unification through war? A way of destroying the treaty? A desperate bid to curb the intimidation of the Catholic minority? Perhaps all of these objectives were contemplated with varying degrees of clarity. In the continuing violence in Belfast, twice as many Catholics as Protestants were killed in the first six months of 1922; a quarter of the Catholics in Belfast had been driven from their homes. In March a Catholic publican and his family were killed in their home in Belfast, apparently by a notorious police assassination squad. Collins and Craig met again at the end of March and once again declared peace, but the IRA launched a disastrous offensive against police barracks in the north in May and Free State army units and IRA fighters occupied two villages on the northern side of the border. When they were forced out by British artillery (seven Free State soldiers were killed) it was clear that Northern Ireland, supported by the imperial government, was impregnable. There also seemed little prospect of further deferring a civil war between the pro- and anti-treaty factions in Dublin.

These remaining slender hopes were largely invested in the constitution being prepared for the new dominion state. Collins tried to assure his opponents that the constitution would supersede the treaty and make Ireland a republic in all but name. He was not being disingenuous; even some of his colleagues in the Provisional Government thought he was naive to believe that the British would allow the treaty signed in London to be trumped by a republican constitution written in Dublin. Collins instructed the team of lawyers drafting and redrafting that it need contain nothing about the king or an oath of allegiance. It must clearly derive its authority from the people, not the monarch, he directed, and be easy to change: it would become a stepping stone to unrestricted sovereignty, as he had promised. The very first article of the draft finally presented to British ministers in London asserted Ireland's sovereignty.

Up to this point, the British government had done everything it could to make it as easy as possible for the Provisional Government to implement the treaty, bending the rules and assuring its critics in parliament that Ireland's new rulers had everything under control. Diehard MPs opposed to the treaty had their own sources in Ireland: British naval officers, loyalists and some newspaper correspondents who were predicting breakdown and chaos. But this was not the message coming from Churchill's man on the spot, Andy Cope. Now the chief liaison officer with the Provisional Government, his interpretation of every alarming development in Dublin was the same as the line he took during the uncertainties of the truce period: everything would work out in the end. Sending the troops back to Ireland would be an admission of failure by British ministers who congratulated themselves for erasing the Irish question from British politics. Churchill confessed his dread at being dragged back into 'that hideous bog of reprisals'. But he could also quickly forget his distaste for intervention in Ireland.

At the end of March a British naval ship carrying more than a thousand rifles, revolvers and machine-guns was intercepted off the Cork coast by anti-treaty IRA men in a tugboat. They forced it to dock at a small harbour where hundreds of lorries and men were waiting. Working through the night, and fortified by whiskey from a local hotel they had forced to stay open, they carted away hundreds of rifles, dozens of machine-guns and over 300,000 rounds of ammunition. The incident provoked panic in Whitehall. Churchill, already coming around to the view that the Provisional

Government was 'feeble' and 'apologetic', was at his bombastic best when he told his cabinet colleagues that the seizure of the ship and the weapons demonstrated that 'we are in contact with revolutionaries who will stop at nothing, who are capable of brilliantly conceived operations and who have facilities and resources at their unhampered disposal both in money and arms of a kind and on a scale never previously experienced'. He had already made plans for what would happen if the anti-treatyites attempted a coup and the Provisional Government failed to respond. If they took control of Dublin, British forces would attack; if they established a government outside the capital, the British would occupy Dublin and send flying columns to attack the republicans in the countryside. The south of Ireland would be blockaded from bases in the north and by the British navy.

Could Britain do this without outraging international opinion? Lloyd George in particular was deeply concerned to avoid being seen to crush an experiment in self-government in a new dominion. Fortunately for him, newspapers, politicians and diplomats in Europe and the United States who had been previously sympathetic to Irish independence could not grasp why Ireland was now on the verge of civil war given that it had won its freedom. The intricacies of the treaty and the abstruse arguments between the rival wings of Sinn Féin were lost on a world that regarded the Irish Free State as an independent country, fulfilling a historical struggle for self-determination. Instead of taking their place in the world the Irish seemed consumed by pointless and destructive factionalism. 'Ireland had every reason to expect to become recognised as the First of the Small Nations,' the minister for foreign affairs, George Gavan Duffy, told the Dáil in April. 'It would, however, be idle to gloss over the fact that we have lost our prestige in recent months . . . If we are to retrieve the splendid position we held, we must take steps at home without delay to prove that we are a nation and not a rabble.'

So when British ministers were presented with the election pact (which provoked Churchill to accuse the Sinn Féin leaders of imitating Lenin and Trotsky) and the draft constitution (which Lloyd George regarded as the proclamation of a republic in thin disguise, treating the British monarch as an archaic joke rather than a mystical symbol of a great worldwide commonwealth) they were sure they would have the support of their dominion partners and the rest of the world in demanding that Ireland fulfil its treaty obligations. Irish ministers were summoned to London. 'We made a big concession to you in the shape of the Free State,' Churchill told them, 'disbanded the army, handed over the revenues, placed you in a position of authority. We said "No republic", but you have made one surrender after another to the republicans.' Then he demanded another surrender. 'You will find that we are just as tenacious on essential points – the Crown, the British Commonwealth, no republic – as de Valera and Rory O'Connor, and we intend to fight for our points.' The new constitution and its symbols turned out to be more important for the British than the election pact. They insisted on recognition for the authority of the Crown, an oath of allegiance to the king and the abandonment of the idea that there could be ministers in the Irish government who did not accept the treaty. To Lloyd George's surprise the Irish representatives accepted almost all of the changes they demanded: the new constitution now recognised the treaty, instead of ignoring it; the king was restored as head of state. But they managed to convince Churchill to accept the electoral pact that he feared might open the way for de Valera to take power. If there was no pact the anti-treatyites would use violence to prevent an election, the Irish ministers argued. More importantly, they were sure that the election would confirm a popular majority for the treaty.

In this they were proved right, although the result of the election, which went ahead in June 1922, was no great endorsement of the Provisional Government itself. Candidates who belonged to neither wing of Sinn Féin won a larger share of the votes than either the pro- or anti-treatyites. All of the neutrals supported the treaty because it finally offered stability. Both sides of the bitter divide in Sinn Féin regarded as an affront the challenge to a sacred national movement by Labour, the newly formed Farmers' Party and others. The runaway success of one Labour candidate was attributed to his being the only candidate 'who gave the electors a chance of breaking the old chain of silence that has bound them since 1918'. The new constitution had been published on the morning of the election. Anti-treatyites denounced it as 'a shameful document' but it is unlikely that voters had enough time to study it. They voted for peace rather than any of the competing arguments over the precise nature of Irish sovereignty. The combined vote for pro-treaty candidates amounted to nearly 80 per cent, a result that gave the treaty legitimacy. It also allowed the Provisional Government to proclaim that it had a democratic mandate.

On the morning of 22 June, less than a week after the election in Ireland, Field Marshal Sir Henry Wilson unveiled a war memorial at Liverpool Street station in London unaware that two young members of the IRA, Reginald Dunne and Joseph O'Sullivan, had arrived with the intention of shooting him. The big crowd gathered at the station to watch the unveiling made a clear shot impossible, especially since O'Sullivan had lost a limb serving with the British army in France and moved slowly on his wooden leg. Instead, they decided to go to Wilson's home in fashionable Eaton Place in Mayfair to await his return. At 2.30 p.m., after Wilson had stepped out of a taxi near his house, O'Sullivan approached him and fired twice from a distance of a few yards. Wilson managed to stagger towards his door but then Dunne stepped close, firing three more quick shots. As Wilson tottered across the pavement, bent over and crying out in pain, O'Sullivan shot him one final time and the field marshal collapsed in the street. Their escape slowed by O'Sullivan's limp, the gunmen shot and wounded two policemen who gave chase before being surrounded and captured by an angry crowd. The assassination of one of the most prominent and decorated figures in the British armed forces on his own doorstep shook the cabinet. Lloyd George and his ministers feared they would be the next targets and ordered emergency security precautions. The possibility of introducing passports for travel between Ireland and Britain was raised in parliament. Both the Provisional Government and the IRA leadership in the Four Courts denied any involvement in Wilson's murder. But an alarming British intelligence report from Dublin indicated that the order had originated in the Four Courts and could be the start of a campaign against other targets in London, Belfast and even the remaining British troops in Dublin. The following day, Friday, the cabinet ordered General Macready to return to Dublin to prepare for the capture of the Four Courts within forty-eight hours in an operation deploying tanks, artillery and aeroplanes. On the Saturday he was told to go ahead the following day. However, Macready was having second thoughts about the reliability of the intelligence reports. He had become convinced that an assault on the Four

Courts by British troops would destroy relations with the Provisional Government, reunite the IRA and invite condemnation of the British government for breaking the truce and causing the civilian casualties that would be an inevitable consequence of such a spectacular attack. He sent his senior staff officer to London and persuaded the cabinet to call off the assault; ships heading across the Irish Sea to transport hundreds of prisoners away were redirected. Instead, the cabinet authorised Churchill to deliver an ultimatum in a speech to the House of Commons on the Monday. If the Provisional Government did not take action against the Four Courts very soon, Churchill told angry MPs, Britain would regard the treaty as dead. It would feel free to reconquer Ireland.

19

Call to Arms

On Wednesday, 28 June 1922, Denis Johnston woke to be told by his mother that her sleep had been disturbed in the early hours by the noise of explosions. The late edition of the newspaper reported that Free State troops had attacked the Four Courts; the civil war had started. Denis dressed quickly and raced into town on his bicycle. Sackville Street appeared calm but he noticed thick columns of smoke pouring from the upper storeys of a building in Parnell Square to the north, which had been occupied by anti-treaty forces. A crowd was watching the fire brigade battering down the door as Denis approached. They threw ladders against walls that had been chiselled by flying bullets. Overhead there was still the occasional crack of rifle fire, which seemed to be coming from the other side of the square. The building had been attacked before the main assault on the Four Courts began. As the fire and the excitement abated, Denis rode back down Sackville Street, dropping off a note for his friend Geoffrey Tickell inviting him to a tennis party that afternoon, before crossing back over the river, past Trinity College and up Dame Street, where he saw Free State lorries and troops gathered in large numbers in front of City Hall and Dublin Castle. A little further on he found a vantage point to look down on the Four Courts across the Liffey. The buildings all around him had

been occupied by Free State soldiers. From somewhere down
on the quays they appeared to be firing a field gun. This was
not the kind of street ambush Dubliners had become used to
over the past few years; it was more like the bombardment
of the Post Office in 1916. A field gun, Denis thought, was
probably the only thing that would get the anti-treatyites out.
Down below by the river, Rosamond Jacob stood in a crowd
that had gathered at the corner of Parliament Street, held back
by a line of soldiers in green uniforms. Everyone stared at the
dome of the Four Courts 'in a senseless sort of way' as the
big gun boomed near by. Rosamond kept thinking that it was
extraordinary that the army could attack so easily. She spent
the rest of the afternoon wandering the streets around the
quays, possessed like the other onlookers by 'a diseased spirit
of curiosity'. Seeing all he needed to, Denis cycled back to
Lansdowne Road for lunch. Then he cut and rolled the lawn
and marked out the tennis court before his friends arrived.
The pop of serves and volleys, the shouts and laughter around
the court, were punctuated by the distant booms of the gun
and the occasional crackle of rifle fire.

After Churchill's speech in the House of Commons it was
no longer possible for the Provisional Government to resist
pressure from London to end the occupation. They had
enquired about the possibility of borrowing British guns to
launch an assault, even though they could not be certain that
the army would obey orders to fire on their former comrades.
This changed when the republicans in the Four Courts kidnapped the popular deputy chief of staff, Ginger O'Connell,
in reprisal for the arrest of a republican. The assault could
now be portrayed as a necessary and unavoidable assertion of
the government's authority in the face of blatant provocation;
with the republicans themselves seemingly split, the whole

affair would be over in days and some accommodation reached. On the evening of Wednesday, 27 June, men from the Dublin Guard took up positions around the Four Courts. At 3.30 a.m. an ultimatum was given to evacuate the building. The first shell was fired at 4.15 and then one every fifteen minutes after that, the rhythm of booms that had woken Denis Johnston's mother from her sleep four miles away.

As dawn broke Ernie O'Malley climbed a ladder on the dome of the Four Courts, momentarily holding still as bullets whistled past. The new day was slowly unfolding along the river below and he noticed how the light gradually illuminated the buildings in shade, taking pleasure in the variety of roof heights and the colour contrasts of shopfronts. Towards the west slight flashes in the dissipating murk revealed sniper positions. Across the river he saw the field gun recoiling as it fired towards the corner of the Courts, pulverising the top storey. Gaps were appearing in the walls, so the anti-treaty soldiers took their captive, Ginger O'Connell, to a safe room in the centre of the building. O'Malley worried that he might be bored. 'What about books, Ginger? I have a pile in my room and can bring them over. This isn't as exciting for you as it is for us.' *War and Peace*, O'Malley suggested, would be perfect reading in the circumstances. He remembered that Ginger was diplomatic: 'I'd like to read it, but I think it will be browsing because I won't have time to finish.' O'Malley returned with an armful of military books, including the recently published account by the German general Paul von Lettow-Vorbeck of his guerrilla campaign, which tied up British forces in East Africa throughout the war. Ginger was unenthused; to O'Malley's disappointment he did not seem very anxious to read. Other books had more practical uses. In the room where they had set up their field hospital, an operation to extract a

bullet from the ankle of a wounded Volunteer was persistently interrupted by sniper rounds splintering through the door.
The chaplain, Father Dominic, remembered the Law Library
near by and took two men to empty its towering shelves of
bound statutes and legal textbooks hundreds of pages thick,
which they piled in columns against the door. At night they
sat leaning against a wall under the dome and talked about
everything except the shortage of food, the lack of ammunition and their extremely hopeless position, unspoken realities
that would become the motif for their entire campaign.

Although they had launched the assault on the Four Courts
under intense pressure from the British government, the one
thing the Provisional Government had to avoid was to appear
to be carrying out British orders. Cope wrote from Dublin insisting that there must be no suggestion that Michael Collins
was responding to a request of the British government. He
was worried that the British press might credit it to 'the crack
of the English whip'. Churchill was prepared to accommodate him: 'I will of course make it clear that action is spontaneous.' Cope initially thought the Four Courts could be
repossessed before lunchtime on the same day the bombardment started. With no sign of surrender twenty-four hours
later, Churchill was already making plans for the British to
finish the job themselves. On Thursday afternoon he strongly
advised Collins to allow British howitzers to shell the Four
Courts from the Phoenix Park and drop bombs from the air:
'Aeroplanes used by untrained persons for bombing would
be a grave danger to you and very likely lead to blowing up
of a lot of women and children. Our aeroplanes manned by
[our] own pilots will carry out any action necessary; they
could be quickly painted [in] Free State colours to show that
they were an essential part of your forces.'

The inexperience of the Free State troops was the main reason why the assault appeared to be fruitless. The men were unfamiliar with the field guns they had borrowed from General Macready's arsenal. One shell landed on the lawn of British military headquarters in the Phoenix Park. When the officer in charge of the assault, General Emmet Dalton, went to apologise, he was himself nearly hit by another stray round. While the Provisional Government desperately searched for some ex-gunners who had served with the British army, Dalton was forced to take control of a gun himself for three hours. At night many men involved in the attack were falling asleep at their posts. Dalton worried that if the guns stopped firing his troops would simply abandon their positions. The British sent them fifty rounds of shrapnel to fire at intervals during the night just to make sure the guns did not fall silent.

By Friday, however, the sheer cumulative relentlessness of the bombardment had made up for its lack of military finesse and efficiency. The ability of the anti-treatyites in the Four Courts to resist was gradually crumbling. Overnight Free State troops had stormed the building at the western side and to the rear. O'Malley and his comrades were forced to retreat to the east wing, leaving behind in the archives department of the Public Records Office, the repository of the administrative history of two centuries of Irish life, a series of booby-trapped mines. Life under siege in the republican headquarters was becoming intolerable. Walls shook, showers of masonry and plaster suddenly crashed from ceilings blocking passages and corridors. No room was safe from a falling shell. Flames were creeping across the complex. There was little time for reading.

Ernie O'Malley had gone out to the main entrance and was wondering about blowing up the armoured car that had been jammed against the gate to block their exit when a thundering explosion sucked the air and knocked him over. A thick dark cloud of smoke rose hundreds of feet above the dome; from across the river it momentarily looked solid, like an enormous black fungus sprouting from the Four Courts. Spinning and swirling against the glowering backdrop were the precious documents carefully archived over two hundred years, now blown to the wind. Thousands of strips of singed white paper drifted in eddies onto the quays and the surrounding streets. Two miles away Fullam's coffee shop shook and Denis Johnston and his friends, taking a coffee after the excitement of watching the street sniping, heard shattered plate glass from shop windows on Grafton Street dashing against the pavement. At a Red Cross post on the quays Rosamond Jacob was attending to two wounded civilians. One man was panicked by the sight of his wounds and as she tried to calm him while tearing a shirt into strips for bandages the window shattered beside her and the air was filled with a repulsive burning smell.

A few hours later a white towel draped over a sweeping brush was thrust through a window in the Four Courts and the anti-treatyites began to emerge, some of the wounded helped along gently by Free State soldiers as if they were on the same side. After firing a last few impotent 'enraged volleys' at the field guns that had broken them, the republicans had cried in despair when they realised surrender was inevitable. They dismantled their guns with such ferocity that their hands were bleeding, poured paraffin on the pile of stocks and barrels and set it alight. An officer insisted they wipe their faces with handkerchiefs to obliterate the tear tracks before they lined up on the quays for inspection by the soldiers in green uniforms, former comrades who had insisted on an unconditional surrender. Ernie O'Malley spotted a Free

State captain he knew and passed him some papers for safe-keeping before tossing his Parabellum pistol over the quay wall and into the dirty water of the Liffey. A photographer began to set up his tripod to capture the image of the defeated republicans, the officers standing looking helpless in their Sam Browne belts with empty holsters. O'Malley threatened to throw him too into the river. He took down the tripod and 'melted away'.

The attempt to take the photograph of the beaten republicans was a sign of how the Provisional Government, well schooled in presenting Ireland's case to the world, grasped that propaganda would also be crucial to their survival. Strict censorship was imposed – even the British military was ticked off for discussing events in Dublin with their London superiors. As the civil war developed the press was instructed always to refer to the government forces as the 'National Army' but never to refer to the anti-treaty fighters as 'forces' or even 'troops'. They could be described as 'Irregulars' or, even better, merely 'armed men'. The press was even forbidden to use the term 'Provisional Government' in case the suggestion of contingency would dilute its legitimacy. Instead, it was simply the 'Government'. Editors who deviated from the prescribed usage were chided and harangued: the *Irish Independent* was chastised for giving the impression that the war was a conflict between two factions, and even the *Irish Times*, then the voice of Irish unionism, was accused of 'misleading the average mind' by referring to 'Republicans' instead of 'Irregulars'. Later Michael Collins argued that funerals of government soldiers should be filmed and shown in every cinema to drive home that they 'were shot maintaining the People's supremacy'. The anti-treatyites were reduced to circulating their publicity sheets by hand. Women glued copies of *Republican War News* to postboxes in the street; Denis Johnston collected a whole set. From the start of the conflict their exclusion from the mainstream media defined republicans as marginal. 'Is the majority always right?' asked one of their plaintive slogans daubed on walls in Dublin.

The surrender of the Four Courts did not mean Dublin was in government control. Anti-treaty fighters had occupied hotels along Sackville Street, including the Hammam and the Gresham, beloved of commercial travellers. They sandbagged the windows looking onto the street and smashed through the interior walls to join one room to another. The centre of Dublin became a shooting gallery that attracted a continuous stream of spectators. Many observers of the fighting remarked how the Dublin public seemed oblivious to danger. Girls in white frocks calmly sold charity flags for a hospital in streets where bullets were humming overhead. Crowds gathered to watch Free State soldiers kneeling behind the newly painted green postboxes to fire at the windows of the republican positions high above them. Warning shots fired over their heads to make them leave made no impression; instead they pressed forward to get a better view of the action. Several were keen to record their presence at a moment in history, holding up their pocket Kodak cameras as a Free State armoured car drove towards the Gresham Hotel under a hail of bullets. Sniping would halt to allow gawkers to duck back into safety. Within a few days Dubliners had once again become accustomed to rifle fire.

Making her way home one evening through what sounded like an 'orgy' of sniping, Rosamond Jacob asked a man if there had been much shooting down the street she was about to take. 'Oh any amount!' he said with a generous smile, as if he thought she was seeking it out for pleasure. Denis Johnston was walking down Westmoreland Street when a friend beckoned him into a side street where people were sheltering from spasms of firing from government snipers on the roof of the Bank of Ireland aiming towards republican positions near the bridge. 'A few shots went off, but still quite a considerable number of people kept going to and fro about their business in the street,' Denis noted with amazement in his diary. 'We're a GREAT city, Dublin; there's no doubt about it. The way business is carried calmly on in the face of all this sort of thing is amazing.' Often there was noise and dust but no sign of the combatants, so it was easy to wander into crossfire. A hatless woman in a navy-blue jacket and skirt ran in half-circles when she realised she was exposed, waving her arms until a Red Cross worker rushed from a side street and dragged her into shelter.

Denis was soon tired of the excitement: 'It's not at all pleasant cycling through the deserted streets of your home town and not knowing from what window or corner a bullet is going to flick past you. One can have enough of it in time.' A delegation of politically active women who tried to negotiate a truce was told by Cosgrave, Griffith and Collins that they would not allow the republicans to leave the hotels without giving up their guns. Rosamond Jacob joined a deputation to the republicans in the Hammam Hotel; they approached the rear entrance in an ambulance and made their way through a garage strewn with petrol tins and bicycles, past exhausted, unshaven men with revolvers jammed in leather belts. In an upper room, busy with the comings and goings of nurses, soldiers and messengers, the commanding officer, Oscar Traynor, received them. Tall and slim in a dark suit with a revolver in his belt and a Sacred Heart badge in his buttonhole, his face was tired and worn, his voice quiet though civil. He referred to his opponents as 'these people', as if they had never been part of the same movement. The delegation relayed what Collins had said: that they would be fools not to melt away quietly, taking their guns with them. He told them he no longer had faith in anything Collins said. Rosamond was struck by the utter lack of trust between the two sides.

As the buildings they occupied burned ever more fiercely, the republicans began to evacuate the hotels. De Valera slipped away to a safe house. A small group staggered out waving a white flag. On Wednesday, 5 July, a white flag appeared over the Hammam. Republican fighters then started to emerge. The last to give up were led by Cathal Brugha, who had presided over the first meeting of the Dáil. As they stood in the lane waiting for their leader to follow, Brugha appeared in the doorway, blackened by soot, carrying a revolver in each hand. He rushed out, firing blindly, and was cut down by a bullet that severed an artery in his thigh. Two days later he died in hospital. Clouds of smoke hung over Sackville Street and the city was bathed in a red glow at sunset. On Sunday Rosamond went up to the Mater Hospital to see Cathal Brugha's body lying in state. A queue stretched a quarter of a mile from the door of the mortuary, which was crammed with republican women. Brugha lay in an ill-fitting uniform (no uniform small enough to fit him could be found). Rosamond thought he looked different from her remembrance of him – his hair was nearly black and his face looked very thin and stern and ascetic. She noted how queer the hands of a dead person looked: a livid pale yellow. Alongside Brugha was a boy who had been shot outside Mountjoy Prison, a great clot of blood on his forehead.

The week's violence had left 65 people dead but Winston Churchill was most impressed by the indifference of the Free State government to the destruction of some of the great buildings of Dublin: 'Look at that great historic street of the historic capital of Ireland which was the property in the national sense . . . of this new government. They have not even hesitated, in order to stamp out the armed resistance to the Treaty, to . . . destroy even their own property worth millions of pounds.' The *Irish Builder and Engineer* cast a more parochial eye on the ruins of central Dublin, wondering if the civil war might further deflate the already depressed building trade. 'On the other hand, the destruction wrought affords the melancholy satisfaction that it will provide considerable work for architects and builders. The destruction in 1916 provided the building industry in Dublin with several million pounds' worth of work that not only tided it over the worst years of the war, but supplied almost a "boom".'

Since the Four Courts battle began Denis Johnston had viewed it as an IRA quarrel and a venting of spite: 'I can't conceive the mentality of a man behind his sandbag in the [Four Courts], what he thinks is going to be the end of it, how he imagines he's going to affect anything by hanging on there and shooting at other Irishmen, and even if he were victorious over the Free State Army how he intends to deal with the British when they come back in these [circumstances]. Beyond me. They are a set of fanatics. "Fighting for Ireland" be damned, with those election results!' The day after the Dublin siege ended a 'Call to Arms' was published in the newspapers, asking for men to sign up with the new national army for six months. Denis read that there were queues waiting to enlist at a recruiting station in Brunswick Street but when he went there he found it shuttered and barricaded. At City Hall they suggested he go to Wellington Barracks or Portobello Barracks, although they seemed doubtful as to whether there might be recruiting stations at either of these places. Feeling he had done his duty Denis went to play tennis for the afternoon.

The army being assembled by the Free State government was as chaotic as the recruiting process. There were barely 10,000 men, many of them without uniforms or guns. Khaki cloth was imported from Britain and dyed green. Those who had weapons were frequently taught how to use them on their way to an engagement. Units often had no transport and were forced to confiscate cars and motorcycles from civilians. Men joined for secure wages and regularly found they did not get paid. Soldiers developed a reputation for surrendering their weapons, drunkenness and desertion. More reliable recruits might have joined up solely out of loyalty to a commanding officer. Although they served the Provisional Government, many still thought of themselves as republicans. Some leading officers were keen to negotiate with republicans rather than fight them.

They were lucky that the republican forces were not really prepared for all-out war either. There was a marked reluctance to kill their old comrades. Several anti-treaty leaders declared their neutrality. Many were arrested in Dublin because their Provisional Government counterparts knew where to find them. As the government troops advanced on their positions after the end of the fighting in Dublin, the republicans dispersed. The shooting of a national-army soldier in Limerick was the trigger for ending the truce there on 18 July. The republicans burned the barracks they had occupied and retreated. For a week at the end of July there was some serious fighting in the countryside near Limerick after republicans took control of an armoured car and machine-guns. But their overall response to attack was to evacuate, burn their positions and retreat.

In much of Ireland any advantage the republicans possessed was weakened by the fact that they were blamed for the war. They could not hold prisoners. They had to loot and commandeer to survive, and this increased their unpopularity. Censorship denied them the opportunity to communicate with the public. Government propaganda emphasised the destruction of railways, roads and property by the retreating republicans. In interviews with foreign reporters de Valera complained that they bore all responsibility for the war but had no voice. Attacks on the railways left many areas without mail or newspapers. In the weeks after the attack on the Four Courts rumours circulated that Collins had resigned, that thousands of English troops had disembarked in Dublin Bay and that half of Dublin was burned.

As the fighting moved south many small towns were cut off by fighting in the surrounding areas. Thurles in County Tipperary was occupied by Free State troops but there were constant rumours of an imminent attack from republicans who controlled the countryside. Travellers brought stories of how the republicans were boasting they were going to surround the town, starve it into submission and then burn it to the ground. In the surrounding areas, young men were being ordered to stop their work in the hayfields to dig trenches and fell trees, and farmers were forced to feed republican fighters. In Thurles the people got used to soldiers sauntering about town, playing handball with local boys in the evenings and flirting with girls. At night drunken privates fired off their rifles; on Sundays the churches were full of soldiers taking Holy Communion. One afternoon several army lorries went out to engage the republicans, returning with 55 prisoners to cheers from the townspeople. But they also brought the body of an eighteen-year-old sergeant shot by republicans hidden in a farmhouse. A few days later, as the sergeant's coffin was being taken away for burial, soldiers started firing into the air. 'One soldier was drawing his revolver when it went off accidentally and the bullet hit a girl in the abdomen,' Father Maher wrote in his journal. The girl was the sister of the local brigadier. 'They took her to Dublin that evening but the wound proved fatal and she died this morning. The remains have just arrived and practically the whole town was present when they laid the coffin in the Cathedral at midnight.'

But over the next two weeks the republican fighters melted away. Cycling out of the town for the first time, Father Maher noticed the remains of barricades and trees that had blocked the road and the collapsed arch of a bridge: 'I met no armed men, as the people were busy everywhere saving hay.' The republican collapse all over the rest of the south was equally swift. The capture of Waterford by Free State forces was followed by looting of shops that had been occupied by republicans. Fire sales were held along the quay. One dry-goods-store owner offered bullet-riddled blankets at a reduced price. Sea landings of troops along the west coast resulted in the capture of several towns with little fighting. The heaviest resistance was in County Kerry, where Free State forces suffered 11 dead and 114 wounded.

By August 1922 Cork city was the last major area still under control of the anti-treatyites. They had requisitioned local retailers to send provisions to fighters elsewhere. Trench-coats, boots, thousands of pairs of socks and commercial vans were confiscated and sent to Limerick. Priests denounced them as robbers and looters. At the beginning of July the republicans took over the customs house and began collecting the duty on the goods still being shipped into the port. Lodging £12,000 a week to a bank account, they were able to write cheques to pay for supplies rather than sequestering them. As the summer passed Cork enjoyed a strange isolated normality. It was cut off from the rest of Ireland but the racing results from England still came by wire. Concerts and theatre performances continued in the evenings and hurling matches, athletics meetings and the annual Cork regatta went ahead as planned. Thousands of people made excursions to the seaside by train on the bank-holiday weekend. And hundreds of sightseers headed out along the coast to see the carcass of a 25-foot basking shark that had been skewered by the mail-boat and washed up on shore. The gaiety concealed the slow constriction of the city's commerce. The government cut off payment to municipal services; construction projects stalled and dockers were laid off as merchants stopped importing. Unemployment soared and homeless men were sleeping on the quayside.

In the early hours of 8 August IRA lookouts watching the wide entrance to Cork harbour noticed a ferry heading for the port. They thought it must be the Cork–Holyhead steamboat returning to port for urgent repairs. But on board were 500 Free State soldiers commanded by General Emmet Dalton. They had sailed around the coast from Dublin the previous day. Dalton held a pistol to the pilot's head to make sure he landed them safely at a point close to the city. The Free State troops and their artillery had disembarked safely before the IRA, caught unawares, was able to offer any serious resistance. Within two days the government forces were at the entrance to the city. The republicans decided to destroy the city's infrastructure before they retreated. Forty men with sledgehammers smashed the printing press of the *Cork Examiner* and the *Cork Constitution*. Military posts were set alight using large barrels of oil and by the late afternoon an acrid cloud of smoke hung over the city, the sun barely visible through the haze. IRA fighters seized delivery lorries, motorcycles and private cars and loaded them up with type-writers, a radio transmitter and small printing presses. At three o'clock a long line of vehicles sped through the city packed with war supplies, republican fighters standing on the running boards or clinging onto the rear. As thousands of on-lookers watched from across the river the last fighters tipped dozens of lorries, cars and motorbikes from Union Quay barracks into the river. Then, having cut the water mains so that the fire brigade would be unable to douse the flames, they set fire to the barracks, exploding its store of grenades and ammunition. By five o'clock the last republican fighters sped away. Before the government troops arrived two hours later looters had taken what they could from the burning barracks and the shops in the centre of the city. Crowds lined the streets to welcome the Free State army, waving their handkerchiefs and passing out cigarettes. Explosions continued into the night. People made a circuit of the seven fires burning around the city to celebrate the end of the siege.

In Macroom Castle twenty miles away, where Seán Ó Faoláin had speedily relocated the workshop in which he had been making grenades all summer, they heard the routed republicans arrive from Cork: 'We could hear them coming all night long, in trucks, private cars, by horse and cart, using anything and everything they could commandeer, and when we rose the next morning we surveyed the image of a rout. Some of these men had been fighting nonstop for a week and as they had poured in to the grounds of the castle they had fallen asleep where they stopped, on the grass, in motor cars, lying under trucks, anyhow and every how, a sad litter of exhausted men. The extraordinary sight left us under no illusions as to our "army's" capacity to form another line of battle'. Over the next few weeks the republican troops who managed to evade capture scattered further into the mountains of west Cork, hoping to continue a guerrilla campaign. The bombmakers found an abandoned house on the edge of a remote valley where they could resume mixing their powders and acid: 'In our cottage we laboured over our bombs into the late autumn while the wet clouds lowered on the mountaintops, the rains fell, and the river rose in spate until we could hear the grumbling of its brown waters outside our door above the roar of the spirit lamps, the rattle of our pestles in the mortars, the hiss of the shaken sifters.' Unlike the war against the Black and Tans, Ó Faoláin now found the local people 'at best sullen and uncooperative at worst hard against us'. Ten days after his forces had taken Cork, the commander-in-chief of the Free State army, Michael Collins, arrived in the city to inspect the banks. He wanted to track down the £100,000 of customs revenue that the IRA had lodged over the summer.

20

'Terror Will Be Struck into Them'

On the Saturday before he left Dublin for Cork, Michael Collins, accompanied by Hazel Lavery, had been to dinner at Kilteragh, the home of Sir Horace Plunkett, the Anglo-Irish champion of the cooperative movement. It was a convivial evening and the other guests were thrilled to be joined by the leading personality in the government. George Bernard Shaw read aloud to him from an article he had just published in the *Irish Times*. Although Collins made pleasant conversation, Shaw divined that 'his nerves were in rags' and could not help noticing how he persistently slapped the revolver strapped to his thigh, either from fear or as a ritual of reassurance, he could not tell. Only a few days before Collins had walked through Dublin for the funeral of Arthur Griffith, who had died of a cerebral haemorrhage after months of declining health. The equanimity with which the government absorbed the passing of the founder of Sinn Féin and the most fervent advocate of the Anglo-Irish Treaty showed how power had shifted. The civilian members of the government had led the procession but all eyes were on Collins as the cortège marched from the Pro-Cathedral to Glasnevin Cemetery, past the ruins of the hotel buildings on Sackville Street where the republicans had staged their last stand the previous month. Lady Gregory was relieved that her request for a ticket to attend the funeral had gone unanswered. On the day she was busy with rehearsals at the Abbey and preoccupied by the empty seats that would be usually be filled by English visitors in evening dress during Horse Show week. When she finally managed a break at lunchtime she stepped out just in time to catch the funeral passing. The dignity of the occasion, the immense crowds, the simple coffin covered by a tricolour impressed her greatly. A wonderful ending, she marvelled, for a man who had spent his best years 'in the office of an obscure journal in a back street in Dublin'. And there was Michael Collins marching boldly despite the danger of assassination and looking 'very much the soldier' in his general's uniform. It was a triumph of appearances. Lady Gregory did not notice the troops at the head of the cortège ducking down side streets and rejoining at the rear of the procession to hide the embarrassment that not enough men knew how to march in time.

Though exhausted, Michael Collins was now the commander-in-chief, the shimmering symbol of an army in the ascendant. In some of the photographs of this time Collins's pose bears a striking resemblance to that of Alexander Kerensky, 'the first people's minister of war' in the Russian Provisional Government of 1917, briefly hailed as the hero of civic patriotism before he was overthrown by the Bolsheviks. As did Collins, Kerensky had taken delight in his late switch from business suit to a general's uniform. One tabloid version of Collins's career published after his death had him fighting the war against the British on a white charger; Kerensky was also imagined by his adoring supporters as a warrior of liberty on a white horse. The title of commander-in-chief was coined by Collins himself in a memo to his colleagues in July. It announced – in the guise of a suggestion – the formation of a war council comprising Collins himself, Richard Mulcahy as minister for defence and Eoin O'Duffy, commander of forces in the south-west, where the fighting was most active. He even dictated the outline of a message to be published as the first 'order of the day' to his troops: 'It should be pointed out that in the present fighting the men we have lost have died for something, that the wounded are suffering for something . . . for the same principle that we fought the British for – the People's right to live and be governed in the way they themselves choose . . . What they are fighting for is the revival of the Nation [and] this revival and restoration of order cannot in any way be regarded as a step backwards, nor a repressive, nor a reactionary step, but a clear step forward.'

The dominating figure in a government standing for the defence of democracy was a charismatic general who projected the image of a national saviour. Most of the key posts in the army were given to trusted fellow conspirators in the IRB or former members of the Squad. Although he no longer attended cabinet meetings, no major decision was taken without consulting Collins. When civilian ministers pressed him for reports about the conduct of the war or demanded that the army be made more accountable, Collins ignored them. He trusted his own gifts as a micro-manager to transform a collection of lazy, incompetent and inefficient recruits into a disciplined army. Inspection tours to the countryside prompted endless detailed reprimands to officers berating their toleration of long hair, slovenliness, dirty mattresses, oversleeping, defective transport and slipshod paperwork. He also invested considerable faith in the force of his own personal authority to control the strong personalities in the army and, even more importantly, to offer the anti-treatyites a way of ending the war with their honour intact. Instead of abusing their opponents, Collins insisted that his colleagues in the Provisional Government should treat them as sincere but misguided and offer to meet them in every way save the fundamental principle of adherence to the treaty. It was no wonder then that his visit to Cork in August should have been accompanied by rumours of discreet peace feelers and secret meetings with old comrades including, most sensationally, de Valera.

With his business completed in the liberated city, the journey Collins embarked on early in the morning of 22 August had the hallmarks of a homecoming tour through the small towns and villages of his own constituency. Bystanders waved and cheered when they recognised the commander-in-chief in the back seat of his open-topped touring car, escorted by an army motorcyclist, a lorry load of riflemen and a Rolls-Royce armoured car. They stopped in pubs and hotels where General Collins stood rounds of drinks for his entourage and anyone who joined them. Their progress was remarkably slapdash considering that the area was full of anti-treaty fighters. They needed a local taxi driver to guide them around demolished bridges and trenched roads. The armoured car stalled on a hill and the soldiers had to put down their rifles and push it until it restarted. Collins himself had to get out and help to saw through a tree blocking the way. His driver took a wrong turn and they were separated from the convoy; Collins pored over the inscriptions on tombstones in a village churchyard while they waited for the rest of the convoy to catch up. The engine of his touring car overheated more than once and they had to stop to fetch water to fill the radiator. At one point early on they had stopped to ask a man outside a pub for directions. He turned out to be a republican sentry and an ambush was prepared in the unlikely event that the convoy carrying the commander-in-chief would be foolish enough to return later by the same route.

After hours spent watching the road, which they had blocked with a dray cart, most of the ambush party decided to give up waiting when the light began to fade just before eight o'clock on a drizzly summer evening. Six men were still lingering in the field overlooking the road when the convoy approached and stopped in front of the barricade. Immediately alert to the danger, Emmet Dalton, who was sitting alongside his commander-in-chief, shouted, 'Drive like hell!' but at the first shots Collins ordered his men to get out and fight. The armoured car roared backwards and forwards along the road as the machine-gunner sprayed the ambushers with bullets that cut into the grass all around them. They feared they were about to be killed until the machine-gun jammed. Now they were facing rifle fire, including, though they were unaware of it, volleys from the commander-in-chief concealed behind his car. The ambushers had given up hope of success and were now only covering their retreat. As Collins noticed them withdrawing he abandoned his position behind the car and stood in the open firing his rifle. An ex-British-army marksman took one last shot at the tall officer standing in the road. The bullet hit Collins behind his right ear and left a gaping exit wound in the side of his head. A minute passed before his men realised that Collins had fallen. They bandaged his wound and set off for Cork, Dalton cradling Collins in his lap. Their journey back in darkness was as chaotic as their daytime travels, blocked roads and wrong turns leading them through fields, distraught soldiers pushing the spinning wheels of the car carrying the body of their commander-in-chief out of the mud. It took them nearly four hours to travel the nineteen miles to the city. Collins's body was brought to a hospital and news of his death was wired to Dublin. At 3 a.m. army lorries spread through the deserted streets of the capital bringing the news to government ministers and senior army officers. The cabinet met in emergency session from 4 to 7.30 a.m. and chose William Cosgrave as the new chair of the Provisional Government. Within hours of the news breaking, Hearst newspapers contacted Dalton in Cork offering him £1,000 for his account of Collins's last hours. It was a celebrity death, shocking and tailor-made for conspiracy theories. The weeks leading up to it were reconstructed to reveal dark portents and premonitions. Sensation bred new rumours: that de Valera was dying of cancer or had shot himself; that Griffith had been poisoned and his body was to be exhumed.

The leadership of the Provisional Government passed from its most flamboyant soldier to W. T. Cosgrave, its least charismatic career politician, whose skills were honed in the debating chamber of Dublin Corporation. But rather than prompting a softening of the government's position, a turn towards concession and conciliation, the ascendancy of Cosgrave and the other civilian ministers who had toiled in the shadow of Collins signalled a new determination to defend their authority mercilessly. The government's legal adviser, Hugh Kennedy, counselled his colleagues that they would need to learn the lesson of history, that every national government that had overcome a serious challenge to its right to rule had succeeded 'by prompt, effective, vigorous and utterly ruthless action'. His example was the crushing of the revolutionary uprising in Weimar Germany four years earlier. In cases where governments had hesitated, haunted by scruples and 'a mistaken idea of humanity', disaffection had overwhelmed them. Here, he pointed to the fate of Kerensky, who had hopelessly underestimated the Bolsheviks. In an interview with an American newspaper correspondent in April, Collins himself had also drawn comparisons between

Ireland's travails and the civil wars in Poland, Germany and Finland to make the point that transition was invariably accompanied by disorder. In those countries there had been 'appalling loss of life' but Ireland would not be as bad. 'We may be depended upon to deal with the disorder in our midst just as effectively, and just as thoroughly, as those several governments dealt with it in their sphere. Our methods may be different but the results will be equally satisfactory.' Four months later Kennedy seemed to be saying that Ireland might not have the luxury of a more irenic solution to its civil war. Belief in their own legitimacy, Kennedy warned his colleagues, would be useless if they were weak-willed. Democrats could not afford pity towards those who would destroy them.

Finally convening parliament as its critics demanded, the government armed itself with new powers that made it look more like a military dictatorship than in the months when Collins and his war council were calling the shots. A Public Safety Bill introduced by the end of September established military courts with the power to order the execution of anyone found in illegal possession of a gun or who had helped an attack by republicans. Cosgrave appeared convinced by the Weimar precedent: 'Although I have always objected to a death penalty, there is no other way I know of in which ordered conditions can be restored in this country, or any security obtained for our troops or to give our troops any confidence in us as a Government. We must accept the responsibility.' Another minister, Ernest Blythe, mused that the reluctance to take life had weakened the government's case.

It was as if they were talking themselves into a posture of callous righteousness. Notions of peace moves, keeping channels open and creative experimentation with the treaty had no currency in this new dispensation. Key clauses of the treaty could no longer be altered by the Dáil. Elected members involved in the anti-treaty campaign were liable to arrest. In one final flourish of the old impulse for conciliation, Richard Mulcahy secretly met de Valera in early September, confiding in only one of his cabinet colleagues. The encounter was a failure: de Valera said he was merely a humble soldier. Furious that he had taken a risk for nothing, Mulcahy decided compromise was impossible and abandoned all his reservations about military courts.

Largely for propaganda purposes an amnesty was offered for those who handed in their weapons before the middle of October. A month later came the first executions. Four young men, all aged between eighteen and twenty-one, picked up at night in Dublin carrying loaded revolvers and thought to be preparing a street ambush, were shot at 7 a.m. on 17 November in Kilmainham Gaol, the same prison where the 1916 leaders had been executed. The firing squad, carefully chosen for their loyalty, were inured to the dark ironies of history; later that morning they were seen swinging their revolvers as they returned to their base. Like the many executions to follow, the men were condemned and shot before any public announcement. A new official form was prepared – 'Remains of _____ coffined and buried' – and copies despatched to the deceased's next of kin; reading a son's or brother's name written into the blank space was how their relatives found out they had been executed. This bureaucratic insensibility was likely more calculated than thoughtless. When a laconic communiqué was published in the evening newspapers its bald brevity made the news of the executions even more shocking. In the Dáil the Labour leader, Thomas Johnson, predicted public revulsion if more information was not given. But Richard Mulcahy said the executions were intended to 'astound the country' and make people realise 'what a grave thing it is to take a human life'. Many remarked that the executed men were unknown or even 'nonentities', but Kevin O'Higgins argued that their very ordinariness would make their fate more of a deterrent because they could not be exonerated by special circumstances: 'If you took as your first case some man who was outstandingly active or outstandingly wicked in his activities the unfortunate dupes through the country might say, "Oh he was killed because he was a leader" or "He was killed because he was an Englishman."'

This was taken as a reference to Erskine Childers, captured at the house of his cousin a week previously. Unknown to the public, Childers had been sentenced to death that same day for possession of a small automatic pistol. An attempt by his lawyers to challenge the legality of the military courts was struck down on the grounds that the state of war that Childers himself had helped to create meant civil law was suspended. One of his legal team complained bitterly that he was being condemned according to 'black man's law . . . the law applied to negroes and hindoos under the English Privy Council'. O'Higgins and his colleagues were obsessed with demonising Childers. Grossly overestimating his influence on the IRA campaign, their propaganda created an image of a fanatical renegade, depicting him as the director of the campaign to destroy bridges and railways in order to engineer social and economic collapse. In fact, he scarcely knew how to fire the gun he carried; it was more an affectation than a weapon. At 8 o'clock on the morning of 24 November he was taken to a shed at the back of Beggars Bush barracks. In the winter murk he struggled to make out the figures in the firing party ('There were no Irishmen . . . they were Irishmen who were in the British army,' his guard recalled). The roof over his head had been removed so that he was illuminated by daylight as he was shot.

Secrecy bred rumours about petty indignities and worse torments allegedly inflicted on the condemned men. It was said that Childers was refused the comfort of choosing the cleric who would give him the last rites. But a much more serious failure of religious compassion for republicans was the absence of any comment on the executions from the Catholic Church. Instead of extending solace to the condemned men the bishops had spiritually stood behind the firing squad. In a remarkably unequivocal pastoral letter to all Catholics a few days before the deadline for the amnesty expired, the bishops had proclaimed that, in the eyes of God, the Provisional Government was the sole lawful authority in the land. The republican resistance could not be fairly judged a war, merely 'a system of murder and assassination of the national forces', for which the penalty would be excommunication, the denial of the sacraments and the suspension of any priest prepared to administer them to republican fighters. Unlike Church pronouncements on violence during the War of Independence, which castigated the British as much as the IRA, there was no criticism of the Provisional Government or the conduct of its army. The suspicion that the Church had given moral sanction to the execution policy was confirmed by the letter Cosgrave sent to the Archbishop of Dublin the day after the execution of the anonymous four in Kilmainham. The bishops' statement had provided the moral grounds to justify the many more death sentences that would follow. The government would be acting 'in the spirit of the solemn teaching of our highest moral authority', Cosgrave wrote, quoting the pastoral letter's judgement that it was not a matter of 'mere politics but what is morally right or wrong according to the Divine Law'.

Assessing how much the Church influenced public opinion is not straightforward. After all, denunciations from the pulpit of the assassination of policemen were ignored by many who regarded themselves as conscientious Catholics. That the bishops were now acting in concert with an Irish government – not censuring violent resistance to a foreign ruler – would make it much harder to escape their moral leadership. But the bishops were also tapping into a profound weariness with the endless chaos of the troubles and a sense that, whatever the defects of the treaty and the idealism of some of those prepared to make a stand for a republic, it was no longer a comprehensible war or one worth continuing. There was a strong sense that it should have been settled by now and each new death described in the newspaper – one day, a train driver killed when his engine hit torn-up track in Kerry; the next, a bank clerk shot by soldiers at a checkpoint in Dublin – were grotesque dramas of pointlessness. Even before the retaking of Cork, Michael Collins had been very optimistic that peace and a return to consensus were not far off. Once the army had driven the republicans out of their strongholds in the south, he told ministers a few weeks before his death, there would no longer be a military problem – the Dáil could be reconvened and the normal rule of law resumed, with judges and policemen in charge instead of soldiers. The one remaining issue, Collins believed, was that the activities of small bands of republicans had left ordinary people 'cowed'. Typically, Collins expressed the solution to this problem as an issue of educating his opponents that the game was up, not crushing them under an iron heel. If the army could extend itself beyond the towns and cities where it had been hailed as a saviour, the republicans would realise 'that they had lost their grip on the people' and lose all hope of continuing. But the republicans refused to get the message. They persisted in believing that popular opinion would turn against a coercive government. Instead, bank robberies and sabotage made daily life impossible, but the republicans seemed too obtuse to notice. People whose tolerance of trees blocking the roads was exhausted were dismissed – 'We have the whole island to think of and you only of your miserable trees.' Indiscriminate firing in crowded streets, the killing of a commercial traveller who blundered into an ambush laid for government troops led some even to suggest they were as reckless and unpredictable as the Black and Tans. One report said armed men had taken over the land of a farmer whose wife had given republican soldiers the worst breakfast they had ever received – they got only skimmed milk.

It is extraordinary, given their own clear awareness of the importance of propaganda, how little the republicans seemed to consider the impact of their campaign. In December 1922 George Russell addressed an open letter to the anti-treatyites calling on them to abandon their struggle because most people now regarded them, not the government, as the cause of their suffering. It was inconsistent, Russell argued, to maintain that people voted for the treaty only because of Britain's threat of war and then use fear to get the public to yield to the anti-treaty policy. It was February 1923 before the republican chief of staff, Liam Lynch, seemed to appreciate how much robberies in particular were infuriating the public, issuing a proclamation that 'it is hereby solemnly notified that robbery will be sternly suppressed and that persons falsely representing themselves to be soldiers of the Irish Republican Army will be dealt with summarily'. Ironically, the leader on the anti-treaty side who took most public blame for showing contempt for the popular desire for peace was the one most

prepared to be candid with his comrades about the unpopularity of their cause. Their greatest weakness, de Valera told
the republican commanders in the autumn of 1922, was that
the majority was not on their side. But, to Lynch, de Valera
really was just another soldier in his army. And de Valera
was well aware of his impotence, reflecting how he was
watching the war 'as through a wall of glass, powerless to
intervene effectively'. Believing that there was no hope of
success he advised on new, creative ways of accepting the
treaty; at the same time he was putting his name to press
statements pledging the anti-treatyites to 'victory or utter
defeat and extermination'. Like the American defense secretary Robert McNamara and Vietnam in the 1960s he was
the public face of a war he no longer believed in. Not that de
Valera had a public profile any longer. Bearded, ragged,
haunted and seized by intense bouts of despair, he was un-
recognisable as the nationalist hero who bestrode the world
stage in New York and London. Most crushingly of all his
opponents had written him off as a politician. Dismissing
any more talk of a negotiated peace, Cosgrave was wither-
ing: 'So far as I can ascertain Mr de Valera is not in a position to "deliver the goods" as the Americans say and I do
not know of any person that is.'

On 6 December 1922, the first anniversary of the signing of
the treaty, the Irish Free State came into existence. Its Irish
name, 'Éire', appeared on a new postage stamp, the nation
represented by an image of the island with no trace of a border. The new governor general, Tim Healy, was sworn in at
five o'clock in the afternoon and members of the Dáil took
their seats in the lecture theatre of the Royal Dublin Society,
housed in Leinster House, the eighteenth-century mansion
whose lawn was the launch pad for the first balloon to take

flight in Ireland. For half an hour members took the oath of allegiance to the king and Cosgrave was elected president of the Executive Council, the new cabinet. The mood was subdued, understandably so since the deputies now faced the threat of assassination.

The executions had extinguished any remaining embers of trust between the leaders of the new state and their former comrades. Lynch's riposte to what he called the 'bad faith, dishonest methods and barbarous acts' of the government was to order his subordinates to kill parliamentarians, newspaper publishers and several other categories of government supporters. The day after the foundation of the new state, a member of the Dáil, Sean Hales, was shot dead, and its deputy speaker, Pádraic Ó Máille, was wounded in an attack in Dublin. The dead man's brother had helped to organise the ambush on Michael Collins. The assassination had not been planned; a member of the Dublin IRA was passing a hotel on the quays as the deputies were leaving after lunch. The newspapers were forbidden from publishing Lynch's order for reprisals, so the public was unaware that the attack might signal the implementation of a new policy. Members of the Dáil and new Senate knew full well what might follow. Some fled the city, pursued by intelligence agents determined to bring them back for their own safety. Convinced that this was merely the beginning of the threatened assassination campaign and fearful that establishment figures might be so intimidated that they would withdraw support for the new state, army officers recommended shooting four prisoners captured after the surrender of the Four Courts in the summer as a devastating reprisal. Richard Mulcahy put their request before an emergency cabinet meeting that night. One account of the decision taken by the seven ministers present suggested

that Kevin O'Higgins had argued against the summary
executions for some time before finally agreeing. But in an
unpublished memoir, Ernest Blythe (who went on to be
managing director of the Abbey Theatre for twenty-six years)
described a brisk, even cool, consideration of the army's proposal. Blythe arrived slightly late because his watch was
running slow: 'As I moved from the door to my usual place at
the table, I heard the list of names being read out . . . I gathered the proposal was that they should be executed in the
morning without trial . . . On the instant I mentally accepted
the suggestion which . . . was being made.' Following a very
brief discussion the question was put and Blythe was one of
the first to vote in favour. He recalled that O'Higgins 'was
prepared to take a more studied view of many problems than
the rest of us. He asked whether any other measures would
suffice. The answer he got from two or three was that it would
not. His hesitation did not last more than a minute and he
did not ask more than two or three questions. The rest of us
waited in silence watching him and he finally said, "Take
them out and shoot them."'

Mulcahy signed official notices for the shooting of each
prisoner that made no pretence that his orders possessed the
legal authority conferred on the military courts. It was
explicitly an act of retaliation: 'You are hereby notified that,
being a person taken in arms against the Government, you
will be executed at 8 a.m. on Friday 8th December as a
reprisal for the assassination of Brigadier Sean Hales T.D., in
Dublin, on the 7th December, on his way to a meeting of Dáil
Éireann and as a solemn warning to those associated [with]
you who are engaged in a conspiracy of assassination against
the representatives of the Irish People.' Later that morning,
Rory O'Connor, Liam Mellows, Joe McKelvey and Dick

Barrett, who had all surrendered after the fall of the Four Courts, were shot by firing squad in Mountjoy Prison. In the Dáil, Labour leaders said it was murder. In London, *The Times* asserted that the British government had never stooped to such drastic measures. O'Higgins, one of only two members of the cabinet to express misgivings before agreeing to the executions, said the decision was taken after 'the coldest of cold discussions', which must have been an act of supreme willed detachment on his part since he had been best man at O'Connor's wedding less than a year previously: 'There was never an act done through personal vengeance, and never an act done through hot blood. We have no higher aim than to place the people of Ireland in the saddle in Ireland, and let them do their will, but we will not acquiesce in gun-bullying, and we will take very stern and drastic measures to stop it. Personal spite, great heavens! Vindictiveness! One of these men was a friend of mine.' With that he sat down, apparently overcome. Cosgrave claimed that the night before the shooting on the quays, he and Mulcahy had agreed that it was time to show clemency to anyone facing a death sentence from a military court. Then came the assassination of 'one of the most inoffensive members of this Dáil'. It was now a psychological battle against an inhuman conspiracy: 'It is where terror meets terror . . . There is only one way to meet it, and that is to crush it and show them that terror will be struck into them.'

As the leaders of an internationally recognised state, Cosgrave and his colleagues did not have the option of behaving like the underground government they had run during the war against the British. Then, being ingenious, fugitives had given a sense of reality to a makebelieve regime, but now their credibility depended on remaining visible occupants of the landmarks of the state in the capital city. The circumstances bred a new sense of mission. Government buildings became a fortress of constitutionalism, behind sandbags and barbed wire. Ministers and civil servants slept in their offices under armed guard, occasionally joined by their wives. The comment by Kevin O'Higgins that the state was established by 'eight young men . . . standing amid the ruins of one administration, with the foundations of another not yet laid and with wild men screaming through the key-hole' refers to the original Provisional Government but was likely inspired by the sense of siege that was at its most intense in the winter of 1922–3. They equated their own fate with the survival of the country, the embodiment of the new state. They could no longer listen to their feelings or doubts or scruples. Desmond Fitzgerald defended the reprisal executions in a letter to a friend: 'We are charged with the responsibility of saving our country and the people in it from ruin . . . In the position we are in we can have only one ideal and that is the continued existence of our country and our people. The fact that existence is jeopardised forces us to take every step, no matter how ruthless it may be, to avert national extinction.' To suppress your better instincts was a form of higher calling.

No matter how exalted they saw their mission they still kept a keen eye on popular reaction. It appeared to be in their favour. One government supporter confided in her diary that she was initially 'startled' and thought reprisals against prisoners was 'taking a leaf out of England's book', but she was soon persuaded (by Blythe's wife) that such killings would save lives in the long run. Mulcahy had given one of his intelligence agents the task of monitoring public opinion. The word was that there was general approval but some disquiet that the men shot had been captured before an amnesty had been offered. Gradually, the new government became increasingly confident that the public would support executions if they could be persuaded that they would stop the war. They were helped to make their case by an arson attack on the home of Sean McGarry – a member of the Dáil who had helped de Valera's escape from Lincoln Prison – in which his wife and two children were badly burned (his seven-year-old son died in hospital). After this Cosgrave took to referring to the republicans as 'people who roast children'. Seven men were executed in Kildare on 19 December, the first executions outside Dublin. Emboldened by the absence of public outrage, the minister for agriculture, Patrick Hogan, pushed for executions to be carried out with 'machinelike regularity'. His ally O'Higgins argued that executions were needed in every county because for republicans in the countryside reading about executions in Dublin was like reading about events in a novel or a history book. 'The people are thirsty for peace, and thirsty for strong ruthless and efficient measures, because they believe such measures will bring peace,' Hogan wrote in a memo to the cabinet. 'There will not be the slightest re-action against any measure we take provided they are strong and efficient, and the people will give us plenty of time to do our work if they feel we mean business.' Their case for bringing executions to the provinces won the day. Units of army officers, many of them not ranked higher than captain, were established as mobile military tribunals, travelling around the country to conduct summary trials of prisoners arrested under the Public Safety Act. The scope of the act itself was extended so that even sympathisers with the republicans tempted to play even the slightest part in sustaining their campaign might face the death penalty.

Thirty-four men were executed in eleven different counties in January. As before, it was a secretive process. The men faced their sentence knowing friends and relations were unaware what was about to happen to them; the only person allowed to see them was a priest approved by the local army commander. Doing the work efficiently did not come as easily to members of the firing squads as it came to Patrick Hogan to propose it; bottles of whiskey were ordered in to steady them after the job was done. The bodies of the executed men were buried in the grounds of the barracks. Only then would next of kin be notified. A woman spent the morning shopping in the town where her son had just been executed and was informed by an official who overtook her on her way home. Occasionally there were small demonstrations. Women who gathered to recite the Rosary outside a prison in Dundalk where three men had been executed were dispersed when revolver and machine-gun rounds were fired over their heads. But overall Hogan's prediction that there would be little reaction was vindicated, so much so that Cosgrave could confidently dismiss a delegation of neutral IRA men trying to start peace talks in February: 'There was a lull after the first executions but once the people saw we were in earnest they came along. We never got so much information as we are getting now. The executions have had a remarkable effect. It is a sad thing to say, but it is nevertheless the case.'

21

Dumping Arms

It was unlikely, the correspondent for the *Ring* wrote with awe, that a major boxing match had ever been staged under such conditions: soldiers with fixed bayonets posted under the ropes, armoured cars patrolling the streets outside the arena, machine-guns trained on the entrance, where fight fans wearing sprigs of shamrock were searched twice by detectives. At 7.30 p.m. on 17 March 1923, nearly two thousand spectators packed La Scala cinema in Dublin to watch the light-heavyweight champion of the world defend his title. A cloud of cigarette smoke drifted over the ring, where a dull warm-up bout staggered to a conclusion under powerful arc lights. The clatter of typewriters rose through the hubbub of conversation among the banks of reporters seated below the ropes, blue, white and red on one side, green, white and yellow on the other. Latecomers trying to locate their seats hurried down the aisles past soldiers, stepping on nutshells and discarded orange peel littering the floor. Cheers went up when the recently defeated world champion, the French matinee idol Georges Carpentier, was shown to his ringside seat. In the gallery, ministers of the Irish Free State government sat near the former British army heavyweight champion.

Without warning, a deep, low boom reverberated through the theatre and the walls appeared to shake. Silence intruded momentarily until spectators turned to each other. Where had the bomb gone off? A mine had been planted by the Pillar Picture House down the street in an attempt to sever the power supply to La Scala. The explosion sent fragments of ceiling plaster crashing onto the audience, who had watched the exit doors being blown in towards them; the violinists and the cellist in the orchestra were propelled from their seats. In the haze of dust, *Peggy Puts It Over* – a comedy about how a liberated young American woman with a civil-engineering degree set about rebuilding her sleepy rural home town and found love on the way – still flickered on the screen. In Sackville Street, the crowd assembled to soak up the excitement of the big fight, now thirty thousand strong, could see the dust rising in the side street. Some ran, thinking La Scala was under attack. But within minutes it was clear that this had been just another wartime incident, a mundane inconvenience of modern city life, not worth worrying about on a night when the eyes of the world were on Dublin. In the boxing arena the lights beamed steadily down on the canvas and the impatient crowd readied itself to give half its attention to one more warm-up bout before the title fight. A bandsman from the Free State army stepped into the ring for a fight with a boxer from London.

Three days earlier, after the execution of seven republican prisoners in the space of forty-eight hours, the IRA had circulated a notice reminding the public of their duties towards the dead: 'It is hereby decreed that, until further notice, the present be observed as a time of national mourning, that all sports and amusements be suspended, that all theatres, picture-houses and other places of amusement and resort be closed, and in particular that all horse racing, hunting, coursing and all outdoor sports be discontinued.' Although the censorship ensured the IRA statement was not published in the press, theatre and cinema managers in Dublin decided to shut their premises the following evening. Threats to blow up La Scala were delivered directly to the promoters of the world-title fight. When the government realised what was happening it sent troops to the foyers of theatres and cinemas in Dublin to order the managers to keep the doors open. Detectives from the Criminal Investigation Department (the CID) took over La Scala to ensure that the management would not be tempted to comply with the republican proclamation.

The fight in La Scala was too important to cancel; Ireland's international reputation depended on it. The defending champion about to enter the ring in Dublin, Battling Siki, was the most notorious boxer in the world. A French war hero from Senegal, who had won a croix de guerre and fought at the Battle of the Somme, Siki had knocked out the reigning light-heavyweight champion, Georges Carpentier, in Paris the previous September. His victory had astonished the growing transatlantic boxing audience created by the screening of major fights in cinemas (among them Rosamond Jacob, who watched the Siki–Carpentier fight in the Masterpiece cinema in Dublin on her thirty-fourth birthday). It was not just that Carpentier was expected to win, or that he was 'the most popular French idol since Napoleon', a decorated fighter pilot in the defeat of Germany and star of *The Wonder Man*, a movie in which he had played a fictional version of himself. ('Signed portraits of the great people of the world all round him', wrote a reporter who visited his apartment in Paris, 'remind him that he, too, is in the front rank of the famous.') The most shocking aspect of Carpentier's defeat was that he had been beaten by a black man: Battling Siki was the first African world champion in any sport.

A scandal erupted when Siki revealed that he had defied an order to lose the fight. Newspapers and magazines in Europe and the United States insisted that France had made an error allowing the fight to go ahead. Hundreds of thousands of black and Arab veterans returning to Africa were a danger to France and the world – with Siki's victory they 'ceased to regard white Frenchmen as unquestionably superiors'. Ho Chi Minh, still in Paris after his failure to make progress at the peace conference, tried to argue that, from the colonial viewpoint, the Carpentier–Siki match was a better advertisement for French rule than a hundred speeches lauding the principle of equality between races. 'Ever since colonialism has existed, the Whites have been paid to bash in the faces of the Blacks,' Ho wrote. 'For once, a Black has been paid to do the same thing to a White.'

Siki was signed up to fight the English champion, Joe Beckett, in London in December 1922. But in November, the British government banned the fight. 'In contests between men of colour and white men, the temperaments of the contestants are not comparable,' the Home Office explained. And since so many persons of colour were subjects of the British Empire, a Siki–Beckett fight in London would not be in the national interest because it might 'arouse passions which it is inadvisable to stimulate'. *The Times* agreed: film of the black American Jack Johnson winning the world heavyweight title in Australia in 1908 had created difficulties for 'white policemen in dealing with natives thousands of miles away'. As a result, 'boxing matches between white men and blacks, to be photographed for the delectation of coloured races all over the world, have become a dangerous anachronism'. Prospects for Siki's next fight looked bleak until his British promoter was approached by an Irish racehorse trainer with an interest in boxing. The trainer had an alternative opponent in mind for Siki, and more importantly an alternative venue. Since the Home Office now had no jurisdiction in the new Irish Free State, the prohibition on matches between black and white fighters would not apply to Dublin, unless the new Irish government objected. The racehorse trainer travelled to Paris and offered Siki a fight against a thirty-nine-year-old Irish-American, Francis McTigue, who was coming to the end of his career. When news broke that Siki had signed a contract to fight in Dublin, the French press proclaimed that Ireland was truly announcing itself as a free state.

Siki's appearance in Dublin was much anticipated. After watching him in the cinema, Rosamond Jacob was excited by the prospect of seeing him in the flesh. Roger Casement's brother Tom told her he had met a woman who was ill at the idea of 'a black savage' being allowed to fight a white man in Ireland's capital city. Tom thought she was cracked. And W. B. Yeats's brother Jack, the painter, also did not think Siki 'a low disgrace' as others did. From the moment he arrived in Ireland Siki was mobbed. Crowds ran onto the platform when his train pulled into Kingsbridge station, calling out his name when he appeared alongside his blond Dutch wife. They clapped him on the back as he made his way to the car waiting for him and jumped on the running board as it drove away, pressing their faces against the windows. A police guard followed Siki on his journeys around Dublin to keep away curious autograph hunters. Thousands of people, many more than were able to get a ticket to see him box McTigue at La Scala, paid to watch him train for the fight at the Rotunda, a concert hall at the top of Sackville Street now used as a cinema, near where some of the 1916 rebels had been held after their surrender. Rosamond discovered she was one of only a handful of women in a crowd of men. She admired Siki's fine figure and 'lovely brown colour' as she watched him skip, spar and work with his medicine ball. He ended the show by leaping around the stage like a wild cat. 'It was awfully interesting and so different from seeing it on the films.'

Tension had risen in the days before the fight. Two soldiers had been shot in Dublin, one of them unarmed as he walked home from the cinema. A lorry filled with soldiers escorted Siki's car in murky drizzle from his hotel in Howth to La Scala. On their way into the city the little convoy had to make its way around a street barricade and as they drove off the soldiers were fired on. Rumours were circulating that new attacks were planned to stop the fight or shoot spectators. Hours before it was due to begin the promoters considered calling off the fight, but the government insisted it must go ahead. Hundreds of extra troops were brought to the city centre in armoured cars.

Everybody had relaxed when they realised that the explosion in the picture-house down the street was not going to spoil the evening. There was even laughter when the arc lights were cut and the searchlight fell on the master of ceremonies in the centre of the ring: 'We have received an order from the military that you must keep your seats until 11.30 p.m.' Georges Carpentier was introduced to the crowd and stepped into the ring to acknowledge the applause. Then it was time for the main event. To most observers it was a one-sided contest. Siki threw heavy punches at McTigue, who skittered away like a crab. Only in the late rounds did McTigue essay a brief flurry of punches, and then Siki went back on the offensive. But when the bell sounded the referee raised McTigue's arm. Even some of the Irish fans protested at such a blatant injustice. It was an hour after the fight ended before the spectators were allowed to leave La Scala. Revolver fire crackled near by; people were knocked over in the rush to safety. The next day Rosamond Jacob read news of McTigue's victory on points. She found this 'very strange and surprising'.

For the Free State government the fight was a demonstration to the world that the civil war was nearly over. The fight was a success from the government's point of view. 'The complete failure to prevent the Siki–McTigue fight and other outdoor sports has proved conclusively how tightly the Government forces hold the reins,' the *New York Times* reported from Dublin four days later. It was not just that the Dublin public had ignored the IRA threats and filled La Scala as well as other theatres and cinemas around the city. The executions had spread demoralisation among the anti-treatyites. In January, one of their most senior commanders, Liam Deasy, awoke in a safe house in Tipperary to find a Free State officer pointing a revolver from the end of his bed. The loaded revolver under his pillow guaranteed a death sentence. Deasy asked for a stay of execution to allow him to try to persuade his comrades to end the war. He was told it would be granted only if he agreed to an unconditional surrender and wrote to all the senior officers of the IRA urging them to do the same. At 4 a.m. on the day of his execution he accepted the terms. His letter to his comrades explained that he had believed for some time that destruction was all that could be achieved by continuing the campaign. Contact with Free State soldiers since his arrest had convinced him that he was deluded in thinking that there might be mass desertion to the republican side. Continuing the war would only create more unemployment, more recruits for the Free State army, 'fodder for the battlefields'. But he identified the executions as the most important issue, the certain prospect of an endless cycle of reprisals and counter-reprisals: 'Then we will have arrived at a point where the war will be waged by both sides against the people . . . in the majority non-combatants, whose only crime is having a son or a brother in either army . . .' Although his appeal was unanimously rejected, the surrender of such a senior and respected figure made it difficult for many to continue a struggle they already doubted. 'It created an air of unreality,' one IRA man said, 'for we weren't sure which of the important officers would go next.'

Despite this, or perhaps in an attempt to counter defeatism, the chief of staff of the IRA, Liam Lynch, proclaimed that his army was 'in a stronger military position than at any period in its history' and that 'victory is within our grasp'. Since the shelling of towns and cities occupied by the anti-treatyites had been crucial to the success of the Free State forces, Lynch believed that if he got hold of even one piece of artillery it would demoralise the Free State forces and end the war. An Irish American supporter embarked on a mission to Germany to secure a field gun that could be dismantled and easily carried by guerrilla fighters; this ended in promising but eventually fruitless contact with one of Adolf Hitler's 'best men' in Munich.

In the meantime the IRA campaign was disintegrating along the lines that Deasy feared. In Wexford, an anti-treaty unit crossed paths with a Free State officer and his troops in a pub. The officer tried to draw his weapon but the IRA commander knocked him to the floor with a burst from his machine-gun. As the soldiers surrendered, the commander bent down and dressed the officer's wounds. When he stood up he marched four of the soldiers to the backyard of the pub and shot them one by one. One of his own men, horrified by what he had seen, abandoned the campaign. Such incidents partly reflected how little opportunity the anti-treatyites had for fighting. Since 'proper jobs' were almost impossible, according to one IRA man, 'the rule of the Torch and Can are proved to be more effective' in trying to make government impossible. As before, Anglo-Irish mansions were an inviting target for arson, which was now directed at the grandees who had been nominated by the government to the newly created Senate. It was a familiar routine: servants woken by armed men in the night, petrol cans spilled across ancient timber floors, some valuables – paintings, silver, furniture – removed to the lawn, from where a family or their faithful retainers watched flames consume the Big House. Many valuable paintings and a historic library were destroyed when Marl-field House, the residence of Senator John Bagwell, near Clonmel in County Tipperary, was burned in January. The family of Daniel Joseph Byrne, a deputy representing the Farmers' Party, was ordered out of his residence in Mullina-hone, County Tipperary, 'at the point of a revolver'.

It was difficult to discern the political aim of this violence and often impossible to work out whether it was carried out by republicans or opportunists posing as republicans. Three men charged with robbery in Sligo told their victims, 'We are Bolsheviks from the Ox mountains and we are starving.' Far from being guerrilla fighters, they had already been tied to the railings of a local church by an IRA unit as a punishment for petty theft. The disturbed circumstances made it very easy to steal timber from the woods behind the high walls surround-ing the Anglo-Irish estates. Was this a political reprisal, equiva-lent in motive to the work of the men with petrol cans, or just looting? It was in rural areas where it was most difficult to disentangle political and social grievances from covetousness. Hay barns were set alight in an attempt to force Catholic farmers to abandon their land so that it could be divided up among their impoverished neighbours. For the anti-treatyites, dissipated and nearly beaten, stoking these grievances was both a means of generating popularity and making the country ungovernable. The minister for agriculture, Patrick Hogan, warned his colleagues that '"land for the people" is almost as respectable an objective as the "Republic" and would make a much wider appeal'. He likened local combinations of tenants to the Ku Klux Klan, burning and shooting their neighbours into submission. Only the army, he believed, could restore order in the countryside – although there was evidence that land invasions were often tolerated when the people involved were related to Free State officers. Hogan argued successfully for the establishment of mobile units of soldiers devoted solely to taking action against land seizures and whose members would have no connections in the areas where they were sent. By the summer of 1923 the Special Infantry Corps had achieved considerable success in clearing occupied farms. The trespassers were not arrested and were generally allowed to keep their animals after paying a hefty fine, but in some cases cattle were seized and taken to Dublin to be sold. These soldiers appeared to be immune from local pressure. Men, women and children rushed towards a unit of the Special Infantry Corps that had arrived to impound cattle on a western farm. The troops fired into the air and the crowd retreated.

In many places anti-treatyite activity, land agitation and labour disputes overlapped. World agricultural prices plummeted as farmers in Canada, Australia and Uruguay took advantage of war shortages in Europe to boost production. In

Britain, Ireland's biggest market, the government could no longer guarantee the price for corn. In the Irish countryside farmers facing falling returns from their barley, potatoes or eggs sought sharp reductions in the wages they paid to their labourers. In the new wave of strikes, firing of crops and sabotage of machinery, both farmers and labourers tried to get the republicans on their side. IRA men, organised by a farmer's son, escorted milk carts through hostile pickets in Cork. Farmers paid republicans to break up pickets or protect workers willing to ignore them. In County Tipperary, the IRA threatened to shoot workers occupying creameries and factories owned by the Condensed Milk Company of Ireland, popularly known as Cleeves. And in several places the farmers established their own militia, styling themselves, in another borrowing from the Russian civil war, as masked 'White Guards' and burning labourers' cottages. As much as the sputtering guerrilla warfare of the anti-treatyites, it was the general unrest, the torching of hay barns, the nighttime shootings, the seizure of property, that provoked the Free State's most articulate ideologues, O'Higgins and Hogan, to increasingly shrill tirades about how Ireland had collapsed into anarchy. For O'Higgins this was not a war but 'organised crime and sabotage on the grand scale, anarchy with arms'. The most telling sign that civilisation was breaking down was the impossibility of recruiting enough bailiffs to impound cattle to enforce payment of debts. What worried him most was the effect on the country's international reputation. The Irish, O'Higgins feared, 'bid fair to be classed with the nigger and the Mexican, as a people unable to govern themselves'. There was some substance to the idea that Ireland could become a failed state and that Britain might even be able to justify re-occupation to restore order. A British observer went so far as to remark that 'Ireland's failure strengthens the cause of those who believe in strong imperial government rather than democracy'. Such a verdict represented a humiliating comedown for a country that had so successfully courted international attention and a revolutionary movement that had been so good at making Ireland a world issue, putting British policy in the wrong.

Moreover, for the Free State government the polarisation of the war had made the treaty – once presented as a malleable and temporary necessity, a diplomatic way station on a journey towards a more expansive freedom – the foundation document of independence. After the break-up of the coalition government in London in the autumn of 1922, Cosgrave wrote to Churchill commending him on the vision and boldness that had produced a settlement: 'We share your faith in the Treaty which our nations have made and ratified and in its fulfilment we look to find goodwill and unity in Ireland and peace at last between Great Britain and Ireland and the fruits of peace.' In this view the treaty established Britain and Ireland as equals rather than condemning Ireland to permanent subordination.

An even bigger problem for the ministers worried about Ireland's reputation was that their own forces were contributing to the sense of anarchy. The national army had grown to more than fifty thousand officers and men, not all of them under control. One reason for the introduction of judicial executions was to prevent reprisals against prisoners. In September 1920 six republican prisoners were taken out and shot on a mountain in Sligo; one of them was the son of the minister for education. Another cabinet member had been passed an account of how the body of an IRA prisoner was found tortured and riddled with bullets in a wood in Kerry. A Free State officer in

Cork officially complained after the shooting of a prisoner by former members of the Squad that had provoked some men under his command to threaten to stop fighting in protest. If this kind of work continued, the officer warned, it could corrupt the entire army: 'If I was taken prisoner I would want to be treated as one. Therefore we must do the same and I oppose that Policy in the strongest way . . .' Only a few months earlier it was one of the ministers so worried about anarchy and the breakdown of law, Patrick Hogan, who had suggested that the army was being 'a little too courteous, a little too ready to take prisoners' after two Free State officers had been shot by IRA men pretending to surrender.

It was not just sections of the army that had developed a reputation for summary justice. Oriel House, the head-quarters of the Criminal Investigation Department, became the base for a squad of armed, plain-clothes detectives who conducted the kind of operations now associated with Argentina during the dirty wars of the 1970s. Established by Michael Collins during the truce to protect independence leaders in the final days of British rule and counter British intelligence, it had by 1923 absorbed other secretive units set up to protect ministers and buildings and gather intelligence. One afternoon in August 1922 two republicans were pulled from a car on a north Dublin street in daylight and shot dead. A British soldier saw three men in army uniform and three men in trenchcoats speed from the scene in a Ford car. In October the bodies of three young men who had been carry-ing anti-treatyite posters and had been picked up by men from Oriel House were found in a ditch in west Dublin. Accounts by prisoners who escaped death spoke of interrogation under torture. Many of the key figures in Oriel House had been part of the network of Dublin gunmen who carried out assassinations on the orders of Michael Collins during the independence struggle, work that an army officer later recalled 'left them anything but normal', constantly seeking out danger and excitement.

The most notorious atrocity carried out by Free State forces, the killing of republican prisoners in Kerry, also involved men who had been personally loyal to Collins. It epitomised the accidental, vengeful nature of civil-war violence, where personal grievance and political allegiance were interchangeable. Its origins lay in a dispute between a farmer in north Kerry and the remaining bands of republican fighters resisting the Free State army, which controlled the major towns after landing from the sea in August 1922. The farmer asked the local IRA commander to take his men out of a field of hay so that he could save it; the commander refused and dismissed him. When a patrol of Free State soldiers arrived in the area shortly afterwards the IRA suspected the farmer had informed on them. They kidnapped him, held him for three days of interrogation and set him free on condition that he pay a 'fine'. When he failed to pay they raided his farm, drove away his cattle and confiscated his pony and trap and a substantial amount of cash. Enraged, the farmer's son enlisted in the Free State army, bringing valuable local knowledge to help the intelligence work. Local republicans forged a letter from a known informant revealing the location of an arms dump and addressed it to the farmer's son at the local hotel the Free State troops had taken over as their base. Guiding a Free State patrol to the supposed location of the arms dump one night in early March 1923, he walked them into a trap. A mine was triggered and five members of the Free State patrol were killed, including two former members of Collins's Squad. The farmer's son was decapitated; arms, legs and pieces of uniform were found hundreds of yards away. In Tralee, the commanding officer of Free State troops in Kerry, Paddy O'Daly, had to be physically restrained by his officers when he heard the news. Twenty-four hours later he issued an order that in future all suspicious obstacles were to be cleared by republican prisoners. Shortly afterwards, nine prisoners were brought from Tralee to a place called Ballyseedy and set down at a barricade on the road; apparently it exploded as they were dismantling it. An eyewitness passing by the following morning saw an enormous hole in the road and pieces of human flesh hanging from the trees. O'Daly issued a statement explaining that the prisoners had been pulling down the roadblock when a concealed mine exploded and all nine were killed. But two days later it emerged that one of the prisoners had survived the explosion, crawling across a river, even though the skin had been burned from his fingers, to seek shelter in a farmhouse. His account, subsequently confirmed years later, was that the prisoners had been tied together around a specially constructed bomb, detonated from a distance by Free State officers. It was a reprisal devised with the support and sanction of O'Daly. Nine other republican prisoners were killed in similar circumstances around the same time. O'Daly was later put in charge of the military inquiry into the incident; it concluded that the barricade had been a trap for the Free State soldiers. Richard Mulcahy read his report into the record of the Dáil, adding that although 'the troops in Kerry have had to fight against every ugly form of warfare', it was inconceivable that they would be guilty of killing the prisoners. The government condemned the 'disgraceful' behaviour of the relatives of the dead men, who had smashed the wooden boxes in which their remains were handed over at the gates of the army barracks in Tralee. But a sympathetic witness said the relatives had been outraged that their dead had been thrown in boxes assembled from painted boards and that while the bodies were being handed over an army band had lined up to play ragtime tunes.

The atrocity at Ballyseedy had no military significance. By then more senior republican officers had concluded that they were beaten. Even if they had been able to realise their dream of provoking the return of British forces, the war had become so bitter that the two sides of the independence movement would not have reunited to fight them. Scorning the pessimism of those around him, the IRA chief of staff, Liam Lynch, still persisted in holding 'great hopes for the future'. At a meeting of exhausted republican leaders in the mountains on the border of Tipperary and Waterford at the end of March 1923, a proposal to call off the campaign was narrowly defeated. Convening the meeting had been a risk and as they broke up they found themselves pursued by Free State troops. On 10 April, Lynch was shot and captured as he scrambled across the Knockmealdown mountains in Tipperary. The same day the new governor-general, Tim Healy, and Cosgrave were attending the races at Punchestown, watching a jockey in his seventies win the main race on a horse called Pride of Arras. As he was being carried shoulder high to be presented to Healy and Cosgrave, it was announced that Liam Lynch had died of his wounds.

Lynch's burial coincided with the opening of a new play in the Abbey Theatre in Dublin. *The Shadow of a Gunman* was the first work by Sean O'Casey to be performed on the stage. Set in the Dublin tenements during the worst guerrilla warfare in 1920, its characters are helpless to escape the violence of the IRA or the Black and Tans. The Abbey was still under armed guard after the IRA threat to the theatres and cinemas in the week of the world-title fight. Lady Gregory found one of the detectives in the green room advising an actor playing a Black and Tan on final adjustments to his costume and demonstrating how to hold a revolver. She was delighted with the big audience that filled the theatre. The programme advised them to stay calm during the play: 'Any gunshots heard during the performance are part of the script. Members of the audience must at all times remain seated.' Seamus Shields, whose room in a city tenement is the scene of all the action, ventriloquised O'Casey's diagnosis of how the revolution had turned out: 'I believe in the freedom of Ireland and that England has no right to be here, but I draw the line when I hear the gunmen blowin' about dyin' for the people, when it's the people that are dyin' for the gunmen!'

It appeared that the message was being heard offstage. The death of Lynch opened the way for the IRA leadership to recognise their hopeless military position and they authorised de Valera to sue for peace. While still rejecting the treaty and the oath, his peace terms announced that the republicans were finally prepared to accept the will of the majority as 'a rule of order'. Even if the people's verdict was not 'right or just or permanent', armed opposition was no longer justified. The new chief of staff, Frank Aiken, suspended military operations from noon on 30 April. But the government demanded the surrender of republican guns to Free State forces before any truce or release of prisoners; the last two republican prisoners to be executed faced the firing squad two days after Aiken's ceasefire order. Acknowledging defeat but refusing to submit to these terms, the republican leadership ordered their followers at the end of May to stop fighting and hide their weapons: 'The dumping of arms does not mean that the usefulness of the IRA is past, or release any member of it from his duty to his country. On the contrary a disciplined Volunteer force, ready for any emergency, will be a great strength to the Nation in its march to Independence. It is clearly our duty to keep the Army Organisation intact.' Peace seemed to descend quickly, taking people by surprise. Three months later Father Maher was struck by the lack of enthusiasm or excitement on the eve of the general election in which the republicans fielded candidates. 'The roads are all cleaned, bridges have been permanently repaired, the railways are working normally, the Dáil meetings have been held in peace, no mansions have been burned, and robberies and violence of all kinds have practically subsided . . . Strikes are the curse of the country now . . . Emigration is going on to an alarming extent through the want of employment owing to stagnation of trade and there seems to be no hope of its cessation until the people will rise to a sense of their duty to the nation as well as to themselves.'

22

Jazz Mad

One evening in November 1919 Rosamond Jacob dropped in on her friends Ned and Lily Stephens in their house near St Stephen's Green in Dublin and found them engrossed in a book on dreams. It was so interesting that they immediately began to talk about it. According to the author, Ned told Rosamond, all dreams emerged from the subconscious; scientific examination of the thoughts swirling through the mind during sleep would reveal the true desires of this hidden self. Most dreams, the book claimed, were about sexual desires that the conscious self was too fearful to acknowledge. This made sense to Ned. He and Lily knew a girl who was terrified of any thoughts about sex entering her head; she was in such 'a half-cracked state of prudery' that she was ashamed to eat in public. They had tried to help her and even seemed to be making progress until she turned against them and stopped coming to their house, excusing herself by saying she disapproved of their Sinn Féin sympathies and the murder of policemen. Later, when Rosamond came to write about the evening in her diary she remarked in a puzzled tone how comparatively few of her own dreams seemed to be about sex. But the book did seem very intriguing, even if she struggled to recall the name of the author, 'some German professor'. A few weeks later Rosamond's sister-in-law loaned her a new book by a woman called Barbara Low: *Psychoanalysis: A Brief Account of the Freudian Theory.*

Although Freud's works began to appear in English translations in 1909, it was after the war that they started to make a major popular impression in Britain and America, partly because his methods were adapted to treat thousands of war veterans suffering from shell shock. Barbara Low's primer was only one of several bestselling books aimed at introducing psychoanalysis to a wide audience. She assured readers that Freud's discoveries made him the equal of Newton and Darwin. His work provided 'new keys by which we can now unlock doors in the human personality hitherto impassable'. The room that looked the most enticing was the secret chamber of sexual desire. Soon Freud's theories were the latest fad among middle-class readers. His books, claimed the *Saturday Review*, were 'discussed over the soup with the latest play or novel'. D. H. Lawrence joked that psychoanalysis had become 'a public danger', with 'the Oedipus complex a household word, the incest motive a commonplace of tea-table chat'. Opportunists saw an opening: one advertisement for an eight-lesson correspondence course in psychoanalysis promised that it would lead to a £1,000-a-year salary. British newspapers such as the *Daily Graphic* published articles investigating 'The Latest Fashionable Cult', to which women seemed particularly susceptible. A major concern was the potential for abuse by quacks, and stories emerged of treatment that ended in seduction or even rape. 'Charlatans Who Prey Upon Women and Weak-Minded Men' were exposed and vilified.

Psychoanalysis was not the only doctrine encouraging women to explore their sexuality. The need for sex education was much in vogue among social reformers. Popular books strove to undermine the inhibitions that made discussion of sex seem perverted instead of normal. In 1918 Marie Stopes published *Married Love*, ostensibly a guide to deepening the joy of conjugal life but intended to be read as a revelation of how women could satisfy a sexual passion as visceral as hunger. Its disclosures were all the more electrifying for being cloaked in coy metaphors to evade the censor. Stopes received hundreds of letters from women (and men) expressing gratitude. It sold two thousand copies within a week and was followed by her birth-control manual, *Wise Parenthood*. The new frankness extended beyond self-help advice and reforming tracts. The New Zealand writer Katherine Mansfield was astounded by the fiction being published in 1920, which revealed 'female writers discovering a freedom, frankness, a license, to speak their hearts reveal themselves as . . . sex maniacs. There's not a relationship between a man and woman that isn't the one sexual relationship – at its lowest.'

In the British popular press the prevailing view was that women were out of control. A lawyer in a notorious divorce case blamed wartime conditions for the collapse of respectable norms: 'During the war women mixed with men to an alarming extent. They did things that would have shocked our ancestors. The result is that you have the new woman of independent or Bohemian habits.' Old-fashioned virtue was passé for this hideously evolved creature. 'Love is a joke,' a newspaper columnist scoffed, 'one of the amusements, one of the sports, one of the recreations of society.' The war had created a demand for recreation itself to be an intense experience. There was 'a constant winding-up of the brain' with cocktails and cocaine. 'It is so easy to take – just snuffed up the nose,' a journalist who investigated the phenomenon in 1916 reported, 'and no one seems to know why the girls who suffer from this body- and soul-racking habit find the drug so easy to obtain. In the ladies' cloakroom of a certain establishment two bucketfuls of thrown-away small circular cardboard boxes were discovered by the cleaners the other day – discarded cocaine boxes.' The death of the twenty-two-year-old actress Billie Carleton from a cocaine overdose after she attended the Victory Ball in the Albert Hall in November 1918 led to the sensational trial of the man accused of supplying her with the drug and provoked a panic about the availability of 'cocaine cigarettes'. In *Ways of Revelation*, the bestselling novel that helped to win Wilfrid Ewart the commission to report on the troubles in Ireland, the wife of the central character is killed by her cocaine addiction.

Every night, as the war raged in Ireland, overwrought accounts of these events made their way across the Irish Sea on the mailboat carrying the English newspapers and magazines. At the turn of the century the Irish-born London-based journalist Michael McDonagh was astonished by the popularity of penny weekly publications such as *Tit Bits* and *Woman's Life*: 'Week after week enormous bundles of these journals are sent to all the chief towns and villages throughout the country.' The continued appetite among their fellow citizens for these debased scandal sheets was an affront to Irish nationalists, some of whom regarded them as rivalled only by the imported stage shows featuring 'nigger minstrelsy' and 'Cockney music-hall singers'. Vigilance Associations were established to harass newsagents, and the IRA regularly seized British papers from street sellers and railway stations and burned them in disgust. Even those who might not have approved of the IRA or Sinn Féin would have commended this crude censorship. A priest won loud applause at the annual conference of the Catholic Truth Society in October 1920 when he demanded 'a merciless war' against English

Sunday papers: 'They must not be stocked or sold in Ireland; they must be driven out.' What would prove to be one of the most influential lay Catholic organisations in twentieth-century Ireland, the Knights of Columbanus, was formally established in 1922 to combat 'a general decadence in moral standards due to the new values being propagated by . . . foreign newspapers and periodicals'.

But all this vigilance was misdirected. Irish newspapers might not have been as brash as their British counterparts but they displayed no high-minded indifference to popular mores in London. On 17 March 1920 the *Irish Independent* carried an article on how the tattoo was 'the latest craze of the leisured ladies of Mayfair'. Quoting the Italian criminologist Cesare Lombroso, who regarded tattooed skin as one of the signs of an inherited criminal tendency, the article suggested with mock solemnity that 'the Dublin girl will not succumb to the fad' because 'she limits herself to the summer tattoo which has just time to wear off before the dancing months begin'. Girls well beyond the big city could familiarise themselves with images of metropolitan chic by opening their provincial newspapers, which carried women's pages syndicated from England with features on Parisian fashions and Hollywood lifestyles illustrated by photographs showing off short dresses and bobbed hair. Gaelic League organisers of traditional ceilidh dances were concerned when girls turned up with Parisian hemlines. Everyone could recognise a flapper in 1920s Ireland. A short story appeared on the 'Woman and Her Home' page of the *Irish Times* in which a daughter commiserated with her mother over the enervating dullness her generation had endured in their youth: 'It must have been deadly: no cinema, no broadcasting, you had not even a motor car, nothing but a push bike. Then think of your dances

. . . no Tango, not a Foxtrot or Two-step . . . Those trailing skirts were the limit, and every morning you had to stick a couple of dozen hairpins in your hair . . . And if you wanted to smoke a cigarette it was in fear and trembling of being found out.'

The English newspapers were not the sole disseminators of vulgar new fashions and fads, and they could also be just as censorious about the drift of modern morals as any Irish Catholic priest. In some quarters in post-war Britain hedonism was viewed as an ideology as dangerous as Bolshevism. Police, vigilance commissions and the popular press led crusades against dancing and drinking. The Bishop of Birmingham oversaw an inquiry sponsored by the National Council of Public Morals into the effect of cinema on schoolchildren. Wandsworth Council in London forbade mixed tennis unless a chaperone was present. Paris was often identified as the fount of corruption and such shameless practices as backless dresses. Once again it was modern women who were regarded as the most disturbing threat to the moral order. An MP suggested making it illegal for girls of sixteen or under to bob their hair, with fines or imprisonment as punishment for offenders. 'The war has profoundly disturbed the feminine mind,' wrote James Douglas in the *Sunday Express*. 'Many millions of young males have been slaughtered, mutilated or deranged. The strange herd-soul of woman, moving in the mass, has taken fright at the sentence of celibacy which has been passed upon her. There are not enough men to go round. Before the war the rivalry of women was acute. Today it is frenzied. Instinctively, the herd-soul of woman is doubling its allurements, trebling its wiles, quadrupling its baits. It has cast modesty to the winds. It has abandoned all its reserves and reticences. The vogue of the jazz dance is one symptom of this frenzy.'

Jazz had also arrived in Dublin. In the autumn of 1919 John P. Mandeville, a veteran of the war from County Tipperary, applied to a court in Dublin for a music and dancing licence for his premises at 35 Dawson Street, across from the Mansion House where the Dáil had assembled a few months previously. Entrance prices would be steep; objectionable customers would be excluded and no alcohol would be served, only lemonade and cake. But the music would be jazz. 'What is jazz?' the judge enquired. A new form of music, probably from Africa, which could best be described as noise, replied the lawyer hired by the Vigilance Association to oppose the licence. It was so wild that it took possession of the personalities of the musicians and they grimaced as they played. 'Do they accompany it by contortions to their bodies?' The lawyer had no idea; he had never been to a nightclub. Captain Cohen, Mr Mandeville's business partner, tried to help the judge. The drummer's contortions were merely a symptom of the difficulty of the beat he had to follow. There was nothing suggestive, nothing 'more voluptuous than early Victorian dances' about jazz. Why then, asked opponents of the licence, had jazz been hunted out of decent ballrooms in Paris and London? They called as a witness the leader of one of the most successful dance bands in Dublin, J. Clarke Barry. Jazz music was excluded from entertainments at the Viceregal Lodge and the Gresham Hotel, he confirmed. In his opinion jazz players were not musicians at all: 'Exaggerated jazz music by nigger musicians is most decidedly suggestive and indecent.' The judge was not so easily swayed. That the grimace of a musician suggested immorality was not a statement he was prepared to accept; some objections to jazz dancing he believed were motivated by humbug and Phariseeism. And he was impressed by the applicant and the two members of the jazz band, who appeared to be respectable young men who had served their country well by fighting in the war. They could go ahead with their scheme but he would ask the Vigilance Association and the police to keep a close eye on their dance club and if there was a suggestion of immorality they would lose their licence.

Dancehalls were inherently suspicious places for the guardians of morality in newly independent Ireland. One bishop described them as 'importations from the vilest dens of London, Paris and New York – direct and unmistakable incitements to evil thoughts, evil desires and the grossest acts of impurity'. Motor cars ran dancehalls a close second as occasions of sin, especially when they were put to other uses than forming raucous convoys at Sinn Féin election rallies or flying-column joyrides. Bishops feared that cars allowed young people to escape parental control. Men and women sat together in cars outside dancehalls and travelled to the beaches, where they indulged in mixed bathing.

Modern times must have appeared genuinely worrying for bishops in newly independent Ireland. A Jesuit priest delivered a series of Lenten lectures in Dublin in 1922 on the 'Idols of Modern Society', which included the 'menace of materialism', the 'collapse of chastity' and 'godless education'. The newspapers were full of developments in politics, science and morals that threatened to undermine confidence in fundamental rules of nature. Bolshevism, Einstein's theories, eugenics and other revolutionary doctrines were just as likely to appear in the news columns as society divorces and the Paris fashions. And they could no longer be avoided in public discussion. Shortly after Marie Stopes opened the first clinic to give out contraceptive products in London on 17 March 1921, she addressed a well-attended public meeting to argue that birth control would preserve the best of the race: there was no point in allowing wastrels to breed. A Catholic priest stood up to protest in vain. Psychoanalysis was particularly threatening because it celebrated sexuality and sought to discredit religious restraint or perhaps even to do away with religion altogether. Writing in a tone suited to a Lenten pastoral, D. H. Lawrence expressed his fear that psycho-analysts 'have crept in among us as healers and physicians; growing bolder, they have asserted their authority as scien-tists; two more minutes and they will appear as apostles . . . doctors are the priests, nay-worse, the medicine men of our decadent society . . . Psychoanalysis is out, under a thera-peutic disguise to do away entirely with the moral faculty in man.' Clerical hostility towards the popular press was a symptom of the panic that these revolutionary ideas were all now accessible in simple prose to anyone who could read. In 1922 the Reverend David Barry warned readers of the *Irish Ecclesiastical Record* that sermons were no match for the papers in shaping the popular mind: 'The influence of the press having attained such dimensions . . . and growing al-most *pari passu* with the emancipation of the masses, it is clear that a sound . . . public opinion regarding the claims of religion and morality can hardly be hoped for, if the exhorta-tions from the pulpit on Sunday, and the edifying example given by those who are comparatively few, have to withstand a debased tone and scandalous reports in the papers to which nearly all have access every day.'

Potentially more menacing than the newspapers, since it materialised from thin air, was the arrival of radio. The BBC began broadcasting in 1922, a few weeks before the foundation of the Irish Free State. Anyone who acquired a radio set could tune in to signals from Hilversum, Helvetia or Budapest. After two years of deliberation, the minister for posts and telegraphs, J. J. Walsh – the man who had supervised the greening of the postboxes – announced in 1925 the establishment of a national radio station funded and run by the government. Those who hoped that native technology might provide some protection from outside influences would not have been reassured by the message of welcome sent to the new station by the director general of the BBC, John Reith, six weeks before its launch on New Year's Day, 1926: 'We are now on the threshold of the international era, in the course of which the medium of the wireless will permit a free exchange of thought and culture between all nations, continents and races.' And their worst fears would have been confirmed by George Russell's prophecy published at the same moment. 'Within a few years,' Russell ventured, 'I doubt if there will be any village in Ireland, any valley however remote amid the hills, where it will not be possible for the country folk to be not only within hearing distance of Dublin, but also London, Paris, Berlin and even the United States. Imagination fails in trying to realise the complexities, the myriad changes in the mentality of the country folk which may come within a generation.'

In their Lenten pastoral in the spring of 1924, the Irish bishops decried a long list of shameful abuses in Irish social life. Chief among them were women's fashions and immodest dress; drink, strikes and lockouts; evil literature, theatrical performances, cinema exhibitions and 'indecent' dancing. Such public pronouncements might well have been influenced by the rise in promiscuity, sexual crimes and illegitimate births in both town and country in the early 1920s. But they also chimed with the prevailing view of the new Irish government that the revolution had not only spawned rancorous political division but disorder in every other sphere. Addressing the Irish Society at Oxford University at the end of October 1924, Kevin O'Higgins celebrated a return to normality in Ireland, epitomised by the lengthy parliamentary debates about whether eggs should be stamped at the farm or by the egg dealer, or butter graded at the ports or in the creameries. He was relieved that the revolutionary period had finally passed since it had been characterised by 'a weird composite of idealism, neurosis, megalomania and criminality' and the sudden outburst of 'savage primitive passion'. While O'Higgins was obviously referring to the violence and destruction of the civil war, he had begun to regard the revolutionary years as an era of more general spiritual collapse that could be repaired only by discipline, determined sobriety and the disavowal of any pursuit of utopias. Political upheaval was conflated with modern restlessness. His diagnosis of Ireland's malaise is indistinguishable from the five plagues afflicting the modern world identified by Pope Benedict XV in 1920: 'Negation of Authority, Hatred Among Brothers, Thirst for Pleasure, Disgust for Work, Forgetfulness of the supernatural objects of life.'

The conduct of women was often singled out as a prime example of the Irish crisis. The revolution had brought women into public life to a degree never seen before. They appeared on public platforms and in the uniforms of Cumann na mBan. They carried arms and documents and ammunition. They were prominent in the debates on the treaty. By the end of the civil war there were more than four hundred women in prison. At this stage the reaction against 'neurotic girls' in public life had begun. Their passion for politics was as unbalanced as their embrace of hedonism. Cosgrave talked of women 'whose ecstasies at their extremest can find no outlet so satisfying as destruction – sheer destruction. Weak men in their atmosphere seek peace in concurrence with their frenzy.' Instead of pursuing politics, republican women 'should have rosaries in their hands or be at home with knitting needles'. When asked in the Dáil whether giving women the vote had been a success, Kevin O'Higgins was more diplomatic, if no less pointed: 'I would not like to pronounce an opinion on it in public.' Commentators worried that the lure of display and assertion were undermining women's proper maternal role. According to the *Irish Independent* there were 'mothers who preferred the fashionable crowded thoroughfare to their own quiet home; there were mothers who preferred talking on a platform or in a crowded council chamber to chatting to their children in a nursery'. Catholic leaders took up the same theme. A bishop in the west of Ireland told a confirmation class of ten-year-olds and their parents that women who helped armed men were furies: 'If I had a little girl friend who took up politics I would give up praying for her . . . Who would respect them or who would marry them? Do your work as your grandmothers did before you.'

Irish women were to embody the qualities of purity, virtue and integrity by which the nation would distinguish itself from the materialism and hedonism of its nearest neighbour. But they were curiously susceptible to foreign influences and needed careful monitoring to ensure that they would live up to the role assigned to them. Women, according to Father J. S. Sheehy of the Catholic Truth Society, had the power to protect or destroy the nation: 'Will you be the bane or the blessing of man: a ministering angel or a wily temptress? . . . Don't so dress that you may give scandal to all right-thinking Christians. Exercise good sense and good taste as well as modesty. Don't be suggestive in dress or movement.' The

Bishop of Galway suggested that parents of wayward girls should 'lay the lash across their backs'. They were not innocent or misled: 'Some of our Irish girls are becoming regular devils, and are a source of disgrace to the countryside. If it were not for the purity of Irish boys there would be far more scandals than there are today. Parents should not allow their girls to wander along countryside roads at night and go to all-night dances where there is drinking.'

Bishops expected Irish Catholics not merely to listen to what they had to say but to submit themselves to their guidance as subjects might defer to sovereign rulers. In October 1922 the prominent Jesuit Father Peter Finlay wrote that bishops were 'divinely appointed teachers' and there was 'no authority on earth' that could defy their commands. One bishop likened himself to the Pope within his own diocese. The chaos of the revolution presented them with invaluable material for refashioning themselves as unerring judges of the right path that would guarantee order and peace. They pointed to those who had ignored the warnings of their priests and bishops and now were filled with regret over the bitterness and vengeance their reckless pursuit of political passion had unleashed. It was time for Irish Catholics to acknowledge the wisdom of their spiritual superiors. In a frightening and insecure world, the bishops would be the best sources of reassurance and protection, so their voices should be heeded on whatever matter they cared to pronounce.

Members of the new Irish government were more than happy to defer to the authority of the bishops. It was not just that the bishops had been a crucial source of support in turning public opinion in favour of the treaty, or that many of the government ministers were themselves devout Catholics. They shared both a political and spiritual vision of Ireland as an exemplary outpost of virtue. And especially because this ideal had been undermined by the bitterness and schisms of the revolution, the purging of indecencies and foreign influence would be a fundamental step towards re-establishing Ireland as a spiritual model for the world, in the sense that many speakers articulated during the treaty debates. One of the first pieces of legislation introduced by the new government was the Censorship of Films Bill. Kevin O'Higgins noted that while he was 'not amongst those who attribute all our present troubles to the cinema', it was 'beyond question' that there was a need for a new censorship regime. 'I think it will be found to be a non-contentious measure and will go through quickly. In view of the considerable and growing demand for the measure I feel justified in asking the Dáil to consider it even in times like the present.'

The demand had come from religious pressure groups who in the eyes of the government were both representative of sound public opinion and also the best way of keeping excessive restlessness in check. Populist invigilation of public morals was a feature of the post-war world in Britain and the United States. But Ireland was one of several European countries where the Pope's exhortation to lay Catholics to involve themselves in moulding mass opinion was heeded. Clubs and associations such as the Catholic Young Men's Society and the Pioneer Total Abstinence Association flourished. The Society of St Vincent de Paul, a charitable organisation founded in France in the nineteenth century to reinforce adherence to Catholicism among the poor, developed a strong presence in Ireland. The Society provided fuel, clothes and shoes to families in need or prepared former prisoners for work. But members also visited families in their homes to ensure they were maintaining their devotional duties, bringing them rosary beads and scapulars. 'Where information was received that persons were negligent in attending Mass or receiving the sacraments,' one Dublin fraternity reported, 'special visits were paid and discreet pressure applied to secure a return to regularity in this [sic] practices.'

This work of St Vincent de Paul was just one of the ways in which the Catholic Church provided social services for a small new state bereft of money, resources and economic ideas and entering a world just emerging from a severe post-war recession. The revolutionaries in power discovered that economic dependence on Britain proved a far greater erosion of sovereignty than the oath of fidelity to the king. By the end of the 1920s more than 90 per cent of Irish exports were sold in Britain and nearly 80 per cent of imports were bought from the neighbouring island. Since the bulk of these exports were food and drink it seemed to follow that making farmers rich would make the nation rich. It was the worst moment for a poorly developed agricultural country to enter the world economy on its own terms. Produce from vast mechanised farms in the New World untouched by the European war had sent agricultural prices plummeting. As electricity and oil became the dominant forms of energy, labour-saving gadgets, not meat and eggs, emerged as the desired merchandise of the 1920s. Across Europe factories established by American multi-national companies popularised consumer brands such as Singer sewing machines, Ponds cosmetics, Remington typewriters and NCR office equipment. 'When a Frenchman installs steam heat;' wrote an American correspondent in Rome, 'or an Italian drinks a cocktail instead of a vermouth; or an Englishman says "I guess"; or a Pole purchases a motor tractor; or a Spaniard chews gum (called *chicle*); or a German produces a motor car in series or hurries over his lunch – he is convinced he is being American.' Fixated on the necessity of maintaining agricultural trade with Britain, Free State ministers dismissed voices suggesting that, rather than passively allowing this tide of consumer durables to wash over the country, Ireland should offer a free-trade zone to American firms manufacturing goods for the European market.

This was not a position forced on them by necessity. The ministers of the new independent state shared an intellectual and temperamental sympathy with the restoration of Victorian norms now being pursued by the British government: the gold standard, balanced budgets, massive reductions in public spending and reduced taxes. It was a policy that favoured wealthy farmers and the professional classes. Women's equality was enshrined in the Free State constitution and the Church was not opposed to the advancement of women if they were middle-class and respectable: 'A good education for a girl is better than a dowry,' in the words of one Catholic bishop. However, for those not deemed to belong to respectable society or who fell out of it through misfortune, there was neither state support nor kindly encouragement from the Church. Children bore the consequence of an unexpected pregnancy or parental disarray. At independence some seven thousand children were confined in industrial schools and reformatories run by religious orders who were paid by the state for each child in detention. Most of these inmates had no criminal convictions. They were confined because their families were unable to care for them: the children of parents who had fallen on hard times, the sons and daughters of unmarried mothers or boys and girls who were homeless or had a father in gaol. Acting on information from a priest or relatives, inspectors from the National Society for the Prevention of Cruelty to Children, known as 'the cruelty men', would bring the children before the courts for committal. Instead of rescue from mistreatment, the children were delivered to a brutal punitive regime of beatings, humiliation and sexual abuse. In addition to the industrial schools, new homes were established by nuns to receive unmarried mothers in secret and protect their families from shame. The children of 'first offenders' were sent to foster parents, while the mothers were re-inculcated with moral discipline so that they became repentant enough to resume a 'respectable life' with due humility. Detention in Magdalen asylums was the solution 'for women who had fallen more than once' and shown themselves as 'sources of evil, danger and expense to the community'.

In the first decade of independence thousands of unmarried mothers escaped years of incarceration by fleeing to England, where adoption was legalised in 1926. Emigration was also the choice of thousands of other young men and women with less urgent reasons for travelling. The spring of 1924 saw a wave of gatherings at rural train stations as defeated republicans saw their comrades heading for Liverpool or New York. The revolution was over. 'There seemed to be a lack of excitement and the whole neighbourhood was very quiet,' Jeremiah Murphy, a Kerry IRA man, recalled. 'Gone were the familiar faces from the village and the list of those who had departed for other parts of the world was a long one. However, many letters had been received indicating that the exiles were doing pretty well and seemed to have no regrets . . . Very little of the new year had gone by when I applied for a visa to the United States.'

Epilogue

'There were no cars in Dublin when I met you again, the streets had been cleared for the funeral of the President who had died.' Neil, the twenty-something protagonist of Neil Jordan's short story, 'A Love', just returned from London, encounters the older woman with whom he had a thrilling affair when he was a teenager, on the day of Éamon de Valera's funeral, 3 September 1975. He watched the crowds thicken on the pavements in the city centre in anticipation of the funeral, women clasping their handbags, their heads bowed. 'I went into a café and it smelt of Dublin, Ireland, the musty femininity of the women waiting on the kerb for the men to pass, dead, heroic, old and virginal. I sat by the plate-glass window and looked at the shiny chrome espresso machine, a cloud of steam rising from it.' Sipping his coffee, Neil could hear the sound of the funereal brass band swell as the cortège slowly approached.

A sense of nostalgia for home was quickly overtaken by a feeling of distance from the scene unfolding outside. It was not a detachment forged in London, he realised, but a change that had come over him long before he left Ireland. 'I knew I was out of step, it was all militarism now, like air in a blister, under the skin, it was swelling, the militarism I had just learned of before, in the school textbooks.' He could remember de

Valera only as an image in his history book, 'his fist raised in a gesture of defiance', but his former lover, a generation older, recalled watching him speak at meetings, a child holding her father's hand as he stood in his cloth cap and trenchcoat and joined in the shouts of 'Up Dev!'

De Valera had come back from his defeat in the civil war to establish himself as the most influential political figure in the independent state. Forming a new anti-treaty party, Fianna Fáil, in 1926, he ended the boycott of Free State institutions and won the election in 1932. From then on Ireland's parliamentary politics would be dominated by the two parties that emerged from the split in the revolutionary movement over the treaty, Fianna Fáil and Fine Gael. During the last week of the summer holidays in 1975, when it was announced that the ninety-two-year-old president was suffering a heavy cold, the news bulletins delivered hourly updates on his final struggle. For some it was the end of an era; teenagers discussed whether de Valera would hang on so that his state funeral would postpone their return to school. The president's death was the most powerful symbol of the passing of the revolutionary generation. In quiet ceremonies in towns and villages all over Ireland throughout the 1970s, mourners gathered to pay their respects to veterans of the independence struggle. Coffins covered in tricolours were carried from churches across country graveyards to be lowered into plots where firing parties, watched by awed children, readied themselves to raise their rifles in a final salute.

On several occasions, however, widows and children declined the honour of a volley of shots. Obituaries of the veterans in local newspapers noted the barest detail of participation 'in the making of the nation'. Reticence, not pride, was often commended. 'Always unassuming and self-effacing he never spoke of his activities in the War of Independence . . .' 'His exploits during this fight are best left to the memory of his comrades.' The profound unease provoked by the Provisional IRA campaign then raging in Northern Ireland was one reason why the rattle of shots in country churchyards disturbed more than the rooks in the tree branches. The bombings and shootings covered nightly on television raised fundamental questions about whether the contemporary campaign to force the reunification of Ireland could be compared to the independence struggle venerated by the state that governed more than three-quarters of the island. But the remorse about violence was not a recent phenomenon; it had descended before the end of the civil war.

In 'The Lessons of Revolution', an essay published in March 1923, George Russell wrote that Ireland was afflicted by a 'moral depression', all the energy of the patriotic spirit squandered by the advocates of physical force. Russell accused them – acting like the militarists in all nations – of having unintentionally 'poisoned the soul of Ireland'. The following year, P. S. O'Hegarty, a long-time Sinn Féin activist but now a civil servant in the new state, published a disenchanted and partisan memoir, *The Victory of Sinn Féin*. Ironically for a friend and admirer of Michael Collins, the master strategist of calibrated violence, O'Hegarty despaired that 'the spirit of the gunman invaded everything' and brought about 'a complete moral collapse' in Ireland. As a symbol of this depravity, both Russell and O'Hegarty offered the popularity among children of games in which ambushes were re-enacted.

At the heart of these reflections was a shocked sense of a fall from grace. In 1927 Liam O'Flaherty recalled the war as a squalid conflict without rules, bar 'the rule of the vendetta', in which the Irish people had shown themselves 'as bloodthirsty and murderous and cruel as the English, the French, the Germans or the Chinese'. Patriotism, wrote Desmond Fitzgerald, some years after he had left politics, was founded on the belief that the Irish possessed 'a natural perfection'. And when the civil war confounded this self-image 'their patriotism suffered shipwreck. They washed their hands of their country.'

The often-mentioned legacy of the Irish civil war is that it tore asunder not just a political movement but almost all other relationships. In Irish, the civil war is known as *Cogadh na gCarad*, the war of the friends. It split families as well as friendships. But O'Flaherty identified a more insidious legacy of the war when he referred to 'the added terror of secrecy' to describe the shadowy nature of much that happened between 1918 and 1923. The truth of many incidents from this time remains unknown or only half apprehended. The consensus that marked Ireland out as one of the few European states born in the broad post-First World War settlement to survive the upheavals of the next twenty years was based on a decision not to settle accounts. The political scientist Tom Garvin believes there was a secret amnesty for acts of theft and murder between the foundation of the Irish Free State on 6 December 1922 and the end of the civil war on 27 April 1923. 'They robbed banks and their agents bought houses in Dublin on their behalf,' one observer recalled fifty years later. 'When the Civil War ended, those new rich moved with impunity into their new shops and undoubtedly enjoyed the fruits of their acumen.'

This awareness of a secret history as well as the insecurity about whether the largest of the two partitioned states in Ireland was truly independent (manifested in recurring disputes about passports, anthems and diplomatic protocols) could vitiate a clear sense of purpose. The novelist John McGahern described in his memoirs how uncertainty was the keynote of the Ireland of the 1930s: 'Though the Free State had been wrested in armed conflict from Britain, it was like an inheritance that nobody quite understood or knew how to manage.' Disillusionment was the prevailing sentiment among veterans whose lives were not improved by a job or a pension. Michael Moran, the cantankerous central figure in McGahern's novel *Amongst Women*, is well into his old age before he talks about the independence struggle to his adult daughters. His recollections mix nostalgia with cynicism. For Moran and his comrades, those times were the best years of their lives – 'Things were never so simple and clear again' – but he is not prepared to romanticise their fight. 'Don't let anybody fool you. It was a bad business. We didn't shoot at women and children like the Tans but we were a bunch of killers.' Worse than his sense that he had never fully readjusted was the result of their sacrifice. Men who 'couldn't tell one end of a gun from the other' ended up with pensions and medals while others who had fought were forgotten, dying young or emigrating. 'What did we get for it? A country, if you'd believe them. Some of our own johnnies in the top jobs instead of a few Englishmen. More than half of my own family work in England. What was it all for? The whole thing was a cod.' It made him sick to think of the state of the mid-century Ireland he lived in run 'by a crowd of small-minded gangsters out for their own good'.

This sense that the revolution was a failure because it did not create a new country was the bitterest feeling of all. Desmond Fitzgerald likened people's expectations of independence to the Bolsheviks' dream of a communist future: 'Implicit in our intense nationalism was the supposition that with the coming of a national Government our lives would be radically changed . . . We had expected an Utopia, an Earthly Paradise analogous to that promised by the Communist religion . . .' The Irish state, free of British cultural influence, never materialised. 'The mass of people in the country continue to think as they did before the revolution,' George Russell pointed out in his essay in 1923. And it would have been little different even if Ireland had become an 'isolated Republic' instead of a member of the British Commonwealth: 'The momentum of the old order carries us along in Ireland hardly deflected a hair's breadth from the old cultural lines.' In their focus on 'De-Anglicising' Ireland the revolutionaries had misconstrued the real challenge to the survival of distinctive national cultures in the twentieth century, epitomised by the observation of the journalist Francis Hackett in 1925 that an Irish emigrant in the United States 'can be told to his face that he has been deplorably and totally Americanised in ten years' without protest.

The utopian dreams had been reduced to the preservation of stability and order. 'The duty of the Irish citizen today is to strengthen the State and the intelligence of the State,' read a government propaganda leaflet on civic duty issued in 1923. 'He who is not with the State today is against it . . . The mind that does not realise these things is part of the slave mind inherited from the days of tyranny.' In these circumstances, the revival of the Irish language or the promotion of Irish culture often became grim defensive manoeuvres instead of a joyous crusade. Little changed when de Valera abandoned the IRA and led Fianna Fáil into power in 1932. Maintaining Irish sovereignty, defending democracy and ensuring stability were de Valera's goals too. In the north, unionists were trapped by a sectarian populism obsessed by the threat posed by the Catholic minority. Both sides in the civil war now accepted the treaty – de Valera set out to achieve what Collins had promised could be done by dismantling the treaty bit by bit until finally, in 1949, when he was briefly out of power, the Irish Free State was declared a republic by the party he had fought the civil war against. For decades Irish politics was frozen in the themes of the revolutionary world of 1918, sovereignty and partition. 'The main cause of all that emigration, of all the poverty, and of anything else that is wrong politically, nationally and economically with the country', a member of de Valera's party intoned in 1937, 'is due to the partition of Ireland.' In the 1950s, British officials worried that persistent unemployment might lead to a civil war in Northern Ireland. In the south the ceaseless flow of emigration gave substance to the idea that the country was dying.

Although thousands of disaffected republicans emigrated, others regrouped to deal with unfinished business. 'I think we have in our ranks a number of men who do not believe we can get the isolated Republic in our generation,' an anonymous anti-treaty fighter declared in 1923, 'but who do believe . . . that we should go on fighting . . . as a protest and then give it to the next generation to finish . . .' The people who continued on this path retained the old idea of the Irish Republican Brotherhood, that their task was beyond mere electoral sanction. In 1933, eighteen months after de Valera had formed his first government, the veteran Irish American republican Joseph McGarrity tried to persuade him to enter a secret alliance with the IRA: 'They can do the things you will not care to do or cannot do in the face of public criticism, while the I.R.A. pay no heed to public clamor so long as they feel they are doing a national duty.' Partition and the plight of the Catholic minority in Northern Ireland provided a rationale for those who kept the IRA alive. And later generations would find other attractions in the bravado of armed struggle. The price of stability in the Republic of Ireland was the restoration of many of the old hierarchies of power and authority. As the revolutionary era faded away, it could appear both exhilarating and mysterious, a permanent source of inspiration to challenge the staid established order. Sitting in the cafe listening to the approach of de Valera's funeral cortège, the central character in Neil Jordan's story 'A Love' recalled the beginning of his teenage affair with the woman he was about to meet: 'I remembered your father's civil war pistol, black and very real, a cowboy gun. It was that that first attracted me, me a boy beyond the fascination of pistols but capable of being seduced by a real gun owned by a lady with real bullets . . .'

Fifty years after independence it was often easy to draw the conclusion that because freedom had been achieved in a flawed revolution, Ireland had an untapped potential to be revolutionary. But the stifling consensus that developed after the 1920s, which feared instability, inculcated sexual repression and conceded inordinate power to the Catholic Church and deference to authority figures, was not merely imposed on an unwilling populace. It suited many people that the country should be run this way.

And just as it is futile to project the glimmerings of more radical alternative futures onto the failed possibilities of 1918–23 – if only a republic had been achieved, if Michael Collins had lived – it is also easy to underestimate the more general failed promise of the revolutionary world in which the Irish state emerged. In Paris on the eve of the signing of the Versailles Treaty, Woodrow Wilson's publicity team summoned the newspaper correspondents for one final sales pitch for the new world order from the embattled American president. 'Think of all the positive achievements of the peace,' Wilson entreated, 'the newly liberated peoples, who had not before dared to dream of freedom . . . It is a colossal business. It is all on paper so far, of course, but it is up to us to see that it is made effective.' The Wilsonian vision held out high hopes for Ireland and all the other new nations figuring on the new map of Europe. But the reality they confronted was that independence and sovereignty, so long coveted, offered limited opportunities to control their destiny in an inhospitable world still shaped by great powers and vast economic forces.

Notes

PROLOGUE Two Funerals

2 *Greenwich Mean Time*: Michael Laffan, *The Resurrection of Ireland: The Sinn Féin Party 1916–1923*, Cambridge University Press, Cambridge, 1999, p. 62; House of Commons Debates, 17 August 1916, col. 2222–33

3 *a concert in St Patrick's Hall*: *Freeman's Journal*, 29 September 1917, p. 3

3 *a letter from the Catholic Bishop of Killaloe*: ibid., 29 September, p. 5

4 *'her three rather grubby little boys'*: 'An Englishman' [Douglas Goldring], *A Stranger in Ireland*, Talbot Press, Dublin, 1918, pp. 31–2

5 *Ernie O'Malley*: Ernie O'Malley, *On Another Man's Wound*, Anvil Books, Dublin, 1994 edn, pp. 60–62

6 *Bohemian picture-house in Phibsboro*: Denis Condon, 'Politics and the Cinematograph: The Boer War and the Funeral of Thomas Ashe', in *Field Day Review*, vol. 4 (2008), pp. 132–45

6 *'a tamed and weary hawk'*: Michael Laffan, 'John Redmond (1856–1918) and Home Rule', in Ciaran Brady (ed.), *Worsted in the Game: Losers in Irish History*, Lilliput Press, Dublin, 1989, pp. 133–4

6 *Redmond's body was taken to Westminster Cathedral*: Denis Gwynn, *The Life of John Redmond*, George G. Harrap & Co., London, 1932, pp. 594–6

7 *one of his earliest memories*: *Freeman's Journal*, 7 March 1918

8 *'another Thomas Ashe tragedy'*: ibid., 8 March 1918

8 *Officials from Dublin Castle had come to pay their respects*: *Wicklow People*, 16 March 1918

9 *Benedictine nuns from the Belgian town of Ypres*: ibid., 16 March 1918

9 *a handful of people would come forward and kneel in prayer*: ibid., 16 March 1918

9 *the winner of the Sinn Féin club raffle*: *Wicklow News-Letter and Arklow Reporter & County Advertiser*, 16 March 1918

9 *Thousands of people gathered around a monument*: Gwynn, *The Life of John Redmond*, p. 596

9 *Chopin's Funeral March*: *Freeman's Journal*, 11 March 1918

10 *'left the whole of England friendly to his country's freedom'*: *Wicklow People*, 16 March 1918

10 *why Ireland should scrap the leaders*: ibid.

10 *'The whole earth trembles'*: Benito Mussolini, quoted in Robert Gerwarth and Erez Manela (eds.), *Empires at War 1911–1923*, Oxford University Press, Oxford, 2014, p. 1

11 *'a laboratory atop a vast graveyard'*: Mark Mazower, *Dark Continent: Europe's Twentieth Century*, Alfred A. Knopf, New York, 1999, pp. ix–x

11 *'Our future is in us, ourselves!'*: quoted in Andrea Orzoff, *Battle for the Castle: The Myth of Czechoslovakia in Europe, 1914–1918*, Oxford University Press, Oxford, 2009, p. 38

12 *'We adjusted our movement to the scope of world events'*:
quoted in Orzoff, *Battle for the Castle*, p. 51

13 *'detect some at least of the influences'*: quoted in Mary E.
Daly, '"Less a Commemoration of the Actual Achievements
and More a Commemoration of the Hopes of the Men of
1916"', in Mary E. Daly and Margaret O'Callaghan (eds.),
1916 in 1966: Commemorating the Easter Rising, Royal Irish
Academy, Dublin, 2007, p. 30

ONE Victory of the Rainbow Chasers

15 *Some people noticed the women*: *Irish Times*, 16 December 1918

16 *The Irish electorate had nearly tripled*: R. V. Comerford,
'Tipperary Representation at Westminster 1801–1918', in
William Nolan (ed.), *Tipperary: History and Society. Inter-
disciplinary Essays on the History of an Irish County*,
Geography Publications, Dublin, 1988, p. 338

17 *'that infernal machine with the foreign name'*: Michael Laffan,
The Resurrection of Ireland: The Sinn Féin Party 1916–1923,
Cambridge University Press, Cambridge, 1999, p. 28

17 *'exactly similar in appearance and manner'*: Mark Bence-Jones,
Twilight of the Ascendancy, Constable, London, 1993, p. 184

17 *'a wave of democracy in the world'*: John Borgonovo, *The
Dynamics of War and Revolution: Cork City, 1916–1918*, Cork
University Press, Cork, 2013, p. 219

17 *'the world's working model of a modern Catholic state'* . . . *'a
medieval fragment'*: A. de Blacam, *What Sinn Féin Stands For*,
Mellifont Press, Dublin, 1921, pp. xv, xvi

17 *'They used to deride us'*: *Nationalist and Munster Advertiser*,
23 November 1918

18 *'No people can be said to have rightly proved their nation-
hood'*: Terence Denman: 'The Catholic Irish Soldier in the First
World War: "The Racial Environment"', in *Irish Historical
Studies*, vol. xxvii no. 108 (November 1991), p. 364

20 *As he went to bed on Easter Monday*: Johnston Diaries, 'A
Schoolboy in the Rebellion'

22 *'They were still shooting rebels'*: Johnston Diaries, 9 May 1916

22 *streams of angry letters*: Terence Denman: *Ireland's Unknown*

Soldiers: The 16th (Irish) Division in the Great War, 1914–1918, Irish Academic Press, Sallins, County Kildare, 1992, pp. 150–51

23 *'lean, hard face'* . . . *'His romantic foreign name'*: Father Pat Gaynor, 'Memoirs', in Eamonn Gaynor (ed.), *Memoirs of a Tipperary Family: The Gaynors of Tyrone 1887–2000*, Geography Publications, Dublin, n.d., p. 74

24 *'the subtle blend of virility and emotion'*: William O'Brien, quoted in Tim Pat Coogan, *De Valera: Long Fellow, Long Shadow*, Hutchinson, London, 1993, p. 107

24 *'We had candles lighting in every window'*: Laffan, *The Resurrection of Ireland*, p. 112

24 *National Aid Fund*: Peter Hart, *Mick: The Real Michael Collins*, Macmillan, London, 2005, pp. 112–19; Caoimhe Nic Dháibhéid, 'The Radicalization of Public Opinion in Ireland, 1916–1918', in *Historical Journal*, vol. 55 issue 3 (September 2012), pp. 705–29

25 *'English people of the better sort'*: John Maxwell Hamilton and Robert Mann (eds.), *A Journalist's Diplomatic Mission: Ray Stannard Baker's World War I Diary*, Louisiana State University Press, Baton Rouge, 2012, p. 112

26 *'brutal military savagery'*: F. S. L. Lyons: *John Dillon: A Biography*, Routledge & Keegan Paul, London, 1968, p. 436

26 *Irish MPs as terrorists carrying sickles, guns and bombs*: Joseph P. Finnan, 'Punch's portrayal of Redmond, Carson and the Irish Question, 1910–18', in *Irish Historical Studies*, vol. xxxiii no. 132

27 *'convinced that women and children will stand in front of their men'*: R. F. Foster, *W. B. Yeats: A Life, vol. 2: The arch-poet, 1915–1939*, Oxford University Press, Oxford, 2003, p. 132

27 *'delicious'*: Jacob Diaries, 27 September 1918

28 *'He had the usual way of saying "men"'*: quoted in Leeann Lane, *Rosamond Jacob: Third Person Singular*, University College Dublin Press, Dublin, 2010, p. 131

29 *'I wish I could go somewhere where I wasn't known'*: Lane, *Rosamond Jacob*, p. 42

29 *a bicycle pump, a green scarf and a large photo of Eamon de Valera*: Jacob Diaries, 13 October 1918

29 *influenza epidemic*: Ida Milne, 'The 1918–19 Influenza

Pandemic in Ireland: A Leinster Perspective', unpublished PhD
thesis, Trinity College Dublin, 2011, pp. 32–59

30 *'His mind was filled with the purest and loftiest ideals'*: ibid.,
pp. 151–2

30 *Kevin O'Shiel . . . watched the commotion with distaste*:
BMH WS 1770; the statements can be searched at
http://www.bureauofmilitaryhistory.ie/bmhsearch/search.jsp

31 *'Ford cars, covered with dust'*: 'An Englishman' [Douglas Gold-
ring], *A Stranger in Ireland*, Talbot Press, Dublin, 1918, p. 103

31 *locked their fathers and mothers in their homes*: Horsley Ussher
Journal, p. 30

31 *voted thirty times*: Oliver Coogan: *Politics and War in Meath
1913–23*, Folens, Dublin, 1983, p. 105

32 *'I have looked in vain'*: Journal of Father Michael Maher,
17 December 1918, St Patrick's College, Thurles

32 *President Wilson had arrived in Paris*: Margaret MacMillan,
*Peacemakers: The Paris Conference of 1919 and Its Attempt
to End War*, John Murray, London, 2001, p. 24

TWO The American Spirit

33 *John Dos Passos found himself in a small Spanish village*:
Donald Pizer (ed.): *John Dos Passos: The Major Nonfictional
Prose*, Wayne State University Press, Detroit, MI, 1988, p. 55

34 *American troops simply redesigned the ports*: Frank Costigliola,
*Awkward Dominion: American Political, Economic and
Cultural Relations with Europe, 1919–1933*, Cornell University
Press, Ithaca, NY, 1984, pp. 169–70

34 *'pinheads of bureaucratic Europe'*: Bertrand M. Patenaude,
*The Big Show in Bololand: The American Relief Expedition to
Soviet Russia in the Famine of 1921*, Stanford University Press,
Redwood City, CA, 2002, p. 30

34 *'the big show'*: ibid., p. 49

34 *Thousands passed through Dublin*: *Irish Times*, 24 April 1919
and 9 September 1919

34 *chewing gum – a practice that had taken off in Europe*: Edgar
Ansel Mowrer, *This American World*, Faber & Gwyer, London,
1928, p. 142

34 *The first Rotary Club in Britain or Ireland*: C. R. Hewitt,
    *Towards My Neighbour: The Social Influence of the Rotary
    Club Movement in Great Britain and Ireland*, Longmans,
    Green and Co., London, 1950, p. 17

34 *'jazz tea'*: *Irish Times*, 21 February 1919

35 *Tallaght Jazz Band at the fashionable Café Cairo*: ibid.,
    22 October 1919

35 *'they seem to take Fords so seriously'*: Elizabeth Bowen, *The
    Last September*, Vintage Classics, London, 1998 edn, p. 46

35 *factory in Cork*: Mira Wilkins, *American Business Abroad:
    Ford on Six Continents*, Cambridge University Press,
    Cambridge, 2011, pp. 70, 102–3

35 *'If we can enlist the support of American capital'*: John J.
    Horgan, 'Ireland and World Contact', in *Studies: An Irish
    Quarterly Review*, vol. 8 no. 29 (March 1919), p. 41

35 *the American spirit*: *Irish Times*, 28 December 1918

35 *'a prestige and a moral influence'*: John Maynard Keynes,
    The Economic Consequences of the Peace, Macmillan & Co.,
    London, 1919, p. 34

36 *'since it speaks a universal language'*: Kristin Thompson,
    *Exporting Entertainment: America in the World Film Market
    1907–34*, BFI Publishing, London, 1985, p. 94

36 *the Wilsons' arrival*: Margaret MacMillan, *Peacemakers: The
    Paris Conference of 1919 and Its Attempt to End War*, John
    Murray, London, 2001, pp. 23–4

36 *Cardinal John Joseph O'Connor addressed thousands of Irish
    Americans*: *New York Times*, 11 December 1918

36 *forty Irish town councils pledged support*: ibid, 23 December
    1918

37 *'Every national question today is international'*: ibid.,
    13 November 1918

37 *'Ireland is out of the corner'*: quoted in Bill Kissane, 'The
    Doctrine of Self-determination and the Irish Move to
    Independence, 1916–1922', in *Journal of Political Ideologies*,
    vol. 8 no. 2 (2003), p. 328

38 *films showing Wilson's face were banned*: Erez Manela, 'Dawn
    of a New Era: The "Wilsonian Moment" in Colonial Contexts
    and the Transformation of World Order, 1917–1920', in

Sebastian Conrad and Dominic Sachsenmaier (eds.), *Competing Visions of World Order: Global Moments and Movements, 1880s–1930s*, Palgrave Macmillan, New York, 2007, pp. 132, 137

38 *In China a collection of Wilson's speeches became a bestseller*: Pankaj Mishra, *From the Ruins of Empire: The Revolt Against the West and the Remaking of Asia*, Allen Lane, London, 2012, p. 193

38 'in the remotest villages': Manela, 'Dawn of a New Era', p. 131

39 '*organise the moral forces of the world*': Patrick O. Cohrs, *The Unfinished Peace after World War I: America, Britain and the Stabilisation of Europe, 1919–1932*, Cambridge University Press, Cambridge, 2006, p. 37

39 '*It would have been as though one of the great teachers of humanity*': Manela, 'Dawn of a New Era', p. 129

40 '*Our attitude should be that Wilson is a sincere man*' and other Griffith quotes: Memo by Arthur Griffith, from Gloucester Prison, 23 January 1919, quoted in Ronan Fanning, Michael Kennedy, Demot Keogh, Eunan O'Halpin (eds.), *Documents on Irish Foreign Policy Volume 1: 1919–1922*, Royal Irish Academy, Dublin, 1998, pp. 3–4

41 *nearly a third of all children born in Berlin were dead within a few days*: Anthony Read, *The World on Fire: 1919 and the Battle with Bolshevism*, Jonathan Cape, London, 2008, p. 140

41 '*hop and caper like troops of ferocious baboons*': ibid., p. 24

41 '*how far Europe is infested with Bolshevism*': ibid., p. 38

41 *a Bolshevist plot to infiltrate the army*: ibid., p. 59

41 '*a dead city, a city of candles*': ibid., p. 84

42 *every country in Europe would soon have to choose*: Jacob Diaries, 7 April 1919

42 *the choice was either Wilson or Lenin*: Mark Mazower, *Dark Continent: Europe's Twentieth Century*, Alfred A. Knopf, New York, 1999, p. 9

42 '*Now that it is all over, and the Empire stands on a pinnacle*': Keith Jeffrey, *The British Army and the Crisis of Empire 1918–1922*, Manchester University Press, Manchester, 1984, p. 1

43 *English residents were dragged off trains*: Lanver Mak, *The British in Egypt: Community, Crime and Crises 1822–1922*, I. B. Tauris, London, 2012, p. 218

43 *the military accounted for more than 80 per cent of government expenditure*: Paul Kennedy, *The Realities Behind Diplomacy: Background Influences on British External Policy 1865–1980*, Fontana Press, London, 1985, pp. 146–7

43 *'There can be no good international system'*: Bertrand Russell, 'National Independence and Internationalism', in *Atlantic Monthly*, May 1917, p. 622

44 *'the whole world is rocking'*: Lord Milner, quoted in Ronald Hyam, *Britain's Declining Empire: The Road to Decolonisation, 1918–1968*, Cambridge University Press, Cambridge, 2006, p. 32

44 *'a world movement which takes different forms'*, Arthur Balfour, quoted in ibid., p. 32

45 *'We have got all that we want'*: quoted in Kennedy, *The Realities Behind Diplomacy*, p. 256

45 *John Buchan reflected in 1907*: Bill Schwarz, *Memories of Empire, Volume 1: The White Man's World*, Oxford University Press, Oxford, 2011, p. 62

46 *'Truly we are a remarkable people'*: Gertrude Bell, quoted in Priya Satia, 'Developing Iraq: Britain, India and the Redemption of Empire and Technology in the First World War', in *Past & Present* 197 (November 2007), p. 228

47 *the most popular man in Britain*: Schwarz, *The White Man's World*, p. 283

47 *'The British Empire . . . is not founded on might or force'*: Jan Smuts, quoted in John J. Horgan, 'Precepts and Practice in Ireland, 1914–19', in *Studies: An Irish Quarterly Review*, vol. 8 no. 30 (June 1919), p. 210

47 *'much nursing'*, Jan Smuts, quoted in MacMillan, *Peacemakers*, p. 108

48 *In an article published in the American magazine* Foreign Affairs *in 1922*: Phillip Kerr, 'From Empire to Commonwealth', in *Foreign Affairs*, vol. 1 no. 2 (15 December 1922), pp. 83–98

THREE Message to the World

51 *Denis Johnston, now seventeen*: Johnston Diaries, 30 January 1919

52 *'We heard that there was a rebellion in Ireland'*: quoted in Paul

Taylor, 'Heroes or Traitors? Experiences of Returning Irish Soldiers from World War One', unpublished DPhil, Oxford University, 2012, p. 39

52 *A grubby, limp tricolour hung from a window*: Daily News, 17 January 1919

53 *Field Marshal Viscount French of Ypres*: Richard Holmes, *The Little Field Marshal: A Life of Sir John French*, Jonathan Cape, London, 1981, pp. 338–61; there is also a good account of French's wartime career in Adam Hochschild, *To End All Wars: How the First World War Divided Britain*, Macmillan, London, 2011

54 *French's official car once stalled in the vicinity of a horse fair*: Major Gerald French, *The Life of Sir John French, First Earl of Ypres,* Casell and Co., London, 1931, p. 354

55 *'swine'*: quoted in Hochschild, *To End All Wars*, p. 326

55 *'I knew, of course, that we had a garrison in Dublin'*: G. K. Chesterton, *Irish Impressions*, W. Collins, London, 1919, p. 69

56 *after-dinner talk here was between Ireland and India*: Nora Robertson, *Crowned Harp: Memories of the Last Years of the Crown in Ireland*, Allen Figgis & Co., Dublin, 1960, p. 26

57 *'we wired them all up inside concentration camps'*: quoted in Eunan O'Halpin, *The Decline of the Union: British Government in Ireland 1892–1920*, Gill and Macmillan, Dublin, 1987, p. 200

57 *'A dear old man Lord French'*: quoted in Michael Hopkinson, *The Irish War of Independence*, Gill and Macmillan, Dublin, 2002, p. 8

58 *'A lady who wished to call attention to her grievances'*: G. C. Duggan, BMH WS 1099

58 *'Under its regime, the nation has had as much to say to its own public policy'*: Thomas Kettle, *The Open Secret of Ireland* [1912], University College Dublin Press, Dublin, 2007, p. 117

58 *'was wholly divorced from the people'*: Lawrence W. McBride: *The Greening of Dublin Castle: The Transformation of Bureaucratic and Judicial Personnel in Ireland 1892–1922*, The Catholic University of America Press, Washington DC, 1991, pp. 254–5

59 *Maurice Headlam*: Deirdre McMahon, 'Ireland and the Empire-Commonwealth, 1900–1948', in *The Oxford History*

of the British Empire, Volume 4: The Twentieth Century,
Oxford University Press, Oxford, 1999, and Duggan, BMH WS
1099

59 *'suspicion and espionage'*: quoted in Fergus Campbell, 'Who
Ruled Ireland? The Irish Administration, 1879–1914', in
Historical Journal, vol. 50 no. 3 (September 2007), p. 624

61 *'haunting' the House of Commons*: Tim Healy, quoted in
Arthur Mitchell, *Revolutionary Government in Ireland: Dáil
Éireann, 1919–22*, Gill and Macmillan, Dublin, 1995, p. 23

61 *how shabby the party's offices appeared*: *Daily News*, 1 January
1919, p. 1; *Daily Mail*, 2 January 1919, p. 2

62 *'so long as Ireland remained under the heel of the English
oppressor'*: *Manchester Guardian*, 1 January 1919

63 *'eventual disintegration of the British Empire'*: quoted in
Margaret MacMillan, *Peacemakers: The Paris Conference
of 1919 and Its Attempt to End War*, John Murray, London,
2001, p. 53

67 *'We had burnt our boats now'*: Maire Comerford, *The First
Dáil: January 21st 1919*, Joe Clarke, Dublin, 1969, p. 51

FOUR 'Where Tipperary Leads, Ireland Follows'

70 *John McCormack was President Wilson's guest*: Gordon
T. Ledbetter, *The Great Irish Tenor: John McCormack*, Town
House, Dublin, 2003, p. 146; also *New York Times*,
27 December 1918

71 *Union Jacks draped over the carriage doors*: *Irish Times*,
17 September 1914

71 *An American journalist attending a performance*: *New York
Times*, 1 November 1914

71 *'where Paddy would find peace and happiness'*: *Irish Times*,
2 May 1915

71 *The* Sphere *sent a photographer*: *The Sphere*, 2 January 1915

74 *'purification'*: Seamus Babbington, BMH WS 1595

75 *On 21 January, a cold, wet, misty morning*: my account of the
ambush at Soloheadbeg relies on Desmond Ryan, *Sean Treacy
and the 3rd Tipperary Brigade*, Alliance Press, London/The
Kerryman, Tralee, 1945; reports in the *Nationalist and Munster*

Advertiser, 21, 25, 29 January, and the interviews given to the Bureau of Military History by Dan Breen, BMH WS 1739, and Seamus Robinson, BMH WS 1721

76 *Treacy had performed a little dance*: Seamus Robinson, BMH WS 1721

76 *Dan Breen told interviewers*: Dan Breen, BMH WS 1739

76 *'were dogs not men'*: quoted in Paul Bew, 'Moderate Nationalism and the Irish Revolution, 1916–1923', in *Historical Journal*, vol. 42 no. 3 (September 1999), p. 738

78 *'the people had to be educated and led gently into open war'*: Maryann Gialanella Valiulis, *Portrait of a Revolutionary: General Richard Mulcahy and the Founding of the Irish Free State*, Irish Academic Press, Dublin, 1992, p. 39

78 *'when the scales fell from people's eyes'*: Dan Breen, *My Fight for Irish Freedom*, Talbot Press, Dublin, 1924, p. 51

80 *'To be killed in action by an enemy'*: ibid., p. 73

82 *On Monday, 23 June, crowds gathered in the market town of Thurles*: the account of the shooting of DI Hunt is based on reports in the *Nationalist and Munster Advertiser*, 25 June 1919, and the following witness statements: Jerry Ryan, BMH WS 1487; Sean McLoughlin, BMH WS 290; Charles Wyse-Power, BMH WS 420; William Hanly, BMH WS 1368; James Leahy, BMH WS 1454; Patrick Kinnane, BMH WS 1475; Thomas Meagher, BMH WS 1541

84 *'who may not have studied the art of winning popularity'*: quoted in Brian Heffernan, 'Catholic Priests and Political Violence in Ireland, 1919–21', PhD thesis, National University of Ireland Maynooth, 2011, p. 47

85 *'We agreed that killing Hunt was very excusable'*: Jacob Diaries, 28 June 1919

86 *'We have our authority in our pockets'*: *Daily Mail*, 19 May 1919

FIVE Over a Policeman's Body

87 *'nearly every turn, every hill and every cross-road'*: George Amyrald de M. E. Dagg, *'Devia Hibernia'*, *The Road and Route Guide for Ireland of the Royal Irish Constabulary*, Hodges, Figgis & Co., Dublin, 1893, p. ii

88 *Ernie O'Malley came across a carriage full of constables*: Ernie O'Malley, *On Another Man's Wound*, Anvil Books, Dublin, 1994 edn, pp. 11, 68

89 *'a modest, pious trusting man'*: Seán Ó Faoláin, *Vive Moi*, Sinclair-Stevenson, London, 1993, pp. 22–3

89 *The policeman was an intrinsic feature of Irish rural life*: see Elizabeth Malcolm, *The Irish Policeman, 1822–1922: A Life*, Four Courts Press, Dublin, 2004

90 *Samuel Waters. His earliest memories*: Stephen Ball (ed.), *A Policeman's Ireland: Recollections of Samuel Waters, RIC*, Cork University Press, Cork, 1999, pp. 23–31

95 *'I'm just as good an Irishman as you'*: Peter Hart, *The IRA and Its Enemies*, Clarendon Press, Oxford, 1998, p. 55

95 *'no decent girl would walk'*: quoted in ibid., p. 60

95 *John Regan, a policeman in Bantry*: W. J. Lowe, 'The War Against the R.I.C., 1919–21', in *Éire-Ireland*, vol. 37 nos. 3 and 4 (fall/winter 2002), p. 81

95 *Patrick Shea . . . remembered his first experience of political prisoners*: Patrick Shea, *Voices and the Sound of Drums*, Blackstaff Press, Belfast, 1981, p. 23

96 *'spies in our midst'*: Eamon de Valera, quoted in Lowe, 'The War Against the R.I.C.', p. 85

96 *'lost souls who have sold themselves to the devil'*: D. M. Leeson, *The Black and Tans: British Police and Auxiliaries in the Irish War of Independence, 1920–1921*, Oxford University Press, Oxford, 2011, p. 193

96 *'Some of them were, like, nasty enough'*: quoted in John D. Brewer, *The Royal Irish Constabulary: An Oral History*, Institute of Irish Studies, The Queen's University of Belfast, 1990, p. 76

97 *a resolution that policemen should be banned*: Oliver Coogan: *Politics and War in Meath 1913–23*, Folens, Dublin, 1983, p. 95

97 *'I'd like to see them [turn down donations]'*: Jacob Diaries, 9 April 1919

98 *'I laughed at the idea of it'*: quoted in Brewer, *The Royal Irish Constabulary*, p. 49

98 *'"War" was already being waged'*: Horsley Ussher Journal, p. 32

99 *'could not believe that anyone'*: ibid., p. 36
100 *'They are burning our quarters now'*: ibid., pp. 37–8
100 *'Are you not afraid we would shoot you'*: Joost Augusteijn, *From Public Defiance to Guerrilla Warfare: The Experience of Ordinary Volunteers in the Irish War of Independence 1916–1921*, Irish Academic Press, Dublin, 1996, p. 201
101 *'If you thought about being targets'*: Brewer, *The Royal Irish Constabulary*, p. 81
101 *'incredulity and fear and horror'*: Shea, *Voices and the Sound of Drums*, p. 27
101 *'I was filled with a fierce anger'*: ibid.
102 *'both eyes blown away'*: Hart, *The IRA and Its Enemies*, pp. 76–7
102 *'fought over a policeman's body'*: *Daily News*, 22 August 1919
102 *'a fratricidal vendetta'*: quoted in D. M. Leeson, *The Black and Tans*, p. 193
102 *Denis Johnston set out with two friends on a cycle tour*: Johnston Diaries, 21–6 July 1920

SIX Ancient Faiths

104 *Ibrahim Rashad embarked on a tour of Ireland*: Ibrahim Rashad, *An Egyptian in Ireland*, private edn, 1920
104 *'In spite of the great regard'*: ibid., p. 9
105 *'for sake of those who enjoy "Bacon and Eggs"'*: ibid., p. 46
105 *'a trivial incident'*: ibid., pp. 70–71
106 *'A social order which is responsible for poverty'*: ibid., p. 90
108 *'I used to think and say, during the War'*: quoted in Terence Dooley, *The Decline of the Big House in Ireland: A Study of Irish Landed Families 1860–1960*, Wolfhound Press, Dublin, p. 122
109 *'There was always a bed for a guest'*: Moritz Bonn, *Wandering Scholar*, Cohen & West, London, 1949, p. 90
109 *curry paste and powder, figs, caviar*: Cormac Ó Gráda, *Ireland: A New Economic History 1780–1939*, Clarendon Press, Oxford, 1994, p. 267
109 *precious Rembrandts, Chippendale furniture*: Dooley, *The Decline of the Big House*, pp. 139–40
109 *'The Big House might be spruce'*: Ernie O'Malley, *On Another Man's Wound*, Anvil Books, Dublin, 1994 edn, p. 79

110 *'All of us were in full evening dress'*: Bonn, *Wandering Scholar*, p. 92

110 *'Nothing counted for about three miles'*: Lionel Fleming, quoted in Ian D'Alton, '"A Vestigial Population"? Perspectives on Southern Irish Protestants in the Twentieth Century', in *Éire-Ireland*, vol. 44 nos. 3 and 4 (fall/winter 2009), p. 21

111 *'smalltime stock'*: William Trevor, *Excursions in the Real World*, Penguin Books, London, 1994, pp. xiii–xiv

111 *some ten thousand Protestants who could be described as working class*: Martin Maguire, 'The Organisation and Activism of Dublin's Protestant Working Class, 1883–1935', in *Irish Historical Studies*, vol. 29 no. 113 (May 1994), p. 65

112 *'on the inner circuit of power'*: Jasper Ungoed-Thomas, *Jasper Wolfe of Skibbereen*, Collins Press, Cork, 2008, p. 49

112 *A pass in Irish was made essential*: Andy Bielenberg, 'Exodus: The Emigration of Southern Irish Protestants During the Irish War of Independence and the Civil War', in *Past & Present* 218 (February 2013), pp. 224–5

113 *'Well, then, what do we want?'*: quoted in Senia Paseta, *Before the Revolution: Nationalism, Social Change and Ireland's Catholic Elite, 1879–1922*, Cork University Press, Cork, 1999, p. 116

113 *'There is something very distinctive'*: D. P. Moran, *The Leader*, 9 February 1901, quoted in Conor Cruise O'Brien, *Ancestral Voices: Religion and Nationalism in Ireland*, The University of Chicago Press, 1995, p. 39

113 *'the first contest after Home Rule'*: quoted in ibid., p. 47

113 *'They desert the country for the town'*: quoted in Tom Garvin: *Nationalist Revolutionaries in Ireland 1858–1928*, Gill and Macmillan, Dublin, 2005, p. 45

114 *'Once people have got a name for deceitfulness'*: Jacob Diaries, 12 May 1920

114 *'My God what bigots they are'*: ibid., 32,582 (34), 18 August 1918

115 *'and a few might even be Roman Catholics'*: Fergus Campbell, 'Who Ruled Ireland? The Irish Administration, 1879–1914', in *Historical Journal*, vol. 50 no. 3 (September 2007), p. 637

115 *'Proddy waddy greenguts, never said a prayer'*: Ungoed-Thomas, *Jasper Wolfe*, pp. 31–2

116 *Colonel Rowley in Summerhill*: Dooley, *The Decline of the Big House*, pp. 172–3

117 *Colonel Mountifort J. C. Longfield*: James S. Donnelly Jr, 'Big House Burnings in County Cork During the Irish Revolution 1920–21', in *Éire-Ireland*, vol. 47 nos. 3 and 4 (fall/winter 2012), p. 155

117 *Timoleague House*: ibid., pp. 150–52

118 *The owner of a car dealership in Tipperary*: Gemma M. Clark, 'Fire, Boycott, Threat and Harm: Social and Political Violence Within the Local Community. A Study of Three Munster Counties During the Irish Civil War, 1922–23', unpublished DPhil thesis, Oxford University, 2010, p. 41

119 *'looked thinner than ever'*: Jacob Diaries, 31 March 1920

119 *'a chance of settling down and making money'*: quoted in Wilfrid Ewart, *A Journey in Ireland 1921*, G. P. Putnam's Sons, London, 1922, p. 49

119 *'It was a house of God'*: Rashad, *An Egyptian in Ireland*, p. 59

120 *'Watching the children performing these religious duties'*: ibid., p. 106

120 *'From childhood to old age'*: ibid., p. 59

120 *'The clergy . . . live by the people, come from the people'*: quoted in Jérôme aan de Wiel, *The Catholic Church in Ireland 1914–1918: War and Politics*, Irish Academic Press, Sallins, County Kildare, p. 163

121 *'into the four provinces of Ireland'*: Don Boyne, *I Remember Maynooth*, Longmans, Green and Co., London, 1937, p. 29

121 *'We have marked the recovery of Ireland'*: Giolla Eoin, 'From the Watch Tower', in *The Irish Monthly*, vol. 49 no. 573 (March 1921), p. 129

122 *'the centre of the empire'*: de Wiel, *The Catholic Church*, p. 167

122 *'have been and are associated with the worst forms of civil tyranny'*: quoted in Patrick Murray, *Oracles of God: The Roman Catholic Church and Irish Politics 1922–37*, UCD Press, Dublin, 2000, p. 22

122 *'quite happy under my tall hat'*: Father Pat Gaynor, 'Memoirs', in Eamonn Gaynor (ed.), *Memoirs of a Tipperary Family: The Gaynors of Tyrone 1887–2000*, Geography Publications, Dublin, n.d., p. 42

122 'I believed that Ireland free': ibid., p. 43

123 'who wish to win the heart of their flocks': de Wiel, The Catholic Church, p. 183

123 'Irish Bishops recommend Sinn Féin': ibid., p. 328

124 'are not different from the rest of the people': quoted in Emmet Larkin, 'Church, State and Nation in Modern Ireland', in the American Historical Review, vol. 80 no. 5 (December 1975), p. 1,271

124 'the very reverse of anti-clerical or anti-religious': quoted in de Wiel, The Catholic Church, p. 328

124 'most exemplary in attending to their Christian religious duties': quoted in ibid., p. 328

124 '"Where is Martin Cullinane"': Brian Heffernan, 'Catholic Priests and Political Violence in Ireland, 1919–21', PhD thesis, National University of Ireland Maynooth, 2011, p. 64

125 The clerk of a chapel in Tipperary: Joost Augusteijn, From Public Defiance to Guerrilla Warfare: The Experience of Ordinary Volunteers in the Irish War of Independence 1916–1921, Irish Academic Press, Dublin, 1996, p. 309, n. 56

126 'There are a class of men going about': quoted in ibid., p. 308

SEVEN The Virtual Republic

127 Just before 8.30 a.m. on the grey and drizzly morning: Alcock's and Brown's arrival and reception in Ireland is described in Graham Wallace, The Flight of Alcock & Brown, Putnam, London, 1955, pp. 256–91, and Brendan Lynch, Yesterday We Were in America: Alcock and Brown, First to Fly the Atlantic Non-Stop, Haynes Publishing, Sparkford, 2009, pp. 209–45

129 'the sunlit clearness and brightness': H. G. Wells, A Year of Prophesying, T. Fisher Unwin, London, 1924, p. 15

130 'a patchwork of various sized internment camps called Independent Sovereign States': ibid., p. 86

130 'It is part of the fantastic nationalism': ibid., p. 50

132 'All subject peoples are filled with hope': quoted in Fredrik Logevall, Embers of War: The Fall of an Empire and the Making of America's Vietnam, Random House, New York, 2012, p. 3. For Ho Chi Minh in Paris, see also Sophie Quinn-

Judge, *Ho Chi Minh: The Missing Years, 1919–1941*, Hurst and Company, London, 2002, pp. 11–41; William J. Duiker, *Ho Chi Minh*, Hyperion, New York, 2000', pp. 51–86, and Pierre Brocheux, *Ho Chi Minh: A Biography*, Cambridge University Press, Cambridge, 2007, pp. 1–28

133 *'among crucified nations, Ireland occupies the foremost place'*: *Sinn Féin*, 29 March 1919

133 *'It seems . . . that the blacks and yellows, all colours and races'*: quoted in Arthur Mitchell, *Revolutionary Government in Ireland: Dáil Éireann, 1919–22*, Gill and Macmillan, Dublin, 1995, p. 29

135 *'the walking bank'*: ibid., p. 56

136 *an encyclopaedic knowledge*: ibid., p. 55

136 *'a cheerfully juvenile figure which flits past'*: quoted in ibid., p. 55

137 *'would cut the ground from under these people's feet'*: quoted in ibid., p. 91

138 *'a good return and first class security for yourself'*: Denis Cogan, BMH WS 1556

138 *'something in English psychology'*: Lionel Smith Gordon, quoted in Mitchell, *Revolutionary Government*, p. 88

139 *'commands the unforced obedience of the Irish people'*: quoted in ibid., p. 62

141 *'incorrigible criminals'*: Simon Donnelly, BMH WS 481

142 *'an extraordinary and anomalous state of affairs'*: quoted in David Foxton, *Revolutionary Lawyers: Sinn Féin and Crown Courts in Ireland and Britain, 1916–1923*, Four Courts Press, Dublin, 2008, p. 172

143 *'every countryman had a pleasant nod or a cheery word for us'*: Johnston Diaries, 21 July 1920

144 *'The Sinn Féin tribunals are jostling British law into oblivion'*: Mitchell, *Revolutionary Government*, p. 142

144 *'Sinn Féin sets up law courts'*: *Daily Mail*, 17 July 1920

EIGHT 'Would You Shoot a Man?'

145 *Dublin prepared itself . . . for the annual Horse Show*: Padraig Yeates, *A City in Turmoil: Dublin 1919–21*, Gill & Macmillan, Dublin, 2012, p. 142

146 'His attendance there would have made everyone rightly nervous': Stephen Gwynne, 'Ireland Week by Week', in the Observer, 15 August 1920

147 'a rotten place to be in': diary of Private J. P. Swindlehurst, in William Sheehan, British Voices From the Irish War of Independence 1918–1921: The Words of British Servicemen Who Were There, Collins Press, Cork, 2005, p. 13

147 'in olive oil or else wagon grease': ibid., p. 19

147 Infant mortality for the city's professional classes: Yeates, A City in Turmoil, p. 35. For overviews of Dublin, see Ruth McManus, Dublin 1910–1940: Shaping the City & Suburbs, Four Courts Press, Dublin, 2002, and Séamas Ó Maitiú, Dublin's Suburban Towns: 1834–1930: Governing Clontarf, Drumcondra, Dalkey, Killiney, Kilmainham, Pembroke, Kingstown, Blackrock, Rathmines and Rathgar, Four Courts Press, Dublin, 2003

148 'a general impression of horror': Lambert McKenna, 'The Housing Problem in Dublin', in Studies: An Irish Quarterly Review, vol. 8 no. 30 (June 1919), p. 280

149 'It is a maze of narrow streets': Record of the Rebellion in Ireland in 1920–21, Volume II: Intelligence, quoted in William Sheehan, Fighting for Dublin: The British Battle for Dublin 1919–1921, Collins Press, Cork, 2007, pp. 138–9

149 Dublin had made exactly the same impression on Sean Treacy: Desmond Ryan, Sean Treacy and the 3rd Tipperary Brigade, Alliance Press, London/The Kerryman, Tralee, 1945, p. 108

149 They cycled to a pub: this account of the attempted assassination of Lord French is based on ibid., pp. 108–23

152 'I'm not letting any young scuts tell me how to do my duty': Tim Pat Coogan, Michael Collins: A Biography, Hutchinson, London, 1990, p. 117

153 '"Would you shoot a man, Byrne?"': Vincent Byrne, BMH WS 423

155 'Are you Mr Bell?': Yeates, A City in Turmoil, pp. 106–8

156 a large oil drum bobbing in the water: Joice M. Nankivell Loch and Sydney Loch, Ireland in Travail, John Murray, London, 1922, pp. 39–40

156 the best-dressed men in Dublin: ibid., p. 76

158 *chasing a woman down the quays who cursed and kicked him*:
Swindlehurst, in Sheehan, *British Voices*, p. 23

158 *'heard a great rattle of a car coming into town'*: Johnston
Diaries, 22 September 1920

158 *'some unspectacular petting'* . . . *'endless opportunities to hide
in gardens'*: Johnston Diaries, January 1920

159 *Wilmot Irwin was a twenty-year-old bookkeeper*: Wilmot Irwin,
Betrayal in Ireland, Northern Whig, Belfast, 1968, pp. 42–3

159 *'manufacturing agents'*: T. Ryle Dwyer, *The Squad and the
Intelligence Operations of Michael Collins*, Mercier Press,
Cork, 2005, p. 13

160 *Almost all the films they exibited were American*: Kerry
Segrave, *American Films Abroad: Hollywood's Domination
of the World's Movie Screens from the 1890s to the Present*,
McFarland and Company, London, 1997, and Victoria de
Grazia, 'Mass Culture and Sovereignty: The American
Challenge to European Cinemas, 1920–1960', in the *Journal
of Modern History*, vol. 61 no. 1 (March 1989), pp. 53–87

160 *'Charlie Chaplin is going into the barracks'*: Sean Healy, BMH
WS 1479

160 *'a French film with plague'*: Jacob Diaries, 25 August 1919

161 *'American men who go in for social life'*: ibid., 17 November
1920

161 *'rows and rows of white spots shining in the dark'*: Johnston
Diaries, 1 January 1923

161 *enterprising fifteen-year-old boy* . . . *using stolen money to buy
magic lanterns*: *Irish Times*, 6 January 1919

162 *'Ain't We Got Fun'*: Irwin, *Betrayal in Ireland*, p. 49

NINE Bolshevism in the Air

163 *'Cruel, humourless, hard'*: John Buchan, *The Three Hostages*,
Polygon, Edinburgh, 2010 edn, p. 19

165 *'the foolish and dangerous ostentation of the rich'*: James E.
Cronin, 'Coping with Labour, 1918–1926', in James E. Cronin
and Jonathan Schneer (eds.), *Social Conflict and the Political
Order in Modern Britain*, Croom Helm, London, 1982, p. 120

165 *'the Irish question* . . . *had more to do with the existing*

industrial unrest': Emmet O'Connor, *Syndicalism in Ireland 1917–1923*, Cork University Press, 1988, p. 72

165 *'Bolshevism was in the air' . . . 'the troublesome uneducated'*: ibid., p. 70

166 *Sylvia Pankhurst, the famous anti-war suffragist*: Stephen Gwynne, 'Ireland Week by Week', in the *Observer*, 18 May 1919

167 *'Good God, you can't cut off lunatics from food'*: Peadar O'Donnell, *Monkeys in the Superstructure: Reminiscences of Peadar O'Donnell*, Salmond Publishing, Galway, 1986, p. 12

167 *'rapidly becoming a vast reservoir of resentment'*: O'Connor, *Syndicalism*, p. 48

167 *'in what English workers consider the half fairyland of eastern Europe'*: 'A Neutral View of Ireland by a Swiss correspondent', in the *Living Age*, 14 August 1920, reprinted from *Neue Zürcher Zeitung*, 13 June 1920

170 *'I have witnessed many strikes in England'*: Daily Express reporter, quoted in Liam Cahill, *Forgotten Revolution: Limerick Soviet 1919, A Threat to British Power in Ireland*, O'Brien Press, Dublin, 1990, p. 83

171 *'There can't be. The people here are Catholics'*: Ruth Russell, *What's the Matter with Ireland?*, Devin-Adair Company, New York, 1920, p. 134

171 *'Isn't it well that communism is to be Christianized?'*: ibid., p. 142

172 *Lady Gregory bought a loaf of bread*: Lady Gregory, *Journals: Books 1–29, 10th October, 1916–24th February, 1925*, edited by Daniel J. Murphy, Colin Smythe, Gerrards Cross, 1978; 13 April 1920, p. 138

173 *'The Volunteer spirit in essentials was hostile*: Ernie O'Malley, *On Another Man's Wound*, Anvil Books, Dublin, 1994 edn, p. 55

174 *'no distinction at table'*: Dan Bradley, *Farm Labourers: Irish Struggle 1900–1976*, Athol Books, Belfast, 1988, p. 48

175 *'The experience of last year's land strikes'*: O'Connor, *Syndicalism*, p. 43

175 *'but any farmer may keep a gun for potting the Transport Union officials'*: *Voice of Labour*, April 1919, quoted in Tom Crean, 'Crowds and the Labour Movement in the Southwest

1914–23', in Peter Jupp and Eoin Magennis (eds.), *Crowds in Ireland c. 1720–1920*, p. 255

176 *'No man had a right . . . to advocate force on the part of one body of Irishmen'*: Bradley, *Farm Labourers*, p. 48

177 *In 1920 conflicts over land raged all along the western seaboard*: Fergus Campbell: *Land and Revolution: Nationalist Politics in the West of Ireland 1891–1921*, Oxford University Press, Oxford, pbk edn, 2005

177 *'utter lawlessness'*: Charles Townshend, *The Republic: The Fight for Irish Independence, 1918–1923*, Allen Lane, London, 2013, p. 28

177 *Godfrey Hardy, a Protestant whose family farmed*: O'Shiel, BMH WS 1770. See also Fergus Campbell and Kevin O'Shiel, 'The Last Land War? Kevin O'Shiel's Memoir of the Irish Revolution, 1916–21', *Archivium Hibernicum*, vol. 57 (2003), pp. 155–200

178 *opened a grave in their uncle's field*: Tony Varley, 'Agrarian Crime and Social Control: Sinn Féin and the Land Question in the West of Ireland in 1920', in Mike Tomlinson, Tony Varley and Ciaran McCullagh (eds.), *Whose Law & Order? Aspects of Crime and Social Control in Irish Society*, Sociological Association of Ireland, p. 57

180 *Going west exposed O'Shiel to the huge social divide*: O'Shiel, BMH WS 1770

TEN A Crowd of Unknown Men

182 *William Joyce*: Mary Kenny, *Germany Calling: A Personal Biography of William Joyce, 'Lord Haw-Haw'*, New Island, Dublin, 2003, especially pp. 24–64, and Rebecca West, *The Meaning of Treason*, MacMillan & Co., London, 1949, especially pp. 10–22

184 *'The trouble is that there is a world wide reaction owing mainly to Russia'*: R. F. Foster, *W. B. Yeats: A Life, Volume II: The Arch Poet, 1915–1939*, Oxford University Press, Oxford, 2003, p. 184

185 *Long was affronted*: Richard Murphy, 'Walter Long and the Making of the Government of Ireland Act, 1919–20', *Irish Historical Studies*, vol. 25 no. 97 (1986), p. 83

185 '8,000 scallywags' . . . 'crowd of unknown men': quoted in
D. G. Boyce, *Englishmen and Irish Troubles: British Public
Opinion and the Making of Irish Policy, 1918–22*, Cape,
London, 1972, p. 54

186 *167,000 fit ex-servicemen*: D. M. Leeson, *The Black and Tans:
British Police and Auxiliaries in the Irish War of Independence,
1920–1921*, Oxford University Press, Oxford, 2011, p. 24

186 'next to the coal question, the grievances of the ex-servicemen':
Stephen R. Ward, 'Intelligence Surveillance of British Ex-
Servicemen, 1918–1920', in the *Historical Journal*, vol. xvi
no. 1 (1973), p. 187

186 'stick at trifles': Bentley B. Gilbert, *British Social Policy, 1914–
1939*, B. T. Batsford, London, 1970, p. 46

186 'for the first time in history, the rioters will be better trained
than the troops': Ward, 'Intelligence Surveillance', p. 179

186 'helped to relieve England of a very dangerous type of
unemployable men': Dorothy McArdle, *The Irish Republic*,
Corgi Books, London, 1968, p. 315

186 *The demobilisation of 200,000 ex-officers*: Martin Petter,
'"Temporary Gentlemen" in the Aftermath of the Great War:
Rank, Status and the Ex-Officer Problem', in the *Historical
Journal*, vol. 37 no. 1 (March 1994), pp. 127–52

187 *a lieutenant-colonel who was reduced to earning his living as
a door-to-door salesman*: Philip Gibbs, 'Social Revolution in
English Life', in *Harper's Monthly Magazine*, vol. 142
(December 1920–May 1921), p. 564

188 *recruited by one of the factions in Mexican Civil War*: Bill
Munro, quoted in James Gleeson, *Bloody Sunday*, Peter Davies,
London, 1962, p. 57

188 *Raymond Cafferata and his friends*: Papers of Colonel
Raymond Oswald Cafferata (1897–1966), Middle East Centre
Archive, St Antony's College, Oxford, GB165–0044 LAIO

189 'the poorer classes in Barcelona': George Orwell, *Homage to
Catalonia*, Penguin Books, London, 2000 edn, p. 109

190 'They weren't going to be like these people from the bogs of
Ireland': John D. Brewer, *The Royal Irish Constabulary: An
Oral History*, Institute of Irish Studies, The Queen's University
of Belfast, 1990, p. 102

191 'Q: What qualification is made indispensable for you as a policeman?': Manchester Guardian, 13 October 1920

191 A Dutchman who had been a medical officer with the Black Watch: Brewer, The Royal Irish Constabulary, p. 108

192 'dodging and scrounging' . . . 'low company': Patrick Shea, Voices and the Sound of Drums, Blackstaff Press, Belfast, 1981, p. 45

192 'They were on their own; hurt one and you hurt them all': Brewer, The Royal Irish Constabulary, p. 111

192 'frightened even those they had come to help': Shea, Voices, p. 45

192 'a counter-murder association': Major-General Sir C. E. Callwell, Field-Marshall Sir Henry Wilson: His Life and Diaries, Volume Two, Cassell & Co., London, 1927, p. 251

193 [Churchill] suggested using aeroplanes: Martin Gilbert, World in Torment: Winston S. Churchill 1917-1922, Minerva Edition, London, 1990, pp. 455-7

193 the same freedom as the police in New York and Chicago: Winston Churchill, The World Crisis: The Aftermath, Thornton Butterworth, London, 1929, p. 287

193 to put down the campaign of the Berbers: Paul Preston, Franco: A Biography, HarperCollins, London, 1993, pp. 27-34

194 Worried about 'attempted revolution': Peter Dennis, 'The Territorial Army in Aid of the Civil Power in Britain, 1919-1926', in Journal of Contemporary History, vol. 16 no. 4 (October 1981), p. 711

194 'a real white man': 'A Woman of No Importance' [Mrs Stuart Menzies], As Others See Us, Herbert Jenkins, London, 1924, p. 94

195 'rascals and rapscallions of the world': quoted in Gilbert, World in Torment, p. 464

195 hunting rabbits and game: Gleeson, Bloody Sunday, p. 62

196 'now about the quietest part of the County': Peter Hart, The IRA and Its Enemies, Clarendon Press, Oxford, 1998, p. 29

196 'swinging their guns': Joost Augusteijn, From Public Defiance to Guerrilla Warfare: The Experience of Ordinary Volunteers in the Irish War of Independence 1916-1921, Irish Academic Press, Dublin, 1996, pp. 127-8

197 *an Englishman living in County Clare*: Letter from R. C. Grey, Killaloe, County Clare, in the *Nation*, 28 August 1920

197 *'You ought to be more careful young man'*: Carl W. Ackerman, 'Inside Irish Parley', *New York Times*, 7 August 1921

198 *'To hear them talk'*: diary of Private J. P. Swindlehurst, in William Sheehan, *British Voices From the Irish War of Independence 1918–1921: The Words of British Servicemen Who Were There*, Collins Press, Cork, 2005, pp. 26–7

198 *'Reprisals Galore'*: Foster, *W. B. Yeats*, p. 181

198 *Black and Tans buying balloons and streamers*: Johnston Diaries, 24 December 1920

198 *Rosamond Jacob listened with horror*: Jacob Diaries, 16 December 1920

198 *The destruction wrought on 20 September in Balbriggan*: Ross O'Mahoney, 'The Sack of Balbriggan and Tit-for-Tat Terror', and David Fitzpatrick, 'The Price of Balbriggan', in David Fitzpatrick (ed.), *Terror in Ireland 1916–1923*, Lilliput Press, Dublin, 2012, pp. 58–102

199 *'Reprisals are wrong'*: Leeson, *The Black and Tans*, p. 212

199 *'The German authorities . . . had nothing for it'*: ibid., p. 213

200 *'I used not to believe the stories of English savagery'*: Lady Gregory, *Journals: Books 1–29, 10th October, 1916–24th February, 1925*, edited by Daniel J. Murphy, Colin Smythe, Gerrards Cross, 1978; 9 October 1920, p. 192

200 *'looking dreadfully worn and changed and his nerves broken'*: ibid., 9 November 1920, p. 199

201 *'done away with'*: ibid., 5 December 1920, p. 209

201 *'Is not this just what I have been hearing of from the crossroads . . . ?'*: ibid., 5 December 1920, p. 209

201 *'When I pray "God Save Ireland"'*: ibid., 5 November 1920, p. 197

ELEVEN The Stigma of Race

202 *'a cup of blue water'*: George Moore, *Parnell and His Island*, University College Dublin Press, Dublin, 2004 edn, p. 1

202 *'made the islands of Ireland and England one island'*: Philip Lecane, *Torpedoed! The R.M.S. Leinster Disaster*, Periscope, Penzance, 2005, p. 21

202 'Every hill, every valley': Johnston Diaries, 13 June 1921

202 'Ireland is a small but insuppressible island': Tom Kettle, The
Day's Burden: Studies, Literary & Political and Miscellaneous
Essays, Browne and Nolan, Dublin, 1910, p. 17

203 'Determined [to think] they were nasty men': ibid., 8 December
1920

205 'a British Mediterranean': quoted in G. R. Sloan, The Geopolitics of Anglo-Irish Relations in the Twentieth Century, Leicester
University Press, Leicester, 1997, p. 23. For Halford Mackinder,
see also Gerard Kearns, Geopolitics and Empire: The Legacy
of Halford Mackinder, Oxford University Press, Oxford, 2009,
and Jerry Brotton, A History of the World in Twelve Maps,
Penguin Books, London, 2013, pp. 337-73

205 'private sea chamber': Halford Mackinder, The Nations of
the Modern World: An Elementary Study in Geography and
History, Volume II: After 1914, George Philip & Son, London,
1924, pp. 237-8

205 'America in a very literal sense is truly the world state':
Will Hays, quoted in Donald Sassoon, The Culture of the
Europeans: From 1800 to the Present, HarperCollins, London,
2006, p. 936

206 'Eamon de Valera, President of the Irish Republic, is in his
native city': Dave Hannigan, De Valera in America: The Rebel
President's 1919 Campaign, O'Brien Press, Dublin, 2008, p. 20

206 A large delegation from the Philippines: Bernardita Reyes
Churchill, The Philippine Independence Missions to the United
States 1919-1934, National Historical Institute, Manila, 1983,
pp. 9-28, and Paul A. Kramer, Race, Empire, the United States
and the Philippines, University of North Carolina Press, Chapel
Hill, NC, 2006, pp. 384-9

206 'to advertise an entire people' . . . 'a mere coterie of savage or
semi-civilised tribes devoid of any sense of nationality': Reyes
Churchill, The Philippine Independence Missions, p. 18

206 the Waldorf-Astoria on Fifth Avenue: Edward Hungerford,
The Story of the Waldorf-Astoria, G. P. Putnam's Sons, New
York, 1925

206 'tremendously international': ibid., p. 195

207 'a compact mass': quoted in Alan J. Ward, Ireland and Anglo-

American Relations 1899–1921, Weidenfeld and Nicolson, London, 1969, p. 229

208 *the same standard of luxury enjoyed by wealthy Americans*: Hungerford, *The Story of the Waldorf-Astoria*, p. 200

208 *'the personal touch'*: Laura E. Nym Mayhall, 'The Prince of Wales versus Clark Gable: Anglophone Celebrity and Citizenship Between the Wars', in *Cultural and Social History*, vol. 4 issue 4 (December 2007), pp. 535–7

209 *'valet, shepherd and manager'*: David Fitzpatrick, *Harry Boland's Irish Revolution*, Cork University Press, Cork, 2003, p. 124

210 *'It is a treat to travel thousands of miles'*: ibid., p. 131

210 *'dark and bloody soil, lovely women'*: quoted in ibid., p. 161

210 *'You Americans, who were looked down upon'*: Eamon de Valera, 'American Liberty and the Spirit of the Irish Republic', in *Current Opinion*, August 1919, p. 83

210 *'We in Ireland recognize'*: ibid., p. 84

211 *'"Dead right, by golly!"'*: Sinclair Lewis, *Babbit*, New American Library, New York, 1961 edn, p. 20

213 *'the greatest medium in conveying Bolshevism to America'*: Colin Grant, *Negro with a Hat: The Rise and Fall of Marcus Garvey and His Dream of Mother Africa*, Jonathan Cape, London, 2008, p. 125

213 *'We new negroes'*: Matthew Pratt Guterl, 'The New Race Consciousness: Race, Nation, and Empire in American Culture, 1910–1925', in *Journal of World History*, vol. 10 no. 2 (fall 1999), p. 325

214 *'a pan-Coloured alliance'*: see ibid., pp. 313–38

214 *'the time has passed when you are entitled to assume'*: Glenda Elizabeth Gilmore, *Defying Dixie: The Radical Roots of Civil Rights*, W. W. Norton, New York, 2008, p. 21

215 *Ku Klux Klan*: see Shawn Lay, *The Invisible Empire in the West: Toward a New Historical Appraisal of the Ku Klux Klan of the 1920s*, University of Illinois Press, Urbana, 1992

215 *'As the Irishman is struggling for the fatherland of Ireland'*: Grant, *Negro with a Hat*, p. 197

216 *Liam Mellows briefed him*: Michael Silvestri, '"The South Needs Encouragement": The Irish Republican Campaign in the

American South and Southern Irish American Identity, 1919–1920', in *Éire-Ireland*, vol. 47 nos. 3 and 4 (fall/winter 2012), pp. 209–10

217 *'Why doesn't Britain declare a Monroe Doctrine'*: Tim Pat Coogan, *De Valera: Long Fellow, Long Shadow*, Hutchinson, London, 1993, p. 161

217 *the war in Cuba was a constant subject of conversation*: W. T. Stead, *The Centenary of 1798 and Its Bearing on Practical Politics of Today*, Review of Reviews, London, 1898, p. 67

218 *'No doubt Cuba was dreadfully governed'*: David W. Ellwood, *The Shock of America: Europe and the Challenge of the Century*, Oxford University Press, Oxford, 2012, p. 25

218 *'America had established a very important precedent'*: Steve J. S. Ickringill, 'Silence and Celebration: Ulster, William McKinley and the Spanish-American War', in Sylvia L. Hilton and Steve J. S. Ickringill (eds.), *European Perceptions of the Spanish–American War of 1898*, Peter Lang, Bern, 1999, p. 97

218 *'by location, helplessness and . . . the sentiment of gratitude'*: Louis A. Pérez Jr, 'Incurring a Debt of Gratitude: 1898 and the Moral Sources of United States Hegemony in Cuba', in *American Historical Review*, vol. 104 no. 2 (April 1999), p. 383

219 *'Rather than living under the "humanitarian Saxon race"'*: ibid., p. 372

219 *'powerful and generous nation, speaking our language, bred of our race'*: quoted in Paul A. Kramer, 'Empires, Exceptions, and Anglo-Saxons: Race and Rule between the British and United States Empires, 1880–1910', in *Journal of American History*, vol. 88 no. 4 (March 2002), p. 1,334

220 *'The world must be made safe for democracy'*: Nym Mayhall, 'The Prince of Wales versus Clark Gable', p. 537

220 *'Yet our hope is here and must be here'*: Peter Hart, *Mick: The Real Michael Collins*, Macmillan, London, 2005, p. 217

TWELVE No Pity

221 *Of the string of stylish cafes along Grafton Street in 1920*: see *Irish Independent*, 25 November 1919; Kevin O'Shiel, BMH WS 1770 part 5; Paul McMahon, *British Spies and Irish Rebels:*

British Intelligence and Ireland, 1916–1945, The Boydell Press, 2008, p. 33

221 *'beastly dear'*: Jacob Diaries, 18 May 1921

221 *'Who are these Sinn Féiners anyway?'*: Johnston Diaries, n.d. [1917]

222 *Frank Saurin and Vinny Byrne from the Squad*: Vincent Byrne, BMH WS 423, and Joseph Dolan, BMH WS 663

223 *'He [said] they were disappearing so fast'*: Carl W. Ackerman Papers, Box 1, Library of Congress, Washington DC, Carl Ackerman, in 'London Notes 1920–21'; 23 October 1920

223 *The most remarkable fact about British agents in Dublin*: this account of the events of Bloody Sunday is based on James Gleeson, *Bloody Sunday*, Peter Davies, London, 1962; Ann Dolan, 'Killing and Bloody Sunday, November 1920', in *Historical Journal*, vol. 49 no. 3 (September 2006), pp. 789–810; Charles Townshend, 'Bloody Sunday – Michael Collins Speaks', in *European Studies Review*, vol. 9 (1979), pp. 377–85; Tim Carey and Marcus de Búrca, 'Bloody Sunday 1920: New Evidence', in *History Ireland*, vol. 11 no. 2 (summer 2003), pp. 10–16; and Mrs Woodcock's memoir, *Experiences of an Officer's Wife in Ireland*, William Blackwood and Sons, Edinburgh and London, 1921

228 *assumed to be his wife*: since the original publication of *Bitter Freedom* I have received information from Mark Newberry, whose late father was Captain Newberry's first cousin, suggesting that the woman in Captain Newberry's flat in Dublin was not his wife, as official statements and Mrs Woodcock's account of Bloody Sunday claimed. According to Mrs Woodcock the woman who witnessed the shooting was pregnant and died giving birth to a stillborn baby a few weeks later. However, Mr Newberry has established while researching his family's history that Captain Newberry's wife, who outlived her husband by eight years, was not pregnant at the time.

233 *Members of the Tipperary team had fought with British soldiers*: Miceál Ó Meára (ed.), *Bloody Sunday 1920–1995: A Commemorative Booklet*, South Tipperary GAA Board, Clonmel, 1995, p. 14

234 *Robert Brennan, was travelling into town*: Robert Brennan,

BMH WS 779, section 3

234 *the journalists Joice Nankivell and Sydney Loch*: Joice M.
Nankivell Loch and Sydney Loch, *Ireland in Travail*, John
Murray, London, 1922, pp. 94–100

236 *Charlie Dalton couldn't get to sleep that night*: Ann Dolan,
'Killing and Bloody Sunday, November 1920', in *Historical
Journal*, vol. 49 no. 3 (September 2006), p. 798

236 *'Are there any more of your English dogs that you want to be
slain?'*: Jacob Diaries, 25 November 1920

237 *the British government reacted in the hard-boiled style*: see
Simon Ball, 'The Assassination Culture of Imperial Britain,
1909–1979', *Historical Journal*, vol. 56 no. 1 (March 2013),
pp. 231–56

237 *'Tragic as the events in Dublin were'*: quoted in Michael
Hopkinson, *The Irish War of Independence*, Gill and
Macmillan, Dublin, 2002, p. 180

THIRTEEN Flying Columns

238 *'not at all a bad looking type'*: Mark Sturgis diary, 25 January
1921, in Michael Hopkinson (ed.), *The Last Days of Dublin
Castle: The Mark Sturgis Diaries*, Irish Academic Press, Dublin,
1999, p. 115

243 *'Wait till I meet your mother'*: Joost Augusteijn, *From Public
Defiance to Guerrilla Warfare: The Experience of Ordinary
Volunteers in the Irish War of Independence 1916–1921*, Irish
Academic Press, Dublin, 1996, p. 326

243 *'I know who you are'*: Hubert Butler, *The Sub-Prefect Should
Have Held his Tongue and Other Essays*, Penguin Books,
London, 1990, p. 54

245 *'The sky looks good'*: Ernie O'Malley, *On Another Man's
Wound*, Anvil Books, Dublin, 1994 edn, p. 322

245 *'After night-fall the neighbours came in'*: ibid., p. 315

246 *'the highest expression of our Nationhood'*: Tom Barry,
Guerrilla Days in Ireland, Irish Press, Dublin, 1949, p. 23

247 *'We soon heard the sound of approaching lorries'*: Sean
Moylan, quoted in William Sheehan, *A Hard Local War:
The British Army and the Guerrilla War in Cork, 1919–1921*,

History Press, Stroud, 2011, pp. 133–4

247 'A bitterness and ferocity': O'Malley, On Another Man's
Wound, p. 316

247 'You being an aggressively anti-Irish person': James S. Donnelly Jr,
'Big House Burnings in County Cork During the Irish Revolution
1920–21', in Éire-Ireland, vol. 47 nos. 3 and 4 (fall/winter
2012), p. 165

248 'no persons shall be regarded': ibid., p. 164

249 In April fifty IRA men seized Upton station: The Times,
16 February 1921, and Frank Neville, BMH WS 443

249 'like a fever chart': Seán Ó Faoláin, Vive Moi, Hart-Davis,
London, 1965, p. 140

249 a barrier consisting of four heavy beech trunks: Wilfrid Ewart,
A Journey in Ireland 1921, G. P. Putnam's Sons, London, 1922,
p. 125

250 sixty-year-old farmer fell dead: Clonmel Chronicle, 22 June
1921

250 driven through the Cork countryside at sunset: ibid., p. 68

250 Emily Horsley Ussher and her family were sitting down to
lunch: Horsley Ussher Journal, pp. 63–4

251 'got mixed up in one of the daily shooting affrays': Johnston
Diaries, 16 April 1921

251 a secret dugout they had prepared in a field: Augusteijn, From
Public Defiance, p. 320

252 'a wholesale wiping out policy': Charles Townshend, The
Republic: The Fight for Irish Independence, 1918–1923, Allen
Lane, London, 2013, p. 259

252 'deport all in favour of the enemy': Michael Hopkinson, The
Irish War of Independence, Gill and Macmillan, Dublin, 2002,
p. 116

253 'Long tongues beware': Augusteijn, From Public Defiance, p. 291

254 One British intelligence officer disguised himself: Major-General
Sir Kenneth Strong, Intelligence at the Top: The Recollections
of an Intelligence Officer, Cassell, London, 1968, p. 1

254 Martin Corry: Sheehan, A Hard Local War, p. 75

254 'All strangers walking or cycling': ibid., p. 294

254 'scarcely normal and not sufficiently intelligent': Fearghal
McGarry, Eoin O'Duffy: A Self-made Hero, Oxford University

Press, Oxford, 2005, p. 66

255 *a Protestant clergyman in Cork*: Ewart, *A Journey in Ireland*, p. 58

255 *One man killed in Cork*: Paul Taylor, 'Heroes or Traitors? Experiences of Returning Irish Soldiers from World War One', unpublished DPhil, Oxford University, 2012, p. 96

256 *In February 1921*: John Borgonovo, *Spies, Informers and the 'Anti-Sinn Féin Society': The Intelligence War in Cork City, 1920-1921*, Irish Academic Press, Dublin, 2007, pp. 37-61

256 *Men in south Roscommon dressed like soldiers*: Townshend, *The Republic*, pp. 262–3

256 *'They saw our tin hats'*: O'Malley, *On Another Man's Wound*, pp. 89–90

257 *Castleconnell . . . IRA ambush*: House of Commons debates, 19 April 1921, CC1689–92; 20 April 1921, C1870; 26 April 1921, CC15–41; 5 May 1921, CC256–64; 16 June 1921, CC588–9

FOURTEEN Frightfulness

258 *a tall handsome young Englishman*: Wade Davis kindly shared his research on George Mallory for his book, *Into the Silence: The Great War, Mallory and the Conquest of Everest*, Bodley Head, London, 2011. See also Peter and Leni Gillman, *The Wildest Dream: Mallory, His Life and Conflicting Passions*, Headline Books, London, 2000, pp. 162–6, and David Robertson, *George Mallory*, Faber and Faber, London, 1969, pp. 124–31

258 *'I want to lose all harshness of jagged nerves'*: Davis, *Into the Silence*, p. 197

258 *'tired of trying to teach gentlemen to be gentlemen'*: Robert Graves, *Goodbye to All That*, Penguin, London, 2000, p. 57

259 *'Perhaps the most important thing about me'*: Gillman and Gillman, *The Wildest Dream*, p. 163

260 *'Don't speak to me about Le Côté de Guermantes'*: Nicholas Allen, *Modernism, Ireland and Civil War*, Cambridge University Press, Cambridge, 2009, p. 54

260 *'You could not see the face of that man'*: Lady Gregory, *Journals: Books 1–29, 10th October, 1916–24th February,*

1925, edited by Daniel J. Murphy, Colin Smythe, Gerrards Cross, 1978; 15 November 1920, p. 201

261 *a hunger strike by sixty-eight communists*: *New York Times*, 30 November 1919

261 *a black prisoner in Pennsylvania serving seven years*: ibid., 12 August 1920

261 *'shriek of agony'*: Anne Oliver Bell (ed.), *The Diary of Virginia Woolf, Volume II: 1920-1924*, Hogarth Press, London, 1978, pp. 72-3

261 *Irish revolutionaries owed a debt to British suffragists*: for the international origins of the hunger strike see Kevin Grant, 'The Transcolonial World of Hunger Strikes and Political Fasts, *c.* 1909-1935', in Durba Ghosh and Dane Kennedy (eds.), *Decentring Empire: Britain, India and the Transcolonial World*, Orient Longman, Hyderabad, 2006, pp. 243-69, and James Vernon, *Hunger: A Modern History*, The Belknap Press, Harvard, 2007, pp. 61-8. For Terence MacSwiney the best source is Francis J. Costello, *Enduring the Most: The Life and Death of Terence MacSwiney*, Brandon Books, Dingle, 1995, especially pp. 157-245

262 *'He is dying to bring all these atrocities before the people of the world'*: Peter MacSwiney, quoted in Paige Reynolds, 'Modernist Martyrdom: The Funerals of Terence MacSwiney', in *Modernism/modernity*, vol. 9 no. 4 (November 2002), p. 538

263 *An American journalist arriving for an appointment with Maud Gonne MacBride*: Ruth Russell, *What's the Matter with Ireland?*, Devin-Adair Company, New York, 1920, pp. 72-9

265 *Many visiting journalists stayed in the Shelbourne Hotel*: *The Shelbourne Hotel [tariff and guide to Dublin]*, Shelbourne Hotel, Dublin, 1902, and Elizabeth Bowen, *The Shelbourne*, Vintage Books, London, 2001

266 *'the incarnation of an Irish bard'*: Wilfrid Ewart, *A Journey in Ireland 1921*, G. P. Putnam's Sons, London, 1922, p. 18

266 *'Personally I am not in favour of violence'*: ibid., p. 20

267 *'were hynotized . . . as a rabbit by a snake'*: Niall Ferguson, *The Pity of War*, Basic Books, New York, 1999, p. 212

267 *'Look at the Irish'*: John Buchan, *The Three Hostages*, Polygon, Edinburgh, 2010, p. 47

267 *'an inspired work of genius'*: quoted in Ferguson, *The Pity of War*, p. 213

267 *'a short clean-shaven man in glasses'*: Ewart, *A Journey in Ireland*, p. 8

268 *'the horrible condition'*: *Manchester Guardian*, 23 October 1920

269 *'That last gibe, the sneer of a nation'*: *Daily News*, 26 February 1921, p. 4

269 *'they are detestable: but the worst is, they are partly true'*: *The Times*, 5 March 1921, quoted in James O'Connor, *History of Ireland, 1798–1924*, Arnold, London, 1925, p. 316

269 *'We followed and there at the back of the houses'*: *The Times*, 5 October 1920

269 *Ethel Snowden . . . spent ten days in Ireland*: Mrs Philip Snowden, *A Political Pilgrim in Europe*, Cassell and Company, London, 1921, pp. 237–70

270 *'Well, ma'am, ye seem to have a kind heart'*: ibid., p. 260

271 *'an episode . . . without precedent'*: quoted in Derek Sayer, 'British Reaction to the Amritsar Massacre 1919–1920', *Past & Present*, no. 131 (May 1991), p. 154

271 *Oswald Mosley*: Oswald Mosley, *My Life*, Thames Nelson and Sons, London, 1968, pp. 151–2, and Robert Skidelsky, *Oswald Mosley*, Macmillan, London, 1981, pp. 98–107

272 *'We think that no words of reprobation'*: 'Letter signed by thirty men from Cambridge University including J. M. Keynes, F. M. Cornford and Arthur Quiller-Couch', in *The Nation*, 27 November 1920, p. 308

272 *'sternly maintained'*: Hansard, HC (series 5), vol. 135, col. 502,494, 24 November 1920

272 *'It seemed to be agreed . . . that there are no such things as reprisals'*: Lord Hugh Cecil, quoted in Martin F. Seedorf, 'Defending Reprisals: Sir Hamar Greenwood and the "Troubles", 1920–21', in *Éire-Ireland*, vol. 25 no. 4 (winter 1990), p. 81

273 *'People in England don't seem to realise'*: Ewart, *A Journey in Ireland*, p. 69

273 *degenerates . . . 'such as would not be indulged in by the wildest savages in Central Africa'*: William Sheehan, *A Hard Local War: The British Army and the Guerrilla War in Cork, 1919–*

1921, History Press, Stroud, 2011, pp. 50–51

273 *'an extremely backward race'*: ibid., p. 59

273 *'the native Irish are . . . the lazy, dirty element'*: Major General Charles Howard Foulkes, 'Some Special Points as Regards Propaganda in Ireland', Foulkes Papers 7/4, Liddell Hart Centre for Military Archives, King's College, London

273 *'I almost begin to believe that these mean, dishonest insufferably conceited Irishmen'*: Mark Sturgis diary, 3 September 1920, in Michael Hopkinson (ed.), *The Last Days of Dublin Castle: The Mark Sturgis Diaries*, Irish Academic Press, Dublin, 1999, p. 35

274 *the ambush was a legitimate tactic of war*: Ewart, *A Journey in Ireland*, p. 39

274 *frightfulness 'in a more or less severe form'*: Charles Townshend, 'Civilization and "Frightfulness": Air Control in the Middle East Between the Wars', in Chris Wrigley (ed.), *Warfare, Diplomacy and Politics: Essays in Honour of A. J. P. Taylor*, Hamish Hamilton, London, 1986, p. 150

274 *'A great popular outcry will be created'*: Sir Hugh Trenchard, 9 October 1920, quoted in Sheehan, *A Hard Local War*, p. 141

275 *'a world problem'*: *The Times*, 11 February 1921

275 *'the more certain does it become that great bodies of opinion'*: quoted in Maurice Walsh, *The News From Ireland: Foreign Correspondents and the Irish Revolution*, I. B. Tauris, London, 2008, p. 93

275 *'of great public importance'* . . . *'the interests of this country'*: quoted in ibid., p. 94

275 *'naturally we should wish to end this uphill, sordid, unchivalrous, loathsome conflict'*: ibid., p. 94

276 *Pacifist*: Mark Sturgis diary, 15 April 1921, in Hopkinson (ed.), *The Last Days of Dublin Castle*, p. 159

FIFTEEN A Republic of Their Own

277 *In 1914 the British clothing firm Burberry*: for the transformation of the trenchcoat from military necessity to fashion essential see Jane Tynan, 'Military Dress and Men's Outdoor Leisurewear: Burberry's Trench Coat in First World War Britain', in *Journal*

of Design History, vol. 24 no. 2 (2011), pp. 139–56

278 *crossing the moonlit street*: Thomas J. O'Carroll, BMH WS 124

278 *'a trenchcoat with all the usual buttons, belts and rings'*:
Colonel Eamon Broy, BMH WS 1280

278 *Eamon de Valera claimed to have made his own contribution*:
Joe Good, BMH WS 388

279 *'Time for me to be off'*: Robert Brennan, BMH WS 779

279 *'rather a pallid, unwashed crowd'*: Brigadier Frederick Clarke,
quoted in William Sheehan, *British Voices From the Irish War
of Independence 1918–1921: The Words of British Servicemen
Who Were There*, Collins Press, Cork, 2005, p. 40

279 *tall, dark, black-haired figure with 'flashing eyes'*: Celia Shaw,
quoted in Joost Augusteijn, *From Public Defiance to Guerrilla
Warfare: The Experience of Ordinary Volunteers in the Irish
War of Independence 1916–1921*, Irish Academic Press, Dublin,
1996, p. 302

279 *'a resolute profile, powerful as a thought'*: Elizabeth Bowen,
The Last September, Vintage Classics, London, 1998, p. 34

280 *'It was the first official intimation we had received'*: Ernie
O'Malley, *The Singing Flame,* Anvil Books, Dublin, 1978, p. 13

281 *Moylett drove four IRA men to Southwark Cathedral*: Patrick
Moylett, BMH WS 767

281 *'to refuse to recognise the Dáil is as futile as to refuse to
recognise the Soviet'*: Michael Hopkinson, *The Irish War
of Independence*, Gill and Macmillan, Dublin, 2002, p. 179

282 *'It is too much to expect that Irish physical force'*: quoted in
ibid., p. 182

282 *Alfred Cope, known to his colleagues as 'Andy'*: Eunan
O'Halpin, 'Sir Alfred William Cope, 1877–1954', in *Dictionary
of Irish Biography Online* and Mark Sturgis diary, in Michael
Hopkinson (ed.), *The Last Days of Dublin Castle: The Mark
Sturgis Diaries*, Irish Academic Press, Dublin, 1999

282 *'I have met quite a number of prominent Sinn Féiners'*: Alfred
Cope, memo dated 16 June 1920, HO 317/59, Public Record
Office, Kew

283 *'Coercion was the only policy'*: Hopkinson, *The Irish War of
Independence*, p. 187

283 *'an unmeasured calamity'*: Ronan Fanning, *Fatal Path: British*

Government and Irish Revolution 1910–1922, Faber and Faber, London, 2013, p. 212

284 *Denis Johnston emerged from La Scala*: Johnston Diaries, 11 July 1921

284 *'Then as the Angelus rang out'*: Frank O'Connor, *An Only Child and My Father's Son: An Autobiography*, Penguin Books, London, 2005, p. 146

285 *'He looks like a young war god'*: Simone Téry, 'French Reporter Visits Volunteers' Training Camp, "Somewhere" in Western Ireland, August 15, 1921', in *Irish Renaissance Annual III*, University of Delaware Press, Newark, 1982, p. 126

286 *'We'll all wake up some morning'*: Michael Laffan, *The Resurrection of Ireland: The Sinn Féin Party 1916–1923*, Cambridge University Press, Cambridge, 1999, p. 299

286 *'In the mind of every soldier was a little republic of his own'*: Fearghal McGarry, *Eoin O'Duffy: A Self-made Hero*, Oxford University Press, Oxford, 2005, p. 77

286 *'would wish to set up a Mexico here'*: Laffan, *The Resurrection of Ireland*, p. 303

286 *'entitled to some consideration for having fought'*: ibid., p. 298

286 *'anyone else who attempted to collect rates'*: ibid., p. 300

286 *'no pressure of any kind is to be used'*: ibid., p. 299

286 *'an aggressive or intolerant attitude'*: ibid.

287 *in conversation with 'gossipy girls'*: McGarry, *Eoin O'Duffy*, p. 77

287 *'We felt very important'*: Michael V. O'Donoghue, BMH WS 1741

287 *'The British Empire is a saving fact in a very distracted world'*: Lloyd George, quoted in *The Times*, 20 June 1921

289 *'to remind us that we are not the army of the Irish Republic'*: Tom Barry, quoted in S. M. Lawlor, 'Ireland from Truce to Treaty: War or Peace? July to October 1921', in *Irish Historical Studies*, vol. 22 no. 85 (March 1980), p. 59

289 *'arrogant and provocative'*: Michael Collins, quoted in ibid., p. 59

289 *'We have either peace or war'*: quoted in ibid., p. 59

290 *'too popular'*: O'Malley, *The Singing Flame*, p. 15

291 *'when the majority of people in small towns'*: Paul McMahon, *British Spies and Irish Rebels: British Intelligence and Ireland, 1916–1945*, Boydell Press, 2008, p. 61

291 *'we have to keep a constant eye on these people'*: ibid., p. 56

SIXTEEN Not Irish in the National Sense

292 *'the rattle of thousands of hammers riveting'*: J. A. Strahan, 'Dublin and Belfast: A Study in Towns and Temperaments', in *Living Age*, 6 September 1919

292 *'premier shipbuilding centre of the entire world'*: quoted in Paul Bew, *Ideology and the Irish Question: Ulster Unionism and Irish Nationalism 1912–1916*, Clarendon Press, Oxford, 1994, p. 36

293 *'One would guess that her people's chief idea of happiness'*: 'An Englishman' [Douglas Goldring], *A Stranger in Ireland*, Talbot Press, Dublin, 1918, p. 42

293 *'Our tunic fronts were often stuffed with them'*: John F. Lucy, *There's a Devil in the Drum*, Faber and Faber, London, 1938, pp. 46–7

293 *'steadily more Protestant and less Irish'*: Joe Devlin, quoted in Thomas Hennessy, *Dividing Ireland: World War I and Partition*, Routledge, London, 1998, p. 146

294 *'sympathy with the world mission of the British Empire'*: Thomas Sinclair, quoted in Philip Ollerenshaw, 'Businessmen in Northern Ireland and the Imperial Connection, 1886–1939', in Keith Jeffery (ed.), *An Irish Empire?: Aspects of Ireland and the British Empire*, Manchester University Press, Manchester, 1996, p. 173

295 *'We have prospered under it and we will take nothing less'*: William Moore, quoted in Hennessy, *Dividing Ireland*, p. 10

296 *'Opposition to Home Rule in Ulster . . . has destroyed all differences'*: The Marquis of Londonderry, quoted in Richard Bourke, *Peace in Ireland: The War of Ideas*, Pimlico, London, 2003, p. 429, n. 56

296 *a ten-year-old C. S. Lewis in suburban Belfast*: Alvin Jackson, 'Unionist Myths 1912–1985', in *Past & Present*, issue 136 (August 1992), p. 165

297 *'We claim that Ireland is a nation'*: John Redmond, quoted in Hennessy, *Dividing Ireland*, p. 20

297 *'solid homogeneous Ulster'*: John Bowman, *De Valera and the*

Ulster Question, Clarendon Press, Oxford, 1982, p. 40

298 'a foreign garrison' ... 'not Irish people' ... 'they would have to go under': ibid., p. 32

298 'The Unionists of Ulster have never transferred their love and allegiance': Father Michael O'Flanagan, quoted in Hennessy, *Dividing Ireland*, p. 147

299 'I used to hold my breath till I got through it': Louis MacNeice, *The Strings Are False: An Unfinished Autobiography*, Faber and Faber, London, 1982, pp. 49–50

300 'The Protestants and Roman Catholics are nearly equally divided in Belfast': Queen Victoria, quoted in S. J. Connolly and Gillian McIntosh, 'Whose City? Belonging and Exclusion in the Nineteenth-Century Urban World', in S. J. Connolly (ed.), *Belfast 400: People Place and History*, Liverpool University Press, 2012, pp. 250–51

300 'The Protestants here are bigots': Wilfrid Ewart, *A Journey in Ireland 1921*, G. P. Putnam's Sons, London, 1922, p. 159

301 'Rest assured that mighty changes are coming in Ireland': Jonathan Bardon, *A History of Ulster*, Blackstaff Press, Belfast, 2005, p. 468

302 'virtually the Governor of Derry': ibid., p. 475

304 'If that's what we get when they have not got their Parliament': Alan F. Parkinson, *Belfast's Unholy War: The Troubles of the 1920s*, Four Courts Press, Dublin, 2004, p. 39

305 This account of the Belfast boycott draws on two articles by Philip Ollerenshaw: 'Business Boycotts and the Partition of Ireland', in Brenda Collins, Philip Ollerenshaw and Trevor Parkhill (eds), *Industry, Trade and People in Ireland 1650–1950: Essays in Honour of W. H. Crawford*, Ulster Historical Foundation, Belfast, 2005, pp. 205–24, and 'Business, Politics and Revolution in early twentieth-century Ireland', in Terry Gourvish (ed.), *Business and Politics in Europe, 1900–1970: Essays in Honour of Alice Teichova*, Cambridge University Press, 2003, pp. 63–81, as well as David S. Johnson, 'The Belfast Boycott, 1920–22', in J. M. Goldstrom and L. A. Clarkson (eds), *Irish Population, Economy, and Society: Essays in Honour of the Late K. H. Connell*, pp. 287–307.

306 *'It does not hit Ulster very hard'*: Ewart, *A Journey in Ireland*, p. 157

308 *'the British government would let Ulster down tomorrow'*: ibid., p. 151

308 *On 22 June the king came to Belfast to open the new parliament*: *The Times*, 17, 20, 23 June 1921; *Daily News*, 23, 27 June 1921

SEVENTEEN The Crown Close at Hand

310 *'no set rules of life and behaved just as it pleased'*: *Daily Mirror*, 10 October 1921

311 *'The task before women today'*: ibid.

311 *'the Sinn Féin mystery man'*: Rex Taylor, *Michael Collins*, New English Library, London, 1970, pp. 119–20

311 *'all three of his own girls [were] dropping from fatigue'*: *Washington Post*, 30 October 1921

312 *'Sinn Féin cook who is a potato specialist'*: *Daily Mirror*, 15 October 1921

312 *'What do you think of the enclosed? Writing all bosh'*: quoted in Margery Forester, *Michael Collins: The Lost Leader*, Sphere Books, London, 1972, p. 217

313 *'We Irishmen were nervous and ill at ease'*: Robert Barton, quoted in Tim Pat Coogan, *Michael Collins: A Biography*, Hutchinson, London, 1990, p. 240

314 *'its mighty navy, its flag on every sea'*: John Darwin, *The Empire Project: The Rise and Fall of the British World-system, 1830–1970*, Cambridge University Press, Cambridge, 2009, pp. 399–400

315 *'It will not survive unless it shows now in the most unmistakable fashion'*: Lloyd George, quoted in Adam Tooze, *The Deluge: The Great War and the Remaking of Global Order, 1916–1931*, Allen Lane, London, 2014, p. 387

315 *'anarchic gunmen'*: F. E. Smith, quoted in John Campbell, *F. E. Smith: First Earl of Birkenhead*, Jonathan Cape, London, 1983, p. 549

315 *'He fancied he had met and defeated the whole might of the Empire'*: Lloyd George, quoted in Peter Hart, *Mick: The Real Michael Collins*, Macmillan, London, 2005, p. 297

316 *'permanent allies'*: Joseph M. Curran, *The Birth of the Irish*

Free State 1921–1923, University of Alabama Press,
Tuscaloosa, 1980, p. 88

317 *'It is the keystone of the arch in law'*: Frank Pakenham, *Peace
by Ordeal: The Negotiation of the Anglo-Irish Treaty, 1921*,
Pimlico, London, 1992, p. 157

317 *'The Crown thousands of miles away would never menace the
Dominions'*: ibid., p. 199

318 *'a propaganda of inanity unparalleled in the world's history'*:
H. G. Wells, quoted in Laura E. Nym Mayhall, 'The Prince of
Wales versus Clark Gable: Anglophone Celebrity and Citizenship Between the Wars', in *Cultural and Social History*, vol. 4
issue 4 (December 2007), p. 536

319 *'the Sterilisation of the Crown'*: Pakenham, *Peace by Ordeal*,
p. 202

319 *'Dublin is the real problem'*: Coogan, *Michael Collins*, p. 242

320 *'sugar coating to enable the English people to swallow the pill'*:
Curran, *The Birth of the Irish Free State*, p. 118

321 *'like a wild beast in a cage'*: Coogan, *Michael Collins*, p. 275

321 *'It was as if the world fell in pieces around us'*: quoted in
T. Ryle Dwyer, *'I Signed My Death Warrant': Michael Collins
& The Treaty*, Mercier Press, Cork, 2006, p. 216

321 *'We heard tonight Ireland is a Free State'*: quoted in Michael
Hopkinson, *Green Against Green: The Irish Civil War*, Gill
and Macmillan, Dublin, 1988, p. 35

322 *'What should I read it for?'*: Tim Pat Coogan, *De Valera: Long
Fellow, Long Shadow*, Hutchinson, London, 1993, p. 283

322 *'The British and Irish Press carried the people off their feet'*:
Austin Stack, quoted in Pakenham, *Peace by Ordeal*, p. 265

323 *Rosamond Jacob's first impression*: Jacob Diaries, 7 December
1921

325 *'In my opinion it gives us freedom'*: Michael Collins, *Dáil
Debates*, vol. 3 col. 32, 19 December 1921

328 *'The British Empire stands to me in the same relationship'*:
Liam Mellows, *Dáil Debates*, vol. 3 col. 231, 4 January 1922

328 *'she will not be allowed to exterminate the people of Ireland'*:
Mary MacSwiney, *Dáil Debates*, vol. 3 col. 119, 21 December
1921

328 *'We have no debt and no great factories'*: Seamus Robinson,

Dáil Debates, vol. 3, col. 290, 6 January 1922

329 *'Ireland must choose extermination before dishonour'*: Mary MacSwiney, *Dáil Debates*, vol. 3 col. 119, 21 December 1921

329 *'essentially a spiritual fight'*: Mary MacSwiney, *Dáil Debates*, vol. 3 col. 118, 21 December 1921

329 *'would rather have the people of Ireland eking out a poor existence on the soil'*: Liam Mellows, *Dáil Debates*, vol. 3 col. 231, 4 January 1922

329 *'a beacon'* . . . *'This downtrodden, this miserable country'*: Liam Mellows, *Dáil Debates*, vol. 3 col. 233, 4 January 1922

329 *'We believe that the Gaelic-Irish outlook of civilisation and culture should permeate and influence the life of every nation'*: Gearóid O'Sullivan, *Dáil Debates*, vol. 3 col. 24, 6 January 1922

329 *'world improvements in problems that have never been solved'*: W. T. Cosgrave, *Dáil Debates*, vol. 3 col. 108, 21 December 1921

EIGHTEEN The Quietest Triumph

331 *'Is human nature universal'*: Letter from the *American Paint and Oil Dealer*, 7 July 1922, vol. 200; American Consulate Dublin Correspondence 1922 RG84, National Archives, College Park, Maryland, US

331 *In an extraordinarily swift reply*: American consul to *American Paint and Oil Dealer*, 24 July 1922, ibid.

332 *a significant revolutionary act*: J. J. Walsh, *Recollections of a Rebel*, The Kerryman, Tralee, 1944, pp. 63–4

332 *'Quite a number of these people imagine'*: Joseph Connolly, quoted in Bernadette Whelan, *United States and Foreign Policy and Ireland: From Empire to Independence, 1913–29*, Four Courts Press, Dublin, 2006, pp. 379–80

332 *the US consulate in Dublin was flooded with requests*: Correspondence of the American Consulate in Dublin 1919, vol. 177, 850.7–865.15

332 *Texan oil magnate*: Ian d'Alton, 'In a "Comity of Cultures": The Rise and Fall of the Irish Statesman, 1919–30' in Mark O'Brien and Felix Larkin (eds.), *Periodicals and Journalism in Twentieth Century Ireland*, Four Courts Press, Dublin, 2014, pp. 96, 100

333 *'America's bounding prosperity'*: quoted in Colum Kenny, 'Tom Grehan: Advertising Pioneer and Newspaper Man', in Mark O'Brien and Kevin Rafter (eds.), *Independent Newspapers: A History*, Four Courts Press, Dublin, 2012, p. 56

333 *'freedom at midnight'*: see David Cannadine, 'Independence Day Ceremonials in Historical Perspective', in Robert Holland, Susan Williams and Terry Barringer (eds.), *The Iconography of Independence: 'Freedoms at Midnight'*, Routledge, London, 2010, pp. 1-15

334 *'seemed scarcely out of their teens'*: Sir Henry Robinson, *Memories: Wise and Otherwise*, Casell and Company, London, 1923, pp. 325-6

334 *'the quietest triumph of all'*: Journal of Father Michael Maher, 16 January 1922

334 *Around the Curragh*: Con Costello, *A Most Delightful Station: the British Army and the Curragh of Kildare, Ireland, 1855-1922*, The Collins Press, Cork, 1996, p. 326

335 *It was the same with the Black and Tans*: Costello, *A Most Delightful Station*, p. 332

336 *'At that time we were in Beggars Bush'*: Michael Hopkinson, *Green Against Green: The Irish Civil War*, Gill and Macmillan, Dublin, 1988, p. 62

337 *handover of the Curragh*: Costello, *A Most Delightful Station*, pp. 336-40

338 *'If a Government goes wrong'*: Rory O'Connor, quoted in Hopkinson, *Green Against Green*, p. 67

341 *'Cannot something be done to hurry up R.I.C. disbandment?'*: Kent Fedorowich, 'The Problems of Disbandment: The Royal Irish Constabulary and Imperial Migration, 1919-29', in *Irish Historical Studies*, vol. 30 no. 117 (May 1996), p. 94

341 *'knocked them Arabs about a bit'*: John D. Brewer, *The Royal Irish Constabulary: An Oral History*, The Institute of Irish Studies, The Queen's University of Belfast (1990), p. 122

342 *The father of the literary critic Denis Donoghue*: Denis Donoghue, *Warrenpoint*, Cape, London, 1991, p. 7

342 *leave within twelve hours or be shot*: Brewer, *The Royal Irish Constabulary*, p. 123

342 *'The man who was going to have to shoot me'*: ibid., p. 125

343 *Some suggested the victims had been chosen*: the 'Bandon Valley massacre' has provoked a bitter historical controversy over whether it was motivated by sectarianism. See Hart, *The IRA and Its Enemies*, pp. 273-92, and John M. Regan, 'The Bandon Valley Massacre as a Historical Problem', in *History*, 97 (2012), pp. 70-98

343 *A local IRA commander issued a proclamation*: Ungoed-Thomas, *Jasper Wolfe*, p. 143

343 *'a fearful squash'*: Jacob Diaries, 12 February 1922

343 *'Collins was blasting away'*: ibid., 5 March 1922

344 *'They would have to wade through Irish blood'*: Joseph M. Curran, *The Birth of the Irish Free State 1921-1923*, University of Alabama Press, Tuscaloosa, 1980, p. 174

344 *'unity at home was more important'*: Hopkinson, *Green Against Green*, p. 98

347 *'that hideous bog of reprisals'*: ibid., p. 54

348 *'we are in contact with revolutionaries who will stop at nothing'*: Winston Churchill, quoted in ibid., p. 73

348 *'Ireland had every reason to expect to become recognised'*: Michael Kennedy, '"Civil Servants Cannot Be Politicians": The Professionalisation of the Irish Foreign Service, 1919-22', in *Irish Studies in International Affairs*, vol. 8 (1997), p. 105

349 *'We made a big concession to you'*: Thomas Towey, 'The Reaction of the British Government to the 1922 Collins-de Valera Pact', *Irish Historical Studies*, vol. 22 no. 85 (March 1980), p. 73

350 *'who gave the electors a chance'*: Michael Gallagher, 'The Pact General Election of 1922', in *Irish Historical Studies*, vol. 22 no. 84 (September 1979), p. 416

350 *On the morning of 22 June*: the account of Wilson's assassination is drawn from Peter Hart, 'Michael Collins and the Assassination of Henry Wilson', in Peter Hart, *The IRA at War 1916-1923*, Oxford University Press, Oxford, 2003, pp. 194-220

NINETEEN Call to Arms

353 *Denis Johnston woke*: Johnston Diaries, 28 June 1922

354 *Rosamond Jacob stood in a crowd*: Jacob Diaries,

28 June 1922

355 *As dawn broke*: Ernie O'Malley, *The Singing Flame,* Anvil Books, Dublin, 1978, p. 97

355 *'What about books, Ginger?'*: ibid., p. 99

356 *'the crack of the English whip'*: Alfred Cope to Lionel Curtis, 27 June 1922, CO 906/21, National Archives, Kew

356 *'I will of course make it clear'*: Winston Churchill, quoted in Michael Hopkinson, *Green Against Green: The Irish Civil War,* Gill and Macmillan, Dublin, 1988, p. 118

356 *'Aeroplanes used by untrained persons'*: Winston Churchill, telegram to Michael Collins, 2.28 p.m., 29 June 1922, CO 906/21, National Archives, Kew

358 *Denis Johnston . . . heard shattered plate glass*: Johnston Diaries, 30 June 1922

358 *Rosamond Jacob was attending to two wounded civilians*: Jacob Diaries, 30 June 1922

358 *'enraged volleys'*: O'Malley, *The Singing Flame,* p. 119

358 *Ernie O'Malley spotted a Free State captain*: O'Malley, *The Singing Flame,* pp. 122–3

359 *'misleading the average mind'*: 'Complaints Against the Press', undated note in Department of the Taoiseach File S1 394, 1922, National Archives, Dublin

359 *'were shot maintaining the People's supremacy'*: quoted in Ann Dolan, *Commemorating the Irish Civil War: History and Memory, 1923–2000,* Cambridge University Press, 2003, p. 125

360 *Girls in white frocks*: 'The Dublin Fighting', in the *New Statesman,* 8 July 1922

360 *'Oh any amount!'*: Jacob Diaries, 5 July 1922

361 *'A few shots went off'*: Johnston Diaries, 30 June 1922

361 *'It's not at all pleasant'*: ibid., 2 July 1922

361 *made their way through a garage*: Jacob Diaries, 1 July 1922

362 *Cathal Brugha's body lying in state*: ibid., 9 July 1922

363 *'Look at that great historic street'*: Winston Churchill, quoted in Dorothy McArdle, *The Irish Republic,* Corgi Books, London, 1968, p. 691

363 *'On the other hand, the destruction'*: Ruth McManus, *Dublin, 1910–1940: Shaping the City & Suburbs,* Four Courts Press, Dublin, 2002, p. 75

363 *'I can't conceive the mentality'*: Johnston Diaries, 29 June 1922

363 *Denis read that there were queues*: ibid., 7 July 1922

365 *Thurles in County Tipperary*: Journal of Father Michael Maher, St Patrick's College, Thurles; 7 July–9 August 1922

366 *Cork city was the last major area*: for events in Cork I rely on John Borgonovo, *The Battle for Cork, July–August 1922*, Mercier Press, Cork, 2011

368 *'We could hear them coming all night long'*: Seán Ó Faoláin, *Vive Moi!*, Hart-Davis, London, 1965, p. 154

TWENTY 'Terror Will Be Struck into Them'

370 *dinner at Kilteragh*: Sinéad McCoole, *Hazel: A Life of Lady Lavery, 1880–1935*, Lilliput Press, Dublin, 1996, pp. 96–7

370 *'his nerves were in rags'*: Peter Somerville-Large, *Irish Voices: An Informal History 1916–1966*, Pimlico, London, 2000, p. 65

371 *'very much the soldier'*: Lady Gregory, *Journals: Books 1–29, 10th October, 1916–24th February, 1925*, edited by Daniel J. Murphy, Colin Smythe, Gerrards Cross, 1978; 20 August 1922, p. 386

371 *troops ducking down side streets*: John M. Regan, *The Irish Counter-Revolution 1921–1936*, Gill and Macmillan, Dublin, 2001, p. 164

371 *Collins . . . on a white charger*: Anne Dolan, *Commemorating the Irish Civil War: History and Memory 1923–2000*, Cambridge University Press, Cambridge, 2003, p. 75

372 *'It should be pointed out'*: Tim Pat Coogan, *Michael Collins: A Biography*, Hutchinson, London, 1990, Coogan, *Michael Collins*, p. 392

373 *the journey Collins embarked on*: see Coogan, *Michael Collins*, pp. 400–415

375 *'by prompt, effective, vigorous'*: Tom Garvin, *1922: The Birth of Irish Democracy*, Gill and Macmillan, Dublin, 1996, p. 161

375 *'a mistaken idea of humanity'*: ibid., p. 162

376 *'We may be depended upon'*: Bill Kissane, *The Politics of the Irish Civil War*, Oxford University Press, Oxford, 2005, p. 154

376 'Although I have always objected to a death penalty':
Hopkinson, Green Against Green, p. 181

378 'If you took as your first case some man': ibid., p. 189

378 'black man's law': Timothy Murphy Breen, 'The Government's
Executions Policy During the Irish Civil War', unpublished PhD
thesis, National University of Ireland Maynooth, 2010, p. 113

378 'There were no Irishmen': John M. Regan, The Irish Counter-
Revolution 1921–1936, Gill and Macmillan, Dublin, 2001,
p. 112

379 'a system of murder and assassination': Michael Hopkinson,
Green Against Green: The Irish Civil War, Gill and Macmillan,
Dublin, 1988, p. 182

379 'mere politics but what is morally right or wrong': quoted in
Patrick Murray, Oracles of God: The Roman Catholic Church
and Irish Politics 1922–37, University College Dublin Press,
Dublin, 2000, p. 87

381 'We have the whole island to think of': Lady Gregory, Journals,
19 December 1922, p. 421

381 'it is hereby solemnly notified that robbery will be sternly
suppressed': Kissane, The Politics of the Irish Civil War, p. 106

382 'as through a wall of glass': quoted in ibid., p. 90

382 'So far as I can ascertain Mr de Valera is not in a position to
"deliver the goods"': ibid., p. 106

383 Several fled the city: Regan, The Irish Counter-Revolution, p. 115

384 'As I moved from the door': Ernest Blythe memoir, quoted in
Martin A. Fitzpatrick, 'Liam Mellows: His Final Tragic Year
and the Management of His Legacy', unpublished MA thesis,
University College Dublin, 2012, p. 36

385 'It is where terror meets terror': Breen, 'The Government's
Executions Policy', p. 152

386 'We are charged with the responsibility of saving our country':
Regan, The Irish Counter-Revolution, p. 116

386 'taking a leaf out of England's book': Regan, The Irish Counter-
Revolution, p. 116

387 'people who roast children': Kissane, The Politics of the Irish
Civil War, p. 146

388 'There was a lull after the first executions': quoted in Garvin,
1922, p. 163

TWENTY-ONE Dumping Arms

389 *a major boxing match*: this account of the world-title fight in
Dublin relies on Andrew Gallimore, *A Bloody Canvas: The
Mike McTigue Story*, Mercier Press, Cork, 2007, pp. 20–56 and
83–149; Peter Benson, *Battling Siki: A Tale of Ring Fixes, Race
and Murder in the 1920s*, The University of Arkansas Press,
Fayetteville, 2006, pp. 1–37

393 *a woman who was ill at the idea*: Jacob Diaries, 9 February
1923

393 'a low disgrace': ibid., 19 February 1923

395 *'The complete failure to prevent the Siki–McTigue fight'*:
New York Times, 21 March 1923

395 *'Then we will have arrived at a point'*: Liam Deasy, *Brother
Against Brother*, Mercier Press, Cork, 1998, p. 120

396 *'It created an air of unreality'*: Michael Hopkinson, *Green
Against Green: The Irish Civil War*, Gill and Macmillan,
Dublin, 1988, p. 232

396 *'victory is within our grasp'*: ibid., p. 229

396 *Adolf Hitler's 'best men' in Munich*: Troy D. Davis, 'The Irish
Civil War and the "International Proposition" of 1922–23',
in *Éire-Ireland* 29 (summer 1994), pp. 101–2

396 *In Wexford*: Aodagán O'Rahilly interviewed in *The Madness
From Within*, RTE documentary broadcast on 21 January 1998

397 *'the rule of the Torch and Can'*: Hopkinson, *Green Against
Green*, p. 228

397 *'at the point of a revolver'*: Gemma M. Clark, 'Fire, Boycott,
Threat and Harm: Social and Political Violence Within the
Local Community. A Study of Three Munster Counties During
the Irish Civil War, 1922–23', unpublished DPhil thesis, Oxford
University, 2010, p. 85

397 *'We are Bolsheviks from the Ox mountains'*: Michael Farry,
The Aftermath of Revolution: Sligo 1921–23, University
College Dublin Press, Dublin, 2000, p. 171

398 *likened local combinations of tenants to the Ku Klux Klan*:
Hopkinson, *Green Against Green*, pp. 221–2

399 *'bid fair to be classed with the nigger and the Mexican'*:

Timothy Murphy Breen, 'The Government's Executions Policy During the Irish Civil War', unpublished PhD thesis, National University of Ireland Maynooth, 2010, p. 187

399 *'Ireland's failure strengthens the cause of those who believe in strong imperial government'*: Bill Kissane, *The Politics of the Irish Civil War*, Oxford University Press, Oxford, 2005, p. 65

400 *'We share your faith in the Treaty'*: ibid., pp. 106–7

401 *'If I was taken prisoner'*: Breen, 'The Government's Executions Policy', p. 83

401 *'left them anything but normal'*: Eunan O'Halpin, *Defending Ireland: The Irish State and Its Enemies Since 1922*, Oxford University Press, Oxford, 1999, p. 11

402 *The most notorious atrocity*: my account of events in Kerry is drawn from the RTE television documentary *Ballyseedy*, directed by Pat Hand, presented by Pat Butler, transmitted on RTE 1, 12 November 1997

404 *Lady Gregory found one of the detectives in the green room*: Lady Gregory, *Journals: Books 1–29, 10th October, 1916–24th February, 1925*, edited by Daniel J. Murphy, Colin Smythe, Gerrards Cross, 1978; 15 April 1923, p. 445

405 *'Any gunshots heard during the performance'*: Declan Kiberd, *Inventing Ireland: The Literature of the Modern Nation*, Vintage Books, London, 1996, p. 218

405 'The dumping of arms does not mean that the usefulness of the IRA is past': Kissane, *The Politics of the Irish Civil War*, p. 123

406 *'The roads are all cleaned'*: Journal of Father Michael Maher, St Patrick's College, Thurles; 23 August 1923

TWENTY-TWO Jazz Mad

407 *Rosamond Jacob dropped in on her friends*: Jacob Diaries, 10 November 1919

407 *Rosamond's sister-in-law loaned her*: ibid., 12 January 1920

408 *'new keys by which we can now unlock doors in the human personality'*: Barbara Low, *Psychoanalysis: A Brief Account of the Freudian Theory*, George Allen & Unwin, London, 1920, pp. 16–17

408 *'discussed over the soup'*: Graham Richards, 'Britain on the

Couch: The Popularization of Psychoanalysis in Britain 1918–1940', in *Science in Context*, vol. 13 issue 2 (summer 2000), p. 212

408 *'the Oedipus complex a household word'*: ibid., p. 197

409 *'female writers discovering a freedom'*: Nicola Beauman, *A Very Great Profession: The Woman's Novel 1914–39*, Persephone Books, London, 2008, p. 175

409 *'During the war women mixed with men'*: George Seldes, *World Panorama 1918–1933*, Hamish Hamilton, London, 1933, p. 63

409 *'Love is a joke'*: quoted in ibid., p. 62

409 *'It is so easy to take'*: Jon Savage, *Teenage: The Creation of Youth Culture*, Pimlico, London, 2008, p. 165

410 *'Week after week enormous bundles'*: quoted in David Dwan, *The Great Community: Culture and Nationalism in Ireland*, Field Day Publications (Field Day Files 5), Dublin, in association with the Keough-Naughton Institute for Irish Studies, University of Notre Dame, Indiana, 2008, p. 157

410 *'nigger minstrelsy'* and *'Cockney music-hall singers'*: *Leader*, quoted in ibid., p. 168

410 *'a merciless war'* against English Sunday papers: *Irish Times*, 23 October 1920

411 *'a general decadence in moral standards'*: Evelyn Bolster, *The Knights of Saint Columbanus*, Gill and Macmillan, Dublin, 1979, p. 48

411 *'the latest craze of the leisured ladies of Mayfair'*: *Irish Independent*, 17 March 1920

411 *'It must have been deadly'*: quoted in Louise Ryan, *Gender, Identity and the Irish Press: Embodying the Nation*, Edwin Mellen Press, Lewiston, New York, 2001, p. 58

412 *The Bishop of Birmingham oversaw an inquiry*: Richard Overy, *The Morbid Age: Britain and the Crisis of Civilisation*, Penguin, London, 2010, p. 152

412 *Wandsworth Council in London*: James McMillan, *The Way It Was 1914–1934*, William Kimber, London, 1979, p. 147

412 *'The war has profoundly disturbed the feminine mind'*: ibid., p. 145

413 *John P. Mandeville, a veteran of the war*: *Irish Independent*, 25 November 1919

414 *'importations from the vilest dens'*: quoted in Gearóid Ó hAllmhuráin, 'Dancing on the Hobs of Hell: Rural Communities in Clare and the Dance Halls Act of 1935', in *New Hibernia Review/Iris Éireannach Nua*, vol. 9 no. 4 (winter 2005), p. 11

414 *'Idols of Modern Society'*: quoted in Maria Luddy, 'Sex and the Single Girl in 1920s and 1930s Ireland', in *The Irish Review*, no. 35 (summer 2007), p. 81

415 *A Catholic priest stood up to protest in vain*: Overy, *The Morbid Age*, pp. 96–8

415 *'have crept in among us as healers and physicians'*: D. H. Lawrence, *Fantasia of the Unconscious and Psychoanalysis and the Unconscious*, Martin Secker, London, 1923, p. 197

415 *'The influence of the press having attained such dimensions'*: quoted in Anthony Keating, 'Setting the Agenda for the Press: The 1929 Case Against the *Waterford Standard*', in *New Hibernia Review*, vol. 16 no. 2 (summer 2012), p. 27

416 *'We are now on the threshold of the international era'*: Christopher Morash, *A History of the Media in Ireland*, Cambridge University Press, New York, 2010, pp. 134–5

416 *'Within a few years . . . I doubt if there will be any village in Ireland'*: ibid., p. 136

417 *'a weird composite of idealism, neurosis, megalomania and criminality'*: Jason Knirck, 'Afterimage of the Revolution: Kevin O'Higgins and the Irish Revolution', in *Éire-Ireland*, vol. 38 nos. 3–4 (fall 2003), p. 219

417 *'Negation of Authority, Hatred Among Brothers'*: Seldes, *World Panorama*, p. 62

417 *'whose ecstasies at their extremest'*: Ryan, *Gender, Identity and the Irish Press*, p. 216

418 *'I would not like to pronounce an opinion'*: quoted in Knirck, 'Afterimage of the Revolution', p. 219

418 *'mothers who preferred the fashionable crowded thoroughfare'*: Maria Luddy, *Prostitution and Irish Society, 1800–1940*, Cambridge University Press, Cambridge, p. 196

418 *'If I had a little girl friend who took up politics'*: Ryan, *Gender, Identity and the Irish Press*, p. 221

418 *'Will you be the bane or the blessing of man'*: quoted in ibid., p. 258

419 'lay the lash across their backs': McMillan, The Way It Was, p. 146

419 'divinely appointed teachers': Patrick Murray, Oracles of God: The Roman Catholic Church and Irish Politics 1922–37, University College Dublin Press, Dublin, 2000, p. 14

420 'I think it will be found to be a non-contentious measure': Kevin O'Higgins, Dáil Debates, vol. 3 col. 587, 3 May 1923

421 'Where information was received that persons were negligent': Eamonn Dunne, 'Action and Reaction: Catholic Lay Organisations in Dublin in the 1920s and 1930s', in Archivium Hibernicum, vol. 48 (1994), p. 113

421 'When a Frenchman installs steam heat': Edgar Ansel Mowrer, This American World, Faber & Gwyer, London, 1928, pp. 135–6

422 'A good education for a girl is better than a dowry': Caitriona Clear, Women of the House: Women's Household Work in Ireland 1926–1961: Discourses, Experiences, Memories, Irish Academic Press, 2000, p. 37

422 some seven thousand children were confined in industrial schools: Mary Raftery and Eoin O'Sullivan, Suffer the Little Children: The Inside Story of Ireland's Industrial Schools, New Island, Dublin, 1999, p. 69

423 'for women who had fallen more than once': Paul Michael Garrett, 'The Abnormal Flight: The Migration and Repatriation of Irish Unmarried Mothers', in Social History, vol. 25 no. 3 (October 2000), p. 332

423 'sources of evil, danger and expense to the community': ibid., p. 333

423 'There seemed to be a lack of excitement': Gavin Foster, 'No "Wild Geese" This Time?': IRA Emigration after the Irish Civil War', in Éire-Ireland, vol. 47 issue 1 & 2 (earrach/samhradh/spring/summer 2012), p. 117

Epilogue

424 'There were no cars in Dublin': 'A Love', in Neil Jordan, Night in Tunisia and Other Stories, Co-Op Books, Dublin, 1976, p. 103

425 'Always unassuming and self-effacing': obituary of 'Miko'

Kennedy, *Clare Champion*, 31 January 1970

426 *'His exploits during this fight'*: obituary of Gilbert Powell, ibid., 23 February 1973

426 *'moral depression'* . . . *'poisoned the soul of Ireland'*: George Russell (Æ), 'Lessons of Revolution', in *Studies: An Irish Quarterly Review*, vol. 12 no. 45 (March 1923), p. 4

426 *'the spirit of the gunman invaded everything'* . . . *'a complete moral collapse'*: P. S. O'Hegarty, *The Victory of Sinn Féin*, University College Dublin Press, Dublin, 1998, p. 38

426 *'the rule of the vendetta'* . . . *'as bloodthirsty and murderous and cruel as the English'*: Liam O'Flaherty, *The Life of Tim Healy*, Jonathan Cape, London, 1927, pp. 305, 309

427 *'a natural perfection'* . . . *'their patriotism suffered shipwreck'*: Desmond Fitzgerald, quoted in Tom Garvin, *1922: The Birth of Irish Democracy*, Gill and Macmillan, Dublin, 1996, p. 150

427 *'the added terror of secrecy'*: O'Flaherty, *The Life of Tim Healy*, p. 305

427 *'They robbed banks and their agents bought houses'*: Garvin, 1922, p. 166

428 *'Though the Free State had been wrested in armed conflict from Britain'*: John McGahern, *Memoir*, Faber and Faber, London, 2005, p. 32

428 *'Don't let anybody fool you'* . . . *'What did we get for it?'*: John McGahern, *Amongst Women*, Faber and Faber, London, 1989, p. 5

428 *'Implicit in our intense nationalism'*: Desmond Fitzgerald, quoted in Garvin, 1922, p. 149

429 *'The momentum of the old order carries us along'*: Russell, 'Lessons of Revolution', pp. 2–3

429 *'can be told to his face'*: Francis Hackett, quoted in Margaret O'Callaghan, 'Language, Nationality and Cultural Identity in the Irish Free State, 1922–7: The "Irish Statesman" and the "Catholic Bulletin" Reappraised', *Irish Historical Studies*, vol. 24 no. 94 (November 1984), p. 243

429 *'The duty of the Irish citizen today'*: Bill Kissane, *The Politics of the Irish Civil War*, Oxford University Press, Oxford, 2005, p. 164

430 *'The main cause of all that emigration'*: Michael Gallagher, *The Irish Labour Party in Transition 1957–82*, Manchester University Press, Manchester, 1982, p. 120

430 *'I think we have in our ranks'*: quoted in Kissane, *The Politics of the Irish Civil War*, pp. 113–14

430 *'They can do the things you will not care to do'*: Joseph McGarrity, quoted in Richard English, '"Paying No Heed to Public Clamor": Irish Republican Solipsism in the 1930s', in *Irish Historical Studies*, vol. 28 no. 112 (November 1993), p. 426

431 *'I remembered your father's civil war pistol'*: Jordan, *Night in Tunisia*, p. 103

432 *'Think of all the positive achievements of the peace'*: Woodrow Wilson, quoted in John Maxwell Hamilton and Robert Mann (eds.), *A Journalist's Diplomatic Mission: Ray Stannard Baker's World War I Diary*, Louisiana State University Press, Baton Rouge, 2012, pp. 442–3

Select Bibliography

I have drawn on many diverse sources in an attempt to convey the experience of living through Ireland's revolutionary years; most are detailed in the Notes. The following is a brief list of some of the works I found most helpful in plotting the political and social narrative of those years and which could be a starting point for readers wishing to find out more about the events and personalities of those times.

Several general histories place the revolutionary period in the context of the broader developments in modern Ireland. Those I found most useful were: Alvin Jackson, *Ireland, 1798–1998: War, Peace and Beyond* (2nd edn, 2010); Paul Bew, *Ireland: The Politics of Enmity 1789–2006* (2007); Diarmaid Ferriter, *The Transformation of Ireland, 1900–2000* (2004); R. V. Comerford, *Ireland* (2003); Dermot Keogh, *Twentieth-century Ireland: Nation and State* (1994); Joseph Lee, *Ireland 1912–1985: Politics and Society* (1989); and R. F. Foster, *Modern Ireland 1600–1972* (1988). The development of Irish nationalism in the context of Anglo-Irish relations is surveyed by Alvin Jackson in *Home Rule: An Irish History, 1800–2000* (2003); Tom Garvin, *The Evolution of Irish Nationalist Politics* (1981) and *Nationalist Revolutionaries in Ireland 1858–1928* (1987); and Oliver McDonagh, *States of Mind: A Study of Anglo-Irish Conflict 1780–1980* (1983).

For the immediate pre-history of the revolution I have drawn on Fearghal McGarry, *Rebels: Voices from the Easter Rising* (2011); Charles Townshend, *Easter 1916: The Irish Rebellion* (2005); and Clair Wills, *Dublin 1916: The Siege of the GPO* (2009). An indispensable source on Sinn Féin is Michael Laffan, *The Resurrection of Ireland: The Sinn Féin Party, 1916–1923* (1999). The debates animating the home-rule crisis are lucidly explored in Paul Bew, *Ideology and the Irish Question: Ulster Unionism and Irish Nationalism 1912–1916* (1994) and Richard Bourke, *Peace in Ireland: The War of Ideas* (2003).

The burgeoning literature on wartime Ireland includes John Horne (ed.), *Our War: Ireland and the Great War* (2008); John Borgonovo, *The Dynamics of War and Revolution: Cork City, 1916–1918* (2013); Ben Novick, *Conceiving Revolution: Irish Nationalist Propaganda during the First World War* (2001); Jérôme aan de Wiel, *The Catholic Church in Ireland 1914–1918: War and Politics* (2003); and Paul Taylor, *Heroes or Traitors? Experiences of Southern Irish Soldiers Returning from the Great War 1919–1939* (2015). The last days of the British administration in Ireland are surveyed in Eunan O'Halpin, *The Decline of the Union: British Government in Ireland 1892–1920* (1987) and Martin Maguire, *The Civil Service and the Revolution in Ireland, 1912–38: 'Shaking the Blood-stained Hand of Mr Collins'* (2008).

The military history of the revolutionary period is comprehensively covered in Charles Townshend, *The Republic: The Fight for Irish Independence, 1918–1923* (2013) and Michael Hopkinson's two volumes, *The Irish War of Independence* (2002) and *Green Against Green: The Irish Civil War* (1988). Joost Augusteijn provides a detailed account of the emergence of the IRA in *From Public Defiance to Guerrilla Warfare:*

The Experience of Ordinary Volunteers in the Irish War of Independence 1916–1921 (1996). The collection of essays he edited, *The Irish Revolution, 1913–1923* (2002), develops several key themes, as does the late Peter Hart in the essays in *The IRA at War 1916–1923* (2003). Arthur Mitchell's *Revolutionary Government in Ireland: Dáil Éireann, 1919–22* (1995) contains a wealth of information on the underground government. Paul McMahon's *British Spies and Irish Rebels: British Intelligence and Ireland, 1916–1945* (2008) is a superb source for the intelligence war.

The story of the emergence of Northern Ireland is told in Jonathan Bardon, *A History of Ulster* (2001); David Fitzpatrick, *The Two Irelands 1912–1939* (1998); Eamon Phoenix, *Northern Nationalism: Nationalist Politics, Partition and the Catholic Minority in Northern Ireland 1890–1940* (1994); Paul Bew, Peter Gibbon and Henry Patterson, *Northern Ireland 1921–1996: Political Forces and Social Classes* (1996); and Michael Farrell, *Northern Ireland the Orange State* (1980) and *Arming the Protestants* (1983).

There has been a steadily growing flow of local studies. Among those I found most useful were: David Fitzpatrick, *Politics and Irish Life: Provincial Experience of War and Revolution* (1998 edn); Peter Hart, *The IRA & Its Enemies: Violence and Community in Cork 1916–1923* (1998); Michael Farry, *The Aftermath of Revolution: Sligo, 1921–23* (2000); Marie Coleman, *County Longford and the Irish Revolution, 1910–1923* (2003); and John Borgonovo, *Spies, Informers and the 'Anti-Sinn Féin Society': The Intelligence War in Cork City, 1920–1921* (2007).

Ronan Fanning deals with the high politics in *Fatal Path: British Government and Irish Revolution 1910–1922* (2013). Thomas Pakenham's *Peace by Ordeal: The Negotiation of the*

Anglo-Irish Treaty, 1921, originally published in 1935, is still an essential guide through the treaty negotiations, as is Joseph M. Curran's *The Birth of the Irish Free State* (1980). On the civil war and its aftermath the essential works are Tom Garvin, *1922: The Birth of Irish Democracy* (1996); John M. Regan, *The Irish Counter-Revolution 1921–1936* (2001); Bill Kissane, *The Politics of the Irish Civil War* (2005) and *Explaining Irish Democracy* (2002); Eunan O'Halpin, *Defending Ireland: The Irish State and Its Enemies Since 1922* (1999); and Anne Dolan, *Commemorating the Irish Civil War: History and Memory 1923–2000* (2003).

Some books on specific themes are exceptionally informative. Emmet O'Connor's *Syndicalism in Ireland, 1917–1923* (1988) is a comprehensive guide to labour unrest during the revolution. Likewise, the best account of the struggle over land can be found in Fergus Campbell, *Land and Revolution: Nationalist Politics in the West of Ireland 1891–1921* (2005) and Terence Dooley, *The Decline of the Big House in Ireland: A Study of Irish Landed Families, 1860–1960* (2001) and *'The Land for the People': The Land Question in Independent Ireland* (2004). For the role of the Catholic Church in the revolution see Patrick Murray, *Oracles of God: The Roman Catholic Church and Irish Politics, 1922–37* (2000) and Brian Heffernan, *Freedom and the Fifth Commandment: Catholic Priests and Political Violence in Ireland, 1919–21* (2014).

The cultural background to the revolution is surveyed in John Hutchinson, *The Dynamics of Cultural Nationalism: The Gaelic Revival and the Creation of the Irish Nation State* (1987); Declan Kiberd, *Inventing Ireland: The Literature of the Modern Nation* (1996); and Terence Brown, *Ireland: A Social and Cultural History 1922–2002* (2004). The pervasive sense of destabilisation in social life and personal beliefs

in the early years of the twentieth century is brilliantly conveyed by Philipp Blom in *The Vertigo Years: Change and Culture in the West, 1900–1914* (2008) and Kevin Jackson's
Constellation of Genius: 1922, Modernism Year One (2012).

Margaret Macmillan, *Peacemakers: The Paris Conference
of 1919 and Its Attempt to End War* (2001) is the essential
guide to global political upheaval caused by the First World
War, as is Robert Gerwarth and Erez Manela (eds.), *Empires
at War 1911–1923* (2014). Jeffry A. Frieden, *Global Capitalism: Its Fall and Rise in the Twentieth Century* (2006) provides a crisp survey in chapters six, seven and eight of the
consequences of the war for the global economy. Similarly the
early chapters of Mark Mazower's *Dark Continent: Europe's
Twentieth Century* (1998) offer a fluent account of the
challenges faced by post-war Europe. Two articles by Robert
Gerwarth and John Horne, 'The Great War and Paramilitarism in Europe, 1917–23', in *Contemporary European History*, vol. 19 no. 3 (August 2010), pp. 267–73, and 'Vectors
of Violence: Paramilitarism in Europe after the Great War,
1917–1923', in *The Journal of Modern History* 83 (September 2011), pp. 489–512, shed new light on how the violence
continued after the conventional armies left the battlefield,
as does Julia Eichenberg, 'The Dark Side of Independence:
Paramilitary Violence in Ireland and Poland after the First
World War', in *Contemporary European History*, vol. 19 no. 3
(August 2010), pp. 231–48.

For biographies of the key figures of Ireland's revolutionary
period see Diarmaid Ferriter, *Judging Dev: A Reassessment
of the Life and Legacy of Eamon de Valera* (2007); Peter
Hart, *Mick: The Real Michael Collins* (2005); Tim Pat
Coogan, *Michael Collins: A Biography* (1990) and *De Valera:
Long Fellow, Long Shadow* (1993); Fearghal McGarry, *Eoin*

O'Duffy: A Self-made Hero (2005); Maryann Gialanella Valiulis, *Portrait of a Revolutionary: General Richard Mulcahy and the Founding of the Irish Free State* (1992); Nicholas Allen, *George Russell and the New Ireland 1905–30* (2003); R. F. Foster, *W. B. Yeats: A Life, Volume II: The Arch Poet* (2003); and Richard English, *Ernie O'Malley: IRA Intellectual* (1998).

Acknowledgements

The idea for this book came from Neil Belton, and without his enthusiasm, patience and encouragement it might never have been finished. He lavished care and attention on the drafts, and his commentaries, themselves a joy to read, were full of insight and advice for improvement. Over lunches and dinners he kept me going when my own zest was flagging. More than anything he endorsed what I was trying to to do – to retell a story traditionally obsessed with ambushes and political intrigue from a much wider perspective – and suggested ways of achieving it.

Many studies of different aspects of the Irish revolution have been published, particularly over the past thirty years, and I am indebted to the many scholars upon whose work I have drawn to shape my narrative. To give a sense of what it was like to live through these events I have used contemporary newspapers, magazines, memoirs and novels but especially a series of diaries and journals chosen, not for the political stance or insider knowledge of the authors, but because each one was keen to notice and vividly record aspects of daily experience beyond political upheaval. I wish to thank the following institutions for permission to quote from their collections: The National Library of Ireland and Rosamond Jacob's grandnephew, Anthony Shanahan, for permission to quote from Rosamond Jacob's diaries; The Board of Trinity College Dublin for permission to quote from the Denis Johnston Papers; The Representative Church Body Library in Dublin for permission to quote from Emily Horsley Ussher's journal; The President of St Patrick's College, Thurles, Father Tom Fogarty, and Diocesan Archivist, Father Christy O'Dwyer, for permission to quote from the journals of Father Michael Maher; The Trustees of the Liddell Hart Centre for Military Archives at King's College, London, for permission to quote from the papers of Major General Charles Howard Foulkes.

In particular I would like to thank James Harte at the National Library of Ireland, Felicity O'Mahoney at the Manuscripts and Archives Research Library at Trinity College, Raymond Refaussé at the Representative Church Body Library, Ailish Larkin and Ruth Talbot at St Patrick's College Thurles and Lianne Smith at King's College archives for their assistance. Glen Dunne and Berni Metcalfe at the National Library of Ireland, Lisa Dolan at Military Archives in Dublin, and Parveen Sodhi at Imperial War Museum in London were extremely efficient in helping me to secure photographs.

Most of my research was done in the upper reading room at the Bodleian Library in Oxford. That it became such a pleasure to work there was due to the kindness, humour, knowledge and skill of the librarians I got to know over the last few years: David Busby, Ernesto Gomez Lozano, Sally Matthews and Vera Ryhajlo. Vera was a great source of fun and conversation and her death after a brief illness came as a great shock and left a void I still feel when I walk into the reading room.

I was fortunate to be the recipient of the Alistair Horne Fellowship at St Antony's College, Oxford, while I worked on the book. My thanks go to Sir Alistair Horne, Avi Shlaim

ACKNOWLEDGEMENTS

and the Warden, Margaret Macmillan, whose warmth and suppport made for a very pleasant year. Penny Cooke offered invaluable assistance in sorting out administrative matters. The interest of the Fellows in my project was a great source of inspiration. In particular I would like to thank Dr Eugene Rogan, Director of the Middle East Centre, and the staff who helped me at the centre's archive.

At Kingston University I have benefited from the support of Beth Brewster, head of the Department of Journalism and Publishing, who made time to release me from marking papers and listened with a straight and sympathetic face as I promised the book would be finished soon. Beth and Brian Cathcart also found money to employ two diligent and perspicacious students, Ruth McKee and Natasha Roberts, to conduct research on my behalf at the British Library newspaper archive. David Rogers has also been a constant source of friendly encouragement and funded my research trip to Washington DC.

A special debt of gratitude is due to the many people who generously shared research or documents. Keelin Bourke made my life immeasurably easier by offering to share her stills of the Jacob diaries within hours of meeting in the National Library. Wade Davis generously sent me the notes he collected while writing *Into The Silence* when I got in touch with a query about George Mallory. Lar Joyce at the National Museum of Ireand presented me with a pile of photocopies of obituaries of IRA veterans from the local newspapers. Catriona Crowe provided crucial help in accessing material. I wish to thank Ida Milne, Paul Taylor, Gemma Clark, Brian Heffernan, Paul McMahon, Georgina Laraghy and Martin Fitzpatrick for sharing their research. Martin Broderick loaned me material on the Limerick soviet.

A great many other people have helped me simply by being prepared to talk about the project. David Edmonds endured many conversations about the book as it took shape and offered wise direction and enlightenment. Richard Bourke's trenchant and often hilariously acerbic counsel has been invaluable. For advice, guidance, ideas, the loan of material or just taking the time to answer my queries my gratitude goes to: Timothy Garton Ash, Brendan Barrington, Mark Brennock, Tom Buchanan, Ray Burke, Michael Coady, Seamus Dooley, Myles Dungan, Diarmaid Ferriter, David Foxton, Juliet Gardner, Kevin Grant, John M. Hamilton, Keith Hopper, John Horgan, Neil Jordan, Declan Kiberd, John L. Knight, Paul Legg, Donal Lowry, Maria Luddy, Deirdre McMahon, Manus McManus, Ruth McManus, Michael Massing, Ida Milne, Mark O'Brien, Hussein Omar, Colm Ó Mongáin, Niamh O'Sullivan, Yetti Redmond, Eugene Rogan, William Sheehan, Frank Shovlin, Colin Storer, Michael Walsh and Vincent Woods.

In addition I was was extremely lucky to have a band of critical readers of my drafts. I am indebted to the following for their perceptive and careful feedback: Mark Brennock, Richard Bourke, David Edmonds, Anna Faherty, Martin Fitzpatrick, Ida Milne, Alison Tickell and Vincent Woods. In addition to general commentary, John Horgan and James Painter subjected the text to a meticulous reading at proof stage. Needless to say, much as I would like to say it was all their fault, all remaining errors of fact and interpretations are mine alone.

At Faber, Kate Murray-Browne has guided the book through the final stages to production with patience, tact and attention to detail. I also wish to thank Julian Loose and Anna Pallai for their help. Jill Burrows has been a terrific copy editor and indexer – exacting, hawk-eyed and a fount of clever solutions to difficult problems, while patiently indulging my delayed responses and last-minute dilemmas. Ian Bahrami's meticulous proofreading snared elusive literals and repetitions.

I owe enormous thanks to my agent, Maggie Hanbury. She has been a source of strength in difficult moments and a resolute defender of my interests at a critical juncture; it has been an enormous relief to have her at my side. Henry de Rougemont designed my website and has done everything he could to prepare me for maximum digital engagement (he may despair that it was still not enough). Harriet Poland has been a model of efficiency at the Hanbury Agency.

Several friends put me up – and put up with me – on my travels to research this book and made those trips infinitely more enjoyable than they would have been without their company. In Dublin, Mark Brennock and Yetti Redmond provided a home from home, where Anna Brennock graciously vacated her bed and Maggie Rose and Alex tolerated my bad jokes. Seamus Dooley and Brian Cooke indulged me with lavish hospitality. Maev O'Leary and my nieces, Deirdre and Siobhan Walsh, made room for me on Marlborough Road. Michael, Frances and May Walsh welcomed me home to Tipperary. In Washington, Alexandre Marc and Patricia Vasquez were terrific hosts and pulled out all the stops to make my stay fun. Neil Johnston and Mark Long lent me their cottage at Lauragh on the Beara Peninsula, a perfect place to write and think (though I will miss the sheep resting against the front door). When I was in danger of becoming too much of a recluse, Val Thatcher and George (who sadly passed away in 2014) and Norman Moore and Cloe Snoek plied me with food and drink.

As ever, my biggest debt is to my family for their forbearance and resilience as I retreated to my little cave in the garden: to Alison, Louis and Kitty my heartfelt thanks and love.

Index